Divination and Human Nature

Divination and Human Nature

A COGNITIVE HISTORY OF INTUITION
IN CLASSICAL ANTIQUITY

Peter T. Struck

PRINCETON UNIVERSITY PRESS
PRINCETON AND OXFORD

Published by Princeton University Press, 41 William Street, Princeton,
New Jersey 08540

In the United Kingdom: Princeton University Press, 6 Oxford Street,
Woodstock, Oxfordshire OX20 1TR

press.princeton.edu

Design concept by Natalie B. Dohrmann
Cover images (from left to right): 1. Alchemy / Alamy Stock Photo, 2. Birds /
Shutterstock, 3. Sketch of the Liver of Piacenza

First paperback printing, 2018
Paperback ISBN 9780691183459

The Library of Congress has cataloged the cloth edition as follows:
Names: Struck, Peter T., author.
Title: Divination and human nature : a cognitive history of intuition in classical
antiquity / Peter T. Struck.
Description: Princeton, NJ : Princeton University Press, 2016. |
Includes bibliographical references and index.
Identifiers: LCCN 2016005144 | ISBN 9780691169392 (hardcover : alk. paper)
Subjects: LCSH: Philosophy, Ancient. | Divination—Greece. | Intuition.
Classification: LCC B171 .S85 2016 | DDC 133.3093—dc23
LC record available at http://lccn.loc.gov/2016005144

British Library Cataloging-in-Publication Data is available

This book has been composed in Minion Pro

Printed on acid-free paper. ∞

Printed in the United States of America

For Roger and Sally

CONTENTS

Acknowledgments   ix

Introduction. Divination and the History of Surplus Knowledge   1

Chapter 1. Plato on Divination and Nondiscursive Knowing   37

Chapter 2. Aristotle on Foresight through Dreams   91

Chapter 3. Posidonius and Other Stoics on Extra-Sensory Knowledge   171

Chapter 4. Iamblichus on Divine Divination and Human Intuition   215

Conclusion. Reconsidering Penelope   251

Bibliography   263

Index Locorum   277

Subject Index   287

ACKNOWLEDGMENTS

THIS PROJECT HAS BENEFITED ENORMOUSLY OVER THE YEARS from generosity of many kinds. I thank the National Humanities Center where the early work began, and the Center for Advanced Studies in the Behavioral Sciences at Stanford, which provided an orientation toward the evidence that informed the whole of the work. A project that began aimed at semiotics took on a cognitive dimension under the eye-opening tutelage of colleagues there. Further, I have benefited greatly from responses to presentations at universities I list here in alphabetical order: the Académie Royale Belgique, Brown, Chicago, University of Cincinnati, Columbia, Corpus Christi College Oxford, Dartmouth, Fordham, Florida State, Indiana University, Kent University, Leiden, Harvard, University of North Carolina, Ohio State, the Scuola Normale Superiore, Smith, Stanford, Toronto, Texas, University of Washington, and Wesleyan. Conversations with colleagues on the *Journal of the History of Ideas* have been continuously challenging and enlightening and helped to reshape the framing of the introduction. And finally, the inspiring community of classicists at the University of Pennsylvania was essential at the many inflection points of the project. Penn's Department of Classical Studies provides continuous evidence of the pleasure of study and discovery, and the salutary benefits of supportive challenge and intellectual rigor. Earlier versions of some parts of the chapters have been previously published. Parts of the introduction appeared as "A Cognitive Approach to Divination in Antiquity," in the *Journal of the History of Ideas* (January 2016); sections of chapter 1 appeared as "Plato and Divination," in *Archiv für Religionsgeschichte* in 2014. An earlier version of a part of chapter 4 awaits the publication of *Divine Powers in Late Antiquity*, edited by Eirini Viltanioti and Anna Marmodoro, from Oxford University Press (2016). I thank Laura Agosto for research work she did for me on Stoic notions of the seed; Alex Ramos for help preparing the manuscript; and graduate students Roshan Abraham, Jae Han, and Daniel Harris-McCoy for their stimulating discussions; but especially Natalie Dohrmann and Adam Struck, who continue to be the prime movers.

Divination and Human Nature

Divination and the History of Surplus Knowledge

> Divination is like this: By the visible it knows the invisible, and
> by the invisible it knows the visible, and by the present it knows
> the future, and by dead things it gains knowledge of the living,
> and it becomes aware from things that have no awareness. The
> person who knows it is always correct, while the person who
> doesn't sometimes is and sometimes isn't. In this way it imitates
> human life and human nature.
>
> Μαντικὴ τοιόνδε· τοῖσι μὲν φανεροῖσι τὰ ἀφανέα γινώσκει, καὶ
> τοῖσιν ἀφανέσι τὰ φανερά, καὶ τοῖσιν ἐοῦσι τὰ μέλλοντα, καὶ
> τοῖσιν ἀποθανοῦσι τὰ ζῶντα· καὶ τοῖσιν ἀσυνέτοισι συνιᾶσιν, ὁ
> μὲν εἰδὼς ἀεὶ ὀρθῶς, ὁ δὲ μὴ εἰδὼς ἄλλοτε ἄλλως. Φύσιν
> ἀνθρώπου καὶ βίον ταῦτα μιμεῖται·
>
> —The Hippocratic treatise *On Regimen* 1.12

FROM ALL CORNERS OF THE ANCIENT MEDITERRANEAN, PEOPLE that
had run up against the limits of their own knowledge brought their remaining questions to a frail, illiterate woman housed in a massive stone
temple at Delphi. She was Apollo's human embodiment on earth and
the most revered source of wisdom in the classical world. As they pre-
pared for their consultation with the mysterious Pythia, seekers would
have read an enigmatic, deceptively simple two-word sentence cut into
the temple wall, "Know yourself."[1] No one could remember where the

---

[1] For a sample of the scholarship, see Eliza Wilkins, "'Know Thyself' in Greek and Latin
Literature" (Ph.D. dissertation, University of Chicago, 1917), 60–77; S. Levin, "Know Thyself:
Inner Compulsions Uncovered by Oracles," in *Fons perennis: Saggi critici di filologia classica*

saying came from or what exactly it was supposed to mean, but this only heightened the aura around it. Why should the god advise those consulting him to know themselves? Wasn't it precisely their lack of knowledge that had led them to him? Perhaps the god was trying to tell us that, in some way or other, knowing oneself is the key to knowing anything at all, and that any inquiry could start only from a condition of self-awareness. Maybe it meant that self-knowledge is not the beginning but rather the end of true wisdom. While we may be looking for answers to other things, what we really come to know in the end is ourselves. Whatever it meant, the position of the inscription, over the entry hall to the inner sanctum, invited those reading it to look at it as some kind of key to the place they were entering. The riddle of the cryptic abundance of divine knowing they were about to experience had been rephrased as a riddle about self-understanding.

The idea of knowing oneself takes a bit of unpacking. From a contemporary vantage, we might first think of knowing one's own tastes and proclivities, the kind of self-discovery that is the stuff of the modern *Bildungsroman*. But for the Greeks it was not so much a question of knowing oneself as a sui generis individual but rather of developing an understanding of oneself as a member of the order of things. To know yourself meant to pursue what it is to be human. Ideas on that question are thick and varied in the ancient sources, but a few shared points of reference set them on the trail. As humans we are composite creatures. On the one hand, we possess an extraordinary intelligence, a knowingness that is so mysterious as to seem to have something to do with the divine. On the other, we also have a bodily nature, a creaturely self, that we share with the other self-propelled organisms we see around us. Although they do not partake in our intelligence, like us they do eat, metabolize, reproduce, and eventually die. For most of day-to-day life in Greek antiquity, this pair of considerations produced

---

raccolti in onore di Vittorio d'Agostino (Turin: A Cura della Administrazione della RSC, 1971) 231–57; Hermann Tränkle, "Gnothi seauton: Zu Ursprung und Deutungsgeschichte des delphischen Spruchs," *Würzburger Jahrbücher für die Altertumswissenschaft* n. F. 11 (1985): 19–31; Christian Gorm Tortzen, "'Know thyself': A Note on the Success of a Delphic Saying," in Bettina Amden et al., *"Noctes Atticae:" Thirty-Four Articles on Graeco-Roman Antiquity and Its Nachleben: Studies Presented to Jørgen Mejer on his Sixtieth Birthday, March 18, 2002* (Copenhagen: Museum Tusculanum, 2002), 302–14; cf. also Pierre Courcelle, *Connaistoi toi-même de Socrate à Saint Bernard*, vol. 1 (Paris: Études Augustiniennes, 1974).

three very broadly understood layers of reality, with humans some-where between the divine realm of gods in the heavens and the world of animal nature.

These are distinct zones, whose boundaries are enforced by founda-tional taboos, such as hubris on the one hand and cannibalism on the other. But the cultural walls that separate them have cracks. Greek myth is filled with figures that blur the lines. Satyrs, centaurs, and other hybrids split the difference between us and the animals, while heroes and spirits populate the other boundary. In more complex cultural for-mations as well, we find both barriers and bridges.[2] For example, in the protocols around sacrifice, one sees all three spheres coming into con-versation, as the animal's embodied self, demanded by the god, both secures divine favor and goes to the enrichment and nourishing of the human organism. As scholars in the last several decades have shown, sacrifice is as much about human nature as it is about the gods or the animals they supposedly desire.[3] I will argue in this book that the kind of thing that took place not just in consultations with the Pythia, but in a kaleidoscopic array of common ancient divinatory practices, per-formed a similar kind of organizing function. Such practices orient us between our weird knowingness, which we share with the divine, and our creaturely selves, which traverse the terrestrial world alongside the other animals. Divination does this by drawing a connection between the two.

For many millennia and across the whole Old World, from Eastern to Western Eurasia, and from the tip of southern Africa to the high-lands of Britannia, people were in the habit of practicing divination, or the art of translating information from their gods into the realm of the human. On a scale whose breadth we have yet to fully appreci-ate, they assumed that clandestine signs were buried in the world

[2] For an illuminating reading of Hippolytus and Heracles that reaches a similar end point by Freudian and structuralist means, see Charles Segal, "Pentheus and Hippolytus on the Couch and on the Grid: Psychoanalytic and Structuralist Readings of Greek Tragedy," *The Clas-sical World* 73.3 (1978): 129–48.

[3] The seminal modern work on the topic is Walter Burkert, *Homo Necans: The Anthropology of Ancient Greek Sacrificial Ritual and Myth*, trans. Peter Bing (Berkeley: University of Califor-nia Press, 1983) (originally published, Berlin: De Gruyter, 1972). Of similar importance is the collection by Jean-Pierre Vernant and Marcel Détienne, eds., *La cuisine du sacrifice en pays grec* (Paris: Gallimard, 1979).

around them. Consultants perceived messages from temple-based oracles, like the one at Delphi, as well as in their dreams, the entrails of the animals they killed, lightning, fire, lots, pebbles, livers, fired tortoise shells, the stars, birds, the wind, and nearly anything else that moved.[4] These practices were not, for the most part, considered esoteric or marginal. The inclinations of the divine, like the weather, were simply a part of the ancient atmosphere, and just about wherever we look in the sources, we find people trying to gauge the prevailing winds. Scholars have yet to take account of the extraordinary diffusion of the phenomenon. It belongs to a small group of rather widely shared cultural forms from antiquity—alongside things like myth or sacrifice. Although no global answer to why this is so will easily be found, it is also true that better local answers will emerge if scholars make a fuller reckoning of this near universal diffusion.

Diverse as they are, the preponderance of divinatory signs in the classical world shares a grounding in natural processes. From climactic phenomena, to animal behaviors, to involuntary human actions like sneezes, twitches, or dreaming, the language the gods spoke was understood to be anchored in the other bookend of the human being—according to the Greek scale—namely, the world of nature and the animal. Even in the case of the more ephemeral, internal states of divine possession, whether oracular trances or unconscious visions, bodily natures are made salient, as the strange, quickened bulk in which our consciousness resides takes on the function of an instrument—whether we ourselves are vibrating in sleep or we witness another human body writhing, twitching, and providing vocal cords to the divine message. The Pythia's legendary illiteracy is consonant with this view. The void in her education makes her creaturely nature all the more prominent; and her gender aligns with this sense of corporeality, since Greek men typically associated women with body over mind.[5] When that realm which lay above us chose to speak, the messages mostly came in and

---

[4] And even some things that don't, including cheese. Artemidorus, 2.69, cited in Sarah Iles Johnston, *Ancient Greek Divination* (Oxford: Wiley-Blackwell, 2008), 8.

[5] On the question of gender and the Pythia, see for example, Lisa Maurizio, "A Reconsideration of the Pythia's Role at Delphi: Anthropology and Spirit Possession," *Journal of Hellenic Studies* 115 (1995): 69–86.

through the one that lay below us. It does not simply stand to reason that the phenomenon would be organized this way.

DIVINATION, MAGIC, AND POLITICS

The study of ancient divination does not typically begin like this. When it has been treated by classicists, it tends to appear in one of two scholarly venues: either as an important component of social and political history—which it clearly was—or as a subset of the study of magic, a field that has been bourgeoning in recent decades. Taking social history first, several important advances have been made. Informed by anthropological studies, and ultimately by Evans-Pritchard, classicists have looked at divination as a means to invoke the ultimate authority of the divine in order to construct and maintain social orders by building consensus and managing conflict.[6] This approach grows pretty naturally from the kind of evidence most often cited in scholarly studies—that is, the captivating tales of divinatory practice recorded by historians and poets, including such famous stories as those of Oedipus, Croesus, or the Athenians' Wooden Wall. These typically unfold according to the literary logic of the puzzle or riddle, and show people trying to grope their ways through life on incomplete and partial information, always in contrast to a divine fullness of knowledge. We see elite figures fastening onto this or that sign and enlisting the gods' voices in the service of their own ends. Such famous cases invite us into high stakes public venues, looking at leaders in politics or war struggling with what something ominous portends for them. By focusing here, one can surely see why some scholars have developed the view that divination was mainly about politics.

[6]For a lucid recent overview, see Michael Flower, *The Seer in Ancient Greece* (Berkeley: University of California Press, 2008), 72–80. For a standard of scholarship, see H. W. Parke and D.E.W. Wormell, *The Delphic Oracle* (Oxford: Oxford University Press, 1956); and the reworking of this tradition by Joseph E. Fonenrose, *The Delphic Oracle: Its Responses and Operations* (Berkeley: University of California Press, 1978); cf. Robert Parker, "Greek States and Greek Oracles," in P. A. Cartledge and F. D. Harvey, eds., *Crux: Essays in Greek History Presented to G. E. M. de Ste. Croix* (London: Duckworth, 1985), 298–326. E. E. Evans-Pritchard, *Witchcraft, Magic, and Oracles among the Azande* (Oxford: Clarendon, 1937); cf. J. C. Mitchell, *The Yao Village* (Manchester: Manchester University Press, 1956), 165–75, and George K. Park, "Divination and Its Social Contexts," *Journal of the Royal Anthropological Institute* 93.2 (1963): 195–209.

Attractive as it obviously is, and as useful as it has been in clarifying political and social history, this approach has limitations. Briefly put, it moves all too quickly away from the divinatory moment itself, classifying it as a pretext for the real work divination does, according to this view, working through a social problem in a political forum. But we may be left wondering why (on earth) the ancients would have chosen these peculiar methods of doing politics. There isn't an obvious logic that explains why such debate would be catalyzed by, and authorized by, the screech of birds or the coloration of a sheep's liver. In addition, current scholarly studies of this variety are sometimes shaped by a rather straightforward picture of an enlightened few manipulating the masses with ostentatious mystery. But such claims rarely take into account that the elites, just as much as the larger public, typically thought divination worked. And further, if divination were really mostly about politics, why would such techniques have been equally useful in private matters, even in questions of intimate and personal concern, in which social manipulation plays no part? When seen as a pretext, the divinatory sign, as a medium, with all its curious characteristics and qualities, is passed over. It becomes a cipher, isolated and irrational, to be bracketed and filled with other more comprehensible—that is, social-historical—content.

The second significant body of scholarship begins from entirely different premises. It treats divination as though it were a part of the underworld of occult practices that thrived in the classical period. The prevalence of the pairing "magic and divination"—to be found in the titles of books, chapters, articles, and conferences, and enshrined in the title of Evans-Pritchard's seminal work of anthropology, *Witchcraft, Oracles and Magic Among the Azande* (1937)—suggests that the two are twinned in the modern imagination.[7] But, from the perspective of the classical evidence, this view also has its limitations. Although magic and divination may seem to us to be complementary, and although they may have been so for Evans-Pritchard's Azande, that is not the Greek and Roman view, and in the classical context we lose something in our understanding of both by lumping them together. While we are learning more in recent years of a learned form of "magic," attached to

---

[7] A modern *locus classicus* for the field is W. R. Halliday, *Greek Divination: A Study of Its Methods and Principles* (London: MacMillan, 1919).

the traditions of the Persian *magoi* in the classical period,[8] the vast majority of the evidence we have for the tradition of magic (γοητεία, μαγεία) makes it out to be a fringe, esoteric, occult activity. This is something divination (μαντεία) was certainly not considered to be. Magic was nearly always malicious and deeply socially stigmatized. It was not something done in polite company. The magician has a reputation as a secretive and nefarious miscreant; the diviner does not—even though he or she can make enemies, as the Pythia does of Croesus or Tiresias of Oedipus. It is the γόης and not the μάντις that becomes simply synonymous with a cheat. Greeks and Romans reserved multiple, prestigious offices for their diviners; no parallel exist for magicians. A few stereotypes, informed by class distinctions, of unscrupulous or charlatan diviners, particularly itinerant ones,[9] do exist, but they find their closest analogues not in treatments of magicians, but in ancient views of technical experts of all kinds, like medical doctors or rhetoricians, whose specialists' knowledge is sometimes an irritant.

It is true that we find many spells in the *Greek Magical Papyri* offering expertise in the divinatory arts, but then again, the writers of these spells claim expertise in all kinds of things.[10] They offer results in the fields of rhetoric, athletics, the making of pottery, medicine, or nearly any other highly skilled craft for which people were accustomed to hiring expert help. That magicians should claim skills as diviners does not mean divination has particularly to do with magic any more than it means medicine does. It is better to say that the two fields have some relationship, but not a bidirectional one. The most famous diviners and oracles—Teiresias, the Pythia, the priestesses of Dodona, and the Sibyl, for example—have no reputation as magicians. It is probably more accurate to position the evidence this way: while on the one hand we have magicians who make rather indiscriminate claims about the range of

---

[8] See James Rives, "Aristotle, Antisthenes of Rhodes, and the *Magikos*," *Rheinisches Museum für Philologies* n. F. 147.1 (2004): 35–54; and Phillip Horky, "Persian Cosmos and Greek Philosophy: Plato's Associates and the Zoroastrian *Magoi*," *Oxford Studies in Ancient Philosophy* 37 (2009): 47–103.

[9] See John Dillery, "*Chresmologues* and *Manteis*: Independent Diviners and the Problem of Authority," in Sarah Iles Johnston and Peter T. Struck, eds., *Mantikê: Studies in Ancient Divination* (Leiden: Brill, 2005), 167–231.

[10] For the most thorough recent treatment of divination in the magical texts, see Johnston (2008), 21–27, 144–79.

their areas of expertise, the practitioners of the other specialties tend to be more circumspect. We find an occasional Gorgias and his equivalent in the parallel arts, who will claim powers to bewitch and beguile, usually to be purposefully provocative, but the claim of affiliation is usually one-sided.[11] For the most part, divination is understood as one of the useful arts—a speculative one, to be sure, but not an occult one. This general picture is supported on the level of simple terminology. It is telling that divination gets a commonly used Greek substantive adjective form in -ικη (μαντική), which ranks it among the other well-known *technai*. The parallel formations hardly exist in the vocabulary for magical practice.[12] Finally, one could highlight the awkwardness of the pairing, magic and divination, by a comparison with sacrifice. One would not get far in classical scholarship arguing that magic and sacrifice were a natural heuristic combination. Although one could imagine a scenario in which sacrifice struck a scholarly audience as mysterious behavior, which could perhaps lead to a positioning of the two as subsets of the same kind of phenomena, this would be a rather obvious mistake. Someone could even support a claim of a relationship between magic and sacrifice from the magical papyri, since magicians also give copious examples and detailed instructions regarding sacrifice. But this makes the pairing no less awkward. We have known for many centuries that sacrifice was a core, nonoccult part of classical religious life, and have achieved a richer understanding of it by letting it stand as a subject of study on its own.

The scholarly approach to divination that treats it as a subset of the study of magic seems to share little with the social-historical one. However, after some reflection a simple, though consequential, similarity comes into view. Both proceed from an irrationalist premise. They participate in an area of classical scholarship that, since Dodds, has received corrective attention under the umbrella of recovering the "irrational" aspects of Greek and Roman life, on which more in a moment; and this context means that both begin with the idea that divination is a form of human behavior that does not, properly speaking,

[11] Gorgias, *Encomium of Helen*, speaks of the power of words to work like a magical charm (Diels-Kranz B11.8, B11.10).

[12] The form γοητική as a substantive is unattested in the literary corpus. The substantive μαγική does appear, but not until the Septuagint and only rarely.

make sense. The question of the logic that might lie behind it is either not asked at all, since it is assumed not to have one, or it is deflected onto other, functionalist grounds. In place of a rational logic, the social historian explores the more comprehensible realm of social capital, while the historian of magic will tend toward the psychological, presenting an ancient mind-set, groping to find effective means of dealing with a sometimes brutal world. These intellectual histories group divination into a cluster of oddities of a past time that emerge from exotic theological commitments, unearthed with a kind of curatorial spirit.[13]

In my view, the current study of divination has been overly functionalized. This has left us with atrophied answers to a question that, in the largest sense, animates the present study. The question is this: Why did it made sense to most Greeks and Romans to think that their gods were sending them messages through the natural world and its creatures, including their own bodies, asleep or awake? Answers in the current scholarship are not very satisfying. They move quickly into generalities like superstition or a desire for social manipulation. These are after all rather broad impulses, and while they are relevant to divination, they don't very directly lead to it. It's not as though with sufficient amounts of superstition and manipulative intent, the idea that the universe is percolating with hidden messages will just emerge. In my view, the question of "Why?" has been positioned too narrowly, doubtless partially as a result of the kinds of source texts that have been the focus of study. Immersed in the case studies of divinatory situations both real and imagined, told by historians or poets, a scholar finds local answers, tactical purposes, specific goals, and targeted outcomes. Croesus sent messengers to Delphi to ask if he should attack the Persians, because he wanted to know if he would win. The kind of testimony about motivations that one extracts from actual instances of divination, told from the point of view of participants, does not offer much purchase on the potential underlying reasons why divination seemed like a reasonable activity to nearly all ancient people in the first place.

There is another kind of answer offered in the classical evidence. It emerges from a set of texts, less well studied than the literary and historical ones. From back to at least Democritus' time, we find a tradition

---

[13] A welcome exception is Johnston (2008), 1–30.

of philosophical reflection on divination. While there is rarely a question that it is poised on the edge of comprehension, these thinkers do not generally assume that it has fallen into the abyss. Only a few of our sources are entirely hardheaded on the subject, like Epicurus[14] and Cicero's own persona in book 2 of the *De divinatione*. These currents of thought, which have been unduly amplified, are only eddies in the main stream. And the outsized influence of Cicero's text, which his academic background leads him to structure as a for-and-against proposition, has lead us to overemphasize the controversial dimension of the topic, and to overlook the earnestness with which nearly all of our sources pursue it. Most ancient intellectuals, in short, take divination more or less seriously. The contrast with magic is again striking: theories of magic are very rare and sketchy.[15] The evidence base is orders of magnitude more robust in the case of divination theory.[16]

Rather than setting out to reckon with the meaning of one particular sign or other, these thinkers explore the premises of the whole enterprise. They study the structure of this language of signs, not particular iterations. Their works provide a remarkably rich vein of thinking on the subject, which has hardly been explored beyond specialized studies of individual texts. They vary in their emphases. Plato and Aristotle devote most of their serious attention to prescient dreams. The Stoics and Neoplatonists open up the consideration to all kinds of divinatory activity. Although one can find some interest in linking the phenomenon to gullibility, manipulation, or superstition, each of these schools also has much more to say about it. In the parts of their studies on which I will focus, they start with what they see as a curious

[14] See Cicero, *De div.* 1.3, 2.40.

[15] The most thorough study is Fritz Graf, "Theories of Magic in Antiquity," in Paul Mirecki and Marvin Meyer, eds., *Magic and Ritual in the Ancient World* (Leiden: Brill, 2002), 93–104. Though, again, the studies of Rives and Horky are beginning to see a tradition attached to the Persian *magoi* that shows philosophical interest, not least in the attribution to Aristotle of a tract called *Magikos* (Rose [1967], F32–F36). It is doubtful that this tradition will be much illuminated by the goetic magic of the *Papyri Graecae Magicae*, etc.

[16] Sarah Iles Johnston is surely right to call divination a "tertium quid" and to point out that this has played a role in keeping divination from being vigorously pursued by scholars. See Sarah Iles Johnston, "Introduction," in Johnston and Struck (2005); and in more depth in Johnston (2008), 21–30. Even after Dodds, while magic had the irresistible attraction of a kind of purity of unreason, divination, which has always been an alloy of sorts, was largely passed over in the rush to the opposite pole.

phenomenon; one that seems to them to be both hard to understand and a more or less observable fact. Certain people are just good at arriving at useful knowledge, in crux situations, in difficult to understand ways. After making a degree of allowance for the speculative nature of the topic, they ask something like: How in the world do they *do* that? The traditional Homeric view, that an anthropomorphic Olympian divinity intervenes in an act of purposeful communication, placing a kind of person-to-person call, is never embraced. Instead, we find a rather long list of singularly powerful minds meditating on what for them is an undeniable sense that we humans sometimes acquire knowledge—on matters past, present, and future—in deeply enigmatic ways. Their very general approach and their purpose of looking behind examples to underlying processes invites a more rudimentary investigation of divination. The way these thinkers examine the question has suggested to me that another, parallel history of divination is also possible to tell, one that sees it not so much as a social or occult phenomenon, but rather as belonging to the history of a certain kind of cognition.

Before going on with this point, it is perhaps useful here briefly to make a distinction between classical Greek ideas of divination and the quite different phenomena of prophecy in the Hebrew Bible or the later development of apocalyptic literature. Some further remarks on these traditions will again become pertinent in the later parts of this study. With very few exceptions, Greek diviners produce incremental advice on tactical matters in the proximate future. These increments may have grand consequences, but the insights themselves are small bore.[17] They provide guidance on whether a particular god is angry; whether this or that time is more advantageous for a military attack, or a business deal, or a marriage; and (commonly from Delphi) whether it's a good time to set up a colony in a faraway place. They do not offer large judgments about the alignment of the universe, or have revelatory visions that open a vantage to the underlying structure of the cosmos. Their knowledge is narrower and meant to be put to use when a small increment of

---

[17] See a similar assessment at Parker (1985), 77. Parker extends this as a general characterization drawn from anthropological treatments of divination across contemporary cultures. On the Greek side, see these testimonia: Xenophon, *Mem.* 1.4.15, *Cyrop.* 1.6.46; Herodotus 1.157.3; Hipparchus 9.9. For the case of the specific evidence at Didyma, Bernard Haussoullier made this point nearly a century ago, "Inscriptions de Didymes," *Revue du Philologie* 44 (1920): 271–74.

knowledge can make a big difference. As we will see in the later material under consideration here, these aspects of the classical tradition undergo some change after the Hellenistic period, and after substantive contact with the Near East. More expansive views like these become rather thoroughly embedded in the work of the Neoplatonists, whose ideas mark a distinct break with their predecessors, though they appear already in imperial prophecies recorded from Claros.[18]

RATIONALITY AND COGNITION

For many years the category of rationality governed modern accounts of the distinctive place of the Greeks in intellectual history. With a few exceptions around the school of Cambridge Ritualists, scholars took them to stand for a stage in which humanity was emerging into a new kind of critical self-awareness, one that, as the story goes, had eluded their predecessors.[19] A half-century ago, after the obvious contributions of the Greeks to the development of rationality no longer seemed to need advocates, E. R. Dodds added powerful nuances to the dominant narrative with his Sather Lectures of 1949–1950, published as *The Greeks and the Irrational*. Dodds showed that Greeks were not, in fact, always and everywhere following the course of *logos*, but instead engaged in a range of practices and held a range of beliefs that would seem, to us at least, to be decidedly *ir*rational. Dodds's landmark study initiated whole fields of inquiry and left us a more balanced picture of classical intellectual culture, but it also, in an infelicitous side effect, reinforced the centrality of rationality (or now its lack) in Greek intellectual history. Too often, in my view, classical cultural forms are thought of exclusively in terms of whether, or to what extent, they are rational or irrational

The most important contributions to the study of divination's place within intellectual history, a study which has never quite achieved critical mass, mainly place the question of rationality/irrationality at the center. A useful but mostly documentary section of Auguste

---

[18] Johnston (2008), 78–82.
[19] See further, Johnston (2008), 18–19.

Bouché-LeClercq's four volumes on the *Histoire de la Divination dans L'Antiquité* (published between 1879 and 1882) deals broadly with divination in its ancient intellectual contexts, and a not well-known dissertation, of Friedrich Jaeger from Rostock University, on *De oraculis quid veteres philosophi judicaverint* (1910) returned to the idea. W. R. Halliday published his *Greek Divination* three years later, embracing, in the wake of the Cambridge Ritualists, a possibility for an irrational, "pre-Olympian" realm of Greek life.[20] Arthur Stanley Pease showed the remarkable depth of Cicero's *De divinatione* in his monumental edition and commentary (1920–1923), which included copious commentary on the philosophical tradition, almost always from the standpoint of source criticism. Since then the topic mostly languished until Dodds's watershed book, where divination appeared as one species of the irrational. A quarter century after Dodds, Jean-Pierre Vernant and his collaborators made important advances in his collection *Divination et rationalité* (1974). These observations were pursued by Detienne within the realm of structuralist anthropology.[21] Valuable studies of Aristotle and the Stoics appeared in the history of science by R. J. Hankinson, followed by pathbreaking contributions by Philip van der Eijk.[22] Friedrich Pfeffer examined some of the same evidence studied here in his *Studien zur Mantik in der Philosophie der Antike* (1976), a study from which I have profited. A revival of interest in ancient semiotics has made promising inroads, in the work of Giovanni Manetti, Ineke Sluiter, and Walter Leszl.[23] More recently, Johnston has set out a clear overview of the whole.[24] Collectively, the main contribution of this area of

[20] See discussion in Johnston (2008).

[21] Marcel Detienne, *Masters of Truth in Archaic Greece* (New York: Zone, 1996), originally published as *Les Maîtres de vérité dans la grèce archaïque* (Paris, Maspéro 1967).

[22] R. J. Hankinson, "Stoicism, Science, and Divination," *Apeiron* 21.2 (1988): 123–60; Philip van der Eijk, *Medicine and Philosophy in Classical Antiquity: Doctors and Philosophers on Nature, Soul, Health, and Disease* (Cambridge: Cambridge University Press, 2005); and his edition and commentary, Aristoteles, *De insomniis; De divinatione per somnum* (Berlin: Akademie Verlag, 1994), is extraordinarily helpful.

[23] Giovanni Manetti, *Theories of the Sign in Classical Antiquity* (Bloomington: Indiana University Press, 1993); Ineke Sluiter, "The Greek Tradition," in Wout van Bekkum et al., eds., *The Emergence of Semantics in Four Linguistic Traditions: Hebrew, Sanskrit, Greek, Arabic* (Amsterdam: John Benjamins, 1997); Walter Leszl, "I messaggi degli dei e I segni della natura," in Giovanni Manetti, ed., *Knowledge through Signs: Ancient Semiotic Theories and Practice* (Turnhout: Brepols, 1996), 43–85.

[24] Johnston (2008), 4–27.

scholarship has been to work through the powerful observation that rationality has a history, and to show the gains we realize by a deeper understanding of cultures whose notions of it are not always isomorphic to our own.[25]

But by letting the category of rationality and its negative twin set the terms for the discussion we have missed out on some of the subtleties of the ways Greeks thought about the topic at hand—and, more important, and in a broader sense, how they thought about thinking in general. The binary of rationality/irrationality is too blunt. It places self-conscious, volitional, discursive, inferential intellectual activity on the one side and absurdity on the other. But according to the general view among the philosophers, while divinatory knowledge arrives via processes that are not quite rational—the mechanisms that lie behind it are not like those of our normal, waking thinking—they are not precisely irrational either, in the sense of being unreasonable, illogical, or absurd.

These texts treat the phenomenon in a different way. They work through the investigation starting from a sense that even if it is sometimes difficult to know how we arrived at a particular insight by using the normal measures and standards for how we know things (vigorous ideas about which vary widely from thinker to thinker) it is still at least possible that there is some accounting to be made for how we got it right. I have come to the view that trying to measure the rationality of divinatory thinking is actually a stumbling block and not a pathway to understanding it. As I hope to justify in the following pages, the contemporary category of cognition (as used in its broadest sense within the cognitive sciences) allows us to describe such intellectual phenomena better precisely because it allows for a study of thinking that is agnostic on the question of rationality. Cognition, as I will be using it, captures all activities of the mind and allows them an equal share of attention. The modes of thinking that the philosophers speculate about in studying divinatory insight, characterized in multivariant and elegantly subtle ways, is best approached from this broad scope.[26]

---

[25] This is an ongoing theme in Johnston and Struck (2005).

[26] Thomas Habinek has already shown the gains that accrue from taking this perspective on Stoicism, in "Tentacular Mind: Stoicism, Neuroscience, and the Configurations of Physical Reality," in Barbara Stafford, ed., *A Field Guide to a New Meta-Field: Bridging the Humanities and Neuroscience Divide* (Chicago: University of Chicago Press, 2011), 64–83.

Surplus Knowledge

Starting from these preliminaries, this study proceeds via a central axiom. It is likely to be relatively uncontroversial, and if it is a good axiom it should have been just as true in antiquity as it is now: *Our ability to know exceeds our capacity to understand that ability.* This means that our cognitive selves are to some (let us say, for now, irreducible) degree mysterious to us. After bracketing entirely the claims of psychics or enthusiasts of ESP, it is not uncommon that we find ourselves in the position of knowing things, about which, if pressed, we cannot quite develop a clear account of how we know them. The messages that we receive from the world around us add up, sometimes in uncanny ways, to more than the sum of their parts.

The residual I am calling "surplus knowledge." By this I mean the quantum of knowledge that does not arrive via the discursive thought processes of which we are aware, and over which we have self-conscious control. Beginning from this axiom, the overall argument here runs like this: Surplus knowledge exists, as a fact of human nature; over the course of history cultures have developed different strategies for getting a grip on it; and divination is just the most robust ancient version in a long series of attempts to do so. By "get a grip," I mean to acculturate it, to fit it into a coherent worldview and to some extent regulate it and make it socially useful. According to this account, divination will be best understood as driven not mainly by exotic theological commitments, nor by primitive minds tempted by superstition, nor by political ambitions to manipulate the masses; but rather by an underlying characteristic of the nature of human cognition. The rich political and social dimensions, then, unfold posterior to—and as an epiphenomenon of—this peculiar zone of knowing. The theology is not the cause, but rather the authoritative local language, if you will, that is the favored classical means to express and describe a durable human experience.

The best modern analogue to ancient divination by this account is not horoscopes, palmistry, or tarot cards, since, in most current valuations, these and similar practices are esoteric and self-consciously marginal. They partake of the occult, in the same way that ancient magic did; and are mostly meant to be engaged in when no one is looking, or at least from the safety of an ironic distance. In the pages that follow I will be working through evidence that positions divinatory knowledge within the classical thought-world in a way that is more or less analogous to the position of the modern concept of intuition, in the way it is generally understood. Both are widely accepted, socially authorized placeholders to mark those things we know without quite knowing how we know them. Neither is fully understood, when used in the common parlance of their respective times, and this undertheorized nature is likely to be part of their point and usefulness for the general audiences that put the categories to use. The categories themselves are provocative, and intellectuals produce studies to try to figure them out. Like modern intuition, divination gave the ancients a way to talk about surplus knowledge, although the whole phenomenon remained (as it still does) somewhat squirrelly.

TECHNICAL AND NATURAL DIVINATION

Of course, this line of argument needs to reckon with a very old division in the field, between the classes of natural and technical divination, to which we find ancient authorities attesting, including Plato (*Phaedrus* 244) and Cicero (*De div.* 1.6, 18; 2.11).[27] Divination by nature happens through an inspiration that produces an oracle, dream, or daytime vision in the recipient's mind, while technical divination proceeds by interpreting signs in the surrounding environment. Although the first is congenial enough to the idea of an alternative mode of cognition, given that it centers on altered states of mind, the second appears not to be, since it seems to proceed by the application of self-conscious inferential logic to empirically gathered external signs. Plato and Cicero both speak of the thought processes involved in these classes as being divided in this way.[28] But there are reasons to see this division as less than a clean line.

---

[27] Contemporary scholars have mostly followed this division, but several have cast doubt on its coherence and importance for ancient thinking; see Flower (2008), 84–91; Johnston (2008), 9, 17, 28.

[28] Plato, *Phaedrus* 244c–d; Cicero, *De div.* 1.2–4.

A recent treatment by Michael Flower has shown the general fuzziness of the lines between these hoary categories in actual practice, outside of the testimony of Plato and Cicero.[29] Technical and natural divinatory techniques often accompanied one another, and dream divination appears on both sides of the divide. Flower has pointed to rhetorical motivations behind both Plato's and Cicero's distinction between the modes of thinking involved in the two forms. As we will see, the Stoic Posidonius will go to some lengths to try to show that the modes of thinking in each case are the same. This brings up another point of note. It holds true in the evidence in this study, albeit not comprehensive on this question, that those who take technical divination seriously (Posidonius) characterize its mode of thinking as partaking in the nondiscursive, while those that call it inferential and discursive (Plato, Aristotle, Cicero, and Iamblichus) do so accompanied by doubts on whether it should count as divination. These observations prompt us to try looking at Greek technical divination in a slightly different light.

We start by noting that in almost all cases for Greeks and Romans, discerning the external sign itself is, after all, a strenuous process that resists neat formulation. The gnarled traditions that try to systematize these practices make this obvious. The loci on which technical divination unfolds are almost never high-contrast evidence of strict black and white. Flights of birds are erratic, entrails have no straight lines, and discerning the degree of greediness with which chickens eat their grain is subject to ambiguity. Even the relentlessly regular movements of the heavenly bodies become so laden with interpretive schemata that the lore of astrology remains, let us say, murky. On the Roman side, the augural laws, like the astrological treatises, are another interesting case. The expanse of the literature, and the profusion of rule making, looks much more like something set up to thwart the application of inferential logic than to facilitate it. It offers any interpreter a wide array of choices, a kind of jurisdiction shopping. Jerzy Linderski's famous efforts to

---

[29] See Flower (2008), 84–91; and see also Philip Peek, "Introduction: The Study of Divination, Past and Present," in Peek, *African Divination Systems: Ways of Knowing* (Bloomington: Indiana University Press, 1991), 12, cited in Flower (2008), 86.

work through the laws help prove the point.[30] And on the Greek side, we simply do not have surviving *any* tract, let alone the collection of tracts one would expect, to attest to an impulse toward the development of standard rules for interpretation in any of the technical varieties of divination, including such prominent ones as entrail- or bird-reading.[31] If such practices had actually been based on discursive inference from the straightforward observation of signs, guided by the collection of lore (such as Cicero describes it) one would have expected to find a convergence on practicable rules. But such a thing, beyond vague generalities, does not exist.

Now, the absence of clarity with respect to such phenomenon, from a functionalist perspective, of course, looks like the diligent production of refuges for the system when particular instances result in failure. This is no doubt the case. But at the same time, from the perspective of this study, there is an orthogonal point to be drawn. From within the cognitive reality of the system, it speaks to a cultural attempt to make space for precipitating a shift in the kind of thinking engaged, a change to a noninferential, nondiscursive mode of knowing, at the moment of observation. It breaks open the normal sequential thinking of long-form wrestling with inference, directs attention away from the details of the problem at hand, and invites more associative and correlative cognition to take over for a while. The reading of livers on the battle-field is closer to a gut-check, so to speak, than to a calculation; and the mode of cognition most salient in riddling out an answer from most of the rest of the technical forms remains as inscrutable as it does in the natural ones.[32]

---

[30] Jerzy Linderski, "The Augural Law," *ANRW* II.16.3 (Berlin: De Gruyter, 1975), 2146–312.

[31] The clearest surviving example of a rule-based record of inferential thinking, ironically, pertains to a mode of divination mostly thought to be based on inspiration, in the case of Artemidorus' *Dreambook*. For a recent, lucid translation and commentary, see Artemidorus, *Oneirocritica*, trans. Daniel E. Harris-McCoy (Oxford: Oxford University Press, 2012).

[32] The case of sortition leads one to entertain exceptions. On the question as a whole, see Sarah Iles Johnston, "Lost in the Shuffle: Roman Sortition and Its Discontents," *Archiv für Religionsgeschichte* 5 (2003): 146–56. The results from the Roman practice of placing names in a jar for the assignment of offices is open to no ambiguity. But it is also true that this has led some contemporary commentators to doubt its status as a divinatory technique (N. Rosenstein, "Sorting Out the Lot in Republican Rome," *American Journal of Philology* 116 [1995]: 43–75, cited in Johnston [2008], 147). And further, since the result of the lot toss was subject to veto by

There is a useful contrast with Babylonian divination, where a different kind of clarity is observable in the crystallizations of tradition that survive in the cuneiform tablets.[33] Long strings of codified if-then statements are preserved in the lore. This should give pause to any global conclusion drawn on the basis of the general messiness of such records on the Greek side. Further work would be needed, however, to determine the precise contours of the contrast. For example, the protases of the Babylonian texts are often not straightforward. One omen warns, "If Jupiter becomes steady in the morning, enemy kings will be reconciled."[34] One could imagine some room for latitude in readings of "steadiness," which would, by the argument here, open space for forms of noninferential thinking; the observation applies even more in the case of an omen like: "If the coils of the intestine look like the face of Huwawa: it is the omen of the usurper king who ruled all the lands."[35] Further, while some have pointed to these texts as a kind of birth of scientific thinking, in the form of inference from empiricism, Rochberg has pointed to doubts, based on the other observable forces, beyond empirical observation, that steer the process of drawing connections between the protases and apodoses.[36] Some are clearly based on paranomastic relations or analogical connection, and other apodoses are in fact impossible situations, which could never have been observed. The system of omens, she concludes, grows up independent of empiricism.

---

an adverse oblative sign, even this seemingly clear form opens a space for interpretation, since adverse, unsolicited signs require observers, and observers will value what they see differently. See Johnston (2008) for further citations of scholarly disagreement on the question.

[33] See Francesca Rochberg, "'If P, then Q': Form and Reasoning in Babylonian Divination," in Amar Annus, ed., *Divination and Interpretation of Signs in the Ancient World*, Oriental Institute Seminars 6 (Chicago: The Oriental Institute, 2010), 19–27.

[34] Erica Reiner and David Pingree, *Babylonian Planetary Omens: Part Four*, Cuneiform monographs 30 (Leiden: Brill, 2005), 40–41 line 1, cited in Rochberg (2010).

[35] Albert T. Clay, *Epics, Hymns, Omens and Other Texts: Babylonian Records in the Library of J. Pierpont Morgan*, vol. 4 (New Haven: Yale University Press, 1923), no. 13:65, cited in Rochberg (2010).

[36] See, for example, J. Bottéro, *Mesopotamia: Writing, Reasoning, and the Gods* (Chicago: University of Chicago Press, 1992), 125–38; for further discussion, see Rochberg, *The Heavenly Writing: Divination, Horoscopy, and Astronomy in Mesopotamian Culture* (Cambridge: Cambridge University Press 2004), 268–71.

FURTHER CONSIDERATIONS

Understanding divination as more closely related to surplus knowing than occult religion helps make more comprehensible why ancient philosophers commonly thought it worthwhile to try to explain it. The philosophers rarely theorize seriously about religious practices.[37] There is a pronounced dearth of ancient thinking on traditional cult practices, including such a fundamental one as sacrifice. When philosophers approach questions having to do with religion, they theorize about the nature of the gods, not praxis. The comparatively rich tradition of thinking about divination is an outlier here. That it piqued the curiosity of philosophers mostly uninterested in religious practices is made more comprehensible when we realize that they could understand it as a way of knowing, an area in which they had developed interests.

On a linguistic level, another curious piece of information, which as far as I know has never been recognized, finds an explanation when the topic is positioned as it is here. Greek has long been appreciated for its rich vocabulary for cognitive processes. There are words for reason (λόγος), calculation (συλλογισμός), discursive reasoning (διάνοια), opinion (δόξα), belief (πίστις), wisdom (σοφία), practical wisdom (φρόνησις), a rational mind (νοῦς), and scientific knowledge (ἐπιστήμη), among many others. But there is no good fit within the standard domain of such cognition terms for what we mean in English when we use the term *intuition*—which the *Oxford English Dictionary* describes as an immediate apprehension of something without the intervention of any reasoning process. Even Greek words for surmising, like ὑπονοέω or ἐπεικάζω, point to unsure, speculative inferences not to insight that arrives *without* inference. If one does a search (which electronic tools make it possible to do) of the English side of the standard Greek and Latin lexica, one finds there that nowhere have scholars seen fit to assign the English term "intuition" to any particular element of the Greek or Latin language.[38] But, then, one might next think that if

---

[37] See Johnston (2008), 4.

[38] There are a handful of exceptions. First, there are a few instances, over the surviving corpus, where such a notion seems fitting (see below, n. 39), and some of these show up in the lexica as well, as an extended sense of a term whose home meaning is not intuition. See, for example, the sense of ἐπιβολή, which likely has a sense for Epicurus that fits within the "rational

Greeks or Romans didn't have a single term for it, perhaps instead they used some standard phrase which might not be picked up at a dictionary-level analysis of the language. If that were the case, we would expect that any such larger phraseology would be captured when translators sat down to render classical texts into English. If one turns next to standard translations of much of the core Greek and Latin corpus made available by the Perseus project, which at the time of this writing, housed English renderings of 17 million words of Greek and Latin literature, one finds that in only precisely six cases did these words suggest to the English translators the term "intuition."[39] The Perseus database is of course not comprehensive, but the result is a nontrivial proxy for what would appear in something that was. Further, while the idiosyncratic interpretive choice of this or that translator would not be probative, the aggregation of the interpretive choices of many scholars, each from his or her own perspective, over a broad swath of the corpus is certainly suggestive. What it suggests to me is either: a) the Greeks didn't think much about the human capacity to know things without self-conscious inference, as contained in my earlier axiom, or b) the English translators had some aversion to the standard way English talks about this phenomenon when they saw parallel ideas expressed in Greek words, or c) the Greeks thought we had such a capacity and just expressed in a cultural form sufficiently different from our own that it shows up in entirely different terms. I will be arguing here for c). Their

---

intuition" tradition (see below), carrying forward early ideas contained in Aristotle' νοῦς, but this is a far cry from surplus knowledge. See Gregory Vlastos, "Cornford's *Principium Sapientiae*," in Daniel W. Graham, ed., *Studies in Greek Philosophy*, vol. 1, *The Presocratics* (Princeton: Princeton University Press, 1995), 118 (= reprint of a review originally published in *Gnomon* 27 [1955]: 65–76). Second, there are a few terms that show up in late Greek, among the Neoplatonists, which LSJ finds stretch over to meaning "intuition (ἐπιβολή, προσβολή, ἀνεννόητος; ἐπαφή could be added, but LSJ does not include it). As will be shown in chapter 4 below, the emergence of a vocabulary that matches our sense of intuition corresponds exactly with the decline in prestige and authority of traditional notions of *mantikê* under the scrutiny of Iamblichus in the *De myst.*; see 3.26.

[39] Plato, *Crat.* 411b (for μαντεύω; trans. Fowler [1926]); Plato, *Laws* 950b (for θεῖον δέ τι καὶ εὔστοχον; trans. Bury [1929]); Plato, *Rep.* 431e (for μαντεύω; trans. Shorey [1969]); Ovid, *Met.* 6.510 (for *praesagia*; trans. More [1957]). The remainder are drawn from Aristotle's development of a category customarily rendered "rational intuition" (νοῦς; trans. Rackham [1926]; see below, and chapter 2), which he references in the *NE* 6.8 and 6.11, for the faculty that apprehends first principles (1142a23–30 and 1143b6). Such a search may well have picked up *Posterior Analytics* 2.19, but did not in this case.

way of talking about the cognitive capacity that in common English parlance is called intuition is through their very robust cultural construction of divination. Consonant with this view: of the six instances where translators introduce the English term intuition into the translations housed in the Perseus database, four of them serve as translations of ancient metaphorical uses of Greek or Latin terms for divination.[40]

DIVINATION IN THE HISTORY OF INTUITION

In another potential gain in our understanding, by setting divination within its cognitive context we open up the possibility for a larger history to come into view. If the overall picture presented here is correct, then surplus knowledge, considered as a result of human cognitive capacity, would presumably have been noticed and made comprehensible in different cultural and intellectual formations over time, and it should be possible to tell a history of it, in which ancient divination and modern intuition would be the bookends of a series of attempts to understand and describe it. Such a study sits well beyond the ken of the current one, but there is enough low-hanging fruit to set out a few very general parameters.

As a first step, it is important to recognize that intuition, at least at this point, has more than one history. Within the field of philosophy, "rational intuition," as it is commonly called, is understood as an immediate apprehension of fundamental prerequisites to discursive intellectual activity, and has a rich scholarly history in the study of epistemology. In a masterful overview of the topic, Richard Rorty marked out the main contours in an article in the *Encyclopedia of Philosophy* (1967). He discerned three principle strands: 1) knowledge of the truth of a proposition not preceded by an inference—he limits these mostly to the form of first-person statements about a psychological state, such as "I feel pain," or underived a priori truths, such as "every event has a cause"; 2) acquaintance with a concept that allows for proper use of it, without being able to give a full explanation of it—under this category are discussed abstractions from concrete sensory data with which one

---

[40] Ibid.

develops a facility through habituation; and 3) nonpropositional knowledge of an entity, including a universal, or the insensible particulars of time and space. This is mostly a carefully circumscribed story about the acquisition of certain bedrock intellectual quanta—concepts, rules of logic, and sensory ground truths—that form the necessary preconditions of knowledge. The discussion makes clear efforts to separate noninferential knowing of these preconditions from any more popular idea of a hunch that turns out to be right, which Rorty identifies as a final, philosophically inconsequential, notion attached to the term "intuition." It is "unjustified true belief not preceded by inference; in this (the commonest) sense 'an intuition' means 'a hunch.' The existence of hunches is uncontroversial and not of philosophical interest." The case will be made in the following pages that there is, in fact, a set of thinkers in antiquity that imagined divinatory insight as something precisely like a hunch, and addressed it as a question of philosophical interest.

In addition to the philosophical tradition of studying "rational intuition," there is another pertinent scholarly literature, bourgeoning in the decades since Rorty's article, which has grown up, mostly without conversation with the discourse of philosophical epistemology. In empirical research in psychology and cognitive science, the salience of phenomena that would fit under the nonspecialist's category of "intuition," has recently risen greatly. "Cognitive intuition," let us call it, speaks not of a capability to acquire fundamental intellectual quanta, but one that results in phenomena closer to what I have here called surplus knowledge. The field has yielded striking results, tracking examples of people knowing things, nondiscursively and without self-conscious inference. Various subfields explore different facets of the topic, as the recent overview by Osbeck and Held has shown.[41] We see understandings of intuition as a primitive cognition that steers evolutionary forces by advancing survival and facilitating adaptation. Other scholars associate it with the category of implicit learning, which takes place underneath the attention of the subject, is associative and works by similarity and contiguity, and is not symbolic, nor does it work by a rule structure

---

[41] Lisa M. Osbeck and Barbara S. Held, eds., *Rational Intuition: Philosophical Roots, Scientific Investigations* (Cambridge: Cambridge University Press, 2014). The introduction of Osbeck and Held (2014) sets out the ground adopted here.

of logically fixed relations. Scholars have further invoked the category to describe one half of various two-process models of cognition—most well-know is Kahneman's "thinking fast and thinking slow"—marking out a region of quick, pre-attentive, preconscious processing.[42] These scholars are after a verifiable description of the modes by which humans process information, and they are expanding our understanding of the multiform ways this happens.

To a greater degree than studies within philosophical epistemology, this line of work shows connections, in subject matter, though not in methodology, with the studies the ancient philosophers undertake of divination. I am cautious to add that contemporary scholars working in these areas may well be quick to resist such an assertion, since a common theme in their work is to dissociate the scientifically observable and verifiable phenomena they are finding in clinical studies from the kind of ill-conceived and popular fantasies that surround the traditions of seers in antiquity. They are understandably cautious to separate their findings from the mystical penumbra of soothsaying or clairvoyance. I can only beg indulgence from this group, in the hope that the whole of the present study justifies the claim of an analogy between their work and the materials under study here: my claim is not about popular fantasies regarding seers, but about the hard-nosed study undertaken in ancient philosophers' accounts, of observable and provocative phenomena, of people sometimes being able to see around corners, or see through things, in ways that defy appeal to the customary modes of our intellects.

A synthetic account of the two traditions—rational intuition on the one hand and cognitive intuition on the other—has not yet been produced. The epistemologists are disinclined to cross into terrain associated with extravagant claims (at least by nonspecialists); and the experimental psychologists needn't, exactly, wrestle with the history of epistemology to measure the effect of implicit learning or alternative information processing in their subjects. Further complicating the matter is the imbalance of scholarly development in the *history* of these two groups. The history of rational intuition has been thoroughly studied, while the history of cognitive intuition has not. Discrete moments have been

---

[42] Daniel Kahneman, *Thinking, Fast and Slow* (New York: Farrar, Straus, and Giroux: 2011).

investigated, but not synthetically assembled. It is likely that they could be, and that some accounting for the parallel presence of the notion of nondiscursive and noninferential knowing in the two discourses would pay mutual benefits.

Studies of the history of rational intuition typically speak of Aristotle as the initiator of the idea, and among the Aristotelian works they enlist are some of the handful of texts mentioned above (fn. 39) in which the English word *intuition* and its cognates appear in standard renderings of core texts from the ancient corpus. According to the still influential reading of Ross, Aristotle attributes to the *nous* an intellectual faculty of apprehending, nondiscursively, basic first principles as fundamental prerequisites for inferential knowledge.[43] The philosophical history proceeds from Aristotle, typically jumping up to Spinoza (although Epicurean ἐπιβολή could be enlisted),[44] who builds up a tripartite view of human ways of knowing. The first is sense-based opinion. The second is reason, which discursively moves from premises to firm conclusions, and by which we infer a cause (a characteristic of God) from its effects (entities in the observable world). Intuition is our third way of knowing and it is a nondiscursive apprehension of a thing as it really is.[45] Descartes' nonsensory *intuitus*[46] along with Kant's *Anschauung*

---

[43] For a recent overview of the question, along with some suggested revisions of the traditional views, see Robert Bolton, "Intuition in Aristotle," 39–54, in Osbeck and Held (2014). Also particularly helpful is the discussion of Victor Kal, *Aristotle on Intuition and Discursive Reason* (Leiden: Brill, 1988). The modern locus classicus is W. D. Ross, *Aristotle's Prior and Posterior Analytics* (Oxford: Oxford University Press, 1949). See also Terrance Irwin, *Aristotle's First Principles* (Oxford: Oxford University Press, 1989), 134–50; Han Baltussen, "Did Aristotle Have a Concept of "Intuition"? Some Thoughts on Translating *Nous*," in E. Close, M. Tsianikas, and G. Couvalis, eds., *Greek Research in Australia: Proceedings of the Sixth Biennial International Conference of Greek Studies, Flinders University June 2005* (Adelaide: Department of Languages-Modern Greek, Flinders University, 2007), 53–62. The Greek *nous* in this Aristotelian context has been regularly rendered with some reference to intuition: see "intuitive reason" (Ross [1949], 608) and "intuition" (Allan [1952], 69); for disagreement, see Barnes (1975), 256–59.

[44] For more on this term, see below, chap. 4, fn. 47.

[45] See Steven M. Nadler, *Spinoza's Ethics: An Introduction* (Cambridge: Cambridge University Press, 2006), 181–85; Yirmiyahu Yovel, *Spinoza and Other Heretics,* vol. 1, *The Marrano of Reason* (Princeton: Princeton University Press, 1989), 154–65. For a fascinating treatment that draws connections between Spinoza and contemporary cognitive science, see Antonio Damasio, *Looking for Spinoza: Joy, Sorrow, and the Feeling Brain* (New York: Harcourt, 2003), 3–24, 274–76.

[46] See especially, Descartes, *Rules for the Direction of our Native Intelligence,* rule 3 in John Cottingham, Robert Stoothoff, and Dugald Murdoch, ed. and trans., *Descartes: Selected Philosophical Writings,* vol. 2 (Cambridge: Cambridge University Press, 1988), 2–4.

anchor the idea in modern epistemology as well. Kant in particular informs the Romantics and their desire for an immediate apprehension of things.[47] Fichte and Schelling each develop a sense of immediate knowing by way of developing Kant's ideas.[48] There are likely to be points of overlap between this line of thinking and the traditions of cognitive intuition, which are waiting to be considered.

On the history of cognitive intuition itself, I will point out a few prospective linking points. First, as we will see in chapter 1, Plato speaks of capacities analogous to those present in Aristotle's *nous*, in his discussion of the immediate, nondiscursive apprehension of the forms. Plato will commonly use the language of divination to express this (these make up most of the rest of the handful of standard translations of classical texts that find use for the English "intuition"). While the scholarship has rightly pointed out the differences between Plato and Aristotle on this question (particularly on their valuing of dialectic as a mechanism), it has given shorter attention to their commonality. While each uses a different language to express it, both imagine a distinctive noninferential character to this cognitive process. According to the history assembled here, Plato represents a moment *prior to* the separation of rational and cognitive intuition, that is, prior to the development of a language of *nous* separate from that of *mantikê*.

It is also surely of interest that when medieval theologians coin the term *intuitus* (which in classical Latin was limited to descriptions of vision) they use it to speak about a nondiscursive knowing that particularly characterizes the divine cognition of angels.[49] This is the avenue by which the term enters the modern European languages. Thomas Aquinas proposes that angels understand things, via intuition, all in a

---

[47] See Jennifer Mensch, "Intuition and Nature and Kant and Goethe," *European Journal of Philosophy* 19 (2011): 431–53.

[48] See Moltke S. Gram, "Intellectual Intuition: The Continuity Thesis," *Journal of the History of Ideas* 42.2 (1981): 287–304; Dale E. Snow, *Schelling and the End of Idealism* (Albany: SUNY Press, 1996), 55–66.

[49] Anselm, *Proslogion*, chaps. 14 and 18; Thomas Aquinas, *Summa Theologica*, 1a56.1, 55.2, 58.6–7. See Harm Goris, "The Angelic Doctor and Angelic Speech: The Development of Thomas Aquinas's Thought on How Angels Communicate," *Medieval Philosophy and Theology* 11 (2003): 87–105. For some further parameters of these developments, see Jerome V. Brown, "Henry's Theory of Knowledge: Henry of Ghent on Avicenna and Augustine," in W. Vanhamel, ed., *Henry of Ghent: Proceedings of the International Colloquium on the Occasion of the 700th Anniversary of his Death, 1293* (Louvain: Louvain University Press, 1996), 19–42.

flash, without recourse to sequential reasoning and inference (*Summa Theologica* 1a58). The mode of angelic intuition likely has connections with how Aristotle's *nous* works, and so it has links to the history of rational intuition. But given that the medieval topic is centrally concerned with divine knowing, it also echoes ancient conceptions of divinatory knowledge. When humans are able to think according to intuition, as certain of the Scholastics imagine they can, they are partaking of a mode of knowing that principally resides with the divine.[50] Of further interest, the appeal to angels in the medieval discussion echoes a consistent appeal to the realm of intermediate divinity (typically under the designation of the Greek *daimonia*) that plays a critical role with regard to divination in classical texts.[51]

This cognitive capacity plays a further part in the work of John Milton, during a conversation Adam has with the archangel Raphael over plates of fruit on his grassy table in the garden of Eden. In the seventeenth century, Milton took bold steps to draw out the connections between divine and human realms. Not only did angels partake of human food, but also humans could sometimes partake of the angelic onrush of knowing. Raphael says reason comes in two varieties: "Discursive, or Intuitive; discourse/ Is oftest yours, the latter most is ours,/ Differing but in degree, of kind the same" (5.488–90).[52] It seems that intuitive reason is precisely what Adam uses to name the animals. Full knowledge of them arrives to him without a need to think about it: "I named them, as they passed, and understood / Their nature, with such knowledge God endued / My sudden apprehension" (8.352–54). This kind of

[50]See in particular the ideas of Duns Scotus, outlined in Robert Pasnau, "Cognition," in Thomas Williams, ed., *The Cambridge Companion to Duns Scotus* (Cambridge: Cambridge University Press, 2003), 285–11. For a connection between intuition and prophecy in Duns Scotus, see Mary Beth Ingham and Mechthild Dreyer, *The Philosophical Vision of John Duns Scotus: An Introduction* (Washington, D.C.: Catholic University Press, 2004), 29. For an overview of Duns Scotus' position in the period as a whole, see Marsha Colish, *Medieval Foundations of the Western Intellectual Tradition: 400–1400* (New Haven: Yale University Press, 1997), 306–11.

[51]The closest English for this term, "the demonic," likely conjures ideas of evil sprites, but in antiquity, the Greek category had nothing to do with the minions of an evil overlord. It referred instead to any deities not as high as gods. After Augustine, this one category is split into two binary opposites: there are purely good ones, the angels, and the term demon is left to name the purely evil ones. No such split is operative in any of the uses of the term in the thinkers under study here.

[52]See Patrick J. Cook, "Intuition, Discourse, and the Human Face Divine in *Paradise Lost*," *Essays in Literature* 23 (1996): 147–64.

knowing could possibly fit into the history of rational cognition, perhaps under Rorty's third category of nonpropositional knowledge of an entity; the scene presents these names as fundamental truths, which are in a way prerequisites for knowledge. But it may also have a place in a history of cognitive intuition. Adam's sudden apprehension provides him knowledge of their full natures, beyond just recognizing them as discrete categories, which suggests something closer to the surplus knowledge at stake in this study. The views at play in Milton's work endure to the doorstep of the Enlightenment. Speaking of angels and brute animals in 1711, the English playwright, essayist, and politician Joseph Addison wrote: "Our superiors are guided by intuition, and our inferiors by instinct" (Joseph Addison, 1711; *Spectator*, no. 162, daily, precursor to the *Guardian*, cited in the *OED*).

As the modern era advances, we see further developments that would be a better fit for a history of cognitive, rather than rational intuition. The work of Erasmus Darwin, physician, natural philosopher, grandfather of Charles Darwin, and poet, whose life spanned the eighteenth century, wrote to moderate acclaim a set of poems along with an accompanying philosophical commentary in which he develops the idea of "intuitive analogy," whereby we nondiscursively and unconsciously assimilate present experiences to our stock of past ones and consolidate our basic sensations. We are able to do this because certain patterns are stamped into nature, ourselves included, and when we sense them in the external world, they are activated internally.[53]

In the nineteenth century, the expanding field of human physiology, energized by the work of Erasmus Darwin's grandson, brought further developments in the history of cognitive intuition. Flush from locating the electrical and chemical impulses that made the human organism function, and working from Descartes and his ghost-in-the-machine dualism, scientists quickened their interest in the phenomenon of reflex action. These muscular movements happen irrespective of our volition, operating by the machinery not the ghost, and they set the physiologists to wondering whether there were analogous cognitive systems at work. These scientists worked over the terrain more thoroughly

[53] See Devin S. Griffiths, "The Intuitions of Analogy in Erasmus Darwin's Poetics," *Studies in English Literature, 1500–1900* 51.3 (2011): 645–65.

than anyone since the ancient thinkers at the center of the current study. William Carpenter, author of the standard anatomy textbook for most of the century, which was reissued in many editions and grew to a thousand pages, took a particular interest in the physiological basis of cognitive functions.[54] He reports his discovery of a subvolitional form of thinking he called "unconscious cerebration." In a special additional textbook on *Mental Physiology*, Carpenter concludes that "a large part of our intellectual activity . . . is essentially *automatic*"[55] (emphasis in the original). Among chapters such as "Of the Nervous System," "Of Sensation," and "Electro-Biology," he devotes one to unconscious cerebration. He describes it as a short-circuiting of normal rational thought, and it hums away, processing information and achieving insights, without our realizing it. It becomes a stewing pot into which insights drop to simmer into full-fledged ideas. Just as, in the system of our musculature, external stimuli may produce impulses that move through the spinal cord to give rise to reflex motor movements, so too in the tissue of our brains we experience "ideo-motor reflexions" that take place along an unselfconscious track of information processing. He provided a chart (see figure 1) as an illustrative aid, which shows the pathway via which unconscious cerebration proceeds.[56]

The idea became widely popular and held a fascination for pivotal literary figures and intellectuals in an era that, as one scholar recently characterized it, was an opening of realism "to the uncertain processes of the organism."[57] Among its propagators were figures as diverse as Oliver Wendell Holmes, Mark Twain, and the inventor of the telephone, Alexander Graham Bell, who wrote:

> I am a believer in unconscious cerebration. The brain is working all the time, though we do not know it. At night, it follows up what we think in

[54] William Benjamin Carpenter, *Principles of Human Physiology* (Philadelphia: Blanchard and Lea, 1842).

[55] William Benjamin Carpenter, *Principles of Mental Physiology* (London: H. S. King and Co., 1874; reissued Cambridge University Press, 2009), 515.

[56] Reproduced from William Benjamin Carpenter, *Principles of Human Physiology* (Philadelphia: Blanchard and Lea, 1860), 441.

[57] Randall Knoper, "American Literary Realism and Nervous 'Reflexion,'" *American Literature* 74.4 (2002): 717. See further Vanessa Ryan, *Thinking without Thinking in the Victorian Novel* (Baltimore: Johns Hopkins University Press, 2012), which despite some controversy in its reception remains a helpful guide.

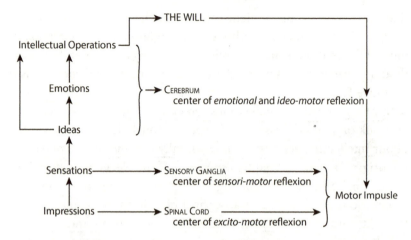

Figure 1. William Carpenter's outline of unconscious cerebration

the daytime. When I have worked a long time on one thing, I make it a point to bring all the facts regarding it together before I retire; and I have often been surprised at the results.[58]

In his preface, Henry James tells that *The American* grew from an abrupt insight that hit him upon his arrival into the sensory rush of Paris, and that he then dropped into a "deep well of unconscious cerebration."[59] And in his *Autobiography* the father of Social Darwinism, Herbert Spencer, recounts a conversation with George Eliot, in which he explained how he came upon his ideas:

> My mode of thinking does not involve the concentrated effort which is commonly accompanied by wrinkling of the brows. . . . It has never been my way to set before myself a problem and puzzle out an answer. The conclusions, at which I have from time to time arrived . . . have been arrived at unawares—each as the ultimate outcome of a body of thoughts that slowly grew from a germ. . . . Little by little, in unobtrusive ways, without conscious intention or appreciable effort, there would grow up a coherent and organized theory.[60]

[58] Cited by Orison Swett Marden, *How They Succeeded: Life Stories of Successful Men Told by Themselves* (Boston: Lothrop, 1901), 33.

[59] Henry James, *The American*, Oxford World's Classics (Oxford: Oxford University Press, 1999), 4.

[60] Herbert Spencer, *An Autobiography*, vol. 1 (London: Williams and Norgate, 1904), 399–400.

The linkage between this tradition and the involuntary nature of dream symbolism in Jung has also recently been pointed out, suggesting further ties to the ancient traditions at stake here.[61]

And reaching to the contemporary period, the advances in the cognitive sciences mentioned above would clearly belong to a history of cognitive intuition. In 2011, Daniel Kahneman set out the memorable pairing of thinking fast (intuitive and nonconscious) and thinking slow (deliberative and self-conscious), a binary that puts the former on a par with the latter in importance. In the decades preceding, scholars and scientists, including Antonio Damasio, Nalini Ambady, Timothy Wilson, Nicolas Epley, Gerd Gigerenzer, and many others, have brought a new kind of respectability to the claim that our ways of knowing are many and diverse.[62] One does not find in this work broad claims about the reliability of such thinking, but there is a consistency in the theme that some nontrivial portion of the knowledge we assemble at any given time arrives to us by ways other than self-conscious, goal-directed, inferential chains of thought.

This body of work has spurred broad interest and many popularizing accounts, one vivid example of which appeared in a newspaper during the height of the recent war in Iraq.[63] While the American army was being menaced by hidden improvised explosive devices, certain soldiers appeared to their comrades to have preternatural abilities to sense the presence of these bombs. The army, in a deeply pragmatic spirit, poured money into studies of such people, trying to see whether there was anything to the anecdotes. Cognitive scientists determined, in a finding not at all surprising to those familiar with the discipline, that some soldiers indeed had more accurate predispositions to sense

---

[61] Sonu Sharmdasani, *Jung and the Making of Modern Psychology: The Dream of a Science* (Cambridge: Cambridge University Press, 2003), 120–21; Farzad Mahootian and Tara-Marie Linné, "Jung and Whitehead: An Interplay of Psychological and Philosophical Perspectives on Rationality and Intuition," in Osbeck and Held (2014), 395–420.

[62] Antonio Damasio, *Descartes' Error: Emotion, Reason, and the Human Brain* (New York: Putnam, 1994; revised Penguin edition, 2005); Nalini Ambady and John Skowronski, eds., *First Impressions* (New York: Guildford, 2008); Timothy Wilson, *Strangers to Ourselves: Discovering the Adaptive Unconscious* (Cambridge, Mass.: Belknap, 2002); Nicolas Epley, *Mindwise: Why We Misunderstand What Others Think, Believe, Feel, and Want* (New York: Knopf, 2014); Gerd Gigerenzer, *Gut Feelings: The Intelligence of the Unconscious* (New York: Penguin, 2008).

[63] Benedict Carey, "Brain Power: In Battle, Hunches Prove to be Valuable," *New York Times*, July 27, 2009.

trouble than others. When the soldiers were asked to describe how they knew something was out of order, they called it a hunch, or a gut feeling. Antonio Damasio, was quoted for the article:

> Not long ago people thought of emotions as old stuff, as just feelings— feelings that had little to do with rational decision making, or that got in the way of it. Now that position has reversed. We understand emotions as practical action programs that work to solve a problem, often before we're conscious of it. These processes are at work continually in pilots, leaders of expeditions, parents, all of us.

It is, of course, more than just uncanny that two millennia ago the single arena in which the seer's gifts were most consistently valued was also the battlefield. According to the Greek military handbook by the first-century CE tactician Onasander, a general should be temperate, self-restrained, vigilant, and hardened to labor—and he should also be a skilled reader of entrails, so he can be personally involved in the readings his diviners are giving him.[64] This is something he would have to do often, since Onasander also says that a general should not initiate any attack, nor any movement of troops at all, for that matter, until after taking omens to determine the optimum time. The diviner meditated on the pulsating innards of slaughtered goats to come up with a judgment, often in the heat of the moment, regarding the likely success of a proposed maneuver. Back in our own age, Antonio Damasio includes pilots alongside military officers, which again parallels the ancient evidence, since, as we will see, ancient pilots (of boats in this case) often appear in discussions in which divinatory knowledge is particularly pertinent. Then as now, people become interested in surplus knowledge precisely in cases where it would be most valued: when the right twitch at the right time makes a big difference, and a lot is riding on people who get the right gut feeling.

I hope to show in the pages that follow that the ancient philosophers' approaches to divinatory phenomena belong to an historical stream of attempts to understand cognitive intuition, or the mechanisms that

---

[64] Onasander, *The General,* 10.10. For more, see Kendrick Pritchett, *The Greek State at War,* part 3 (Berkeley: University of California Press, 1979).

result in surplus knowledge. Although the differences are manifold, there are also likely to be some as yet unfathomed connections between their philosophical attempts to account for divinatory insight, Thomas Aquinas' interest in instantaneous angelic thinking, Milton's idea that humans might be able to do it too, William Carpenter's search for unconscious cerebration, and even the approach of contemporary cognitive scientists. All these investigators try to make an account of the momentary, nondiscursive, apprehension of things by processes that fall outside our self-conscious control. This is not to say that any of the thinkers in this rather long line see the answers as the same—they do not. But they see the problem in a way whose similarly promises to be instructive.

DIVINE SIGNS AND HUMAN NATURE

In addition to the gains already set out, one final insight is advanced when we place ancient studies of divination within this longer history of studies on intuitive thinking. At several moments in that history, the topic of human physiology emerges as a close allied field. The experience that we have some form of nondiscursive knowing is regularly linked with the proposal that this way of knowing is embedded in the natural processes of our natures as organisms. This aspect of the longer history gives a context for something perhaps unexpected in the ancient evidence. As I alluded to above, ideas about divination among the philosophers also show a consistent engagement with questions of human nature, the dimensions of ourselves that we share with the animal realm, as bare organisms. One would think, given the customary Greek habit of linking our knowingnesss in general, and in divination in particular, to the divine realm, that theories about it would try to work their ways mainly through questions about the divine. But while the ancient investigators gathered here engage in a host of related fields—including epistemology, cosmology, causation, empiricism, intentionality, the study of signs, and occasionally questions about the divine—their thinking on divine signs activates and engages most vibrantly a study of human nature.

In the search for alternative systems of information processing, the philosophers appeal frequently to the natural functions of the human organism. We will see that it is not a coincidence that Plato addresses divination most explicitly in tandem with his most detailed discussion in the dialogues about human physiology. In the *Timaeus*, he considers the human organism, the ἄνθρωπος (a usually uninteresting topic for him), as a more or less dynamic piece of the cosmos. This physiological focus continues in a different way in Aristotle's account, which reaches deeply into some of his most profound statements about teleology in general, and specifically its manifestations in the human animal. For the Stoics as well, the critical piece of their understanding rests again on bodily processes, and specifically on their provocative positioning of the human being as a microcosmic corpuscle living within a universe they conceive of, explicitly, as a unified single animal. They will simply equate the coursing semiotic machinery of the cosmos with the messages and purposes that course through an animate, self-sustaining organism. Finally, the fact that ancient thinkers consistently framed the investigation this way also helps make sense of a further counterintuitive aspect in the thinking of the Neoplatonists. Given their association with various kinds of mystical thinking, they would seem likely to find μαντική a congenial domain. But as we will see the opposite proves true. Iamblichus will strike cautionary notes, for the most part, toward traditional forms of divination and advocate instead for what he consistently calls a more disembodied form of introspection, specifically situated outside of traditional μανκτική, which for him is a *too* bodily form of knowing. This position is difficult to understand without fully appreciating the general background in which the Neoplatonists are working. For them, divinatory knowing is, by the most thorough prior traditions that try to account for it, embedded in corporeal functions.

The central idea here is best captured by the notion of the organism, which needs to be disambiguated from a distinct idea with its own long and enduring history, the notion of the body. Since antiquity, and under the influence of Plato, the latter commonly carries the sense of a more or less aimless *corpus*, sitting to some degree external to the center of personhood that regulates one's goals and desires. It answers to the

Greek concept of the σῶμα—Pythagoras' tombstone or, in Platonic thinking, a prison to which we are shackled. From this Platonic positioning, the category of the body holds a tight grip on large swatches of Western intellectual history, in both the ancient and the modern eras. The concept of the organism (Greek ζῷον), by contrast, is more characteristic of Aristotle. It points to a self-generating and self-perpetuating entity that has built into it, and not separate from it, a set of dynamic processes that add up to a teleology of some kind.[65]

One is tempted to conclude that this trope of thinking, this centripetal pull toward questions about human nature in the ancient study of divine signs, illuminates an aspect of divination that we have not yet quite noticed. In addition to revealing divination as a cultural formation around the phenomenon of surplus knowledge, the following studies will suggest why this form has the general shape it does. The embeddedness of divination within the nature of organisms hints that divination serves as an expression of our unique position within the cosmos, poised between the twin wonders of our animate natures and of our self-aware sentience. Typically, as I mentioned at the outset, the Greeks set these two aspects of the experience of being human in opposition to one another. We exist between the regions of the animals and the gods, sharing aspects of both, but mostly witnessing and testifying to their separateness. But, in addition to all its other cultural dimensions in social and political history, divination contains an ongoing testimony about a linkage between the two. This divinatory awareness, this most cryptic and rudimentary region of our own epistemological capacities, is tracked backward and situated not in opposition to our creaturely selves. It is shown rather to emerge from them.

This principle provides a context for the often obsessively corporeal qualities of the most common Greek and Roman divinatory practices. It gives some reasoning behind the odd, almost perverse links made between our remotest insides and our remotest outsides, when astrologers

---

[65] Within the philosophy of biology, there are well placed scruples about the use of the notion of teleology. Here I am using the term to denote a purposiveness to maintain a certain organization of organic components, which, if left to its own devices, the organism performs rather than doesn't perform.

and diviners by viscera find links between their respective domains.[66] The phenomena of divination, in addition to all its other potent cultural dimensions, tightly embraces both our weird knowingness and our creaturely selves. It does this by standing as an expression that, in the end, the former emerges from the latter.

[66] See, for example, Hephaistion of Thebes, a fourth-century CE astrologer, *Apotelesmatica*, book 3, where the parts of the liver are correlated with different heavenly bodies (see D. Pingree, ed. [Teubner, 1973] 254.15ff). For fascinating further discussion on the theme, see Thomas Habinek, "Probing the Entrails of the Universe: Astrology as Bodily Knowledge in Manilius' *Astronomica*," in Jason König and Tim Whitmarsh, eds., *Ordering Knowledge in the Roman Empire* (Cambridge: Cambridge University Press, 2007), 229–40.

CHAPTER 1

Plato on Divination and Nondiscursive Knowing

IN HIS MOST VIVID NARRATIVE OF HIS HERO'S LIFE STORY, Plato has Socrates center his autobiography on an act of divination. The *Apology* shows a man driven by a provocative pronouncement from the Delphic oracle to devote his life to solving its riddle. Pleading his own defense before an Athenian jury, Socrates presents a carefully constructed speech, rich in mythological allusions. He compares himself to Achilles (28c) and likens his life's work to a Herculean labor (22a).[1] A more subtle and also more powerful point of reference is another figure, the Theban hero Oedipus, whose life was as profoundly shaped by the oracle as he argues his own was. But while Oedipus spends his days trying to disprove the oracle, in an archetypal act of intellectual hubris, Plato reverses the main point of the traditional tale, making his story one of intellectual humility. He dramatizes his hero's epistemological caution through counterpoint.

Plato consistently reaches back to myth, usually with an underlying purpose of supplanting a mythic archetype with one of his own more philosophical models—as when Er's trip to the other world is said to supersede Odysseus' narrative ("no tall tale to Alcinous" *Rep.* 614b).[2] It is somewhat surprising, given its prominent place in the corpus, that this particular retelling has not received more attention.[3]

---

[1] For this reading of πόνος here, see Silvia Montiglio, *Wandering in Ancient Greek Culture* (Chicago: University of Chicago Press, 2005), 153–54.

[2] See Kathryn Morgan, *Myth and Philosophy from the Presocratics to Plato* (Cambridge: Cambridge University Press, 2000), 204–10. Montiglio has made an interesting account of the similarity, 153–54.

[3] A reading in this general direction but to a different purpose was forwarded by Jacob Howland, "Plato's *Apology* as Tragedy," *Review of Politics* 70 (2008): 519–46; but the theme, to my mind critical, has as far as I can tell gone otherwise unnoticed.

Socrates makes out his own life to be a kind of propitiation for the general sin of overconfidence in the ability to know (*Apol.* 21b–d, 23b–c), the offence for which Oedipus could well stand. He places the same culturally regnant form of divination, the oracle at Delphi, at the very center of his drama too. The stories of the two figures resonate in specific similarities and inversions. Like Oedipus, Socrates arrives as a foreigner (ξένος 17d) in the land of the courtroom. Both men have given over their lives to solving oracular riddles (αἰνίγματα 21b, 27a, 27d) in order to benefit their cities. Both lose out on wealth and political power because of their wrestling with the Delphic oracle (24a). Even in its staging, the *Apology* resembles the *Oedipus Tyrannus*. In both works, the main character stands in front of a body of citizens who are making judgments, the dicasts resembling the chorus, and defends against accusers from his position at center stage: Socrates' accusers, Anytus, Lycon, and Meletus answering to Oedipus' Creon, Teiresias, and the messengers.

They strongly contrast with each other, though, over their attitude toward the state of their own knowledge. Oedipus deals with the challenge of the Pythia by remaining convinced that the infallible oracle has in his case made a mistake. Since hearing that he would sleep with his mother and kill his father, he has tried to prove it wrong. Bolstered by his victory over the Sphinx, he defensively makes light of Apollo's ability to know. When he gets the message that his Corinthian father is dead, whom he doesn't know was an adoptive one, he goes so far as to vaunt against divinatory knowledge.

> Ah ha!, why then would anyone look to
> the Pythian seer's hearth, or to the
> screeching birds above, under whose guidance
> I was supposed to have killed my very father? But he, now dead,
> lies concealed down in the earth; and I, this man, right here,
> am pure from the spear; unless somehow he died
> by longing for me, and in this way he might have died on account of me.
> But Polybus has taken with him the oracles at hand, worth nothing,
> and lies in Hades.

> φεῦ φεῦ, τί δῆτ' ἄν, ὦ γύναι, σκοποῖτό τις
> τὴν Πυθόμαντιν ἑστίαν, ἢ τοὺς ἄνω

κλάζοντας ὄρνεις, ὧν ὑφ' ἡγητῶν ἐγὼ
κτανεῖν ἔμελλον πατέρα τὸν ἐμόν; ὁ δὲ θανὼν
κεύθει κάτω δὴ γῆς· ἐγὼ δ' ὅδ' ἐνθάδε
ἄψαυστος ἔγχους, εἴ τι μὴ τὠμῷ πόθῳ
κατέφθιθ'· οὕτω δ' ἂν θανὼν εἴη 'ξ ἐμοῦ.
τὰ δ' οὖν παρόντα συλλαβὼν θεσπίσματα
κεῖται παρ' Ἅιδῃ Πόλυβος ἄξι' οὐδενός.

   (OT 964–72)

A certain kind of disagreeing with Apollo is of course authorized by a long tradition of debate with his oracle—famously depicted in Herodotus' stories of powerful men talking back to the Pythia—but Oedipus' challenge is less respectful. He stands outside the oracle's rules by simply declaring it wrong, instead of trying to figure out how it might be right, in a sense that he could live with. When Herodotus' Athenians don't like a particularly dreary oracle they get, by contrast, they ask for a new one (7.140–41). Their query yields them the famous declaration that by taking refuge behind the "wooden wall" they might stand a slim chance against Xerxes' onslaught. This gives them something they can work with, and they argue about the best way to interpret it. Successful interlocutors look for an accommodation. Socrates' stance is much closer to that of Themistocles than it is to Oedipus'. When the oracle declares Socrates to be the wisest of men, he claims to have been incredulous. But he accepts its authority and sets out to see what it might have meant, and in what way it could be true (*Apol.* 21b). Eventually, he declares it is right, understanding his wisdom to consist in a recognition of profound human limitation (20d–e). It turns out to be an oracle itself about divinatory knowledge, in comparison to which the human ability to know functionally vanishes. Precisely reversing Oedipus, he declares in the end that it is human wisdom, not the divine oracle, that is "worth nothing:"

> It's likely, gentlemen, that the god really is wise, and in this oracle is saying this: that human wisdom is worth something very small, even nothing. Although he appears to say this of Socrates, he has just used my name, making me an example, as if he should say, "That man is wisest among you, humans, whoever just like Socrates knows that in regard to wisdom, in truth, he is worth nothing."

τὸ δὲ κινδυνεύει, ὦ ἄνδρες, τῷ ὄντι ὁ θεὸς σοφὸς εἶναι, καὶ ἐν τῷ
χρησμῷ τούτῳ τοῦτο λέγειν, ὅτι ἡ ἀνθρωπίνη σοφία ὀλίγου τινὸς
ἀξία ἐστὶν καὶ οὐδενός. καὶ φαίνεται τοῦτον λέγειν τὸν Σωκράτη,
προσκεχρῆσθαι δὲ τῷ ἐμῷ ὀνόματι, ἐμὲ παράδειγμα ποιούμενος, ὥσπερ
ἂν <εἰ> εἴποι ὅτι "Οὗτος ὑμῶν, ὦ ἄνθρωποι, σοφώτατός ἐστιν, ὅστις
ὥσπερ Σωκράτης ἔγνωκεν ὅτι οὐδενὸς ἄξιός ἐστι τῇ ἀληθείᾳ πρὸς
σοφίαν." (23a–b)

Socrates atones for Oedipus' failing by his own change of attitude, but
further he supplants failure with success. Although Oedipus cannot entirely solve his crucial Delphic riddle, Socrates can. Speaking to the Delphic maxim to "know yourself," Plato makes of Socrates' life a lesson
grounded in a particular kind of self-knowledge. He is indeed the wisest
of men because he at least knows that he doesn't know anything at all.

With vertiginous ingenuity, Plato has made the panoptic knowledge
that most of his peers thought resided at Delphi to occupy a position
perfectly congruent to the kind of knowing Socrates is driven to pursue
throughout his life: a grasp of the real truth of things, as opposed to
tentative knowledge of the shifting surfaces of the shadow world of appearances in which we all sadly dwell. Further, the state of aporia that
results from Socratic elenchus produces an intellectual humility with
which he finds a parallel in that faced by those who tangle with the
oracle. Socrates seems to claim here that he has learned his own most
important lesson from the Pythia: appearances can be deceiving. And
if one could ever achieve secure knowledge of the forms themselves,
that person would be in a kind of higher state of knowing. Xenophon's
version of the story differs in instructive ways. The courtroom drama
is also driven by an oracle, but it isn't about human knowledge. Xenophon has the oracle claiming that no man is freer, more just, nor more
temperate than Socrates (Xen. *Apol.* 14). Socrates then advocates on his
own behalf, arguing for all the ways in which he indeed has more
freedom, justice, and temperance than anyone else.[4] Plato has made a
deliberate choice in the *Apology* to cast Socrates' life as a drama about
epistemology, and by using the oracle as a fulcrum, he indicates divination's power to speak to the human capacity to know. Taking this as

---

[4] Plato includes a characterization closer to Xenophon's in the last line of the *Phaedo* 118a,
where he describes Socrates with the adjectives ἄριστος, φρονιμώτατος, and δικαιότατος.

an invitation to have another look at how divination appears in the corpus, one sees that it comes up more frequently than might be expected. Socrates finds it useful in developing his arguments and illustrating points of his philosophical program. His tone is sometimes ironic and playful, sometimes quite sincerely engaged, sometimes mocking, sometimes serious, and almost never exclusively one of these.

By way of introduction, I will attempt to lay out a general sense of how divination functions in Plato's work. When scholars do take account of this topic, the question of skepticism tends to guide the treatment. We see attempts to determine some point, across a scale leading from negative to positive, corresponding to how Plato, Plato's Socrates, or the historic Socrates might have valued divinatory knowledge.[5] I will engage in a slightly different inquiry. I will not focus on how *seriously* Plato takes divination, but rather on *how* he takes it. Irrespective of any endorsement he may have hinted at toward the idea of knowledge arriving via traditional divinatory pathways, in what particular ways does he talk about it? I will proceed from a sense that Plato uses divination as an authoritative piece of his cultural context, to specify with greater precision his own ideas about ways of knowing; and as he is doing this, he helps us understand the nature of divination, as it is understood in his time.[6]

This approach also mirrors what is probably the standard mode in studies of the complex evidence Plato provides for another traditional, deeply authoritative discourse: poetry. We are used to the idea that even when he is being ironic or critical, we can gain powerful insights from Plato's corpus about poetics and poetry itself. And just as one

[5] Gregory Vlastos forwarded a case against any real investment in divinatory knowledge. Vlastos, *Socrates, Ironist and Moral Philosopher* (Ithaca, N.Y.: Cornell University Press, 1991), 157–78. Vlastos' student, Mark McPherran, embraces the idea that divination played a substantive role for the historical Socrates, *The Religion of Socrates* (University Park: Penn State Press, 1996), 186–88. T. C. Brickhouse and N. D. Smith, *Socrates on Trial* (Princeton: Princeton University Press, 1989), 106–7, 253–54, have slightly more nuanced approaches.

[6] Though this is not the typical approach to the topic, Kathryn Morgan has recently used something like it in a revealing treatment of the many forms of divine language in the *Phaedo* ("The Voice of Authority: Divination and Plato's *Phaedo*," *Classical Quarterly* 60.1 [2010]: 63–81). Morgan traces it back to A. Diès' seminal study of Plato's treatment of mystery cults. Auguste Diès, "La transposition platonicienne," *AIPh* 2 (1913): 267–308. Diès says: "il est difficile de ne pas voir que Platon joue, après d'autres, avec des formules consacrées et qu'il transpose, en ornements du dialogue, croyances et légendes aussi bien que formules" (302).

needn't solve precisely how seriously Plato took poetry in some global sense to gain such insights, so also we can learn about divination from Plato without having first to pin him (or Socrates) down to a single view on the whole of the topic. And as one begins to look in this direction, one finds that his discussions of divination are nearly as frequent as those of poetry, and perhaps even more consequential. In addition to the *Apology*, the topic is woven rather deeply, after all, into the fabric of prominent dialogues, such as the *Phaedrus*, *Phaedo*, and *Symposium*, and shorter references to it pepper other works.

Like poetry, divination often provides a foil for comparison—usually as a point of contrast rather than a topic unto itself. Both discourses carry a background of authority that Plato is keen to co-opt. He measures each art according to the value of its claims to knowledge, and in each case stresses limitations, especially in comparison with philosophy. Both poetry and divination are built on shaky epistemological ground, and they operate via the medium of the phantom image (εἴδωλον)—which for Plato consistently means an imitation of an imitation.[7]

In general in his corpus, I will argue, Plato treats divination (in a rainbow of tones from irony to seriousness) as being based on a claim about a particular form of cognition, one marked especially for being nondiscursive. In his various modes of treating it, it comes to stand for a kind of knowledge that arrives unexpectedly or involuntarily, and stretches beyond our ability to account for it. By consistently highlighting these qualities, Plato attests to a broader view that divination is the locus of surplus knowledge. This aspect of the larger picture has mostly escaped us.

After this broader exploration of the corpus, I will use the view gained to reexamine Plato's most concentrated commentary on the topic, in the fascinating anatomical discussion of human nature in the *Timaeus*. The text is undeniably strange. As we will see, Plato develops an elaborate discussion of the liver as a screen for divinatory images meant to frighten the appetitive soul into submission. But this section of the *Timaeus*, coming as it does at a pivotal inflection point of the dialogue, has provoked a more bemused kind of puzzlement among scholars than perhaps it should.[8] It articulates a complex set of ideas

---

[7] See, e.g., *Rep.* 599d3.

[8] Archer-Hind says: "The keen irony pervading the whole of this very curious and interesting passage is too evident to escape notice." R. D. Archer-Hind, ed., *The Timaeus of Plato* (London:

that are embedded in important components of Platonic epistemology and psychology.[9] And furthermore, in my view, it gives us our most illuminating insights into his ideas on the nature of nondiscursive thought in general, more useful than his more famous discussions of inspiration in the *Phaedrus* and elsewhere. The directness of the remarks in this text makes the discussion in the *Timaeus* as important for understanding divination as the *Ion* or book 10 of the *Republic* are for the study of poetry. The physiological context is entirely in keeping with an enduring current within ancient philosophical commentary, as the subsequent treatments will show. Divination is widely understood as a mode of knowing emergent from the peculiar kind of teleology that inheres in living organisms. But before we turn to the *Timaeus*, we need to build a context for understanding it by taking a broader look across the corpus.

DIVINATION IN PLATO OUTSIDE OF THE *TIMAEUS*

The Diviner as a Craftsman

In many places in his work, Plato talks about divination in the sense of a trade craft or technical expertise. These references are not so illuminating in themselves, but they help set a tone for his more substantive and more plentiful comments on divination as a way of knowing, a consideration of which will follow. In a rather unmarked way, he talks about it as belonging to Zeus at Dodona (*Phaedrus* 275b) and as the

---

MacMillan, 1888 repr. New York: Arno, 1973), 266. Taylor characterizes the discussion of the liver as "a very curious, and obviously far from wholly serious, speculation," A. E. Taylor, *A Commentary on Plato's Timaeus* (New York: Clarendon, 1928), 506. J. E. Raven states that "The effect of much of it is bizarre rather than illuminating," *Plato's Thought in the Making: A Study of the Development of his Metaphysics* (Cambridge: Cambridge University Press, 1965), 238. More recently, Carlos Steel also detects "irony" and claims that the treatment of the liver, spleen, and lungs is "comical," "The Moral Purpose of the Human Body: A Reading of *Timaeus* 69–72," *Phronesis* 46.2 (2001): 113. Cornford is more willing to take the discussion seriously; *Plato's Cosmology: The Timaeus of Plato Translated with a Running Commentary* (London: Kegan Paul, Trench, Trubner and Co.: 1937), 288–89. The claim of irony and lack of seriousness is in each case presented as an observation, typically unaccompanied by argumentation, after which scholars consider various forms of narrower appreciation of compelling aspects of the passage.

[9]See Serafina Rotondaro, "Il ΠΑΘΟΣ della ragione e I sogni: Timeo 70d7–72b5," in Tomás Calvo and Luc Brisson, eds., *Interpreting the Timaeus—Critias: Proceedings of the IV Symposium Platonicum* (St. Augustin: Academia Verlag, 1997), 275–80.

purview of Apollo (*Crat.* 405a–c; *Symp.* 197a; *Rep.* 383b6); and in *Ion*, Socrates includes diviners in a list of craftspeople along with mathematicians, dieticians, doctors, charioteers, and fishermen (531b, 538e–39d). In certain contexts, the sense of the discussion shades more toward the office of the *mantis* than the technique of *mantikê*, as in *Laches* (199a) and especially in the *Laws* (642d7, 686a4). *Phaedrus* adds a value judgment and places diviners in the middle rung of a ladder that ranks the kinds of lives a person could acquire in reincarnation. As souls are reborn, they gain lives according to how powerfully they are drawn to the material world. Those least tempted are reborn as lovers of wisdom and beauty. Next, in descending order, are law-abiding rulers, men of affairs, athletes, and in fifth position diviners. Then come poets, artisans, sophists, and finally tyrants. In the *Statesman*, divination appears as one among the elaborate typology of crafts that he works through according to his cascading tree of binary classifications. It shows up there as an expertise 1) in cognitive or abstract knowledge (γνωστικὴ ἐπιστήμη) rather than knowledge of manual action, that 2) does not just make judgments, but directs actions, and 3) hands on its orders from others (the gods) and does not generate them itself (260e, cf. 299d). The first point already marks his inclination to understand divination as having to do with a way of thinking, rather than an expertise in manual techniques; the second that it is meant to achieve practical results; and the last that it passes on orders but doesn't itself contain wisdom. These will all find echoes elsewhere in the corpus. This dialogue also hints that diviners display a kind of puffed up character: "For the priest and the diviner have great social standing and a keen sense of their own importance. They win veneration and respect because of the high task they undertake" (290d). But along with the class of priests, they belong to a servile class of arts, doing the work of others (in their case the gods), and while they make claims to being one of the ruling classes, this is illusory.

In the *Charmides*, we are asked to consider if human society would thrive and be happy just on the basis of every technical expert knowing his or her craft. Socrates relates a dream he has—whether from the gate of horn or ivory he does not know—where experts have such expertise, and claims that in such a case, while we would be acting according to the kind of accurate tactical knowledge that hits the marks aimed at by various *technai*, we would not necessarily be pursuing the kind of ends that lead to our own true happiness. The general would know how to protect, the physician to heal, and the diviner would know all things (173c), but we would not necessarily be doing any of these things for the kinds of purposes that would lead us to the good. A couple of points are worth noting here. First, the fact that Socrates says he gains this insight via a traditional mantic form is surely relevant. Although it has a playful air to it, the dream reference shows the territory of divination provides a vantage from which a certain kind of knowledge *about* knowledge might be possible. More important, the craft of diviners is one of knowing, and (given the contrafactual quality of the thought experiment) they practice this craft imperfectly, in the way that generals or physicians also sometimes go wrong. And, last, it is not the diviner's art to know purposes and decide normative questions; Socrates' way of positioning them in contrast to those who know good from bad ends suggests that the diviners' expertise is narrower. They know data that others don't know, but they are not themselves particularly possessed of the kind of wisdom that could decide how to value it. In a similar vein, Socrates turns to the example of the *mantis* in the *Laches*, under the consideration of courage. Nicias proposes that courage is a kind of wisdom, a mastery over hope and fear, and provokes a discussion of who might have such wisdom. His interlocutor, pushing him toward an unpalatable claim, suggests in response that the *manteis* would seem then to be courageous, given their reputation for indiscriminate wisdom. Nicias counters the claim by arguing that while the *mantis* may see things coming he is unable to tell whether they are good or bad for the person in question (195e–96d). Here again, Plato portrays the *mantis* as a craftsman with a narrow, technical expertise, akin to that of the physician or warrior. He is able to foresee things, but lacks a sense of what the bigger picture means in order to evaluate them. Both the *Charmides* and the *Laches* speak of an art that knows discrete pieces of knowledge but has no special claim to broader understanding.

We can also locate a cluster of passages where Plato speaks of unscrupulous and charlatan diviners. He mentions them in the *Republic* in a list of craftsmen in the city (389d3) who may potentially lie; and as unscrupulous figures, along with magical priests, who offer wealthy people expiation from their sins for high fees (364b5). In the *Laws* diviners might advise a client to give in to the craven desire to pick up someone else's unattended property (913b2), and so they could be enlisted, in situations where a bit of ethical corner-cutting would be profitable, to tell others what they want to hear. In book 11 in the *Laws* the Athenian is discussing the penalties for poisoning and divides the category into physical poisonings, over which doctors have an expertise, and

> another form that, by certain so-called tricks, incantations, and binding spells, convinces those that dare to perform them that they themselves are doing harm (as much as this sort of thing is able to be convincing) and above all convinces others that they are harmed by those people who are capable of magic.

> ἄλλη δὲ ἢ μαγγανείαις τέ τισιν καὶ ἐπῳδαῖς καὶ καταδέσεσι λεγομέναις πείθει τοὺς μὲν τολμῶντας βλάπτειν αὐτούς, ὡς δύνανται τὸ τοιοῦτον, τοὺς δ' ὡς παντὸς μᾶλλον ὑπὸ τούτων δυναμένων γοητεύειν βλάπτονται. (933a)

Two classes of people are said to have expertise in this arena, the diviner (μάντις) and the τερατοσκόπος (the observer of wonders). Like the doctor, such people deserve a heavier penalty if they are involved in the psychological poisoning that magic amounts to. The language here leaves no doubt that there were figures who practiced both the mantic arts and the magical ones. We see an even more nefarious character near the close of *Laws* 10 (908d), where the Athenian considers different types of atheist. The one with the naturally good character is not particularly harmful. But atheism nurtures a moral lassitude in the one with a poor character. He is a man of subtlety and guile, and from his like come many diviners, tricksters, impostors, tyrants, demagogues, generals, private mystery priests, and sophists. These characterizations of nefarious diviners need to be seen in an overall context in the *Laws*, where, although diviners can go wrong to be sure, so again can any person in a position of authority go wrong. And like those other authority figures, there are good ones too. In fact, in the *Laws*, the Athenian makes many references to diviners as playing important roles in the city. We are told that laws may be changed only exceedingly rarely, and only after consulting with three bodies: all magistrates, the whole popular assembly, and all the oracles (772d). The *manteis* are to be turned to as experts on the gods (885c–d, 792d), to decide on sacrifices and the cities' calendar (828a–b), on matters of law dealing with the regulation of the courts, giving them an apparent super-legal authority (871d). Right on the heels of the reference to a diviner who tells a person to just go ahead and take unattended property, the Athenian tells us that particularly difficult cases of theft are to be sent to the oracle at Delphi, who will be the main arbiter of accusations of theft (914a).

Taken together, these references to the *technê* and office of the diviner tell us of a person to be less admired than philosophers and law-abiding rulers, but more admired than poets, sophists, or tyrants. The diviner is more a conduit and bringer of data than a judge and bringer of wisdom. He or she should not be expected to know what is good or bad, but is generally understood to have information to which others don't have access. The office carries social prestige and authority. It tempts to corruption and offers opportunities for the weak of character to engage in abuse, and conversely it is valuable in securing stability and order in a state when occupied by a person with good qualities.

Divination as a Way of Knowing

MOCKERY AND THE ALOOF SEER

In a larger collection of texts, Plato treats divination not as an office, but as a certain way of knowing. I will here look at the evidence by moving through common themes in increasing order of interest. First, Plato commonly uses divinatory language playfully to describe someone's ability to make an accurate prediction. Socrates is said to have spoken "prophetically" on a number of occasions: when he claims that Theaetetus was going to be someone remarkable (*Theaet.* 142c), when he says that Agathon was going to make a good speech in the *Symposium* (198a), and when he foresees an illustrious future for Isocrates at the close of the *Phaedrus* (279a). Also in the *Phaedrus*, the famous declaration by the Egyptian king Amon that writing will destroy memory is called a prophecy. In the *Republic*, Thrasymachus teasingly says Socrates has mantic powers when he is able to foresee certain implications of Thrasymachus' argument that the unjust person thrives (349a). In the *Statesman*, the stranger uses the verb for "divine" (μαντεύομαι) with a similar tone, to say that he foresees that some classes among the servants and slaves will make claims against the king—and, since one of these classes is indeed that of prophets, a pun is close to hand (289c). In the *Republic*, we see something like this when, in considering the question of whether poets who always speak in direct voice, as if they are the character speaking rather than narrating in the third person, are to be admitted to the city, Adeimantus says he thinks he "divines" that Socrates means to turn the discussion to drama (394d). Finally, in the *Theaetetus*, Socrates mockingly speaks of Protagoras' success, saying no one would have paid such huge sums to study with him if he were not able to convince them that he was better able to see what was going to happen even than a *mantis* (179a).

In the same vein, but with a sharper satirical edge, he makes fun of a few figures who suppose themselves to possess extravagant, or even outlandish, kinds of knowing. Socrates teases Euthyphro's pose as a font of wisdom this way (*Euthyphro* 3e). In the *Meno*, after Anytus expresses his strong dislike of the Sophists, and simultaneously declares that he has never had any contact with them, Socrates wonders how he knows he dislikes people with whom he has had no experience. He answers his own question with a teasing comment: "Well, perhaps you are a *mantis*, Anytus, since indeed I would wonder how else you know about these things, drawing from what you yourself are saying" (μάντις εἶ ἴσως, ὦ Ἄνυτε· ἐπεὶ ὅπως γε ἄλλως οἶσθα τούτων πέρι, ἐξ ὧν αὐτὸς λέγεις θαυμάζοιμ' ἄν [92c]). A similar tone marks the *Lysis* as its argument veers toward the absurdly complex. Socrates and his interlocutors consider whether like is friendly with like or whether opposites attract, and in the middle of some intricate lines of thought, he claims that he "divines" that something neither good nor bad is friendly with what is good (216d). In the *Cratylus*, Plato uses references to divination as bookends to the etymological sections of the dialogue, where he is self-consciously stretching the reach of his own insight. Near the beginning, after Socrates' brief opening run of etymologies, presenting the real truth behind the names of mythic heroes and gods, Hermogenes says to Socrates, "you seem to be suddenly uttering oracles, like an inspired prophet!" (μοι δοκεῖς ὥσπερ οἱ ἐνθουσιῶντες ἐξαίφνης χρησμῳδεῖν [396d–e]). Socrates accepts the ironic compliment with more irony, claiming he was inspired by Euthyphro (whose status as a prophet Socrates has already used as a kind of joke) and then saying that they can use this gift of inspiration for only one day, and tomorrow they will have to conjure it away and find a priest to purify themselves. As Socrates finishes his etymologies later in the dialogue, he hands the discussion over to Cratylus, who makes reference to Socrates' divinatory state of knowledge, and again invokes the name of Euthryphro (428c; cf. 411b).

In the previous clump of evidence, Plato makes salient a theme that will carry forward in what follows. In each case, the texts highlight the idea that divinatory knowing is by definition that which one gets suddenly, and without knowing how one got it. It is a discourse whose authority derives from cultural prestige—analogous to other forms of divine speech, like ritual commandments and mystery formulas—as opposed to reasoned argumentation; and attempts to explain it are presumed to be beside the point. It floats above the realm of proof and assumes its own epistemological value. *Cratylus* furnishes an especially illustrative example, in a slightly different context. As the opening move in the dialogue, Hermogenes describes Cratylus' resistance to explaining one of his own claims:[10]

> When I ask him, eager to know what in the world he's talking about, he clarifies nothing and feigns ignorance. He pretends to be mulling it over internally as though he by himself has private knowledge about it, which if he only wanted to tell clearly would make me also agree and say the very things he himself does. If then you are able somehow to reckon out Cratylus' oracle, I would gladly listen.

> καὶ ἐμοῦ ἐρωτῶντος καὶ προθυμουμένου εἰδέναι ὅτι ποτὲ λέγει, οὔτε ἀποσαφεῖ οὐδὲν εἰρωνεύεταί τε πρός με, προσποιούμενός τι αὐτὸς ἐν ἑαυτῷ διανοεῖσθαι ὡς εἰδὼς περὶ αὐτοῦ, ὃ εἰ βούλοιτο σαφῶς εἰπεῖν, ποιήσειεν ἂν καὶ ἐμὲ ὁμολογεῖν καὶ λέγειν ἅπερ αὐτὸς λέγει. εἰ οὖν πῃ ἔχεις συμβαλεῖν τὴν Κρατύλου μαντείαν, ἡδέως ἂν ἀκούσαιμι. (383b–84a)

In this evidence, then, Plato uses the language of divination to mark a kind of knowledge that seems mostly to hang back, taking refuge in the privilege of silence that its social prestige allows. It does not give an account of itself because its practitioners assume it is not *required* to.

---

[10] For more on Hermogenes' stance toward divination, see Xenophon, *Symp.* 4.47–48.

What joins these texts together is how Socrates positions divinatory knowledge with respect to the need to explain itself: mostly, it just does not seem to bother.[11]

DIVINATION AND ELENCHUS

In a set of texts that cluster around Socrates' final days divination, again positioned as a kind of knowing that sets itself outside of scrutiny, comes into direct conversation with elenchic philosophical discourse. In the *Apology*, *Crito*, and especially *Phaedo*, we have Socrates making poignant and frequent reference to a traditional idea that near the end of life, people have prophetic powers. In the *Apology*, for example, at 39c–d, the long building discussion of Socrates' engagement with the Delphic oracle, culminates with his own prophecy, in the spirit of a curse, when he foresees vengeance for his accusers. In a gentler mode, *Crito* opens with Socrates relating a dream of a woman approaching him quoting a single hexameter line from the *Iliad*, where Achilles rebuffs the embassy in book 9, by saying that "To the pleasant land of Phthia on the third day you will come" (44b). Socrates interprets this as an indication of when he will be put to death. The *Phaedo* carries forward the theme of deathbed prescience, but presses it further. Plato develops the idea in a literary vein with the touching image of the swans, who are traditionally thought to sing louder just before death, and so to have a moment of foresight at the end of their lives (84e–85b). Like *Crito*, *Phaedo* uses the opening device of having Socrates consider a dream to be prophetic, and trying to tease out an oblique message. This dream calls on Socrates to practice "the art overseen by the Muse." Since several different arts fall in the Muses' purview, Socrates has at the last minute taken to covering his bases, in another gesture of epistemological humbleness, by composing poetry. By the end of the dialogue, he has convinced himself that his original interpretation of the oracular dream was correct all along: by telling him to practice *mousikê* the god meant to tell him to devote himself to philosophy, the highest form of music.

---

[11] For more on this theme, see also Morgan (2010); and for a parallel treatment of Pythagoreans by Plato, see Phillip Horky, *Plato and Pythagoreanism* (Oxford: Oxford University Press, 2013), 168–74.

Just as in the case of the *Apology*, an oblique divine message underscores the importance of specifically philosophical inquiry.

As Kathryn Morgan has shown, Plato structures the *Phaedo* as a whole as a cultural refashioning: Socrates takes up the traditional hope to derive knowledge from a divine and infallible authority and subtly argues that we should transpose that aspiration onto a drive to pursue the dictates of logical argument.[12] In this dialogue, divination appears as one among a vast array of divine discourses, including mystery sayings, magical incantations, ritual formulas, mystic doctrines, and esoteric philosophical commandments. Their linking characteristic is that they derive their authority from the cultural prestige of divine speech and not from giving an account of themselves.[13] In contrast to philosophical elenchus, which operates by doubt and is constantly forced to account for itself, divine discourse trades in surety, and does not deign to give its reasons. Over the very personalized stakes of the fate of Socrates' own soul, in the end-of-life dialogues, Plato argues that by allowing ourselves to be led by doubt, we achieve levels of certainty all the more worthwhile for being tested. The discussion famously leads Socrates to declare very near the moment of his death, in what amounts to his parting prophecy, that it is as certain as anything can be that the soul is immortal and indestructible (παντὸς μᾶλλον ἄρα, ἔφη, ὦ Κέβης, ψυχὴ ἀθάνατον καὶ ἀνώλεθρον [*Phaedo* 106e–7a])—although, of course, Simmias confesses to some lingering doubt, reminding us that elenchus never arrives at a finished state.

Plato's line of reasoning is exceedingly clever—he does not just argue for the superiority of *logos* over divine speech. He instead has divine language actively engaged in transferring its own authority. Just as much as he fashions Socrates' philosophical argument, Plato carefully constructs the oracles to underscore the main message as death approaches: philosophical elenchus is the new highest standard of epistemological value. Plato has made all of the oracles that orbit Socrates' final days, like the main one in the *Apology* with which we began, explicitly use their own authority to provide a warrant for philosophical

---

[12] Morgan (2010).

[13] Marcel Detienne has written elegantly on this unipolar approach to discourse, in *Masters of Truth* (New York: Zone, 1996), 62–85.

dialogue. Just before the closing dramatic scenes of the poisoning in *Phaedo*, Socrates relates perhaps his most moving eschatological myth, in which a shining race of humans who live in the upper air are able to get oracles, direct perceptions, and pronouncements from the gods, face-to-face (111b). Their oracles are direct because they are in a state we are not—we do not live in the upper air, but, following the myth, are clustered around a swampy lake wallowing around in muck, which, we have become convinced, is our only world.[14] Elenchus is our real way out, and overinvestment in oracles starts to look presumptuous—it assumes that we are in some status like the people in the shining world and are able to know what the divine wants. Overconfidence in the ability to know, a puffed up sense of human abilities, is, ironically, by Plato's artful and subtle recasting, the teleology of a trust in divine oracles.

INTUITION AND NONDISCURSIVE KNOWING

In the *Laws* a large handful of times Plato uses the verb "to divine" as a rather unmarked synonym for "surmise" or "intuit." The Athenian stranger "divines" correctly the powerful value of a law that prevents young people from challenging laws (634e). Later, after saying that the laws and practices of the Persians seemed sound, the stranger then attempts to "divine" why their prosperity decayed under Cambyses and was recovered under Darius (694c). Examining the public program of hymns and recitals, the stranger says we should be very resistant to changing them, just as we are with the laws, and that is why the ancients gave the name *nomoi* to both hymns and laws. They must have "divined" the similarity in a dream or vision (800a–c, cf. 700b, 722d, 734e). On laws surrounding rites of death, the stranger urges respect for the dead, but also to avoid extravagance. The lawgivers will be the proper judges of the touchy question of what counts as moderation for funeral services; they will "divine" it (952d). Hearkening back to the functions the Athenian gives the office and art of the *mantis* in the *Laws* that we saw above, these examples again point to a super-legal positioning of divinatory knowledge.

Most trenchantly, Plato also uses divination language to express moments of intuitive insight that either seem to, or actually do, pass

---

[14] This image carries resonance with the Orphic traditions likely behind *Phaedo* 69c.

an elenchic test after the fact, but whose origin remains beyond full explanation. In contrast to what we saw above, where divination does not give an account of itself because it presumes it does not *have* to, in this evidence divination does not account for itself because it is *not able* to. Further, the inability to explain is not because of grandiose over-reaching on the part of the knower, but rather is based on an epistemological humility in the face of the inscrutability of the thing known.

We begin looking at this theme in a set of texts that casts the inscrutability of the thing known to derive from its profundity. Aristophanes' famous myth of the origin of erotic love in the *Symposium* is a good illustration. When two lovers, who were originally halves of a whole creature, meet, their desire for one another is profound, and he expresses it as an urge or an impulse, which each soul "is unable to articulate, but each divines what it wants and understands hints of it" (ὃ οὐ δύναται εἰπεῖν, ἀλλὰ μαντεύεται ὃ βούλεται, καὶ αἰνίττεται [192d]). As we saw in the *Apology*, the verb αἰνίττεται is characteristic of divination. The reference to divination marks a fortuitous insight, something like a peripheral vision, whose source is unclear. While no accounting is given for how the insight arrives, neither is there much doubt that it is of value.

Within the frame provided by Aristophanes' myth, we next consider a group of texts that moves to further depths. With some regularity, Plato uses the language of divination to describe an insight of unknown origin that seems to be true, but is so weighty that it would be difficult to understand how any human could get his mind around it. Elenchus may or may not enter into the discussion, but it does not provide the means by which the insight emerges. Some examples within this collection of texts, particularly around the Good, resemble the grasping of fundamental preconditions for knowledge, akin to what those who study epistemology would fit into a history of "rational intuition," such as we defined it in the introductory chapter. We will see Plato use the language of divination to describe such cognitive moments. This is the kind of cognitive event that provokes Aristotle to develop ideas around the category of νοῦς; and scholars of rational intuition typically see this as the crucial beginning point. But when Plato tries to find a language to talk about our nondiscursive apprehension of the forms, he is trying to describe a cognitive phenomenon that is at least analogous. It is of great interest to this study that, when he does, he reaches for divinatory language with at least some regularity. Starting from Aristotle, there will be a different language, but with Plato, there is not. This suggests that Plato is writing at a time before the divergence between what epistemologists have called rational intuition, and what I am claiming in this study to be cognitive intuition, a name for the cognitive function that produces surplus knowledge, for which the cultural form of divination is the main expression in antiquity.

Plato's studies of the virtues are a good place to begin this next part of the investigation. He often treats temperance as a principal virtue, and twice uses notions of divination to describe how one might get a sense of it. In the *Charmides*, one of Socrates' premises in a larger argument is that temperance (σωφροσύνη) is something good. Rather than say he knows this for sure, or try to develop a proof that this is so, he says he "divines" it (μαντεύομαι). The verb is here a shorthand for just knowing something or sensing it, in the absence of discursive proof. In the *Republic*, we find a more elaborated example over the same territory. Socrates senses a similarity between temperance and harmony. First he simply notices a likeness between the two. More than the other great values, temperance "resembles a certain proportion and harmony" (συμφωνίᾳ τινὶ καὶ ἁρμονίᾳ προσέοικεν [430e]). He then looks into the resemblance that caught his eye, and after adducing several reasons that justify the similarity says: "Do you see, then, that we divined plausibly just now that temperance resembles a sort of harmony?" (ὁρᾷς οὖν, ἦν δ' ἐγώ, ὅτι ἐπιεικῶς ἐμαντευόμεθα ἄρτι ὡς ἁρμονίᾳ τινὶ ἡ σωφροσύνη ὡμοίωται;). Here again "divining" describes a particular cognitive state, an intuitive awareness of likeness between two ideas (431e). Also in the Republic, after Socrates moves from his heuristic of examining a whole city, to look for justice on a larger scale, back to the individual, it turns out that the analogy of what they discovered at the larger scale does indeed hold for the smaller scale of the individual. Socrates says that they turn out to have been right, like a predictive dream (443c). Again, resemblance is at stake. The kind of intellectual quantum that is picked up quickly, and without a discursive chain of reasoning. Something of this sort seems to be behind Glaucon's short intervention later in the dialogue, after Socrates describes

with pungent clarity, in a short burst of insights, the decay of souls fix-
ated on material pleasures. "'Socrates,' Glaucon said, 'you are utterly
oracular in describing the life of the many!'" (παντελῶς, ἔφη ὁ Γλαύκων,
τὸν τῶν πολλῶν, ὦ Σώκρατες, χρησμῳδεῖς βίον [586b]). Rather than
give a rigorous proof of such a decay, Socrates strings together moving
speeches that seem to flow one from the next. He earns the designation of being an oracle here for being imbued with specifically nondiscursive powers of insight, and while no elenchic proof of the insights
is made, the dialogue makes it clear that the knowledge offered is
creditable.

Moving even further along the scale of profundity, Plato uses divinatory language to talk about an approach to knowledge of the Good, a
transcendent principle, whose ontological status, let alone its epistemological one, is difficult to discern. He does this multiple times, in the
Republic, and as we will see in a moment, in *Phaedrus*, and *Symposium*
as well. The examples show us the usefulness of divination as a widely
understood cultural language, that allows Plato to discuss something
new and distinctive in his philosophical system. Our apprehension of
the highest truths, which will dwell with Plato's forms, needs to take
place via a mode of knowing that does not move from observations of
the world around us, via sequential inference, to conclusions. Such
forms of knowing are compromised by the unstable and illusory character of the empirical data. And there are even some moments, he will
tell us, when elenchus itself, which stays at the level of the abstract while
using rules of logic discursively, is not quite up to the challenge. There
are some forms of knowing beyond even this, and when Plato speaks of
them, the language of divination is often close to hand. It is perhaps
worth saying in advance that the line I will develop here does not lead
to the conclusion that Plato means this kind of knowing to be identical
to traditional *mantikê*, as further considerations will show, but it is unmistakable that he means it is like *mantikê*.

Just after the parable of the cave in book 7, he returns to the discussion of the educational scheme for the guardians, ongoing since book 2,
which he now understands in terms of the cave's larger implications for
our understanding of where real truth lies. He arrives at the insight
that the guardians should pursue studies that turn the mind away from
the world of material things, generation and decay, and becoming,

and toward the immaterial, unchanging world of being. At the start of the process that reaches this position, Plato begins wondering about their proper studies and then interrupts himself to mention in mid-sentence that some thought has just occurred to him:[15]

> What, then, Glaucon, would be the learning that would draw a soul away from the world of becoming and toward the world of being? This thing just now enters my mind as I am talking . . .

> τί ἂν οὖν εἴη, ὦ Γλαύκων, μάθημα ψυχῆς ὁλκὸν ἀπὸ τοῦ γιγνομένου ἐπὶ τὸ ὄν; τόδε δ᾿ ἐννοῶ λέγων ἅμα . . . (521d)

He then lays out the thing that "just entered," pointing to the idea that abstract pursuits like mathematics (he will go on to add geometry, astronomy, and the theory of music to the list) are the most conducive to turning our minds toward the immaterial and so are the best primary studies in the guardians' curriculum.[16] As he moves the conversation forward to test this idea via elenchus, he makes clear that the original insight arrived via something other than elenchic *logos*:

> I will try, I said, to show what seems right to me at least. Now, either concur or dissent, as a co-observer alongside me, to what I distinguish to be or not to be conducive to the sort of things we're talking about, in order that we might see also this more clearly, whether the matter is as I divine it to be.

> ἐγὼ πειράσομαι, ἦν δ᾿ ἐγώ, τό γ᾿ ἐμοὶ δοκοῦν δηλῶσαι. ἃ γὰρ διαιροῦμαι παρ᾿ ἐμαυτῷ ἀγωγά τε εἶναι οἷ λέγομεν καὶ μή, συνθεατὴς γενόμενος σύμφαθι ἢ ἄπειπε, ἵνα καὶ τοῦτο σαφέστερον ἴδωμεν εἰ ἔστιν οἷον μαντεύομαι. (523a)

He will submit that insight to dialectical scrutiny, but to describe the original flash he makes recourse to the language of prophetic insight.[17] A dialectical section ensues. In closing off this discussion, regarding

---

[15] Such a claim is not uncommon in Plato, and it surely has rhetorical effect (cf. *Rep.* 370a; *Euthyphro* 9c).

[16] This sense is also enacted in the *Meno* in the choice of geometry as the subject for eliciting knowledge from the slave boy.

[17] Similarly, *Philebus* 20b speaks of the happenstance arrival of an idea in divinatory terms: "I imagine some god has recalled to my mind something that will help us," and "I remember a theory that I heard long ago, perhaps I dreamed it."

which arts the guardians are to pursue, Socrates starts to look for commonalities among them, so we can draw larger lessons, and he returns again to divinatory language. Facing such difficult questions, Glaucon "divines" such a thing would be a mammoth task, and Socrates then pivots the discussion to the power of dialectic as an overarching method of study (531d). At the end of considering dialectic's profound value, Socrates wonders about the right time for introducing it, uses a complex thought experiment, and again speaks of "divining" this difficult answer.[18] Such language is repeated (538a4, 538a7, 538a9, 538b9) in a kind of closing punctuation mark on the discussion of what kind of education best guides a person to the Good, the crowning moment of the whole plan for the *Republic*'s ideal city. In these texts, divination marks an insight that is in answer to a problem of great profundity, and that arrives in a flash, not via the processes of elenchus, but is testable by it.

And at the head of this whole discussion, about the right training of the guardians to facilitate an approach to the Good, Plato frames any attempt to know the Good itself again in divinatory terms, as a nondiscursive cognitive event. In book 6, in the discussion leading up to the image of the divided line, Socrates talks about the Good in moving terms:

> That which every soul pursues and on account of which does everything it does, it divines to be something, although it is at a loss and incapable of grasping sufficiently what in the world it is, nor is it able to feel a steady confidence about it, of the sort which it has concerning other things; and on account of this, even if it got some help from other things, it misses the mark. Are we to say, then, with regard to this kind of a thing, and a thing of this magnitude, that those who are best in the city

---

[18] He considers the current state of affairs, in which sophists, who have little investment in the way things truly are (according to Socrates) teach dialectic to young people, who then take a callous disregard for the truth of things and value only manipulation. In trying to figure out when would be a more appropriate time to teach dialectic, he says that in the current situation, he "divines" that people who learn dialectic too young are like young people who are raised in families with abundant wealth, and are then convinced by flatterers that they have been adopted. This knowledge causes them to turn on their families, and graft onto the flatterer. This is the case with those who study dialectic at a young age with sophists. They tell their students that their parental values of temperance, justice, beauty, etc., are not their true parents, but are only shams, and the children attach themselves to the flatterers.

[the guardians] ought to be in darkness also, those to whom we will entrust everything?

ὃ δὴ διώκει μὲν ἅπασα ψυχὴ καὶ τούτου ἕνεκα πάντα πράττει, ἀπομαντευομένη τι εἶναι, ἀποροῦσα δὲ καὶ οὐκ ἔχουσα λαβεῖν ἱκανῶς τί ποτ' ἐστὶν οὐδὲ πίστει χρήσασθαι μονίμῳ οἵᾳ καὶ περὶ τἄλλα, διὰ τοῦτο δὲ ἀποτυγχάνει καὶ τῶν ἄλλων εἴ τι ὄφελος ἦν, περὶ δὴ τὸ τοιοῦτον καὶ τοσοῦτον οὕτω φῶμεν δεῖν ἐσκοτῶσθαι καὶ ἐκείνους τοὺς βελτίστους ἐν τῇ πόλει, οἷς πάντα ἐγχειριοῦμεν; (505e–6a)

The answer is, of course, an emphatic no. Plato then says that proper guardians will need to know how the just and noble relate to the good, as a whole, or they will not be good guardians. He concludes this opening: "I divine that no one will be [a good guardian] until he knows these things sufficiently." His interlocutor tells him that he has "divined well," leaving no doubt about the purposefulness of Plato's use of the description (μαντεύομαι δὲ μηδένα αὐτὰ πρότερον γνώσεσθαι ἱκανῶς. καλῶς γάρ, ἔφη, μαντεύῃ [506a]).

With similar language, at the close of *Philebus*, after a long consideration of the different kinds of pleasures a person might feel, Socrates recapitulates what they have learned from the dialogue. He here endorses some mixture of measured pleasures and reason for a thriving life. A perfect balance will set a person on the way to the highest goal in life, which is, he says:

> to try to learn in this way what on earth is good, both in a human being and in the cosmos, and what in the world one should divine the form itself of the Good to be.

ἐν ταύτῃ μαθεῖν πειρᾶσθαι τί ποτε ἕν τ' ἀνθρώπῳ καὶ τῷ παντὶ πέφυκεν ἀγαθὸν καὶ τίνα ἰδέαν αὐτὴν εἶναί ποτε μαντευτέον. (64a)

He carries forward the use of the verb to describe the approach to the highest truth again shortly after (66b), when speaking of the qualities that will help a human being achieve the right mixture of different kinds of pleasure and reason that will be most conducive to a vision of the Good.

In this prior group of examples, divinatory language seems to Plato an appropriate way of describing our access to the Good. It will be oblique, not straightforward, more like the spotting of a resemblance, or a flash of insight, than a discursive calculus that moves from premises to conclusions.[19]

These texts, which I have presented in a sequence of increasing weightiness of the objects known, might make tempting the conclusion that Plato uses divination to stand particularly for a way of knowing transcendent entities. But this would be specious, since, with equal facility and equal force in the *Republic*, Socrates relates divination to knowledge of precisely the opposite end on his ontological scale. In his discussion on the allegory of the cave in book 7 of the *Republic*, perhaps the most powerful epistemological description of the material world in the corpus, he characterizes human attempts to draw conclusions about it as a form of *mere "divining"* (ἀπομαντευόμενος; 516d). In this evidence the inscrutability of the thing known derives not from its profundity but from its baseness, and in both cases divination is emblematic of knowledge that can't explain itself. While some may read this characterization from the cave allegory as simply derogatory, there is more to it than that. Just before it, in the *Republic* book 6, Plato also considers potential knowledge of material things, via his image of the divided line. The line measures the great distance between the material world, which comes to be and passes away, and the immaterial world of mathematical truths, and further up, eventually the forms. The world of matter is too unstable to be truly known, and is only apprehensible by opinion (508d, 510a). The best we can do with reference to it is to have true opinion, which he consistently defines as a kind of knowledge that happens to be right but is incapable of explaining itself. This sets out a context very familiar from the many texts we have already seen, in which divinatory knowing is an apposite phenomenon for Plato to use, and it suggests an answer, more precise than simple derision, as to why he describes attempts at knowledge of the material world as a kind of "divining" in the cave text. The critical characteristic here is that we are discussing knowledge that is incapable of making an account of itself.

The *Meno* confirms, in its discussion of the epistemic category of right opinion, that this class is comparable with divination. In that

---

[19] For a similar conclusion, using the evidence in Plato's *Phaedrus*, see Daniel S. Werner, "Plato on Madness and Philosophy," *Ancient Philosophy* 31.1 (2011): 47–71.

dialogue, Socrates works through many sides of the discussion of whether virtue is knowledge (which would make it capable of being taught). At the close, he considers the case of successful statesmen. He suggests that since they are unable to teach their skills to others (which we know because great past statesmen were unable to do so) their ability to thrive as statesmen must not be based on secure knowledge. This leads him to a consider right opinion as the basis for their success and this again brings divination into the discussion:

> Then if it isn't knowledge, the thing left is right opinion; by using this thing statesmen guide their cities, and they are no different with respect to their knowledge than oracles and *manteis*. For these men also in an inspired state say many true things, and yet they know nothing of what they're saying.

> οὐκοῦν εἰ μὴ ἐπιστήμη, εὐδοξία δὴ τὸ λοιπὸν γίγνεται· ᾗ οἱ πολιτικοὶ ἄνδρες χρώμενοι τὰς πόλεις ὀρθοῦσιν, οὐδὲν διαφερόντως ἔχοντες πρὸς τὸ φρονεῖν ἢ οἱ χρησμῳδοί τε καὶ οἱ θεομάντεις· καὶ γὰρ οὗτοι ἐνθουσιῶντες λέγουσιν μὲν ἀληθῆ καὶ πολλά, ἴσασι δὲ οὐδὲν ὧν λέγουσιν. (99b–c)[20]

He elaborates, "Then, Meno, are we right to call these men divine, whoever, although he has no sense, succeeds in doing and speaking many great things?" (οὐκοῦν, ὦ Μένων, ἄξιον τούτους θείους καλεῖν τοὺς ἄνδρας, οἵτινες νοῦν μὴ ἔχοντες πολλὰ καὶ μεγάλα κατορθοῦσιν ὧν πράττουσι καὶ λέγουσι;).[21]

This further evidence, in which Plato uses divination to describe a very lowly kind of knowledge, helps us avoid the mistake mentioned above. It is not, in fact, out of a sense of the transcendence of a given object of knowledge that divination is pertinent in the discussion. Whether he characterizes the highest kind of knowing to which we could dare to aspire (*Rep.* 523a, 505e–6a; *Phil.* 64a) or the lowest kind (*Rep.* 516d), Plato invokes divination with the same purpose.

---

[20] Another apposite text here is surely *Statesman* 309c:

> Τὴν τῶν καλῶν καὶ δικαίων πέρι καὶ ἀγαθῶν καὶ τῶν τούτοις ἐναντίων ὄντως οὖσαν ἀληθῆ δόξαν μετὰ βεβαιώσεως, ὁπόταν ἐν [ταῖς] ψυχαῖς ἐγγίγνηται, θείαν φημὶ ἐν δαιμονίῳ γίγνεσθαι γένει.

[21] He compares correct δόξαι to images in a dream at *Meno* 85c.

Irrespective of the thing known, divination is useful as an emblem for a kind of knowing that happens in a flash, without being able to account for itself. This evidence fits perfectly with the general conclusions we have recovered in the rest of the corpus.

DIVINATION IN THE *PHAEDRUS* AND *SYMPOSIUM*

From this vantage, we turn to two dialogues that give a particular prominence to divination in their overall thematics. In the *Phaedrus*, Plato famously examines the benefits of madness, and counts divination among them. The dialogue is peppered with gestures in the direction of divine inspiration, from seemingly gratuitous mentions of Delphi (229e, 235d); to the mythic rapture of Oreithyia, a human literally carried away by a god (229b); to subtler intrusions of the motif of possession: a "divine experience" (θεῖον πάθος [238c]), "The place seems truly to be divine" (τῷ ὄντι γὰρ θεῖος ἔοικεν ὁ τόπος εἶναι [238c–d]), a "νυμφόληπτος," or possession by divine nymphs settling on Socrates (238d, cf. 241e). Early on, Socrates references the Delphic inscription, "know yourself," as a way of saying he can't agree with natural scientists' ambitious explanations of myth, since he has yet to figure out what kind of a creature he himself is (229e). As Socrates gets closer to delivering his central speech, he makes the claim we mentioned above, that he himself has become an oracle (241e–42d). He says he has advanced past dithyrambic poetry and up to the level of hexameters (the meter of inspired oracles), calls his soul "something divinatory" (μαντικόν γέ τι καὶ ἡ ψυχή), and says he needs to heed a call from his customary divine sign to reconsider the low evaluation of the lover he forwarded in his first speech. He later mentions that his knowledge of rhetoric must have come from some sort of divine possession, since the speeches just happen to have led to an unexpected insight (262d). The references are thick on the ground, and set up the main theme of the first part of the dialogue: an attempt to theorize the limits of discursive reason and explore the power of spiritedness to expand beyond them into a more visionary form of thought. As was the case with the *Republic*, here allusions to divination help adumbrate the nondiscursive character of the thought by which we might have knowledge of the forms.

The dialogue pivots with Socrates' attempt to rehabilitate the lover, whom the earlier speeches claimed is afflicted with an irrational madness. His strategy is to delineate the benefits of irrationality. This leads to a provocative and well-known hierarchy of modes of thought, in the articulation of which divination plays a pivotal role. Plato tells us that certain forms of irrationality have a precedence over rationality. After speaking generally about the blessings derived from the frenzied prophetic utterances of the Pythia, the priestesses at Dodona, and the Sibyl, he then connects *mantikê* etymologically with *mania*, and by this connection means to tell us that our valuation of madness should be elevated by its connection with knowing via inspired divination. He contrasts this with an example of more sober thinking, but the example he chooses is also, interestingly, a form of divination:

> When they named the investigation of the future by people in their right minds, through the behaviors of birds and other signs, they called it the oio-no-istic art, since out of discursive reasoning [*dianoia*] they furnish to human opinion [*oiêsis*] intellect [*novs*] and empirical knowledge [*historia*], which a new generation of people now call *oiônistic*, giving it an air of solemnity with the long ô. So, the ancients testify that by just as much as divination in a frenzy [*mantikê*] is more authoritative and higher in rank than sober-minded divination, both in name and in fact, by this much madness, which comes from god, is superior to a sound mind, which is of human origin.

> ἐπεὶ καὶ τήν γε τῶν ἐμφρόνων ζήτησιν τοῦ μέλλοντος, διά τε ὀρνίθων ποιουμένων καὶ τῶν ἄλλων σημείων, ἅτ’ ἐκ διανοίας ποριζομένων ἀνθρωπίνῃ οἰήσει νοῦν τε καὶ ἱστορίαν, οἰονοϊστικὴν ἐπωνόμασαν, ἣν νῦν οἰωνιστικὴν τῷ ω σεμνύνοντες οἱ νέοι καλοῦσιν· ὅσῳ δὴ οὖν τελεώτερον καὶ ἐντιμότερον μαντικὴ οἰωνιστικῆς τό τε ὄνομα τοῦ ὀνόματος ἔργον τ’ ἔργου, τόσῳ κάλλιον μαρτυροῦσιν οἱ παλαιοὶ μανίαν σωφροσύνης τὴν ἐκ θεοῦ τῆς παρ’ ἀνθρώπων γιγνομένης.[22] (Phaedrus 244c–d)

The most important aspect of the argument for our purposes is that he does not simply set that which is ἄλογον ahead of λόγος, as this famous

---

[22] Text from Harvey Yunis, ed., Plato, *Phaedrus*, Greek and Latin Classics (Cambridge: Cambridge University Press, 2011).

passage could be taken to suggest. Such a proposition would be jarring and easy enough to place into the large bin of more or less counterintuitive positions that Plato toys with for a time and then sets aside. But his terms are more specific than that. Here, two forms of knowing are compared. Plato contrasts inspired forms of divination, that is, those that take place in an irrational frenzy, with apparently more rational technical forms, where practitioners empirically correlate signs in their surroundings with some future outcome, making comparisons to past sets of data in a state of intellectual sobriety.[23] The classification of the second as divination at all is in doubt.[24] The split is not an ad hoc gesture here. As we will see, it recurs in the critical section of the *Timaeus*, where Plato sets out his most explicit ideas on divination. In both cases, Plato draws the taxonomy to mark a distinction, familiar in the texts already examined, between nondiscursive and discursive knowing, where he marks the former as somehow superior. In the context being developed here, the state of inspired divination serves as a proxy for nondiscursive insight of substantial truths (as it did in *Philebus* and *Republic* 6 and 7), while divination by empirical observation stands in for sequential thinking that gathers observations of the material world to reach conclusions via empiricism. Rather than understand this famous passage as a momentary enthusiasm for the irrational, then, we are more right to read him here raising the rather trenchant possibility that nondiscursive thinking might carry an intellectual weight, in certain circumstances, that exceeds discursive thinking. Plato uses the language of divination to enter this consequential cognitive territory. In this particular case he uses different forms of divination (technical and inspired) for both sides of the equation, whereas more typically he references only inspired and it only stands on the nondiscursive side.

As the *Phaedrus* progresses from the typology of madness, Plato speaks specifically of nondiscursive knowing as the way to access the highest truths, different in kind from our normal modes of thinking. This leads through the famous description of the soul as a winged

---

[23] At *Phaedo* 96a Socrates characterizes limitations of this kind of thinking as well. He uses ἱστορία περὶ φύσεως to characterize Socrates' youthful and ultimately mistaken pursuit of knowledge from the observation of causes in the natural world (cf. *Sophist* 267e).

[24] See introduction, pp. 16–19, for further discussion.

chariot ascending upwards through reality. Given the prominence of themes of divination in the dialogue, we are not wrong to follow the suggestions of it that appear in this critical image—at least some way. At the peak of the climb one has an irreducible moment of insight, which appears like a wondrous vision. It begins this way:

> If a man makes correct use of these reminders [iterations of the form of Beauty], and performs always perfect mysteries, he alone becomes truly perfect. Standing aside from human pursuits, and becoming close to the divine, he is rebuked by the many as being out of his wits, for they do not know that he is possessed by a deity.[25]

> τοῖς δὲ δὴ τοιούτοις ἀνὴρ ὑπομνήμασιν ὀρθῶς χρώμενος, τελέους ἀεὶ τελετὰς τελούμενος, τέλεος ὄντως μόνος γίγνεται· ἐξιστάμενος δὲ τῶν ἀνθρωπίνων σπουδασμάτων καὶ πρὸς τῷ θείῳ γιγνόμενος, νουθετεῖται μὲν ὑπὸ τῶν πολλῶν ὡς παρακινῶν, ἐνθουσιάζων δὲ λέληθε τοὺς πολλούς. (*Phaedrus* 249c–d)

The connection to divination here is not direct. After all, Plato does not call "divinatory" the form of madness that propels our ascent to the divine truths; rather, the vehicle is a different one of his four types of irrationality, the erotic. Second, Plato calls "mind" (νοῦς) the "pilot" of the soul steering it upward (247c). This is Plato's core term for the intellect that is the center of discursive reason (cf. *Tim.* 51d), and this makes it clear that he does not envision a thoughtless frenzy. But still the proximity to divinatory language in the vision from the chariot is suggestive, with visions, possession, frenzy, and closeness to the divine. Given the larger background assembled here, we can understand the prominence of divinatory themes in the dialogue as expressing a certain kind of cognition that works via insight and not by inference.

Plato continues, expanding on nondiscursive thinking by associating it with another of his core topics: his theory of recollection, which was already hinted at in the passage above (ὑπομνήμασιν). Our souls before they were born had unmediated visions of the forms, and these earlier glimpses reappear to us in faint memories after we are born into bodies. Socrates memorably pursues the idea in the *Meno*, where he

---

[25] Compare the description of recollection as a similarly associative mode of knowledge at *Phaedo* 73c–75c.

elicits knowledge of geometry from an uneducated slave boy. While no one has ever seen a perfect circle in the material world, nevertheless we know what one is and are able to measure the circles we do see against this ideal perfect one. In both *Meno* and *Phaedrus*, Socrates claims that we have inside us, in ways we don't fully fathom, an innate, latent kind of knowing (cf. *Theaet.* 150d).

> As has been said, every human soul has beheld by nature the real realities, otherwise it would not have entered into a human animal, but it is not easy for them all to be reminded of those things, from these earthly things, neither for those that saw them only briefly at that earlier time, nor for those that, after falling to earth, were so unfortunate that they were turned toward the unjust by some acquaintances and maintained their forgetfulness of the sacred things they once saw. Few then are left who have a sufficient recollection of them; but these when they see here any likenesses of the things there, are knocked out of their wits and no longer have control of themselves.

> καθάπερ γὰρ εἴρηται, πᾶσα μὲν ἀνθρώπου ψυχὴ φύσει τεθέαται τὰ ὄντα, ἢ οὐκ ἂν ἦλθεν εἰς τόδε τὸ ζῷον· ἀναμιμνῄσκεσθαι δὲ ἐκ τῶνδε ἐκεῖνα οὐ ῥάδιον ἁπάσῃ, οὔτε ὅσαι βραχέως εἶδον τότε τἀκεῖ, οὔθ' αἳ δεῦρο πεσοῦσαι ἐδυστύχησαν, ὥστε ὑπό τινων ὁμιλιῶν ἐπὶ τὸ ἄδικον τραπόμεναι λήθην ὧν τότε εἶδον ἱερῶν ἔχειν. ὀλίγαι δὴ λείπονται αἷς τὸ τῆς μνήμης ἱκανῶς πάρεστιν· αὗται δέ, ὅταν τι τῶν ἐκεῖ ὁμοίωμα ἴδωσιν, ἐκπλήττονται καὶ οὐκέθ' αὑτῶν γίγνονται. (*Phaedrus* 249e–50a)

While it is triggered by discursive collections of evidence from engagement with the world, this mode of knowing centers on a nondiscursive component: knowledge of the forms will be akin to memories that flit back into consciousness, responses to a triggering perception, rather than goal-directed inference. In the *Meno*, the boy's correct knowledge of geometry, without any education, is compared explicitly to a dream (85c). This is already in close proximity to the contexts in which divination language appears in the preponderance of evidence above (cf. *Phaedo* 72e–77a, esp. 75c). The salient aspect of the theory of recollection for our purposes is its nondiscursive nature. It happens in a quick flash, a shock by which one is knocked outside oneself (ἐκπλήττεται). The purpose of Plato's copious references to divination in the *Phaedrus*, then, is best understood as deriving from the general importance of this mode of thought for knowing the forms.

Finally, in the *Symposium*, notions of divination have a noteworthy prominence, and provide a culmination for the observations assembled here. The main topic of love is chosen for the dinner party conversation and is illuminated from the different vantages of its participants, with multiple references to inspired speech in general and divination in particular. Phaedrus proposes a discussion of love based in valor and honor, and calls the lover "more divine" than his beloved because he is "inspired" (θειότερον γὰρ ἐραστὴς παιδικῶν· ἔνθεος γάρ ἐστι [180b]). Eryximachus, a medical doctor, claims that divination, along with sacrifice, governs "the association of gods and men with one another" (ταῦτα δ' ἐστὶν ἡ περὶ θεούς τε καὶ ἀνθρώπους πρὸς ἀλλήλους κοινωνία [188c]). He includes it in a short list of human crafts that he says operate by moderating lusty love and enhancing higher-order love in knowing when and how to bring things together (the others are medicine, of course, music, athletics, and agriculture). The subject of divination also inserts itself after Agathon has rendered his flowery paean to the god Eros. Socrates makes his sly opening into the dialogue at the close of the speech with his remark to Eryximachus, which was referenced above, saying that he "prophetically" thought that Agathon would make a wondrous speech (198a–b). He continues the theme of *ekstasis* when he claims that anyone would be knocked out of his wits (ἐξεπλάγη; 198b) upon hearing Agathon's fine phrases. We see divination again as part of Aristophanes' speech, also noted above. It is the way he expresses the mode by which the lovers sense their primal connection with one another, as two parts of a broken whole.

The most powerful moment of the dialogue comes in Diotima's closing speech, on which several observations regarding the present concerns can be made. First, Plato regularly chooses to pair her name, which connects her with honor from Zeus, with a locative epithet. And since he has her coming from Mantinea, the designation for the pivotal figure in the dialogue, Μαντινικὴ Διοτίμα, turns out to be a conspicuous pun for μαντικὴ Διοτίμα, "the divinatory woman honored by god." As Diotima introduces her main point—that erotic love is an expression of human desire for the Fine itself (τὸ καλόν)—Socrates again turns to divinatory language to describe the way we might know the very highest truths, when he says, in order to understand "what on earth you are talking about will require divinatory power" (μαντείας δεῖται ὅτι ποτε λέγεις [206b]). Carrying forward a theme from the *Phaedrus*, Plato here develops the heady idea that reproductive urges in mortal things are an expression of the desire for the immortal, and, ultimately, the "great ocean" (τὸ πέλαγος) of the beautiful itself (210d). An even higher version of this desire shows in the urge to create nonmaterial, intellectual things—such as philosophical knowledge, poems, and laws. When one moves up the rungs of the ladder that lead to higher and higher forms of beauty, one eventually has a vision of the Beautiful itself, which is sudden:

> When a person has been instructed up to this point in matters of desire, contemplating a succession of beautiful things in the proper way, just as he approaches the final goal of the objects of desire suddenly he will see something wondrous, beautiful in its nature—this is that thing, Socrates, on account of which all his previous toils were made.

> ὃς γὰρ ἂν μέχρι ἐνταῦθα πρὸς τὰ ἐρωτικὰ παιδαγωγηθῇ, θεώμενος ἐφεξῆς τε καὶ ὀρθῶς τὰ καλά, πρὸς τέλος ἤδη ἰὼν τῶν ἐρωτικῶν ἐξαίφνης κατόψεταί τι θαυμαστὸν τὴν φύσιν καλόν, τοῦτο ἐκεῖνο, ὦ Σώκρατες, οὗ δὴ ἕνεκεν καὶ οἱ ἔμπροσθεν πάντες πόνοι ἦσαν. (*Symp.* 210e)

The moment has more in common with a prophetic revelation than with a logical conclusion.[26] As with the *Phaedrus*, the thick references to divination in the dialogue as a whole are best understood as adumbrating the nondiscursive character of the kind of knowledge that we aspire to have when we aspire to know the forms. It is important to reiterate that in neither case does he say that our mode of knowing forms a kind of divination. But in both cases it is clear that it *is like* divination, insofar as it will be nondiscursive.

---

[26] To drive home the divine character of this kind of knowing, Diotima claims that the one who achieves it can become a "friend of god" (θεοφιλής; 212a) and "if it belongs to any human being to be immortal, it is to that one" (εἴπέρ τῳ ἄλλῳ ἀνθρώπων ἀθανάτῳ καὶ ἐκείνῳ [212a]).

DIVINATION AND PLATO'S DIVINE SIGN

And finally, before arriving at the *Timaeus*, we turn to what Socrates calls his own form of divination. He famously claims to get messages from a kind of guardian angel. He names it τὸ δαιμόνιον, which is best understood as an abbreviation of τὸ δαιμόνιον σημεῖον ("my divine sign"),[27] and which he calls "my customary form of divination" (ἡ γὰρ εἰωθυῖά μοι μαντικὴ ἡ τοῦ δαιμονίου [*Apol.* 40a–b]). Plato leaves more unsaid than said about the nature and operation of this messaging system. He explains it most thoroughly in his trial in the *Apology*. He says that the verdict against him is not to be lamented, but is actually "something wondrous" (θαυμάσιόν τι γέγονεν), and he knows this because his *daimonion* did not hold him back from anything leading up to the trial. He calls the *daimonion* a "voice" and a "sign" that on occasion appears to him in order to hold him back from doing things, like an early-warning radar. Plato tightly circumscribes the message it is capable of carrying. Specifically, the spirit only ever has one thing to say—no. It warns Socrates away from doing something disadvantageous, and never impels him into a course of action. It prevents him from entering into political life (*Apol.* 31d, *Rep.* 496c), and on three occasions it prevents him from leaving an argument in the middle (*Theaet.* 151a; *Euthyd.* 272e; *Phaedr.* 242b–d).

The sign's typical mode of operation is fully in accord with his comments on divine signs such as we have gathered: it arrives suddenly and is not the result of a deliberative process. The *Phaedrus* shows this vividly:

> When I was about to cross the stream, my good friend, my *daimonion* and customary sign that comes to me came—it always holds me back from something I am about to do—and I thought I heard a certain voice

---

[27] For this reading, see Luc Brisson, "Socrates and the Divine Signal according to Plato's Testimony: Philosophical Practice as Rooted in Religious Tradition," in Pierre Destrée and Nicholas D Smith, eds., *Socrates' Divine Sign: Religion, Practice, and Value in Socratic Philosophy*, special issue of *APEIRON: A Journal for Ancient Philosophy and Science* 38.2 (2005), 1–12; and Vlastos (1991), 280. The scholarship is vast, for the most succinct comprehensive overview of the various schools of thought, see Brickhouse and Smith, "Socrates' *Daimonion* and Rationality," in Destrée and Smith, *Socrates' Divine Sign*, 43–62; see also Vlastos (1991), 280–87. This particular reference at *Apol.* (40a–b) follows immediately after he lays down his "prophecy" foreseeing that his accusers will meet their own form of reckoning.

from it that forbade me from leaving before I made an expiation, on the grounds that I had committed some sin against the deity. And so I am a seer, not a very good one, but, just as the bad writers say, good enough for my own purposes; so now I understand clearly my error. How prophetic the soul is, my friend! For a long while, as I was making my speech, something bothered me, and as Ibycus says, "I was distressed lest I buy honor among men by sinning against the gods." But now I have seen my mistake.

Ἡνίκ' ἔμελλον, ὦγαθέ, τὸν ποταμὸν διαβαίνειν, τὸ δαιμόνιόν τε καὶ τὸ εἰωθὸς σημεῖόν μοι γίγνεσθαι ἐγένετο—ἀεὶ δέ με ἐπίσχει ὃ ἂν μέλλω πράττειν—καί τινα φωνὴν ἔδοξα αὐτόθεν ἀκοῦσαι, ἥ με οὐκ ἐᾷ ἀπιέναι πρὶν ἂν ἀφοσιώσωμαι, ὡς δή τι ἡμαρτηκότα εἰς τὸ θεῖον. εἰμὶ δὴ οὖν μάντις μέν, οὐ πάνυ δὲ σπουδαῖος, ἀλλ᾽ ὥσπερ οἱ τὰ γράμματα φαῦλοι, ὅσον μὲν ἐμαυτῷ μόνον ἱκανός· σαφῶς οὖν ἤδη μανθάνω τὸ ἁμάρτημα. ὡς δή τοι, ὦ ἑταῖρε, μαντικόν γέ τι καὶ ἡ ψυχή· ἐμὲ γὰρ ἔθραξε μέν τι καὶ πάλαι λέγοντα τὸν λόγον, καί πως ἐδυσωπούμην κατ᾽ Ἴβυκον, μή τι παρὰ θεοῖς "ἀμβλακὼν τιμὰν πρὸς ἀνθρώπων ἀμείψω." νῦν δ᾽ ἤσθημαι τὸ ἁμάρτημα. (242b–d)

Socrates casts his divine sign as a form of knowing that just arrives to him, which is not explainable, and (as with a certain number of the examples we saw above) nevertheless turns out to be accurate. It occurs to him while he is occupied in an otherwise completely separate train of discursive thought (while he is stringing together his first *logos* on love). It was a nagging feeling (τι ἐμὲ ἔθραξε) that he, in the end (νῦν δὲ), realizes had an intellectual content, telling him that his speech was in error.

While Socrates' demon shows up only a handful of times in Plato's work,[28] his attitude toward it is much discussed among scholars, most of whom are interested in what epistemological value it could possibly have. Rationalists have argued that the demonic sign is a literary construction, a metaphor meant to stand for intuitive knowledge (a rational "hunch" in Vlastos's formulation).[29] Vlastos is surely right to point out that Plato's divinely inflected messenger yields a kind of knowledge that looks a lot like what modern English speakers would

[28] See in addition *Euthyphro* 3e and *Apol.* 40a.
[29] See Vlastos (1991), 280–87.

call "intuition." It just arrives, is not the result of purposeful deliberation, sometimes expresses itself as a gut feeling, and when it is accurate, it has an uncanny feel. Others claim that Socrates really means to invoke a kind of divination in these references, and that he does sincerely propose some supernatural aspect of the message.[30] This debate perfectly captures the coherence between the ancient understanding of divination and the modern notion of intuition. The Socratic δαιμόνιον in both aspects—as intuition and as divination—is actually precisely an embodiment of the consonance. The way Greeks talked about an involuntary, gut-feeling sort of knowledge was precisely via divinatory language. So it would be much *more* strange to see Socrates speak of such insights in a way that was *not* couched in divination language. It is, on my reading, wholly expected for him to have labeled such knowledge divinatory, and at the same time to have described it in ways that look, to us, like intuition. In my view, the resemblance of this mode of Socrates' knowing to our modern notion of intuition does nothing to separate it from ancient divination.

It is easy to draw a link connecting this δαιμόνιον to a culminating statement from Diotima's speech in the *Symposium*. Although she does not speak directly of Socrates' divine sign, she provides apposite information about the class of *daimonia* as a whole, and she explicitly links it to divination. Diotima claims that love is "a great *daimôn*," and this leads her to discuss "the *daimonion*," which she calls a region "intermediate between divine and mortal." Socrates asks her what power it has, and she replies as follows:

> It interprets and transports human things to the gods and divine things to humans; from the one prayers and sacrifices, and from the other guidance and gifts in return for sacrifices. Since it is in the middle, it helps each fulfill the other, so that the whole is combined in one. Through it go all divinatory arts and the sacred arts concerning sacrifices, rituals, and incantations, the whole of divination and sorcery. The divine does not mingle with the human, rather the gods have all contact and communication with humans through the medium of the *daimonion*, both when we are awake and asleep.

[30] See Mark McPherran, *The Religion of Socrates* (University Park: Penn State Press, 1996), 185–208.

Ἑρμηνεῦον καὶ διαπορθμεῦον θεοῖς τὰ παρ' ἀνθρώπων καὶ ἀνθρώποις
τὰ παρὰ θεῶν, τῶν μὲν τὰς δεήσεις καὶ θυσίας, τῶν δὲ τὰς ἐπιτάξεις τε
καὶ ἀμοιβὰς τῶν θυσιῶν, ἐν μέσῳ δὲ ὂν ἀμφοτέρων συμπληροῖ, ὥστε τὸ
πᾶν αὐτὸ αὑτῷ συνδεδέσθαι. διὰ τούτου καὶ ἡ μαντικὴ πᾶσα χωρεῖ καὶ
ἡ τῶν ἱερέων τέχνη τῶν τε περὶ τὰς θυσίας καὶ τελετὰς καὶ τὰς ἐπῳδὰς
καὶ τὴν μαντείαν πᾶσαν καὶ γοητείαν. θεὸς δὲ ἀνθρώπῳ οὐ μείγνυται,
ἀλλὰ διὰ τούτου πᾶσά ἐστιν ἡ ὁμιλία καὶ ἡ διάλεκτος θεοῖς πρὸς
ἀνθρώπους, καὶ ἐγρηγορόσι καὶ καθεύδουσι. (202e–3a)

By giving his divine sign the name τὸ δαιμόνιον, Socrates assigns it to
the region here described, between humans and gods. The demonic
will also figure into the *Timaeus'* account of divinatory signs. That dialogue speaks of inferior gods that minister to human affairs in a direct,
hands-on way, from which the highest god remains aloof. The eternal
god hands over to them the duty to construct human beings. Plato's
inheritors had little trouble settling these divinities into the role that
we have already seen Diotima claim for the demonic realm. The later
tradition consistently calls the intermediary divinities of the *Timaeus*
daimones. Plato only speaks of demons once in the dialogue (40d). It is
in the context of intermediate divinities, and specifically in reference to
the traditional pantheon.[31] These beings carry a certain resemblance to
Socrates' δαιμονίον, a likeness that Plato's Middle Platonist successors
are quick to notice. The association between the demonic realm and
divination will deepen with fascinating richness in Aristotle.

DIVINATORY KNOWLEDGE DERIVES FROM A NATURAL DISPOSITION

The discussion of the Socratic *daimôn* hints at an additional insight.
Socrates' divine sign seems to function a bit like a twitch, or an involuntary movement, as when he describes it above as a nagging feeling
(τι ἐμὲ ἔθραξε). This aspect of divinatory knowledge will appear in a
prominent way in the critical *Timaeus* account, to which we will turn
shortly, and it shows clearly in two additional texts as well. In the
Apology, with which we began this survey, Socrates speaks of the different classes of reputedly wise people, whom he interrogates in his

---

[31] Later, he calls the highest part of the soul our *daimôn*, claiming that it is a divine thing that
guides us up toward the gods (*Tim.* 90a).

exploration of the oracle. He gets to the poets and finds they are unable to understand what they have written any better than anyone else. This leads him to a conclusion:

> So in turn I recognized this also concerning the poets in short order, that they did not compose what they did compose by wisdom, but by a certain natural disposition and enthusiasm, just like the diviners and the givers of oracles: For these also say many fine things, but they know nothing of what they are talking about.

> ἔγνων οὖν αὖ καὶ περὶ τῶν ποιητῶν ἐν ὀλίγῳ τοῦτο, ὅτι οὐ σοφίᾳ ποιοῖεν ἃ ποιοῖεν, ἀλλὰ φύσει τινὶ καὶ ἐνθουσιάζοντες ὥσπερ οἱ θεομάντεις καὶ οἱ χρησμῳδοί· καὶ γὰρ οὗτοι λέγουσι μὲν πολλὰ καὶ καλά, ἴσασιν δὲ οὐδὲν ὧν λέγουσι. (22b–c)

The skill that makes a poet a poet, and also a diviner a diviner, is something in their natures, a certain constitution (φύσει τινὶ). It is not exactly an intellectual power, but a disposition that results in a cognitive capacity. The *Philebus* elaborates on this a bit more. The discussion on pleasures has circled around to the objections of some unnamed natural scientists who claim that pleasures do not exist at all. This strikes Socrates as a wrong, but not uninteresting, position. He says that the scientists are onto something without quite knowing it. Their objection grows out of a certain innate quality in their natures which causes them, entirely rightly, to be suspicious of any idea that pleasure could provide a benefit. This stance agrees with Plato's general sense that real pleasure lies in the contemplative approach to the truth and not in things that seem gratifying. Speaking of such scientists, he recommends that:

> We put them to use, just like certain seers, who divine not by an art but by a certain resistant streak in their natures, not ignoble, which belongs to those who very much hate the power of pleasure and consider it nothing salutary, so that even the very attractiveness of it they consider to be trickery and not pleasure.

> ὥσπερ μάντεσι προσχρῆσθαί τισι, μαντευομένοις οὐ τέχνῃ ἀλλά τινι δυσχερείᾳ φύσεως οὐκ ἀγεννοῦς λίαν μεμισηκότων τὴν τῆς ἡδονῆς δύναμιν καὶ νενομικότων οὐδὲν ὑγιές, ὥστε καὶ αὐτὸ τοῦτο αὐτῆς τὸ ἐπαγωγὸν γοήτευμα, οὐχ ἡδονήν, εἶναι. (44c)

Plato here compares the particular knowledge these scientists have to that of inspired diviners *because* it arrives by a certain innate quality in their natures, which causes them to reach a plausible conclusion. Like the successful statesmen in the *Meno* who perform well not by teachable knowledge, or the poets who seem to just arrive at what they know, these people's natures cause them to land on an opinion that turns out to be true. Compare the close of the *Philebus* (67b), where Plato speaks of divination as residing in animal instinct. He contrasts it (in this case negatively) with the results of reasoning in normal discursive philosophy. Of course, Plato can produce an opposite valuation of this theme as well, as we already saw in the swansong from *Phaedo* (84d–85d). In all these cases, divinatory knowing lines up with physical instinct—as opposed to inferential argumentation.

DIVINATION IN THE *TIMAEUS*

So far, we have seen Plato use divination as a trope to illuminate nondiscursive knowing. It comes in a momentary flash, akin to a recollected image, it may or may not be confirmable by discursive reasoning, and it is tied to instinct. This survey provides context for a deepened understanding of a critical section of the *Timaeus* that remains to be considered. In it he makes his most direct comments on divination, analogous to his treatment of poetry in the *Ion* or book 10 of the *Republic*. His fascinating anatomical discussion of human nature in the *Timaeus* as a whole is undeniably strange. In the part most pertinent to this investigation, he sets out a view of the liver as a screen for images of rational thought that are meant to frighten the appetitive soul into submission, and at the same time to serve as a receptacle for divinatory visions. But it is also true that this section of the text comes at a pivotal inflection point of the dialogue. As the Italian scholar Serafina Rotondaro has shown, it articulates a complex set of ideas that connect with many aspects of Platonic epistemology and psychology.[32] I will focus here on building a further understanding of divination as a peculiar form of cognition.

[32] See Rotondaro (1997).

We begin by marking a contrast and tension between the *Timaeus* and the rest of Plato's work. The value of the natural world in the rest of the corpus is tenuous. In fact, he doesn't take it entirely seriously. The *Phaedo* offers a particularly well-turned testimony:

> I, when I was young, Cebes, was marvelously set on the kind of wisdom that they call investigation of nature. I thought it was a splendid thing to know the causes of each thing, why each one comes into being and why it passes away and why it exists. . . . And I investigated the phenomena of heaven and earth until finally I came to understand that I was by nature totally useless for this investigation.[33]

> ἐγὼ γάρ, ἔφη, ὦ Κέβης, νέος ὢν θαυμαστῶς ὡς ἐπεθύμησα ταύτης τῆς σοφίας ἣν δὴ καλοῦσι περὶ φύσεως ἱστορίαν· ὑπερήφανος γάρ μοι ἐδόκει εἶναι, εἰδέναι τὰς αἰτίας ἑκάστου, διὰ τί γίγνεται ἕκαστον καὶ διὰ τί ἀπόλλυται καὶ διὰ τί ἔστι. . . . καὶ [σκοπῶν] τὰ περὶ τὸν οὐρανόν τε καὶ τὴν γῆν πάθη, τελευτῶν οὕτως ἐμαυτῷ ἔδοξα πρὸς ταύτην τὴν σκέψιν ἀφυὴς εἶναι ὡς οὐδὲν χρῆμα. (96a–c)

Likely having been influenced by Heraclitus' observation that nothing in the physical world is ever stable, Plato finds his intellectual home in an ontology based on a set of stable forms. Working from precedents in Parmenides, he introduces to philosophy his unchanging realities, existing beyond both the natural world and our abilities to perceive it. The contrast here with Aristotle, as will be apparent in the next chapter, could not be more striking. In most of the dialogues, Plato's quasi-divine forms, nearly always conceptualized as atemporal and synchronic, do not guide the unfolding of causal chains into the material cosmos, they rather sit back transcendent above the unfolding into decay of the material world below them. On these heady topics, the views of the *Timaeus* are quite a different matter altogether. Plato moves his consideration into the world of the material, and causes, and the physiological dimension of human existence, and this general stance is important in reckoning why the most straightforward consideration of divination in the corpus is visible here, further testimony that it is a kind of thinking that sits in proximity to the forces of nature.

---

[33] After Fowler (1926).

Overall Structure of the Timaeus

The dialogue sets out a rather broad agenda: "to speak beginning from the origin of the cosmos and ending at the nature of humans" (λέγειν ἀρχόμενον ἀπὸ τῆς τοῦ κόσμου γενέσεως, τελευτᾶν δὲ εἰς ἀνθρώπων φύσιν· [27a–b]). It can be divided into three main sections, which can be seen as moving from the outside inward, from the cosmos toward the human body. The first centers on the creation of the universe, which closes with the mention of the four classes of beings— heavenly, airy, watery, and earthly—and with the highest god making his charge to his minions to go about creating humans (27c–41d). Next, Timaeus initiates a long discussion of the basic building blocks of material bodies, which ushers in a consideration of the φύσις and, at the same time, how humans sense it, the fullest consideration in the corpus of how sensation works (41d–69a). Third, he moves from this discussion of the outside world and how it makes impressions upon the outer border of the human, and moves inside the human body to close out the dialogue with a lengthy discussion of the different bodily organs and how they function. The topic of divination comes up at the beginning of the third section, just at the point that he ventures into the body and physiology (70e). Its introduction is marked by a break in the rhetorical flow as pronounced as any in the dialogue. The discussion occupies an intermediate space, akin to what Diotima had set for the topic in the *Symposium*: Plato is turning away from questions of the divine and the larger cosmos and toward the human being, and also away from the immaterial soul and toward the material human body. Having just come to a pause in his long discussion of the causes behind the creation of the cosmos,[34] and human sensation of it, Timaeus tells us that it is time to revert to the beginning of the discussion, in order to "try now to set an end to our story, a fitting crown to what has come before it" (τελευτὴν ἤδη κεφαλήν τε τῷ μύθῳ πειρώμεθα ἁρμόττουσαν ἐπιθεῖναι τοῖς πρόσθεν [69b]). This culmination will be a description of the form and function of the human organism and an account of the placement of the soul inside it. He considers divination at this crux point. To

---

[34] The three are the intelligent causes that enact the plan of the eternal god, the necessary causes deriving from the material out of which the world is made, and the wandering causes in the orbit of the Nurse or receptacle.

understand its significance requires some further consideration of the whole.

The visible cosmos must have come into existence at some point. It is observably subject to change, and things of that character belong to the world of becoming, not the eternal world of being. Timaeus tells us that a divine first principle, about which we know very little, set about ordering a clump of disordered material by fashioning it into an image of an ultimate form, "the perfect creature." He was good and did not begrudge that everything should be as good as possible too, so when he saw the disorder and ugliness of the unformed cosmos, he set about fashioning it into a single organism.

> So, then, according to the likely account, we must say that this cosmos has in truth emerged as a living creature endowed with soul and reason through the foresight of god.
>
> οὕτως οὖν δὴ κατὰ λόγον τὸν εἰκότα δεῖ λέγειν τόνδε τὸν κόσμον ζῷον ἔμψυχον ἔννουν τε τῇ ἀληθείᾳ διὰ τὴν τοῦ θεοῦ γενέσθαι πρόνοιαν. (30b, cf. 69)

The universe is made up of a body (the visible cosmos), which is circular and turns (34a–b), and itself has a soul. Knowing that rational things are more beautiful than irrational, and wanting the cosmos to be as beautiful as possible, the god constructs it as a single *rational* animal. And any creature that has reason needs a soul into which it can be placed, and so he implanted a soul in the cosmos' body, and then reason within the soul. In more precise terms, the cosmic body exists within the soul (not the other way around): the soul is diffused through its entirety and surrounds it like a cloak (34b, cf. 36e). For later thinkers, particularly the Stoics, the idea that the cosmos is a single organism will support the idea that it has visible signs tucked away within it, making divination something akin to medical symptomology. Just as an organism produces readable symptoms of future states in sometimes distant portions of the body, so also the cosmos as a whole does. The notion of co-feeling or "sympathy" (συμπάθεια) will become critical in this cluster of ideas, though it is not present, in this context, in Plato.

The divine demiurge creates the soul, Plato says, out of hunks of sameness, difference, and being. He fashions sameness and difference into two strips (35), and then bends the strips into hoops. The circle of the Same spins horizontally. It allows us to recognize sameness, and it has an affinity with the world of being. The other hoop orbits slightly oblique to the horizontal. It is the circuit of difference, and is connected to the world of becoming. Timaeus says this structure is observable in the two main visible circuits in the astronomical spheres (39a–b). He likens the circle of the Same with the unchanging, spinning horizon of the fixed stars, which move in perfect synchronic circular motion from East to West every night, in a path described by the celestial equator. The circle of Difference moves analogously to the ecliptic, the band of space within which the planets (the wandering stars) are observable from Earth. They move at various speeds also East to West across the sky, in a circuit that is offset 23.5 degrees to the celestial equator. As astronomers of the ancient Near East had known for many centuries, while the planets, including the sun and moon, rotated around the earth daily, they lost a little ground each day when compared against the fixed stars. The amount of ground lost is uneven and varies from planet to planet. This allows for calibration of time, Timaeus says, claiming that the planets were made for this purpose.

More gods are created by the one timeless creator and are fixed into the heavenly bodies. They are in turn charged, since the highest god wanted the world to be as good as possible, to imitate the process by which they were created and to fashion human beings. But the eternal god does not delegate the entire task to his staff. He himself first creates a "divine part" of humans, the immortal soul, by remixing a residue that remained after he created the soul of the cosmos (41d). This will be the highest part of a human soul, reason, that dwells in our heads. He hands this over to his minion gods and commands them to fashion humans around it. They start by forming their own imitation of a soul, which becomes a human's mortal soul (our spirited and appetitive parts) which will be the instrument of divination. Finally they fashion the physical body to act as a vehicle to carry the immortal and mortal soul about.

The core principle of organization at each stage of the creation is that of microcosm and macrocosm. In the Greek literary corpus, there is no shortage of evidence on the idea of some kind of a relationship like this. The notion that the human is a *"mikros kosmos"* or a world in miniature probably dates back to Democritus.[35] But in the later tradition the *Timaeus* takes pride of place as the source of it. Plato claims explicitly that the smaller parts of the cosmos unfold as copies of the grand whole. The visible cosmos itself is an image (both an εἰκών [29b] and a μίμησις [39e, 47c]) of the "perfect creature." And when the highest god orders the lower gods to create humans, they carry out the order by copying the whole: the human being is formed and shaped as an image of the image. Human physiology mirrors the universe in specific ways. The round shape of the head, for example, is said to imitate the spherical form of the universe (44d). And heavenly circuits (περίοδοι) and revolutions are mirrored by circuits (περίοδοι) and movements of the soul within the body (39c, 44a–d). In other words, the larger whole is thought to recapitulate itself *in nuce* in the smaller piece of itself that is the human being. This fractal-like structure makes the human an epitome of the cosmos, and allows us to see larger forces at work on a screen that reduces them to a manageable size. Of interest here is a statement, in the context of digestion:

> And the process of filling and evacuating happens just as the motion of everything in the universe does, according to which everything kindred moves toward itself. For what surrounds us on the outside is always dissolving us and sending off and distributing to each kind of thing what is akin to it; the particles of blood, which are in tiny pieces within us and

---

[35] "And just as in the whole we see things that only are in charge, for example divine things; and things that are both in charge and are subject to things, for example the human realm (for this both is subject to the divine and rules over senseless creatures); and things that only are subject to other things, like senseless animals. In the same way also in a human, since he is a *mikros kosmos* according to Democritus, these things are observed. Things that only are in charge, like reason; and things that both are subject to and rule things, like the *thumos* (for it is ruled from reason, and rules over appetite), and things that only are subject to things like the appetite." (Democritus, Diels-Kranz 68 B 34 = David of Nerken, [Armenian philosopher, fl. 490 CE] *Prolegomena*, chap. 12 [= *Commentaria in Aristotelem graeca* vol. 18.2, p. 38.14–21, ed. A. Busse (Berlin: Reimer, 1904).

contained within the frame of each animal, just as under heaven, are compelled to imitate the motion of the universe.[36]

ὁ δὲ τρόπος τῆς πληρώσεως ἀποχωρήσεώς τε γίγνεται καθάπερ ἐν τῷ παντὶ παντὸς ἡ φορὰ γέγονεν, ἣν τὸ συγγενὲς πᾶν φέρεται πρὸς ἑαυτό. τὰ μὲν γὰρ δὴ περιεστῶτα ἐκτὸς ἡμᾶς τήκει τε ἀεὶ καὶ διανέμει πρὸς ἕκαστον εἶδος τὸ ὁμόφυλον ἀποπέμποντα, τὰ δὲ ἔναιμα αὖ, κερματισθέντα ἐντὸς παρ' ἡμῖν καὶ περιειλημμένα ὥσπερ ὑπ' οὐρανοῦ συνεστῶτος ἑκάστου τοῦ ζῴου, τὴν τοῦ παντὸς ἀναγκάζεται μιμεῖσθαι φοράν. (81a–b)

He does not indicate that the compulsion arises because the macrocosm at some moment in time wills it, which would be evidence of ongoing discrete acts of communication between large whole and small whole, but the isomorphism creates a parallelism of processes too. We will see congruent kinds of thinking in each of the great schools of thought to follow, including in Aristotle and among the Stoics. And in the following chapter, we will consider a striking example of it in the fourth book of the Hippocratic treatise *On Regimen*, which we will examine in connection with Aristotle's dream theory.

Divination and the Organism

Timaeus moves into the topic of the body by considering the placement of the soul. In accord with the better known tripartite presentation in the *Republic*, the human soul has three parts. The minion gods fashion the head as a home for the human being's divine part, or the immortal soul handed over to them by the eternal god. In an attempt to protect this part as much as possible from the riotous sensations that vie for sway over the rest of the body, the head is attached only via the thin "isthmus" of the neck (69e). They then fabricate the lower, mortal soul, which the eternal god directed them to make, and house it in the trunk. This lower soul has two pieces. The courageous part is placed in the upper chest cavity and is especially associated with the heart, which the

---

[36] Compare Democritus, Diels-Kranz 68 B 164.

creators "placed in the guard house" (εἰς τὴν δορυφορικὴν οἴκησιν κατέστησαν [70b]. When high spirits are needed, the heart pumps the message to rouse the rest of the body to action (70b). The lungs conversely aid in cooling the passion when appropriate.

The lower part of the mortal soul is housed in the lower trunk, below the midriff.[37] It governs the appetites, which drive people to meet the needs of their bodily natures. It is also, interestingly enough, the seat of divination. This part of the soul has a sinister cast. The creators had to "bind this one down there like a wild beast" (κατέδησαν δὴ τὸ τοιοῦτον ἐνταῦθα ὡς θρέμμα ἄγριον [70e]). Its desires threaten to overrun reason and take control of people. As a safeguard against this, the gods created the organ of the liver, and here begins a single period that runs some 24 lines of the OCT text. It contains manifold ideas and repays close consideration. The minion gods were aware that this part of the soul would not listen to reason, and that even if it got hold of some part of reason through the faculty of sensation (to which it does have access), it would not heed it (71a). The language to which it responds is one of εἴδωλα—"phantoms"—and φαντάσματα—"visions." These terms are common descriptions of dream visions in classical Greek. Also, in Plato's thought, they mark the lowest tiers on his ontological scale, the images of images that result from imitations of the material world found in artistic representations. These phantoms and visions ψυχαγωγοῦσι the lower soul—that is, they "attract" but more particularly "beguile" or even "bewitch" it. This happens "night and day," Plato says, broadening the context, already opened up with φαντάσματα, for understanding this part of the soul to be engaged in dreams.

To regulate the lower soul, the gods settle the liver there, parallel to the placement of the heart and lungs within the spirited part. The liver, which is dense, smooth, and shiny (as well as being both bitter and sweet) functions as a kind of screen or mirror on which the highest part of the soul, contained in the head, can issue a display aimed at guiding the lower soul. Correctives are sent out from above in the form of "discursive thoughts" (διανοήματα) which the liver's surface translates

[37] For a recent study of this part of Plato's soul, treating physiology and psychology, see David Wolfsdorf, "Timaeus' Explanation of Sense-Perceptual Pleasure," *Journal of Hellenic Studies* 134 (2014): 120–35.

into the imagistic language that the lower soul understands. Such a translation is necessary because the lower soul does not operate by discursive thinking. The liver receives impressions (τύποι) from above and mirrors back phantom images (εἴδωλα). These displays take two forms, frightening and soothing, which are correlated with the liver's bitterness and sweetness respectively. The frightening ones attempt to scare the beastly soul into submission. The power from above uses the liver's bitterness (a harshness to which the lower part is akin) to make it contract and wrinkle and turn bilious colors. It also contorts the liver's shape:

> And with respect to the lobe and receptacle[38] and the gates,[39] by bending down the first from its correct position and shriveling it up, and by clogging shut the other two, it produces pain and nausea.

> λοβὸν δὲ καὶ δοχὰς πύλας τε τὸ μὲν ἐξ ὀρθοῦ κατακάμπτουσα καὶ συσπῶσα, τὰ δὲ ἐμφράττουσα συγκλείουσά τε, λύπας καὶ ἄσας παρέχοι. (71c)

Although he has not yet mentioned divination, this part of his discussion is deeply and slyly engaged with it. As we know from Euripides (c. 485–406 BCE), the language of lobes, receptacles, and gates is distinctive of the science of liver-reading, where the disposition of these elements, along with the livers' color, texture, and overall appearance, manifest the divine will (*El.* 826–29).[40] When Plato uses it here, he gives us an alternative explanation for the traditional disfigurations of livers, on which hepatoscopic diviners had built their discipline, borrowing from the cultures of the Near East. Rather than thinking of them as marks produced by a god, Plato says they are actually the physiological manifestation of the reasoning part of the soul manipulating the liver in order to shock the lower soul and make it listen to reason. This sense receives support from a vivid statement he makes near the close of his

---

[38] Gall bladder.

[39] Portal vein.

[40] The connection with Euripides is noted by A. E. Taylor, *A Commentary on Plato's* Timaeus (New York: Clarendon, 1928); and Archer-Hind (1888). For more on early Greek hepatoscopy, see Walter Burkert, *The Orientalizing Revolution* (Cambridge, Mass.: Harvard University Press, 1992), 46–53; and Derek Collins, "Mapping the Entrails: The Practice of Greek Hepatoscopy," *AJP* 129.3 (2008): 319–45.

treatment: when the individual creature is alive, the liver holds signs that are rather clear (τὸ σημεῖα ἐναργέστερα ἔχει [72b]), but when stripped of life, it becomes blind, and the omens it presents are too obscure to indicate anything clearly (τὰ μαντεῖα ἀμυδρότερα ἔσχεν τοῦ τι σαφὲς σημαίνειν [72b]). He thereby seems to be giving tradition-alists a nod by claiming that there is actually something to divination by the liver, since it is a vestige of an underlying internal cognitive state, but what sense the practice has is not due to the traditional ex-planations. This appears to be a fascinating bit of rationalization. However, it does run into a problem. He could not strictly be meaning such an explanation since only human livers would have a rational soul to produce such disfiguration, and we have no tradition of read-ing the livers of humans. Perhaps, though, he means to suggest some analogous process happening in other large mammals.

In addition to the frightening images, the liver can also make a display of gentleness, and it is during this process that divination ex-plicitly enters his account. When the liver produces calmness and serenity, the hunger-driven part of the soul spends its time during the night performing divination through dreams, Plato says:

> And when, in turn, a certain inspiration from discursive reasoning paints opposite images of gentleness, and provides a respite from the bitterness, because it refuses to move or to touch what is naturally opposite to it, and by using the sweetness innate throughout the liver, and by setting it all back into correct alignment, making it smooth and unencumbered, it makes the part of the soul settled around the liver gentle, and it is in good order. And it passes the night in a mea-sured state, experiencing divination during sleep, since it has no share of reason and purposive intelligence.

> καὶ ὅτ' αὖ τἀναντία φαντάσματα ἀποζωγραφοῖ πραότητός τις ἐκ διανοίας ἐπίπνοια, τῆς μὲν πικρότητος ἡσυχίαν παρέχουσα τῷ μήτε κινεῖν μήτε προσάπτεσθαι τῆς ἐναντίας ἑαυτῇ φύσεως ἐθέλειν, γλυκύτητι δὲ τῇ κατ' ἐκεῖνο συμφύτῳ πρὸς αὐτὸ χρωμένη καὶ πάντα ὀρθὰ καὶ λεῖα αὐτοῦ καὶ ἐλεύθερα ἀπευθύνουσα, ἵλεών τε καὶ εὐήμερον ποιοῖ τὴν περὶ τὸ ἧπαρ ψυχῆς μοῖραν κατῳκισμένην, ἔν τε τῇ νυκτὶ διαγωγὴν ἔχουσαν μετρίαν, μαντείᾳ χρωμένην καθ' ὕπνον, ἐπειδὴ λόγου καὶ φρονήσεως οὐ μετεῖχε. (71c–d)

Plato's language is very suggestive in this section. His term for inspiration here, ἐπίπνοια, is not ambiguous. It commonly means a precisely divine inspiration (e.g., Aesch., *Supp.* 17), and it exclusively means this in the handful of other times it appears in Plato's corpus.[41] The images cause the lower soul to become gentle and propitious (ἵλεων) and bright, prosperous, and flourishing (εὐήμερον). It becomes well ordered, like a good household or colony (κατῳκισμένην). The word choice here draws again from the register of omens, as ἵλεως is commonly used to refer to the beneficent aspect of a divinity. The term εὐήμερον is not common and it is likely chosen here to invoke a sense of daytime-level clarity, provocatively available during this nighttime condition. The lower soul passes the night in a measured way (ἔχουσαν μετρίαν), achieving the state of proportion that typically eludes it. But it does this not in the way the upper soul does, since it does not partake in sensible discursive reason (λόγου καὶ φρονήσεως). Just as in his more general treatment in the rest of the corpus, he frames divinatory thinking as specifically nondiscursive, operating by images that appear in a flash.

One possible reading is that Plato intends further to rationalize dream divination, in the way he seems to do with hepatoscopy. Perhaps he is claiming that what has traditionally been understood as a divinatory dream, is actually a psychological processes by which the reasoning soul moderates the appetitive part. Such a view has a certain consistency with his idea that the upper soul is the divine part in us, the only part that is constructed by the demiurge himself as opposed to his minions. And later in the dialogue, he even refers to the reasoning soul as the "*daimôn*" in each of us, so this would provide a further connection, by linking the upper soul with the demonic, which, as we heard from Diotima in the *Symposium*, is the seat of divinatory agency (*Tim.* 90a, c). But the claim that Plato overwrites divination with rational psychological action runs aground in the section of text directly following. There Plato makes clear he sees divination as something quite distinct from the psychological dynamics he has just set out. Reason, he says explicitly, has nothing to do with it. While it plays the preparatory role of

[41] It is the term Plato uses of mantic inspiration from Apollo at *Phaedrus* 265b. See also *Rep.* 499c; *Laws* 738c, 747e, 811c; *Crat.* 399a, of Euthyphro's inspiration; and *Symp.* 181c, of inspiration from Eros.

calming, making the lower soul receptive, the upper soul is not at all involved in the actual divinatory moment:

> God gave *mantikê* to human senselessness, for no one lays hold of inspired and true divination when in his right mind, but when the power of his purposive intelligence [φρονήσις] is shackled during sleep, or when he is in an altered state due to disease or on account of some inspiration.

> μαντικὴν ἀφροσύνῃ θεὸς ἀνθρωπίνῃ δέδωκεν· οὐδεὶς γὰρ ἔννους ἐφάπτεται μαντικῆς ἐνθέου καὶ ἀληθοῦς, ἀλλ᾽ ἢ καθ᾽ ὕπνον τὴν τῆς φρονήσεως πεδηθεὶς δύναμιν ἢ διὰ νόσον, ἢ διά τινα ἐνθουσιασμὸν παραλλάξας. (71e)

Plato allows for a place for reason again later in the process, but only after the divinatory vision has subsided. Reason is capable of pulling the visions out of memory and discerning (διαιρέω) by means of rational calculation (λογισμός) what the vision means and for whom. This sets up another connection with the general survey of Plato's use of divination as a trope above. There we saw him referring to something that popped into his head like a divinatory image, which then provoked discursive, elenchic evaluation. This further testimony accords with the idea that Plato imagines the arrival of the divine sign to be its own process, separate from the conscious and deliberate actions by which the upper soul guides the lower soul, through berating or soothing, using the liver as medium.

So, first, discursive reason flashes images on the liver to regulate the lower soul. When those thoughts are gentle and calming, they facilitate a second process in which the lower soul passes the night temperately and is receptive to divinatory images, and this happens *only* when reason is absent. Then reason re-enters to evaluate the image. One would have liked him to be a bit more specific about the middle process. But there are clues in his account that help us understand it better. They come to the surface from a closer look at the precise language he uses to describe the condition of the lower soul when it is soothed. He talks about it becoming straightened out (ὀρθά) and settled (κατῳκισμένην), and the main verb that Plato uses here is an odd one for him—rare in his corpus and one that he develops a liking for only in the later dialogues. The upper soul puts the lower soul into alignment—ἀπευθύνω. The clue to what he means by this comes in an apposite usage of a cognate term that helps us pin it down. The accounting of it starts with a better understanding of rational intelligence in the *Timaeus*. Briefly, it is related to spinning, which is itself dependent on alignment.

As we saw above, the rational soul is constructed of two nested circular bands each spinning with its own circular motion. One spins horizontally and detects sameness; the other spins slightly oblique to the horizontal and it detects difference. Like invisible gyroscopes, these spinning motions orient people and allow them to make judgments about what is around them. But this is an end state of intelligence that is reached only after a human being enters maturity. From birth until the onset of adulthood the human (Plato assumes male) soul isn't quite spinning right yet, and this makes it subject to great perturbing flows of sensation—exacerbated by the youth's strong need for food to produce growth—and so the soul moves chaotically, not having yet settled into its orbits.

He connects this ontogenetic process with a corresponding, and vividly expressed, phylogenetic stage. As is the case with individual souls, the whole human race has an irrational beginning. Plato narrates the origin of the species, as the minion gods place souls inside bodies for the first time and subject them to the roiling currents of the material world. It is a violent and frightening process:

> The souls bound in a great river neither got control of it nor were controlled by it, but violently they were carried along and endured, so that the whole of the living creature was set going, but in such a random way that its progress was disorderly and irrational.
>
> αἱ δ' εἰς ποταμὸν ἐνδεθεῖσαι πολὺν οὔτ' ἐκράτουν οὔτ' ἐκρατοῦντο, βίᾳ δὲ ἐφέροντο καὶ ἔφερον, ὥστε τὸ μὲν ὅλον κινεῖσθαι ζῷον, ἀτάκτως μὴν ὅπῃ τύχοι προϊέναι καὶ ἀλόγως (43a–b)

He goes on to compare these early humans to people held upside down and unable to see anything for what it really is. He claims this tumultuous stage to be the advent of the perceptions, as the soul is battered by exterior movements. He describes it as flooding in and streaming out and producing collisions against the embodied soul. The connection between this early stage of the human race, the early development of individual humans, and the moments when the irrational soul is ascendant are obvious, even down to the link with the hunger-drive.

But this stage does not last forever, thank goodness, neither for the proto-humans the minions created, nor for each of us individually during our youth. Eventually, as we reach maturity, the inflow and outflow subside, and the soul is calmed and can develop its rational capacities by achieving the state of spinning outlined above—and here is where the clue enters.

> But when the stream of growth and food enters in less volume, and the revolutions calm down and proceed on their own path, becoming more stable as time proceeds, then at length, as the circles move each according to its natural track, their revolutions are aligned, and they designate sameness and difference correctly, and thereby they render their possessor of sound mind.

> ὅταν δὲ τὸ τῆς αὔξης καὶ τροφῆς ἔλαττον ἐπίῃ ῥεῦμα, πάλιν δὲ αἱ περίοδοι λαμβανόμεναι γαλήνης τὴν ἑαυτῶν ὁδὸν ἴωσι καὶ καθιστῶνται μᾶλλον ἐπιόντος τοῦ χρόνου, τότε ἤδη πρὸς τὸ κατὰ φύσιν ἰόντων σχῆμα ἑκάστων τῶν κύκλων αἱ περιφοραὶ κατευθυνόμεναι, τό τε θάτερον καὶ τὸ ταὐτὸν προσαγορεύουσαι κατ’ ὀρθόν, ἔμφρονα τὸν ἔχοντα αὐτὰς γιγνόμενον ἀποτελοῦσιν. (44b)

We can observe a congruence between the process of calming and alignment that leads to the advent of rationality in the maturing adult and the calming and alignment of the lower soul by the upper soul in preparation for divination. The echoing of the rare term ἀπευθύνουσα (71c) and κατευθυνόμεναι (44b) points to the conclusion that, during divination, the lower, irrational soul has a momentary episode of cognitively productive spinning. Just as the immature soul must get aligned with the motions of the heavens before it can partake of reason and become ἔμφρονα, so too the lower soul occasionally becomes aligned—and it is on these occasions that it too can partake of a certain kind of cognition it can on occasion achieve.

The theme of alignment is of some further importance in the dialogue as a whole. Running from 89d through 90d Plato closes the *Timaeus* with a discussion of the proper training of the soul. He says that "with special care we must prepare the part that is to be the guide to the best of our power, so that it may be as fair and good as possible for the work of training" (τὸ δὲ δὴ παιδαγωγῆσον αὐτὸ μᾶλλόν που καὶ πρότερον παρασκευαστέον εἰς δύναμιν ὅτι κάλλιστον καὶ ἄριστον εἰς τὴν παιδαγωγίαν εἶναι). Plato describes this process as attending to the proper motions of each of the three parts of the soul. In this context the upper soul received the designation of *daimôn* mentioned above (90a). It is the point by which we are suspended from the heavens, and it has the job of seeing to it that each part of the soul enters the motions that are proper to it (90c). For the highest part of the soul, the motion is as follows:

> For the divine part in us, the natural motions are the discursive thoughts and revolutions of the universe. Each one of us must, by following these, and by straightening out [ἐξορθοῦντα] the revolutions in our heads, which were distorted at our birth, through learning the harmonies and revolutions of the universe, make the part that thinks like the object of its thought, according to its original nature, and, after he has likened it, achieve finally the goal of that life which is set out for men by the gods as the best, both for the present and for the future.

> τῷ δ' ἐν ἡμῖν θείῳ συγγενεῖς εἰσιν κινήσεις αἱ τοῦ παντὸς διανοήσεις καὶ περιφοραί· ταύταις δὴ συνεπόμενον ἕκαστον δεῖ, τὰς περὶ τὴν γένεσιν ἐν τῇ κεφαλῇ διεφθαρμένας ἡμῶν περιόδους ἐξορθοῦντα διὰ τὸ καταμανθάνειν τὰς τοῦ παντὸς ἁρμονίας τε καὶ περιφοράς, τῷ κατανοουμένῳ τὸ κατανοοῦν ἐξομοιῶσαι κατὰ τὴν ἀρχαίαν φύσιν, ὁμοιώσαντα δὲ τέλος ἔχειν τοῦ προτεθέντος ἀνθρώποις ὑπὸ θεῶν ἀρίστου βίου πρός τε τὸν παρόντα καὶ τὸν ἔπειτα χρόνον. (90c–d)

So the whole point of living is to align our motions with the cosmos. A mature, well-functioning upper soul does this often; the lower soul does so on occasion, and in those cases partakes of prescient dreams.

In his closing remark on divination, just before he goes off to describe the gall bladder and the other organs, Plato tells us: "The nature of the liver then is on account of these kinds of things, and it is naturally in the place which we have said, for the sake of divination" (ἡ μὲν οὖν φύσις ἥπατος διὰ ταῦτα τοιαύτη τε καὶ ἐν τόπῳ ᾧ λέγομεν πέφυκε, χάριν μαντικῆς [*Tim.* 72b]). The liver as an organ functions purposively,

for the sake of producing divination for us. But on the evidence explored here, there are actually two ends the liver seems to fulfill. It has
the role of regulating the lower soul, and the more abstruse one of being
the organ of divination. There is a seeming redundancy of purposes.
Just this kind of redundancy is actually a deep-running and powerful
feature of the dialogue generally. When analyzing natural phenomena
in the *Timaeus*, Plato typically looks for two kinds of causes at play, in
an adumbration of Aristotle's more developed, and better-known, mul-
tifold treatment of causes.[42] First of all, there is a set of causes for things
in the world that derives from necessity. These are attributable to the
characteristics and qualities of the material used to construct things.
They provide physical-level explanations for why things are the way
they are. Plato uses the term of "ancillary causes," more literally co-
causes, for these (συναίτιον [46c7, 46d1, 76d6]). Secondly, there is the
divine cause, which tells us not how some process unfolds due to the
material characteristics of things, but rather why the divine creator
bothered to make that thing or process in the first place. These are the
primary, final, or divine causes, and these press always toward the goal
that what exists in this world should be good—remembering the demiurge's injunction. His discussion of sight is a well-known illustration of
the principle.[43] He reasons for a long time over the optics of light and
how vision works via the nature of the materials involved, but closes
by considering the final cause of sight, or the reason that god shaped
the physical world in such a way as to make sight emerge. The god did
it so that we, by looking up at the sun, the moon, and the stars, would
contemplate the universe, develop the habit of inquiry into the ways
of the cosmos, and from there develop philosophy. So the "for the
sake of which" of sight turns out to be philosophy.[44]

From this perspective, what seem to be the multiple stories Plato
tells about the liver can be understood to be entirely compatible. The

---

[42] See 47e–48a; cf. summary statement at 68e–69a. On this topic, see Carlo Natali, "Le cause
del Timeo et la teoria delle Quattro cause," in Calvo and Brisson (1997), 207–13. He also adds to
this the wandering causes in the orbit of the Nurse or receptacle, which cause like to congregate
with like (48a). For further discussion and context, see Dana R. Miller, *The Third Kind in Plato's
Timaeus* (Göttingen: Vandenhoeck and Ruprecht, 2003), 66–71.

[43] For a full treatment see Carlos Steel, "The Moral Purpose of the Human Body: A Reading
of *Timaeus* 69–72," *Phronesis* 46.2 (2001): 112.

[44] See Cornford (1937), 157, cited in Steel (2001), 112, n. 22.

first, in which the reasoning part of the soul uses the liver to produce phantoms to regulate the appetites, explains the process on the level of mere physicality, and provides an account based on the ancillary or co-causes embedded in the material world. The raging materiality of the lower soul needs a harness. But his discussion of divination also gives us the primary cause for these characteristics of the liver—the "for the sake of which"—the divine set it up to regulate the lower soul in this particular way. As he gets to his conclusion that the purpose of the liver is divination, he tells us that divination was granted to the lower part of our soul as a compensation to it. The minion gods who make our mortal natures recalled that the demiurge ordered them "to make the mortal kind as good as they possibly could" (τὸ θνητὸν ἐπέστελλεν γένος ὡς ἄριστον εἰς δύναμιν ποιεῖν [71d–e]). As mentioned above, this is a powerful guiding principle in the creation of the cosmos. Following this command, Plato says, again speaking of alignment, that "they straighten out the vile part in us by establishing divination there, so that it might in some degree lay hold of the truth" (οὕτω δὴ κατορθοῦντες καὶ τὸ φαῦλον ἡμῶν, ἵνα ἀληθείας πη προσάπτοιτο, κατέστησαν ἐν τούτῳ τὸ μαντεῖον). Divination, then, turns out to be the final cause of our appetites.[45] To put it another way, it is not that divination is overwritten by the physiological architecture, it is underwritten by it.

It is important not to overplay how Plato would view the usefulness of this knowledge. Within his epistemological scheme it is about as far down the ladder of reliability as one can get. We recall that he governs his account by an especially hypothetical version of the idea of likeness, anchored to the notions of *eidôlon* and *phantasma*. The lower soul is incapable of listening to *logoi*, and so it must be cajoled, soothed, forced, or beaten down by phantoms. As mentioned above, these are terms he uses to label not first-order images (*eikones*) but rather images of images. And here we get back to the kind of analysis Plato makes of poetry. Both discourses are at a third remove from the truth, and neither should be relied on to grant us secure knowledge. Perhaps this explains why seers are placed fifth in Plato's scale of incarnations listed at

[45] This point has been made in a fascinating study by Anne Freire Ashbaugh, *Plato's Theory of Explanation: A Study of the Cosmological Account in the Timaeus* (Albany: SUNY Press, 1988), 79.

Phaedrus (248d), just below a gymnast, but in fact above poets, artists, and craftsmen.

This observation also helps us reflect back on the larger set of testimonies above, in which Plato uses the idea of divinatory knowledge as a metaphorical descriptor for a variety of forms of daytime, waking knowing. We saw above that these examples were united by being non-inferential, nondiscursive, and unable to account for themselves. As we saw in the treatment of the broader corpus above, he nowhere claims that people are gaining these insights (whether, in the examples above, a dislike of Sophists, a recognition of the resemblance between temperance and harmony, a spotting of one's soul mate, or a scintilla of light from the highest Good itself) via their irrational souls, or via the liver as an intervening organ. Rather these kinds of waking cognitive events seem to him like divination, because they are imagistic, nondiscursive, and unable to give an account for themselves. Of course, such knowing may or may not be accurate, and sturdy elenchus gives us the best possibility to test whether it is.

CHAPTER 2

Aristotle on Foresight through Dreams

INTRODUCTION

In contrast to Plato, the surviving portion of Aristotle's corpus is made up of his esoteric works—lectures, essays, and sometimes apparently just notes, meant for an audience already at the advanced stage. One salutary aspect is immediately apparent. Aristotle has little use for dramatic irony and deals with issues more directly and systematically than Plato does. On the other hand, the particular challenges for Aristotle's readers are apparent as well. Whereas Plato could be said to present sometimes too many words, elaborating long and intricate lines of argument in which his investment remains indeterminate, Aristotle nearly always presents too few. Using compressed expression and a schematic vocabulary, he will outline even fundamental concepts with nothing more than prepositions and pronouns. His compression produces two immediate results. It puts a great deal of pressure on each component of the sentence; the reading of even a single particle can change sometimes essential points of interpretation, leaving broad areas of disagreement among specialists. It also exacerbates the concerns raised by the textual problems that crop up in the corpus, sometimes at important points, where basic issues will turn on small discrepancies in the manuscript tradition. To work with Aristotle's corpus is a lesson in humility, and the most lasting gains accrue to the judicious rather than the bold.

As with Plato, his most detailed thinking on divination centers on dreams. He positions noncoincidental prescient dreams as examples of surplus knowledge that are provocative, and he sets out to attempt to explain them. The cognitive event underlying them is nondiscursive, happens in a lower region of the soul, and emerges from the cusp of physiology and psychology. Unlike with Plato, we do not have a range of references to the phenomenon across the corpus, which we might aggregate and use to discern facets of his views. We instead have a concentrated treatment in one treatise, *On Divination during Sleep*. The text has the distinction of being the shortest in his surviving corpus, and it is entirely justified to take this as a rough index of its importance to him, relative to such larger issues as ethics, the structure of animal bodies, or causation. One would be further justified to see it as nonetheless noteworthy that Aristotle chooses to treat the topic at all. Once again, we are not in territory like Plato's corpus, where one senses a certain motivation to touch on widely shared points of cultural reference—including phenomena like magic, drinking bouts, or mystery initiation—as an instrument to drive home an abstract philosophical point to a broad audience. We instead see a teacher and his students assembling materials on topics that in their judgment are most worthy of consideration.

In order to understand this text, dotted with references to specialized concepts developed in other parts of his corpus, one is led on a rather long and circuitous path: through Aristotelian positions in the fields of physics (regarding the origins of movement in both animate and inanimate objects), psychology (regarding sleep, perception, imagination, and especially the psychic dimensions of the states of incontinence, luckiness, and melancholy), and even ethics (regarding volition, impulse, and desire), as well as allied traditions of dream reading in the medical corpus—and each of these topics entails others of greater or lesser magnitude. It turns out to be a rather large undertaking. At the end, we will find Aristotle's treatment to be not at all a detour into an exotic tributary, but one deeply engaged in, and mutually illuminating of, adjacent regions of his thinking. I will begin with a detailed paraphrase of the text, which will be necessary to set out in full, in which I will flag four points where further investigation will follow. There remain important disagreements among scholars on several issues of text and interpretation. I have addressed only the more consequential ones directly here.[1]

---

[1] The scholarship on the *On Divination during Sleep* is relatively meager. The great contribution is Philip van der Eijk's outstanding edition and commentary for the series: *Aristoteles Werke in deutscher Übersetzung: Parva Naturalia. De insomniis. De divinatione per somnun,*

Like a nested doll, the *On Divination during Sleep* sits inside larger units. It is a part of the larger grouping of the *Parva Naturalia* (*PN*), comprised of seven short empirical works investigating topics that emerge out of the more theoretical and substantial treatise *On the Soul*. At the opening of the *PN*, he tells us that, after now having investigated (in the *De anima*) the basic potencies or attributes (δυνάμεις) of the soul, considered as the general principle of all living things, he will now investigate the most common behaviors in which living things engage: sensation, memory, inhalation and exhalation, growing old, sleeping, dreaming, and having predictive dreams. These are the subjects of the seven works that follow. It is for him obvious that all of these have to do with body and soul in common (φαίνεται δὲ τὰ μέγιστα . . . κοινὰ τῆς τε ψυχῆς ὄντα καὶ τοῦ σώματος); they all involve sensation, and sensation "arises in the soul through the body" (διὰ σώματος γίγνεται τῇ ψυχῇ [*Sens.* 436b6–8]). Insight through dreams will be based on something of this character, it will require a reckoning with both psychology and physiology.

Moving inside to the next shell, the treatise is the last in a collection of three on sleep set within the *PN*, which Aristotle considers as a group: the *On Sleep and Waking*, *On Dreams*, and *On Divination during Sleep*. The triptych begins with his offering overviews of the three treatises. In the last one, he says, he will investigate "whether it is possible to foresee the future or not possible, and if it is possible in what way" (καὶ πότερον ἐνδέχεται τὰ μέλλοντα προορᾶν ἢ οὐκ ἐνδέχεται, καὶ τίνα τρόπον εἰ ἐνδέχεται·), and he then specifies further:

καὶ πότερον τὰ μέλλοντα ὑπ᾽ ἀνθρώπου πράσσεσθαι μόνον, ἢ καὶ ὧν τὸ δαιμόνιον ἔχει τὴν αἰτίαν, καὶ φύσει γίγνεται ἢ ἀπὸ ταὐτομάτου. (*Somn.* 453b21–25)

There is an obvious curiosity immediately in Aristotle's invoking the notion of the demonic (τὸ δαιμόνιον), referencing the "demonic as a

vol. 14, part 3 (Berlin: Akademie Verlag, 1994); see his bibliography at pp. 102–32; and van der Eijk's collection, *Medicine and Philosophy in Classical Antiquity* (Cambridge: Cambridge University Press, 2005). Also important are W. D. Ross, *Aristotle: Parva Naturalia* (Oxford: Oxford University Press, 1955; repr. 2000); David Gallop, *Aristotle on Sleep and Dreams: Text and Translation with Introduction, Notes, and Glossary* (Oxford: Aris & Phillips, 1996); and Mor Segev, "The Teleological Significance of Dreaming in Aristotle," *Oxford Studies in Ancient Philosophy* 43 (2012): 107–41.

cause," in this compressed summary.[2] It will recur in a prominent position in the treatise. Solving what he means by this will be the largest question addressed below. To a certain extent, Philip van der Eijk must be correct that the demonic here comes out to mean something "beyond human control."[3] After all it is explicitly set in opposition to actions performed by humans, a contrast backed up by his use of the verb πράσσεσθαι, his preferred way of talking about self-conscious, deliberative human behavior.[4] On the other hand, we would then be left to wonder why he didn't just say *that*. Students of Aristotle are rarely faced with a situation of overly flowery language being used in a way that obscures a rather straightforward point. Just the opposite is more often the case. If Aristotle meant nothing more than "what is beyond human control," he has ways to say that and, in fact, employs a kind of technical vocabulary for the idea—ὃ μὴ ἐφ' αὑτοῖς/τοῖς ἀνθρώποις ἐστι, for example (*EE* 1223a3, 1225a29; *Phys.* 226a35, 259b11; or *Rhet.* 1360a1) or ὡς οὐκ ἐφ' ἡμῖν ὑπάρχει (*NE* 1179b21–22)—and one might have expected him to use such a phrase, or even a more prosaic, ἃ μὴ ὑπ' ἀνθρώπου πράσσεται, if he had meant only to signal what is beyond human control. That he uses a term that for him, as we will see, consistently means a realm of intermediate divinity between us and the highest level of the divine is not without significance.

Even just the general sense of the overview sentence presents difficulties. There is one way to read it, which modern translators typically follow, that makes it into a taxonomy of the kinds of events dreams might foresee.[5] It would render into English something like this:

[2] This term in the Greek has nothing to do with evil sprites. For further comment on the demonic in this study, see the introduction, n. 52.

[3] Philip van der Eijk, *Medicine and Philosophy in Classical Antiquity: Doctors and Philosophers on Nature, Soul, Health, and Disease* (Cambridge: Cambridge University Press, 2005), 143.

[4] See discussion below, p. 135.

[5] Beare, Hett, Gallop, Mugnier (French), Repici (Italian), and Siwek (Latin) all take it this way; as does Ross in his commentary ad loc. on the *Parva Naturalia*. See J. I. Beare, "On Sleep," in Jonathan Barnes, ed., *The Complete Works of Aristotle*, Bollingen (Princeton: Princeton University Press, 1984); W. S. Hett, *On the Soul, Parva Naturalia*, Loeb Classical Library 391 (Cambridge, Mass.: Harvard University Press, 1936); Gallop (1996); René Mugnier, *Aristote: Petits traits d'histoire naturelle* (Paris: Les Belles Lettres 1953); L. Repici, *Aristotele: Il sonno e i sogni* (Venice: Marsilio, 2003); Paul Siwek, *Aristotelis Parva Naturalia graece et latine* (Rome: Desclée, 1963).

And whether it is possible to foresee only future events that are performed by a human, or also those of which the demonic contains the cause, and come to be by nature or from the spontaneous.

But there is a problem with this interpretation. It is difficult to find in the treatise any interest, at all, on Aristotle's part in trying to discern whether we are able to foresee events caused by humans vs. natural or spontaneous ones (which would somehow have demonic causes), let alone a sufficiently large interest that it would make sense for the treatise to be summarized this way. He has different interests with respect to the kinds of events dreams might predict. The overriding distinction he deals with is between predicting internal states of the body vs. external events at a distance. In neither of these categories does the question of the agency responsible for the event even come up, let alone make a difference with respect to the event's predictability. In the case of internal bodily states, agency is not involved; and as for events at a distance, while human causation could be relevant, Aristotle never makes it so.[6] Further, such a rendering of the overview sentence allows no adequate account of why Aristotle would have invoked the demonic here, in a statement meant to be an epitome. These doubts and the work that follows will lead me to propose another possible reading of this passage:

And whether, with respect to foreseeing future events, it is an act performed by humans on their own, or is also among the things which have the demonic as the cause, and arise by nature or from the spontaneous.

[6]To expand on this: measuring whether an event takes place within us or far away from us does not line up with the question of whether it has a self-conscious human cause or not. In the case of medical dreams, centered on in the first part of the treatise, he examines an event that emerges unselfconsciously as a symptomatic expression during sleep, which is irrelevant to human willed πρᾶξις. When he looks at dreams of things far away, in the second chapter, this part of the investigation again does not line up with either category of humanly or not-humanly caused. He speaks of "all those that are both extravagant and whose origin is not within the dreamers themselves, but concern naval battles and faraway events." He cannot mean here a class of events beyond human πρᾶξις otherwise the choice of naval battles would not make sense. He really has in mind the question of proximity to the sleeper, and not the question of whether the event to be foreseen originated from human action or not. This is confirmed also when, after medical dreams, he looks at those that have starting points "that are exotic in time, or place, or magnitude" (*Somn.* 463b1–3); and near the opening, tells us that "it would seem to be beyond human wit to discover the origin of certain people's foresight concerning events at the Pillars of Hercules or the Borysthenes river" (462b24–26). The main point of distinction here, confirmed in the details of the treatise, is how far away from the dreamer is the precipitating cause of the dream.

καὶ πότερον τὰ μέλλοντα ὑπ' ἀνθρώπου πράσσεσθαι μόνον, ἢ καὶ ὧν
τὸ δαιμόνιον ἔχει τὴν αἰτίαν, καὶ φύσει γίγνεται ἢ ἀπὸ ταὐτομάτου.
(*Somn.* 453b21–25)

The following pages will attempt to justify this reading.

Turning to the *On Divination during Sleep* itself, summarizing the
whole is a nontrivial exercise.[7] The treatise is divided into two chapters. To start the first, Aristotle picks up the subject by saying that it is
difficult to have confidence in divination via dreams but also difficult
to dismiss it. Its widespread acceptance is for him, in contrast to Plato,
evidence that there is something to it.[8] Another reason to trust in it
comes from a subset of predictive dreams for which it is possible to construct "a certain account." This is his initial reference to his main concern in the first chapter: a medical stream of thought, attested in the
surviving Hippocratic corpus—the focus of part one below—that sees
dreams as predictive of physiological pathologies. However, on the
other side of the issue, one sees no plausible account for the cause of
dreams that predict things beyond the anticipation of bodily states.
One cause that people suggest, that god sends dreams, is not convincing since, in addition to its being generally at variance with the way god
acts,[9] it is also true that predictive dreams do not happen to the best
and wisest, but to common people, and if god were the sending agent,
god would surely send them to the best people. But if one removes the

---

[7] For the text on which this summary is based, I have followed Siwek (1963), with van der
Eijk's (1994) emendations, with these exceptions: Because of the felicity of the particle, I have
followed Ross' δὴ ἀπιστεῖν where Siwek follows the manuscripts διαπιστεῖν at 462b20. I take
Ross' ταύταις where Siwek follows the manuscripts' τούτοις at 463a25; and the ἀρχὰς of mss. Z
and H instead of Siwek's ἀρχὴ at 463a28. I read ὅπη for ὅποι at 464a12. I make a section break
after περὶ τῶν τοιούτων at 464a19. I read a comma after οἱ ἐμμανεῖς at 464b2.

[8] This mode of valuing ideas—in which the width of attestation of an idea across a popula-
tion serves as a gauge of its trustworthiness—represents a sharp departure from most previous
thinkers, prominently including Plato of course, and the Stoics adhere to their own version of
it, in part of their thinking on divination as well (see chap. 4). This view is twinned, both in
Aristotle and the Stoics, with a view that perception is not systematically defective and whole
populations therefore represent a kind of collective set of sensors detecting the contours of the
world, and the larger the set, the larger and more persuasive the data gathered.

[9] The notion of being generally at variance with the way god acts, van der Eijk's (1994) suggestion, is the best solution, in my judgment, to the otherwise absent antecedent of ἄλλη in
Aristotle's πρὸς τῇ ἄλλῃ ἀλογίᾳ. This leaves us with something like: "in addition to the rest
of its unreasonableness"; it is also absurd for the specific reason he goes on to articulate. This
makes Aristotle suggest that upon simple inspection the proposition is inconsistent with what
we know.

idea that god is the cause, no other cause appears to be convincing. To find the source of dreams that predict events outside the body, and even in faraway and unfamiliar locations, would seem to be beyond human wit.

Anticipatory dreams that hit the mark must either be causes (as the moon causes an eclipse), signs (as a star appearing in daytime is a sign of an eclipse), or coincidences (as when a person takes a walk and an eclipse just happens to occur). Coincidences (συμπτώματα) are not interesting to him, since they do not take place under any general rule. In a crisp rhetorical question and answer, Aristotle next prepares his audience for his taking seriously the possibility that dreams could be signs:

> Among dreams aren't some causes and others signs, for example of things that happen concerning the body? Yes, even the accomplished among the medical doctors say that one must pay very close attention to dreams. And it is reasonable also for those who, while not skilled professionals, are examining something philosophically to take this view.

> ἆρ' οὖν ἐστι τῶν ἐνυπνίων τὰ μὲν αἴτια, τὰ δὲ σημεῖα, οἷον τῶν περὶ τὸ σῶμα συμβαινόντων; λέγουσι γοῦν καὶ τῶν ἰατρῶν οἱ χαρίεντες ὅτι δεῖ σφόδρα προσέχειν τοῖς ἐνυπνίοις· εὔλογον δὲ οὕτως ὑπολαβεῖν καὶ τοῖς μὴ τεχνίταις μέν, σκοπουμένοις δέ τι καὶ φιλοσοφοῦσιν. (463a3–7)

The strength of the language here (ἆρ' οὖν, γοῦν καὶ, σφόδρα) is worth noting, since it suggests the importance he places on the medical tradition. It serves as a proof of concept and anchoring background context for the first half of the treatise. Aristotle then characterizes the line of reasoning behind medical uses of dreams with some care: In sleep, when the more dynamic daytime movements of the soul are quieted, since we are not engaged in perception or gross motor movement, the soul may detect motions caused by even small imbalances in the body, which most ancient theorists saw as the seeds of disease. He cites examples of dreamers magnifying subtle stimuli around them into vigorous dream images. So even though the imbalances in the body that are the beginning points of disease start out tiny, the medical evidence shows that the soul can detect them during sleep; and it then amplifies them in dream images. Dreams might also *cause* future actions by "paving the way" for them (διὰ τὸ προωδοποιῆσθαι 463a28–29). Just as we can observe daytime actions paving the way for nighttime dreams, so also nighttime dreams might prompt us into certain daytime actions.

Most dreams that correspond to the future, though, he says, will do so coincidentally, especially those having to do with extravagant and unfamiliar settings. The phenomenon is akin, he says, to the case of a person making casual mention of something and then having that thing happen. The person's saying it surely wasn't a sign or cause of that thing happening. Furthermore, one would expect many such coincidences (συμπτώματα) as this to happen.

At this point, the second chapter starts, which Aristotle devotes to a speculative exploration of the causes of dreams that predict events outside the body. He begins with the most serious interpretive challenge of the essay, and one of Aristotle's most famously surprising sentences. He tells us:

> ὅλως δὲ ἐπεὶ καὶ τῶν ἄλλων ζῴων ὀνειρώττει τινά, θεόπεμπτα μὲν οὐκ ἂν εἴη τὰ ἐνύπνια, οὐδὲ γέγονε τούτου χάριν, δαιμόνια μέντοι· ἡ γὰρ φύσις δαιμονία, ἀλλ' οὐ θεία. (463b12–15)

which I translate:

> Speaking generally, since also certain of the other animals dream, dreams couldn't be god sent, nor have they arisen for the sake of being a divine message,[10] however they are demonic; for nature[11] is demonic, but not divine.

[10] Hett (1936) takes the antecedent of the τούτου as being functionally μαντική, supplying it in a footnote. The interpretation faces the impediment of gender, which might be explained on the notion that the topic has here been generalized into a "thing," as Aristotle sometimes does. But the greater impediment is that it goes too far for the context, which suggests a narrower issue is at stake. The topic of the sentence in which this clause is embedded focuses on the issue of a dream being "θεόπεμπτον," by which Aristotle means to reference the traditional view that a dream is a discreet act of divine communication with the receiver. While οὗ ἕνεκα is the commonest way for Aristotle to express the notion of final cause, χάριν is used as well (see GA 789b5; Meta. 1050a9; NE 1094a15, 1097a18, 1176b30; Pol. 1280b40, 1325a7, 1339b36; Juv. 469a8; cf. De anim. 407a24).

[11] I have not followed van der Eijk's (1994) suggestion ad loc. that "nature" here refers to the nature of the dreamer, rather than nature as a whole. He is surely correct to point out that Aristotle's lexicon just as easily allows one meaning as the other. But here the context does not support "the nature of the dreamer," since we have no proximate discussion of a dreamer here toward which the article might point. On the other hand, as will become clear below, on my interpretation, there is little substantive difference between the two possible readings, since Aristotle in fact intends the dreamer insofar as he or she is a piece of the natural world, rather than as a human

Now, since we have already encountered the term *demonic* (δαιμόνιος) in the two-line summary of the treatise earlier in the *Parva Naturalia*, we are right to focus on it. It represents the key to this sentence, and in my view the sentence holds the key to understanding the essay as a whole. It leads off a paragraph that contains further challenges, the interpretation of which are interdependent with it, to be addressed in a detailed discussion of the demonic, the focus of a second section below.

Aristotle then sets out the mechanics for how future-leaning dreams could work, saying that it may be that something at a distance from us disturbs the air nearby it, and that this disturbance then stirs up the air adjacent to it, and so on in turn, until the movement reaches the sleeping soul, like a ripple traveling over water. That movement then produces a mental image by contact with the body. He situates his theory in contrast to that of Democritus (who attributed dreams to phantom effluxions, εἴδωλα, that cascaded off objects in the world).[12] Instead of imagining the existence of such exotic things, Aristotle has movements of air producing a palpable impression on the sleeper, and the impression produces a mental image that is then inserted into the dream. Since the air is less turbulent at night than during the day, these movements are less likely to be broken up by other intervening currents. Also, returning again to the medical theory, he claims that by the same principle that people magnify internal bodily states during sleep, dreamers might be able to detect even the small disturbances produced by distant objects. Sleep is a prerequisite to these perceptions, he repeats, since by day the usual movements of perception in the soul overwhelm the faint ripples from far away.

Aristotle then moves on to describing how a sleeper winds up foretelling something from the detected disturbances—another complex idea. He links the account with his observation that such predictive dreams tend to appear to the empty headed. Their lack of intellectual

---

being that achieves rational wishes, or even as an ensouled creature that initiates motion, just as an organism with a teleology—that is the referent here. My translation here is in accord with the 1923 translation of Beare (Ross, ed.), who cites Zeller (1879) and contradicts Bonitz ([1890] see fn. ad loc.).

[12] For Democritus' theory, see Diels-Kranz 68 A 77–79 and B 166. We are also assured on the importance of such εἴδωλα in the idea of foreseeing in general, since Diogenes Laertius testifies to a work written by him under the title *Peri eidôlôn ê peri pronoias* (Diog. Laert. 9.46), in other words, setting up the topic of these images to be equivalent to the topics of foresight.

capacity is not only not an impediment to their having such dreams, it actually enables them to. Since their discursive intellects are ineffectual, vacant, and empty of everything (ἡ γὰρ διάνοια τῶν τοιούτων οὐ φροντιστική, ἀλλ' ὥσπερ ἔρημος καὶ κενὴ πάντων 464a22–24), they present fewer intervening stimuli, and their minds are carried off the by the agency of the distant mover ([ἡ διάνοια] κινηθεῖσα κατὰ τὸ κινοῦν ἄγεται). This also suggests to Aristotle why some who are in an ecstatic state (ἐκστατικοί)[13] are able to foresee things, since their internal movements are knocked away, allowing the outside vibrations to take the lead. Next comes an observation that when one is better acquainted with someone, one is more likely to have premonitions about that person, since one knows the other's movements well and can recognize that person more quickly, just as familiar people are recognizable by sight from far off. The melancholic, on account of their intensity,[14] are "good shots" who can hit the mark. This is a claim, in my reading, that they are able to sift through the potential futures built into the current state of affairs to find the ones that will emerge. They are also particularly malleable, so that they can follow a string of events into the future, taking the sequential leaps of imagination toward a presentiment of what comes next. Both these last observations about the melancholic—that they are good shots, lighting on the right current of air, and that they are good at projecting from this one to the future—will require more consideration, including a detailed look at Aristotle's ideas on luckiness, which will occupy parts three and four below.

He closes his essay with a note on the ability to interpret dreams. This talent is distinct from the capacity to receive predictive ones. He

[13] The word ἐκστατικός does not on its own indicate an ecstatic state as readily as its English descendant does. In this case, though, the translation is pushed in this direction since, of the available meanings Aristotle conveys with this word, a vehement passion that displaces a person's or animal's typical behavior is the most apposite. The more typical meaning in Aristotle of a change from one state to another (a displacement in that sense; see *Phys.* 222b16) is hardly likely here. The particular vehement passion, which the more general word must be indicating here, is a clairvoyant trance under the influence of which oracles made their pronouncements (cf. *EE* 1229a25; *NE* 1145b11; *Cat.* 10a1; see also the noun form at *Part. an.* 651a4).

[14] Siwek (1963) is surely right in his note ad loc.: "eorum 'impetuosities,' i.e. intensities imagine." On melancholy, see Philip J. van der Eijk, "Aristotle on Melancholy," in van der Eijk (2005), 139–68.

says it is a skill of seeing likenesses (the same quality he claims for those good at metaphor).[15] The dream image is broken up by other movements in the soul and so is fragmented, like a reflection in rippled water, and a distinct skill is required to reassemble it. A short concluding statement serves as a closing for the three works on sleep, and seems to look forward to the treatise on the *Movement of Animals*, which would place it at the end of the *Parva Naturalia*, at variance with the traditional Bekker ordering of the texts:

> What then sleep is,
> and what a dream is, and on account of what cause each of them arises,
> and further concerning divination from dreams, the whole of it, has been
> discussed; and concerning the common movement of animals we must
> talk.

> τί μὲν οὖν ἐστιν ὕπνος
> καὶ τί ἐνύπνιον, καὶ διὰ τίν' αἰτίαν ἑκάτερον αὐτῶν γίνεται,
> ἔτι δὲ περὶ τῆς ἐκ τῶν ἐνυπνίων μαντείας εἴρηται περὶ πάσης·
> περὶ δὲ κινήσεως τῆς κοινῆς τῶν ζῴων λεκτέον. (*Div. somn.* 464b15–18a)

The final linking clause here is treated by Ross as an intrusion of later copyists. The variant ordering is in fact attested in the manuscripts, and two recent modern editors, van der Eijk and Siwek, both take this particular linking clause as genuine.[16] In any case, the appearance of a bookend like this one reaffirms that Aristotle considers his works *On Sleep*, *On Dreams*, and *On Divination during Sleep* to form a group. And if the final linking clause is genuine, it also provides an interesting clue, which will be revisited below, that the subject of predictive dreams leads into a discussion of the origins of movement in animals more generally, which is the rather expansive topic of the treatise *On the Movement of Animals*. This reinforces that for Aristotle, the topic occupies a middle position between movements of the soul and the physical movements

---

[15] Compare *Poetics* 1459a8: πολὺ δὲ μέγιστον τὸ μεταφορικὸν εἶναι. μόνον γὰρ τοῦτο οὔτε παρ' ἄλλου ἔστι λαβεῖν εὐφυΐας τε σημεῖόν ἐστι· τὸ γὰρ εὖ μεταφέρειν τὸ τὸ ὅμοιον θεωρεῖν ἐστιν.

[16] See van der Eijk (1994) n. ad loc., and 69–70, n. 67; Siwek (1963) n. ad loc. See further discussion by Martha Nussbaum, ed., *Aristotle's De Motu Animalism* (Princeton: Princeton University Press, 1985), 9.

produced by bodies embedded in nature, which is entirely consonant with the overall reading to be presented here.

The Central Puzzle

Scholars often take Aristotle's main point in the treatise to be a debunking of divine causation, and a naturalizing of the phenomenon.[17] That he discusses "movements" (κινήσεις) of air reaching the soul, that are then translated into perceptions (αἰσθήσεις) when they become mental images (φαντάσματα) inserted into the dream places it in proximity to his general theories of perception, as presented in *De anima* 2.5–3.2 and in *On Sense and Sensible Things*.[18] The senses have to do centrally with the transference of movements from the outside world to the sensing soul.[19] Divination, then, seems to be a special case of perception via extremely subtle stimuli carried along by air currents, and susceptible to explanation via physiology.[20] That Aristotle explicitly says that dreams are not sent by god is of course pertinent as well. Let us call this the debunking argument.

Two problems remain for this reconstruction, though, and they are insurmountable. First, it leaves unanswered the question of how it is that a vibration from faraway current events becomes assembled into a prescient message about future ones. It gives us a story about movements transmitted through the air striking against a sleeping body; through tactile contact an internal image is formed, on analogy with

[17] See, e.g., W. V. Harris in his chapter on "Naturalistic Explanations," in *Dreams and Experience in Classical Antiquity* (Cambridge, Mass.: Harvard University Press, 2009), 229–78. And those leaving an opening to the divine have not specified how it might operate. See M. A. Holowchak, "Aristotle on Dreaming: What Goes On in Sleep When the 'Big Fire' Goes Out," *Ancient Philosophy* 16 (1996): 420–22; and Jose Kany-Turpin and Pierre Pellegrin, "Cicero and the Aristotelian Theory of Divination by Dreams," in W. W. Fortenbaugh and P. Steinmetz, eds., *Cicero's Knowledge of the Peripatos* (New Brunswick, N.J.: Transaction, 1989), 220–45.

[18] On the whole topic of Aristotle on perception, see the recent treatment of Anna Marmodoro, *Aristotle on Perceiving Objects* (Oxford: Oxford University Press, 2014). See also, with discussion of the scholarship, Victor Caston, "The Spirit and the Letter: Aristotle on Perception," in Ricardo Salles, ed., *Metaphysics, Soul, and Ethics, in Ancient Thought* (Oxford: Clarendon, 2005), 245–320.

[19] See the concise presentation of Victor Kal, *Aristotle on Intuition and Discursive Reason* (Leiden: Brill, 1988), 68–70.

[20] See below, fn. 12, with reference to Democritus.

what happens in medical symptoms. But then we are left without an explanation for how these get turned into an anticipatory image. Second, and as I will argue entirely related, such a reading leaves out the key sentence cited above—and, like an extra piece left over after reassembling a delicate machine, the omission renders it suspect. If something like naturalistic debunking were his position, why in the world would Aristotle say, after dismissing that dreams are god-sent, that they "are however demonic; for nature is demonic, but not divine"? And why would the notion of the demonic appear among the few dozen words he chooses to summarize the treatise at the beginning of the triptych of works on sleep? If Aristotle truly were debunking divine causality, he would have no need to reference the category, and certainly no need to make the expansive claim that all of the natural world is demonic. Alternative translations of the term *demonic* are not satisfying. We saw the problems with van der Eijk's suggestion of it meaning only "beyond human control." There are equal problems with suggesting Aristotle simply indicates something wondrous, as some take it to mean.[21] He has a perfectly accessible way to express that via θαυμαστόν, a common Aristotelian descriptor.[22] He instead opts for a much rarer adjective (δαιμόνια), which, following common usage (a good place to start with Aristotle), will mean "having a divine character."[23] It would be uncharacteristic if Aristotle did not mean something like this in using the term, and, as we will see below, he consistently *does* mean something like this in all parallel uses in his corpus.

To unravel these problems and understand the *On Divination during Sleep* as a whole, the analysis below will be divided into the four sections flagged in the summary above. First, since Aristotle devotes a consequential chunk of the compact treatise to summarizing what he sees as the ideas behind medical dream reading (20 of the total of 133 lines in the work), and since he offers the medical doctors' use of dreams as evidence for the basic plausibility of the proposition that dreams might

[21] Beare (1984), 737, opts for "mysterious."

[22] Aristotle's uses of the term are too numerous to list.

[23] Aristotle regards common usage as a source of authority, regularly beginning from everyday terms and, while he makes refinements, retaining the core notion from common usage in his technical vocabulary. His treatment of *mythos* in the poetics, where he takes a common term for "tale" and distills it into a technical term for "plot," is a well-known case in point.

project future events, we will first devote attention to the medical background. As it happens, a pertinent treatise survives in the Hippocratic corpus, and it repays close attention. Second, we will focus on Aristotle's sense of the demonic, a notion that is not prominent in his corpus. It requires detours through basic Aristotelian physics, cosmology, and ontology, and will prepare the way for marking out a very specific role for the divine within predictive dreams. Both the medical background and a firmer sense of the demonic prepare the way for the third and fourth sections, which will both address the question of how certain people are able to move from dream images having to do with current states of faraway events to anticipatory images about what will happen subsequently. Part three will focus on lucky people, whom Aristotle treats as a parallel case to accurate dreamers, and for whom the demonic also plays a crucial part; and four will turn back specifically to dreaming, and examine the dreamers' instinctive capacity to project premonitory visions. The total picture presented here will show Aristotle framing the glimmers of insight that come through divinatory dreams as examples of a peculiar cognitive capacity built into the rudiments of the human organism. The knowledge resulting from it is nondiscursive, and not the result of self-conscious deliberation or volition. It is a surplus that is accessible to all of us, but for most people the higher-order intellects occlude this lower-order information processing system. The lower one realizes itself just in the special case of those who have weak higher-order ones.

PART 1: MEDICAL THINKING BETWEEN PLATO AND ARISTOTLE

For Aristotle, the notion that some dreams are predictive symptoms of hidden internal bodily states provides the pivot for thinking seriously about those that might refer to external states. This suggests the medical background is pertinent for understanding Aristotle's ideas, and a closer look proves it to be so. Within the Hippocratic corpus, as it happens, a text survives that preserves a detailed discussion of the significance of dreams in making diagnoses: book 4 of the *On Regimen*, which is also our earliest surviving tract on preventive medicine.[24] It is likely, though we can't be certain, that Aristotle is referencing this text.[25] We know that he would endorse some of the specific claims made in it, and it is surely the case that it represents the kind of thinking to which he is referring. Consonant with Aristotle, we will see the Hippocratic author of *On Regimen* 4 claim that:

- In the earliest stages of a disease, when it is still too early for a pathology to manifest visibly, a coded message about it may emerge during sleep (cf. *Div. somn.* 463a18–20);
- During sleep, we are particularly capable of subtle self-detection, since intervening perceptions are quieted (cf. *Div. somn.* 463a7–11);
- We can sense even the tiny somatic imbalances from which diseases arise, and dreams emerge that signify these imbalances (cf. *Div. somn.* 463a20–21);
- The language dreams speak is not straightforward but is scrambled (cf. *Div. somn.* 464b8–9).

Going further than Aristotle, the Hippocratic author claims that the code in which dreams speak is premised on a detailed correspondence between anatomy and cosmology.

This piece of the text is reminiscent of ideas in the *Timaeus* that we discussed in the previous chapter, and digging a bit further into it shows instructive similarities and differences with Plato's thinking as well. Like Plato, the Hippocratic author explains how dreams work by embedding them in very expansive claims about the universe as a whole. While the date of the Hippocratic text is uncertain, and it may have appeared before Plato's work, considered topically, it serves a fascinating

---

[24] For the text, see Robert Joly, *Hippocrate: Du régime*, Corpus medicorum graecorm 1.2.4, rev. ed. With dimon Byl (Berlin: Akademie-Verlag, 2003). Useful recent studies include: G. Cambiano, "Une interpretation 'materialiste' des rêves: Du Régime IV," in Mirko Drazen Grmek, ed., *Hippocratica: Actes du Colloque Hippocratique de Paris* (Paris: Éditions du Centre national de la recherche scientifique, 1980); Jacques Jouanna, "L'interprétation des rêves et la théorie micro- macrocosmique dans le traité hippocratique de *Régime*: sémiotique et mimesis," in K. D. Fischer, D. Nickel and P. Potter, eds., *Text and Tradition: Studies in Ancient Medicine and Its Transmission*, Studies in Ancient Medicine 18 (Leiden: Brill, 1998), 161–74; S. M. Oberhelman, "Dreams in Graeco-Roman Medicine" *ANRW* II.37.1 (Berlin: De Gruyter, 1993), 121—56.

[25] Van der Eijk is persuasive on this, van der Eijk (2005), 198. His treatment emphasizes differences between the medical writer and Aristotle, 198–200. I will be more concerned with similarities.

bridging function from Plato to Aristotle, drawing connections between two distinct sets of ideas. Work on the specifics of the *On Regimen* pays dividends in both directions.

In book 1, the author claims like Plato that the human body is an image of the cosmos. The great cosmological principle of fire, in his account, produces individuals by copying the macrocosm. The author elaborates the correspondences, some specifics of which mirror those of the *Timaeus*.[26] The belly is an imitation of the sea, the flesh of the earth, the body's inner circuit imitates the circuit of the moon, its outer circuit mirrors that of the stars. In the fourth book, the author makes his claims about dreams, and their hidden diagnostic messages—they speak a language that is based on the correspondences between body and cosmos. A star plunging into the sea in a dream, for example, is a sign for disease of the belly, a star falling earthward is a symptom of nascent tumors in the flesh. Dreaming of a rough surface of the earth indicates impure flesh, dreaming of high or low rivers indicates high or low blood levels.

These are more expansive than Plato's claims. While Plato also made out the human body to be a copy of the universe, the Hippocratic author adds the idea that the human organism copies the universe in return in the language of its dreams. The first position suggests a fractal-like structure, the second understands an inclination of the microcosm to reach back toward the macrocosm, a process that guides the production of messages readable to those in the know. The Hippocratic text is a kind of missing link between Plato's thought about models and copies, and what we will see is Aristotle's fascinating scheme of a certain congruence between the movements of organisms (in the case of dreaming, ourselves) and the larger vectors that steer the cosmos as a whole. The key insight for both Aristotle and the Hippocratic author emerges from examining the complex forces that produce the significant dream. Though the particulars of the modes of that production are quite different, each author makes out a human to be fulfilling an outcome that

[26] See, Jacques Jouanna, "The Theory of Sensation, Thought, and the Soul in the Hippocratic Treatise *Regimen*: Its Connections with Empedocles and Plato's *Timaeus*," in Philip van der Eijk, ed., *Greek Medicine from Hippocrates to Galen: Selected Papers,* trans. Neil Allies (Leiden: Brill, 2012), 195–228.

engages below the level of our self-conscious awareness and is encoded by the larger cosmos, in which our corporeal selves are embedded.

In the case of the Hippocratic author, the account proceeds in the following way. On one level, the human agent seems responsible for the dream. The author claims in book 4 that the soul produces it (*On Reg.* 4.87). However, the matter is complicated because book 1 teaches us that the soul does all manner of the things it does as part of a large, interconnected cosmos. He envisions the individual and the cosmos not just as model and copy, but also as a pair of coinciding and interconnecting opposites, in a mode similar to Heraclitus. The author considers this kind of a relation to hold in general, and explicitly considers dozens of pairs of opposites that are in actuality "the same." For example:

> Coming to be and passing away are the same thing, mixing and separating are the same thing, growth and diminution are the same thing . . . the individual in relation to the universe and the universe in relation to the individual are the same thing.

> γενέσθαι καὶ ἀπολέσθαι τωὐτό συμμιγῆναι καὶ διακριθῆναι τωὐτό· αὐξηθῆναι καὶ μειωθῆναι τωὐτό . . . ἕκαστον πρὸς πάντα καὶ πάντα πρὸς ἕκαστον τωὐτό· (*On Reg.* 1.4)

While they appear to lie at opposite poles, the individual (ἕκαστον) and everything else (πάντα) are actually the same when one considers their relations with one another. Like Heraclitus' views, this is suggestive, but hardly lucid.

We gain some help from the author's general statement in the section following:

> Everything, both divine and human, goes up and down, exchanging places. . . . The things of the other world come here, the things of this world go there, always and everywhere those things accomplish things here, and these things in turn accomplish things there.[27] And what men do, they don't know, and what they don't do they think that they know;

---

[27] Among the modern translators, W.H.S. Jones (*Hippocrates I*, Loeb Classical Library 147 [Cambridge, Mass.: Cambridge University Press, 1923]) renders "the things of the other world do the work of this, and those of this world do the work of that." Joly ([2003], 7) opts for the more elegant, but less exact, "jouent le rôle." Translations of the *On Regimen* here and following draw on Jones.

and what they see they do not understand, but nevertheless all things take place for them through a divine necessity, both what they wish and what they do not wish. As the things of the other world come to this and these go to that and they combine with one another, each accomplishes its allotted fate, both on the grand scale and on the small scale.

Χωρεῖ δὲ πάντα καὶ θεῖα καὶ ἀνθρώπινα ἄνω καὶ κάτω ἀμειβόμενα . . . φοιτᾷ κεῖνα ὧδε, καὶ τάδε κεῖσε, πᾶσαν ὥρην, πᾶσαν χώρην διαπρησσόμενα κεῖνά τε τὰ τῶνδε, τάδε τ' αὖ τὰ κείνων. Καί τὰ μὲν πρήσσουσιν οὐκ οἴδασιν· ἃ δὲ οὐ πρήσσουσι δοκέουσιν εἰδέναι· καί τὰ μὲν ὀρέουσιν οὐ γινώσκουσιν· ἀλλ' ὅμως αὐτοῖσι πάντα γίνεται δι' ἀνάγκην θείην καὶ ἃ βούλονται καὶ ἃ μὴ βούλονται. Φοιτῶντων δε κείνων ὧδε, τῶν δέ τε κεῖσε, συμμισγομένων πρὸς ἄλληλα τὴν πεπρωμένην μοῖραν ἕκαστον ἐκπληροῖ, καὶ ἐπὶ τὸ μέζον καὶ ἐπὶ τὸ μεῖον. (*On Reg.* 1.5)

Humans, as small parts of the cosmos, are mirroring the whole of it without realizing they do so. The author tells us that "all things happen by a divine necessity" irrespective of our desires (καὶ ἃ βούλονται καὶ ἃ μὴ βούλονται), and with us unaware of what's happening: "what men do, they don't know." Things up "there" and things down "here" *accomplish* (διαπρησσόμενα) predetermined instructions (μοῖρα) of mutual entailment. And this happens despite the fact that humans are not fully aware of it. The term διαπρησσόμενα is used only a handful of times in Hippocratic writings outside the *On Regimen* but quite frequently inside it.[28] It shows in several significant contexts, and lies at the heart of our author's theory of links between the microcosm and macrocosm.

When an individual διαπρήσσεται, that individual performs involuntary operations that are allotted to it in the structure of nature. In *On Regimen*, it is clear that *most* of what we do is describable under this predicate. In book 1, he works through a long list of human crafts, and tells us that when we perform these, we are unaware that we are recapitulating / accomplishing (διαπρήσσεται) some other analogous process in the larger cosmos (1.14, 23, 24). While we may think we are in command of what we are doing when we forge metals, card wool,

---

[28] This is also true of the term "soul" (ψύχη) which is much more frequently used in this text than in any other in the corpus. This was already noticed by Werner Jaeger, *Paideia*, vol. 3 (Oxford: Oxford University Press, 1986), 38.

perform carpentry or cobbling, play music, cook, or make pottery, and so on, we are really following actions that are set down for us in the large scheme of things, and we do this in ignorance:

> For though humans employ arts that resemble human nature, they are unaware. For the mind of the gods taught them to imitate their own functions—while they know what they are doing, even still they do not know what they are imitating.

> τέχνῃσι γὰρ χρεώμενοι ὁμοίῃσιν ἀνθρωπίνῃ φύσει οὐ γινώσκουσιν· θεῶν γὰρ νοῦς ἐδίδαξε μιμεῖσθαι τὰ ἑωυτῶν, γινώσκοντας ἃ ποιέουσι, καὶ οὐ γινώσκοντας ἃ μιμέονται. (On Reg. 1.11)

It is noteworthy that the author explicitly ties the regulating forces ultimately responsible for these operations to the divine, a link that also appeared in the text from 1.5 about the regions "there" and "here." The divine mind (θεῶν νοῦς [1.11]) and divine necessity (ἀνάγκη θείη [1.5]) govern the unfolding of these actions, while humans remain unaware of their participation in the larger cosmological structure. Under the logic encoded in διαπρήσσεται, an understanding of humans as autonomous volition centers becomes rather deeply nuanced.

The case is furthered in book 2, when the author describes the various foods we eat as "accomplishing" (διαπρήσσεται) their functions of drying, moistening, and so on—meaning the verb can govern equally well the activity of nutritive matter activating its natural properties in the one that consumes it.[29] One sees here an interconnected cosmos of which the patient is very much a part—extending the basic premise of such an important Hippocratic treatise as Airs, Waters, Places.[30] Just as a person's health is shown to be the result of larger forces in the atmosphere, so also here, our seemingly independent and self-guided actions are embedded in processes working themselves out in the whole cosmos.

Most relevant for the current purposes, διαπρήσσομαι also serves as a predicate for the relationship between the body and the soul during dreaming. Just before he moves into a consideration of specific examples

[29] On Reg. 2.40, 45, 54. Metabolism is also a particularly graphic way to represent the broader Heraclitean principle of coincidence of opposites. The outside world physiologically becomes "the same" as the inside world, as external hunks of it are assimilated into individuals and become part of themselves.

[30] For more on the overlap between the two treatises, see Jaeger (1986), 36.

of dreams and the symptoms they indicate in book 4, the author says twice that while dreaming, the soul itself διαπρήσσεται all the functions of the body during the night.

> As many as are the functions of the body or the soul, the soul accomplishes all these in sleep.

> ὅσαι τοῦ σώματος ὑπηρεσίαι ἢ τῆς ψυχῆς, πάντα ταῦτα ἡ ψυχὴ ἐν τῷ ὕπνῳ διαπρήσσεται. (*On Reg.* 4.86)

And:

> Whenever the body is at rest, the soul, set in motion and awake, manages its own household and itself accomplishes all the activities of the body.

> ὅταν δὲ τὸ σῶμα ἡσυχάσῃ, ἡ ψυχὴ κινεομένη καὶ ἐγρηγορέουσα διοικεῖ τὸν ἑωυτῆς οἶκον, καὶ τὰς τοῦ σώματος πρήξιας ἁπάσας αὐτὴ διαπρήσσεται. (*On Reg.* 4.86)

By using this verb here, the author suggests that, while the soul and body may seem to have opposite characteristics, they are in some fundamental way the same. It also carries forward the nonvolitional quality that we saw from the earlier parts of the treatise. The dream state fits congenially enough into the category of activities over which we do not have self-conscious control. But putting dreaming under διαπρήσσεται assigns the agency behind the dream to the large processes embedded in the cosmos. Just as we do not realize that in practicing our crafts, we are recapitulating the workings of the larger world, so also in our dreaming we are doing this. As he works out the theory, he comes to his claims about a star plunging into the sea, for example, meaning disease of the belly. During dreaming, the soul unconsciously reflects, by a nondiscursive cognitive process, what is happening in the physical body by transmitting a message encoded in the universal structures in which it partakes.

From this perspective, the dream has a message because our intellectual messaging center is shaped by the central processes that constitute both us and the cosmos, and dreaming unfolds according to a principle of divine intention or necessity.[31] Of course, in accordance

---

[31] Just as the cosmological principle of fire has produced the individual body by making a copy of the cosmos, so too the soul reciprocates, and it "produces" a cosmos within the dream

with the custom of his discipline, it is entirely understandable that the Hippocratic author explicitly dissociates himself from diviners and those who spend their time only asking the gods for help. In perhaps the best known part of the treatise, the author says:

> Now such dreams as are divine, and foretell to cities or to private persons things evil or things good, have interpreters in those who possess the art concerning such things. But all the states of the body the soul foretells—an extreme of surfeit or depletion of what is natural, or a change to an unexpected state—these also the diviners interpret, sometimes with, sometimes without success. But in neither case do they know why it happens, neither what they get right nor what they get wrong. They advise us to take precautions lest something bad take hold of us. But they give no instruction how one must take precautions, but only order prayers to the gods. Prayer indeed is good, but while calling on the gods a person should himself lend a hand.

> ὅσα μὲν οὖν τῶν ἐνυπνίων θεῖά ἐστι καὶ προσημαίνει ἢ πόλεσιν ἢ ἰδιώτῃσιν ἢ κακὰ ἢ ἀγαθὰ [μὴ δι᾽ αὐτῶν ἁμαρτίην], εἰσὶν οἳ κρίνουσι περὶ τῶν τοιούτων τέχνην ἔχοντες. ὅσα δὲ ἡ ψυχὴ τοῦ σώματος παθήματα προσημαίνει, πλησμονῆς ἢ κενώσιος ὑπερβολὴν τῶν συμφύτων ἢ μεταβολὴν τῶν ἀηθέων, κρίνουσι μὲν καὶ ταῦτα· καὶ τὰ μὲν τυγχάνουσι, τὰ δ᾽ ἁμαρτάνουσι, καὶ οὐδέτερα τούτων γινώσκουσι, διότι [οὖν] γίνεται, οὔθ᾽ ὅ τι ἂν ἐπιτύχωσιν οὔθ᾽ ὅ τι ἂν ἁμάρτωσι, φυλάσσεσθαι [δὲ] παραινέοντες, μή τι κακὸν λάβῃ. οἱ δ᾽ οὖν οὐ διδάσκουσιν, ὡς χρὴ φυλάσσεσθαι, ἀλλὰ θεοῖσιν εὔχεσθαι κελεύουσι. καὶ τὸ μὲν εὔχεσθαι ἀγαθόν· δεῖ δὲ καὶ αὐτὸν συλλαμβάνοντα τοὺς θεοὺς ἐπικαλεῖσθαι. (*On Reg.* 4.87)

The author is ruling out a traditional set of appeals to ad hoc divine causation, and casting doubt on certain people who claim authority to analyze these phenomenon. But then again, the treatise certainly doesn't rule out the divine from having a role in the process. After all, we have the divine forces (θεῶν νοῦς, ἀνάγκη θείη) governing the whole of it. They play an attenuated and mediated role, akin to what we have seen in

---

by imitating the body's internal corporeal condition, using features of the cosmos to depict the subject's condition. The two processes, then, are put into the relationship of opposites that finish each other off and are in some sense, "the same." Dreaming recapitulates ontogenesis.

Plato's *Timaeus*; and we will see different kinds of similarities with Aristotle's views.

The details of this system stand in contrast to the views we will see endorsed by Aristotle. However, it is beyond doubt that the plausibility of medical accounts such as this one shows him that dreams can in fact be connected with future states in the body, and shortens the leap he must make to consider that dreams could be related to future events outside the body too. This is the leap that Aristotle makes in the second part of his work, which begins by invoking the idea of the demonic.

PART 2: PRESCIENT DREAMS OF EXTERNAL EVENTS: INTRODUCTION TO THE DEMONIC

The Sensitive Instrument Argument

The second part of Aristotle's treatise begins with the sentence on the demonic, marking out the pivotal puzzle mentioned above.

> Speaking generally, since also certain of the other animals dream, dreams couldn't be god sent, nor have they arisen for the sake of being a divine message, however they are demonic; for nature is demonic, but not divine.

The expository considerations that follow offer a first clue as to what he means:

> Here is a proof: very simple people are clairvoyant and have correct dreams,[32] not because god is the sender, rather in just the way in which, whoever has a nature that is talkative and melancholic sees visions of every sort; for on account of their being moved in many and diverse ways they strike on visions resembling reality, and they are successful in these contexts just as some people steal the contest; for just as it is also said that "If you throw many times, sometimes you will throw one thing, sometimes another," also in this case this happens.

---

[32] Agreeing with Bernd Effe, *Studien zur Kosmologie und Theologie der Aristotelischen Schrift "Über die Philosophie"* (Munich: Beck, 1970), 85 n. 49; and not van der Eijk (2005), 145–46. See further discussion in fn. 86 below.

ὅλως δὲ ἐπεὶ καὶ τῶν ἄλλων ζῴων ὀνειρώττει τινά, θεόπεμπτα μὲν οὐκ
ἂν εἴη τὰ ἐνύπνια, οὐδὲ γέγονε τούτου χάριν, δαιμόνια μέντοι· ἡ γὰρ
φύσις δαιμονία, ἀλλ' οὐ θεία. σημεῖον δέ· πάνυ γὰρ εὐτελεῖς ἄνθρωποι
προορατικοί εἰσι καὶ εὐθυόνειροι, ὡς οὐ θεοῦ πέμποντος, ἀλλ' ὅσων
ὥσπερ ἂν εἰ λάλος ἡ φύσις ἐστὶ καὶ μελαγχολική, παντοδαπὰς ὄψεις
ὁρῶσιν· διὰ γὰρ τὸ πολλὰ καὶ παντοδαπὰ κινεῖσθαι ἐπιτυγχάνουσιν
ὁμοίοις θεωρήμασιν, ἐπιτυχεῖς ὄντες ἐν τούτοις ὥσπερ ἔνιοι ἁρπάζουσιν
ἐρίζοντες· ὥσπερ γὰρ καὶ λέγεται "ἂν πολλὰ βάλλῃς, ἄλλοτ' ἀλλοῖον
βαλεῖς," καὶ ἐπὶ τούτων τοῦτο συμβαίνει. (*Div. somn.* 463b15–22)

On the most common scholarly reading, the "proof" that is being offered here is a proof only of the first half of the pivotal sentence: the idea
that dreams are not god-sent. By this interpretation, Aristotle is claiming that empty-headed or melancholic people have so many random
visions that, just because of the sheer number, they will turn out to be
correct occasionally, out of coincidence. This reading is supported with
the reference to dice throwing and by the verb ἐπιτυγχάνω, which can
well mean coincidentally bumping into something. Let us call this the
randomness argument.[33]

However there are difficulties with this, and they relate to the difficulties we already saw in the debunking argument. It again leaves the
reference to the demonic entirely without context, leaving out the second
half of the sentence for which the "proof" is offered. It is, of course, difficult to see how a statement about the demonic character of dreams, and
nature as a whole to boot, could be related to the idea that, within a
huge enough basket of supposedly random mental fantasies, one of them
is bound to be correct.[34] But the truly insurmountable difficulty becomes
apparent when Aristotle rounds out his "proof" in the subsequent

[33] Some translations significantly augment a dimension of randomness available in the Greek
in the English they choose: see Beare ([1984], 737), "For, inasmuch as they experience many
movements of every kind, they just chance to have visions resembling objective facts, their
luck in these matters being merely like that of persons who play at even and odd"; Hett ([1936],
381), "for since they respond often to any kind of stimulus, they chance upon visions similar to
events, doing so by sheer luck, like men playing odd and even"; Gallop [1996], 107), "for it is because they experience many movements of every kind that they just happen to encounter sights
resembling real events, being fortunate in those, like certain people play at odds and evens."

[34] Even if we opted to translate the demonic as something like "wondrous" or "beyond
human control" (neither of which is compelling in my view), we would be at the same impasse.
Neither of these senses would be "proved" by random fantasies lining up out of coincidence—
unless perhaps one wanted to attribute an entirely uncharacteristic irony here to Aristotle.

sentence. He sets out to explain with precision why some of these visions fail to be predictive. This would be entirely unnecessary, and even perverse, if he had meant that they were random:

> That many of their dreams do not turn out to happen, is not surprising; for neither do many of the signs (σημεία) in the body and in the sky, like those of rain and wind; for if another stronger movement meets up with this one, the movement that was going to happen from which the sign (σημεῖον) arose, does not happen, and many of the things that ought to happen, although thoroughly intended, are broken off due to other stronger origins of movement. Simply put, not everything that was going to happen happens.

> ὅτι δ' οὐκ ἀποβαίνει πολλὰ τῶν ἐνυπνίων, οὐδὲν ἄτοπον· οὐδὲ γὰρ τῶν ἐν τοῖς σώμασι σημείων καὶ τῶν οὐρανίων, οἷον τὰ τῶν ὑδάτων καὶ τὰ τῶν πνευμάτων· ἂν γὰρ ἄλλη κυριωτέρα ταύτης συμβῇ κίνησις, ἀφ' ἧς μελλούσης ἐγένετο τὸ σημεῖον, οὐ γίνεται, καὶ πολλὰ βουλευθέντα καλῶς τῶν πραχθῆναι δεόντων διελύθη δι' ἄλλας κυριωτέρας ἀρχάς. ὅλως γὰρ οὐ πᾶν γίνεται τὸ μελλῆσαν. (463b22–31)

This sentence leaves no doubt that Aristotle is operating from the premise that the profusion of images in these impulsive people's heads actually *are* signs connected with potential future events. The reason they sometimes fail is because some streams of causation of which the impulsive people are picking up signs turn out to be weaker than others, and they get overrun. This has nothing to do with the perceiver's detection system running amok; rather, the opposite. It is too acute. Their dream images are genuine signs. The problem comes up because not all the external movements result in the future states they were on course to produce. Some of them are false starts. This is an argument that has to do with conflicting vectors of causation, a rich topic for Aristotle that will detain us at length below. As we will see, for Aristotle, the current state of the aggregate of causes in the natural world points toward a variety of possible future states, some of which are derailed by others. A final point against randomness arises from the taxonomy Aristotle has set out in chapter 1 of the treatise. We saw that there he set coincidence dreams explicitly apart from dreams that are signs. But in the text above he is without doubt focused on the idea that the dream *is* a sign, a σημεῖον; and, as we would expect, his term for coincidence dreams, συμπτώματα, does not appear here.

For these reasons, he cannot be making an argument based on randomness. Instead, when Aristotle claims that "on account of their being moved in many and diverse ways they strike on visions resembling reality," he must mean something closer to the idea that the extra-sensitive constitutions of certain people make them hyper-reactive, and so they simply do not miss anything that is floating around in the nightly air. They are super-sensitive instruments for picking up vibrations in the atmosphere, and producing reactions from them. Let us call this the *sensitive-instrument argument*.

Two parts of the text present difficulties for the sensitive-instrument reading, but there are countering considerations. The verb ἐπιτυγχάνουσιν does indeed have an established context in discussions of randomness. However, similar to the English "strike," it can just as easily mean hitting a mark, as in succeeding,[35] as it can bumping into something randomly. This leaves the dice. There is another possible reading of the adage, "If you throw many times, sometimes you will throw one thing, sometimes another" (ἂν πολλὰ βάλλῃς, ἄλλοτ' ἀλλοῖον βαλεῖς).[36] It comes from a parallel discussion in the *Eudemian Ethics*, on which we will focus in part 3 below. There we will be introduced to a class of

---

[35] For examples in Aristotle, see *Pol.* 1331b33; *NE* 1106b33, 1146a23; *Meta.* 981a14; *Rhet.* 1354a9.

[36] Dice are not mentioned in the Greek, but it seems likely that he has dice throwing in mind. As van der Eijk (1994) discusses ad loc., the adage is an iambic trimeter, which led Kock to assume it must have come from comedy; *Commicorum Atticorum Fragmenta*, vol. 3 (Leipzig: Teubner, 1888), No. 448. It appears as well in the Byzantine *Collection of Proverbs* from Michael Apostolius, who glosses it as something said, "with a view to many and all sorts of words and deeds that hit the thing sought after or the goal" (ἐπὶ τῶν ἐπὶ πολλῶν καὶ παντοδαπῶν λόγων ἢ ἔργων ἐπιτυγχανόντων τοῦ ζητουμένου ἢ τοῦ σκοποῦ). Another pertinent passage comes from Plutarch's *De def. Or.* (437f):

> The cause of this [not seeing many dreams] is the temperament of the body, just as, in turn, that of the melancholic, at the other extreme, is subject to many dreams and visions, and it seems they have correct dreams; since they turn now to this and now to that in their imagery, just like persons who shoot many arrows, they manage to hit the mark often.

> αἰτία δ' ἡ κρᾶσις τοῦ σώματος, ὥσπερ αὖ πάλιν ἡ τῶν μελαγχολικῶν πολυόνειρος καὶ πολυφάνταστος, καὶ δοκεῖ τὸ εὐθυόνειρον αὐτοῖς ὑπάρχειν· ἐπ' ἄλλα γὰρ ἄλλοτε τῷ φανταστικῷ τρεπόμενοι, καθάπερ οἱ πολλὰ βάλλοντες, ἐπιτυγχάνουσι πολλάκις.

These further glosses do not advance the idea that the adage refers to random chance rather than to extrasensitive sorts. Plutarch could just as well be referring to someone who, via habitual practice, succeeds at the shooting of arrows.

people whom Aristotle explicitly connects to those who are good at divination via dreams: consistently lucky people. He mentions dice there also, in language similar to the text above (*EE* 1247a21–23). But the point of the dice example there is to underscore explicitly that there are some cases, where randomness seems to hold sway, in which certain people are able, counterintuitively, to produce *non*random outcomes. Consistently lucky people are illustrated as those that can throw dice in a lucky throw regularly: differently at different times, but at each time they throw what is required. In a further connection with the questions at stake in divination, he claims there that those who are lucky cannot be so from the specific intentional love of a divinity, because, again by his observation, it is common and empty-headed people who are lucky, not the wise. Aristotle in that text proposes a more diffuse divine origin for consistent good fortune. He explicitly ties this condition to the propensity to have anticipatory dreams. This will align perfectly with the sensitive-instrument argument.[37]

We will set out next to show how the sensitive-instrument reading yields a better understanding of what is at stake in the "proof" being offered. The pivotal sentence that is being proved has two parts: the denial that dreams are sent by god *and* the positive claim that they belong to the sphere of the demonic. The randomness argument ignores the second. The sensitive-instrument does not; and to see how this is so, we will need to do much more work on the notion of the demonic. As a prelude, we clear up a small but important point about the first part of the pivotal sentence. As we will discuss further below, van der Eijk has convincingly shown, partly by way of reference to the *Eudemian Ethics* text, that the denial that dreams are god-sent denies a discrete, ad hoc act of divine favor (as Homer has it, for example), the sending of a particular dream to a particular dreamer on a particular occasion.[38] This leaves open a more diffuse kind of divine involvement,

---

[37] The connection between these two texts is noted by Michael Woods, trans. and comm., *Aristotle: Eudemian Ethics, books I, II, and VIII*, Clarendon Oxford Series (Oxford: Clarendon, 1992; originally published 1982), 171 and advanced greatly by van der Eijk (2005), 238–58 (originally published 1989).

[38] Van der Eijk (2005), 191. Already in section 1, right near the beginning of the treatise, Aristotle ruled out the idea of god sending dreams, because if god did send them, they would go to the best people and not to common ones (*Div. somn.* 462b20–22). This aligns with him denying intentional discrete acts of a divinity.

such as the category of the demonic typically references, and helps us get a glimpse of how this pivotal sentence might make sense. Aristotle's point is to sharpen the question of divine involvement, not to rule it out altogether. And to advance this point requires a closer look at the demonic in Aristotle's corpus.

The Demonic in Aristotle

Gathering Aristotle's references to demons and the demonic produces a not overly large data set. At several points, he speaks in an unmarked way about the demonic, using the term in a traditional sense to mark a class of reality with a divine character that is either less specific than a particular divinity, as in something "numinous," or refers to a divinity subordinate to a higher one. In the *Nicomachean Ethics* (1122b21) the adjective occurs in a description of different kinds of public investments that are worthy of praise, in a way roughly synonymous with something "divine." He lists investments having to do with gods (τὰ περὶ θεούς)—including votive offerings, buildings and furniture, and sacrifices—"likewise also with the whole of the demonic." He includes a list of offices related to these things, which incorporates sacrificial priests, guardians of temples, treasurers of sacred revenues, and so on. Similarly, when in the *Politics* (1322b31) Aristotle divides up the necessary public offices in a city, he speaks of some that have to do with "demonic matters." Other categories in this text are war, revenue and expenditure, the market, the city, the harbors, the countryside, judicial proceedings, and public deliberations. So Aristotle uses the adjective to talk about the realm of religious affairs in general. A smattering of apposite texts in the fragments show Aristotle using the term as a marker of a divinity, usually subordinate (*Frag.* 6.3, 44.21, 487.4, 490.2),[39] and at one point specifically of the guardian-angel variety we saw in treating Plato's views (*Frag.* 192.3 and 193.13). These references seem hardly even to refine common usage, and are largely descriptive rather than technical in character. They are of limited relevance to the problem at

---

[39] Numeration refers to texts from V. Rose, *Aristotelis qui ferebantur librorum fragmenta* (Leipzig: Teubner, 1886; repr. Stuttgart, 1967).

hand, although they do show the correspondence with common usage that one would expect.

In the *Metaphysics* we find more instructive evidence. In book 5, given over to lemmatic definitions of technical terms, Aristotle defines four uses of the designation "substance." The term can apply to a) an essence that is causal of a thing's existence, as a soul is of an animal; b) a formal and universal definition; or c) a critical and limiting subpart that constitutes a *sine qua non*; but the most important of the definitions of substance, he says, is d) as a complete body, which he elaborates in this way:

> Simple bodies are called "substance"—for example earth, fire, water, and these sorts of things—and on the whole bodies and things constructed from them, both animals and demonic bodies, and their parts. All these are called substance since they are not predicated of a subject but everything else is predicated of them.

> Οὐσία λέγεται τά τε ἁπλᾶ σώματα, οἷον γῆ καὶ πῦρ καὶ ὕδωρ καὶ ὅσα τοιαῦτα, καὶ ὅλως σώματα καὶ τὰ ἐκ τούτων συνεστῶτα ζῷά τε καὶ δαιμόνια καὶ τὰ μόρια τούτων· ἅπαντα δὲ ταῦτα λέγεται οὐσία ὅτι οὐ καθ' ὑποκειμένου λέγεται ἀλλὰ κατὰ τούτων τὰ ἄλλα. (1017b10–14)[40]

"Substances" in sense (d) play an important role in Aristotle's corpus.[41] Such bodies are his preferred unit of analysis.[42] It is telling that Aristotle makes the term bodies (σώματα) prevalent when he speaks of substances, since he exhibits an additional preference for specifically living things as the archetypal examples of substances.[43]

So, demonic (δαιμόνια) bodies are among the classes of complete things to which one might apply a set of predicates. They appear paired with biological organisms (ζῷα), and are more complex than the simple

[40]Cf. *Meta.* 7 1028b34–36.

[41]The scholarship is vast. For a start, see M. L. Gill, *Aristotle on Substance* (Princeton: Princeton University Press, 1989) and more recently, Michael V. Wedin, *Aristotle's Theory of Substance: The Categories and Metaphysics Zeta*, Oxford Aristotle Studies (Oxford: Clarendon, 2000).

[42]Such a position leads to claims like that at *Meta.* 1035b6–12, where Aristotle examines the sense in which a human body is more fundamental than a finger.

[43]See, for example, *Meta.* 1032a19 (ἃ [ἄνθρωπον ἢ φυτὸν] δὴ μάλιστα λέγομεν οὐσίας εἶναι). For a lucid account of this, see Jonathan Barnes, "Metaphysics," in Barnes, ed., *Cambridge Companion to Aristotle* (Cambridge: Cambridge University Press, 1995), 99–102.

substances of earth, fire, and so on. If one is wondering where one might find a class of such things in Aristotle, with the divine character that would merit his calling them "demonic," and that are like living organisms, one does not have very hard hunting. As is well known to specialists in Aristotle's astronomy and metaphysics, he commonly speaks of a whole class of living, divine entities. For him, the divine regions are the spheres of the heavens beyond the sphere of the moon (see, e.g., *Phys.* 196a34), and he often refers to the heavenly bodies as being divine and as being living things (*Cael.* 285a29, 286a9–11, 292a20-b2, 292b32; *Meta.* 1074a30–31).[44] They get the designations θεία or δαιμόνια interchangeably; the terms can be synonymous in these contexts (this was also the case in the example on divine offices from the *Politics* above). In such cases, both words will mean something like "with a divine character." In the *Nicomachean Ethics*, he claims, "there are other things much more divine in their nature even than a human, for example, most conspicuously, the bodies of which the heavens are framed" (καὶ γὰρ ἀνθρώπου ἄλλα πολὺ θειότερα τὴν φύσιν, οἷον φανερώτατά γε ἐξ ὧν ὁ κόσμος συνέστηκεν [*NE* 1141a34–b1]). And in the introduction to the *Parts of Animals*, Aristotle famously gives a rather poetic justification for studying even the lowliest bodies in the animal kingdom, via a comparison to the study of the heavenly bodies:

> Of substances constituted by nature some are ungenerated, imperishable and eternal, while others are subject to degeneration and decay. The former are excellent and divine (θείας), but less accessible to knowledge. The evidence that might throw light on them, and on the problems which we long to solve respecting them, is furnished scantily by sensation, whereas respecting perishable plants and animals we have abundant information, living as we do in their midst. . . . Having already treated of the celestial world, as far as our conjectures could reach, it remains to speak of animal nature.

> Τῶν οὐσιῶν ὅσαι φύσει συνεστᾶσι, τὰς μὲν ἀγενήτους καὶ ἀφθάρτους εἶναι τὸν ἅπαντα αἰῶνα, τὰς δὲ μετέχειν γενέσεως καὶ φθορᾶς.

[44] For further discussion, see Geoffrey E. R. Lloyd, *Aristotle: The Growth and Structure of His Thought* (Cambridge: Cambridge University Press, 1968), 133–39.

συμβέβηκε δὲ περὶ μὲν ἐκείνας τιμίας οὔσας καὶ θείας ἐλάττους ἡμῖν ὑπάρχειν θεωρίας καὶ γὰρ ἐξ ὧν ἄν τις σκέψαιτο περὶ αὐτῶν, καὶ περὶ ὧν εἰδέναι ποθοῦμεν, παντελῶς ἐστιν ὀλίγα τὰ φανερὰ κατὰ τὴν αἴσθησιν, περὶ δὲ τῶν φθαρτῶν φυτῶν τε καὶ ζῴων εὐποροῦμεν μᾶλλον πρὸς τὴν γνῶσιν διὰ τὸ σύντροφον. . . . Ἐπεὶ δὲ περὶ ἐκείνων διήλθομεν λέγοντες τὸ φαινόμενον ἡμῖν, λοιπὸν περὶ τῆς ζωϊκῆς φύσεως εἰπεῖν. (644b22–45a6)

All these texts suggest that Aristotle's "demonic bodies" that we saw him refer to above in *Metaphysics 5* are the heavenly bodies, and two final pieces of evidence solidify the case. Both are also from the *Metaphysics*, one in book 7 and another in book 8. They treat the topic of substance, in a way parallel to the treatment we saw above. They make short lists of the kinds of things that would count as a substance, and at the parallel point in his list "heavenly bodies" show up in a position comparable with the place of "demonic bodies" in the enumeration above,[45] leaving no doubt that the "demonic bodies" of the *Metaphysics*' discussion of substances are the heavenly bodies.

His theology provides further context. It has many layers of complexity, and scholars have tried to work out the relationship between the critical *Metaphysics* book 12 and the rest of the corpus. Nonetheless, Aristotle has a conspicuous centerpiece around which he forms

---

[45] From *Meta.* 7:

"Substance" is thought to belong most obviously to bodies; and so we say that both animals and plants and their parts are substances, and so are natural bodies such as fire and water and earth and everything of that sort, and all things that are parts of these or composed of these (either of parts or of the whole bodies), for example the heaven and its parts, stars and moon and sun (trans. Barnes [1984]).

δοκεῖ δ' ἡ οὐσία ὑπάρχειν φανερώτατα μὲν τοῖς σώμασιν, διὸ τά τε ζῷα καὶ τὰ φυτὰ καὶ τὰ μόρια αὐτῶν οὐσίας εἶναί φαμεν, καὶ τὰ φυσικὰ σώματα, οἷον πῦρ καὶ ὕδωρ καὶ γῆν καὶ τῶν τοιούτων ἕκαστον, καὶ ὅσα ἢ μόρια τούτων ἢ ἐκ τούτων ἐστίν, ἢ μορίων ἢ πάντων, οἷον ὅ τε οὐρανὸς καὶ τὰ μόρια αὐτοῦ, ἄστρα καὶ σελήνη καὶ ἥλιος (1028b9–13).

And then *Meta.* 8:

Those [substances] generally recognized are the natural ones, i.e. fire, earth, water, air, and the rest of the simple bodies; secondly, plants and their parts, and animals and the parts of animals; and finally the heavens and the parts of the heavens (trans. Barnes [1984]).

ὁμολογοῦμεναι μὲν αἱ φυσικαί, οἷον πῦρ γῆ ὕδωρ ἀὴρ καὶ τἆλλα τὰ ἁπλᾶ σώματα, ἔπειτα τὰ φυτὰ καὶ τὰ μόρια αὐτῶν, καὶ τὰ ζῷα καὶ τὰ μόρια τῶν ζῴων, καὶ τέλος ὁ οὐρανὸς καὶ τὰ μόρια τοῦ οὐρανοῦ· (1042a7–11).

this area of his thinking.[46] In *Metaphysics* 12.7, he starts calling the primary unmoved mover "god." In this text, other features begin to populate the divine realm of the heavens, including a choir of 49 or 55 unmoved movers adjacent to the Prime Mover that act as proximate causes of the motions of the planets. He constructs the fixed stars as the, if you will, "prime moved" reality; and the planets as the next tier. These bodies are set in motion by their aspirations for their corresponding unmoved movers. He nowhere refers to the heavenly bodies as "gods" themselves.[47] They are clearly parts of nature (as is made plain in the introduction to *Parts of Animals* cited above). Nor are they, however, just any living creature in nature; they are consistently that part of it that is most divine. One way he has of phrasing this is particularly interesting. At *Metaphysics* 1026a18–20, he refers to the stars as the visible aspects of the divine (τὰ φανερὰ τῶν θείων), and at *Physics* 196a34 he calls the heavenly bodies "the divinest of visible things." Such statements position the stars between the divine and us, attributing to them both a natural, perceptible dimension, and a divine character. For this kind of being, the Greek term *daimonion* (a marker for just such a neither-fish-nor-foul entity) could hardly be more appropriate.

---

[46] See S. Alexandru, *Aristotle's Metaphysics Lambda: Annotated Critical Edition Based upon a Systematic Investigation of Greek, Latin, Arabic and Hebrew Sources* (Leiden: Brill, 2014); and Silvia Fazzo, *Il libro Lambda della Metafisica di Aristotele*, Elenchos 61 (Naples: Bibliopolis, 2012). For the breadth of the current scholarship, see the essays in Michael Frede and David Charles, eds., *Aristotle's* Metaphysics *Lambda: Symposium Aristotelicum* (Oxford: Clarendon, 2000).

[47] He comes closest in his discussion in *Meta.* 12.8, in which he articulates his thoughts on the unmoved movers this way:

> It has been handed down from even our most ancient ancestors, left behind for posterity in the form of a myth, that these [stars] are gods and the divine surrounds the whole of nature. The rest of it by this time has been added in mythic form for the persuasion of the many and for use in their laws and their advantage. For they say that these gods are in human form and like some of the other animals, and other things that follow from and are similar to these that have been mentioned. Of these things, if someone should separate out and take only the first, that they used to think the first substances to be gods, one would deem him to have spoken divinely.

On the importance of this text for understanding the history of allegorical reading—it goes on to claim that over the long course of history advances in science have been made, lost, and preserved in mythic fragments—see Luc Brisson, *How Philosophers Saved Myths* (Chicago: University of Chicago Press, 2004), 38. The relevance of this text for allegory is often overlooked, as it was by me in *Birth of the Symbol* (Princeton: Princeton University Press, 2004).

These are the main uses of the demonic in the corpus. The heavenly bodies are the most salient examples of the things that merit the label. In order to see why Aristotle claims a demonic component to dreaming, one might first imagine that the heavenly bodies have something to do with it, but this finds no support in the corpus. Further work will show it to be more promising to understand that the idea of the demonic is a way for Aristotle to talk about the projection of divine power into the natural world. The heavenly bodies merit the designation "demonic" for being visibly moved by the divine, and not moved by anything else, with each unmoved mover acting as a final cause. After further work, we will claim something similar to be the case for dreams. Being mindful of Aristotle's qualification, we need to be careful to steer away from the idea that dreams result from discrete acts of divine will. But, taking seriously his use of the demonic, we equally need to steer clear of the idea that the divine is not involved, such as the debunking argument, as well as the randomness argument, will have it. The next step is to clarify the nature and mode of this involvement by looking more closely at role of the divine in producing motion in general.

The Divine as Origin of Movement

While Aristotle has nothing like the divine immanence we will see in the Stoics, he is not hesitant to speak of a causal connection between divine and natural realms. That such links exist is not controversial, nor does it require large exegetical leaps, but it does require a long list of careful qualifications and clarifications. Many scholars have worked on the question. The richest discussion takes place under the topic of teleology.[48] There are several unresolved issues, among which a few are relevant here, and there are areas of broad agreement that are entirely pertinent as well. Scholars generally agree that there are two different ways in which the divine, in the form of the first unmoved mover, produces effects in the world below. In the first mode, it is a direct final cause that produces the motion of the heavens, not in a mechanical

---

[48] See, recently, Monte Ransome Johnson, *Aristotle on Teleology*, Oxford Aristotle Studies (Oxford: Clarendon, 2005), who includes an outline of the current state of the scholarship, 1–6.

way, but as an object of desire. The fixed sphere of the heavens and the substances in it are alive, as we have seen, and are capable of rational desire. Their desire for the Prime Mover causes them to move kinetically, and the firmament, or the outer sphere of the fixed stars, whirls nightly around the earth. In addition, following earlier astronomers, Aristotle accounts for the motions of the planets through a system of smaller nested spheres, each of which rotates on an axis that is anchored to the already moving massive sphere of the fixed stars, and each of which is propelled along its particular kind of motion by desire for its own unmoved mover. Since the axes do not align, the system can model the extraordinarily complex movements needed to describe the planets' wanderings from a geocentric perspective. The motions of the sun and lesser planets are all caused by their respective unmoved movers, which produce circuits within the simpler circular motion of the fixed stars. The minimum number of such spheres necessary to account for the movements is difficult to determine, Aristotle says, but he thinks the two most likely figures are the 49 or 55 mentioned above.

The second mode of the primary unmoved mover's causation happens indirectly. The elements of the celestial system are responsible for causing *all* the kinetic changes and motions in the sublunary world via their cycles, especially the heating and cooling produced by the sun. Therefore, the primary unmoved mover, sitting behind the heavenly motions, is the ultimate source of *all* motion and change in the cosmos: directly as an object of desire for the heavenly bodies, indirectly for the sublunar world as the heavenly bodies produce the motions down below. Aristotle states this clearly near the opening of the *Meteorology*, a treatise dedicated to the intermediate zone between the heavens and the earth:[49]

> The cosmos as a whole surrounding the earth is made up of these bodies [fire, air, water, earth], and we now take up the properties that are characteristic of it. And it is necessarily continuous with the upper motions; consequently, all its power is steered from [κυβερνᾶσθαι] above. For the originating principle of motion for all things must be designated the

---

[49] On this fascinating and understudied text, see the whole of Malcolm Wilson's welcome *Structure and Method in Aristotle's* Meteorologica (Cambridge: Cambridge University Press, 2014), and for the present purposes, particularly pp. 73–114.

first cause. . . . And it is necessary to consider fire and earth and the elements like them as the material causes of the events of this world (meaning by material what is the passive subject of change) but we must assign causality in the sense of the origin of motion to the power of the eternally moving bodies.

ὁ δὴ περὶ τὴν γῆν ὅλος κόσμος ἐκ τούτων συνέστηκε τῶν σωμάτων· περὶ οὗ τὰ συμβαίνοντα πάθη φαμὲν εἶναι ληπτέον. ἔστιν δ' ἐξ ἀνάγκης συνεχὴς οὗτος ταῖς ἄνω φοραῖς, ὥστε πᾶσαν αὐτοῦ τὴν δύναμιν κυβερνᾶσθαι ἐκεῖθεν· ὅθεν γὰρ ἡ τῆς κινήσεως ἀρχὴ πᾶσιν, ἐκείνην αἰτίαν νομιστέον πρώτην. . . . ὥστε τῶν συμβαινόντων περὶ αὐτὸν πῦρ μὲν καὶ γῆν καὶ τὰ συγγενῆ τούτοις ὡς ἐν ὕλης εἴδει τῶν γιγνομένων αἴτια χρὴ νομίζειν (τὸ γὰρ ὑποκείμενον καὶ πάσχον τοῦτον προσαγορεύομεν τὸν τρόπον), τὸ δ' οὕτως αἴτιον ὅθεν ἡ τῆς κινήσεως ἀρχή, τὴν τῶν ἀεὶ κινουμένων αἰτιατέον δύναμιν. (*Meteor.* 339a19–32)

This text and others like it set up a world in which all kinetic motion and change will ultimately have a divine lineage.[50] The lineage may be long and circuitous, and overwritten by layers and layers of intervening causes crisscrossing this lower world; it is nevertheless Aristotle's unmistakable position that events in the physical world "down here" are ultimately set in motion by causes located "up there." This is the clearest sense in which the natural world below might be said to be connected with the divine, the very broadest reach of the penumbra of god, since its motions ultimately trace back up to it. The famous claim of *Metaphysics* 12 (1072b14) should also be reckoned here, in which, after defining the Prime Mover, Aristotle says: "From such a principle, then, depend the heavens and nature" (ἐκ τοιαύτης ἄρα ἀρχῆς ἤρτηται ὁ οὐρανὸς καὶ ἡ φύσις; cf. *Mot. an.* 700a5). Such statements have provoked extensive discussion around the idea of determinism, a debate unnecessary to enter here.[51]

[50] For a collection of texts of similar scope, see Charles H. Kahn, "The Place of the Prime Mover in Aristotle's Teleology," in Allan Gotthelf, ed., *Aristotle on Nature and Living Things: Philosophical and Historical Studies* (Bristol: Bristol Classical Press, 1985), 183–205.

[51] The most important texts to consider are *Int.* 9; *Meta.* 6.3; *NE* 3.1–5. A formative discussion takes place in Richard Sorabji, *Necessity, Cause, and Blame* (Chicago: University of Chicago Press, 1980); see also Gail Fine's essay in review of it, "Aristotle on Determinism," *Philosophical Review* 90.4 (1981): 561–79; and more recently, Yungwhan Lee, "Aristotle and Determinism: An

Neither of these modes of divine involvement in motion offers us much help in trying to understand why Aristotle would refer to dreams and nature as a whole as having the kind of divine quality that would lead him to call them demonic. The idea that the Prime Mover is directly responsible for the motions of the heavens, and indirectly responsible for all kinetic motion that flows from it, hardly provides insight into the specific phenomenon of dreaming. It is too remote.

The Impulse Hypothesis

In a further sense, though, the Prime Mover may act as a cause for the things of this world. The treatment by Charles Kahn from nearly thirty years ago, which updates and modifies earlier positions of Zeller, Joachim, Lovejoy, and others,[52] represents the most coherent formulation of this position.[53] In exploring the question, Kahn points to studies in the middle of the last century, by figures like Ross and Solmsen, that tend to minimize any further dimension of divine involvement in the world below, beyond indirect kinetic causation.[54] These scholars were carrying forward, a reaction against earlier views, traceable back to the Middle Ages, according to which the Prime Mover is seen as a demiurgic agent (which it surely cannot be). Looking through Neoplatonic lenses, the medieval commentators made the divine out to be a kind of busybody, providing the efficient cause setting in motion all kinds of entities that populate the universe. Later scholars reacted against this idea, but the later modifications went too far, Kahn suggests, and

---

Interpretation of Aristotle's Theory of Causation, Necessity, and Accidents" (Ph.D. dissertation, Princeton University, 2009); and P. L. Donini, *Aristotle and Determinism* (Louvain: Peeters, 2010).

[52] E. Zeller, *Die Philosophie der Griechen in ihrer geschichtlichen Entwicklung*, 3rd ed., vol. 2 (Leipzig: Fues, 1869–1879), 373–75; H. H. Joachim, *Aristotle on Coming-to-be and Passing-away* (Oxford: Clarendon, 1922), 256; and Arthur O. Lovejoy, *The Great Chain of Being: A Study of the History of an Idea* (Cambridge, Mass.: Harvard University Press, 1936), 55. Cited and discussed further at Kahn (1985), 203 fn. 1.

[53] Kahn (1985), 183–86.

[54] Ross, *Aristotle*, 5th ed. (London: Methuen, 1949), 177–82; and Friedrich Solmsen, *Aristotle's System of the Physical World: A Comparison with His Predecessors* (Ithaca, N.Y.: Cornell University Press, 1960), chs. 10 and 20. See Kahn (1985), 203 fn. 2.

steered students of Aristotle to an overly restricted view of the Prime Mover's effect on events down here.

Kahn reads the Prime Mover as continuously influencing the world below, beyond its role as the ultimate, most remote indirect cause of kinetic motion. Briefly, it operates as the ultimate final cause, or "thing for the sake of which" (using Aristotle's terms) any change occurs: it provides the impulse that leads each entity to complete the immanent causality of its specific nature, and to become the thing that its inner nature is set up for it to become. The specific characteristics any substance is to have are provided by nature, but the inclination to achieve them comes from outside. The Prime Mover gives the oomph, if you will, to the acorn to grow into the oak its inner nature causes it to become. Its becoming an *oak* is a product of nature as a cause,[55] but its *becoming* an oak is attributable to the Prime Mover acting as the ultimate final cause for it. And in the case of inanimate substances, it functions as well, causing each thing to move from potentiality to actuality, and to achieve its own good. It is in fire's nature to be hot (and of heat to move upward), but it is the Prime Mover that is continually causing (as ultimate final cause) this nature to be actualized. And in human

---

[55] For more on nature's role, see for example, the *On Generation and Corruption*, where he refutes ideas of Empedocles on the salience of chance and the spontaneous in the natural world. Nature is consistent as a cause, while chance is inconsistent: "Then what is the cause of human coming to be from human, and wheat (instead of an olive) coming to be from wheat, either always or for the most part? Are we to say that bone comes to be if the elements be put together in just the right manner?" (Τί οὖν τὸ αἴτιον τοῦ ἐξ ἀνθρώπου ἄνθρωπον ἢ ἀεὶ ἢ ὡς ἐπὶ τὸ πολύ, καὶ ἐκ τοῦ πυροῦ πυρὸν ἀλλὰ μὴ ἐλαίαν; ἢ καὶ ἐὰν ὡδὶ συντεθῇ ὀστοῦν; [333b7–9]); cf. *Phys.* 196a31–32. In telling us that the overwhelming consistencies in nature should rule out the idea that it is governed by chance, he indicates that it is nature's causal role to determine each thing's natural endpoint. Kahn's argument claims that it is the Prime Mover's role to move each piece of nature toward realizing that endpoint. And again at *Part. an.* 641b23–28, he constructs a similar argument against the idea that the cosmos emerges from spontaneity rather than from design:

Whenever there is plainly some final end, to which a motion tends should nothing stand in the way, we always say that the one is for the sake of the other; and from this it is evident that there must be something of the kind, corresponding to what we call nature. For a given seed does not give rise to any chance living being, nor spring from any chance one; but each springs from a definite parent (trans. Barnes [1984]).

πανταχοῦ δὲ λέγομεν τόδε τοῦδ' ἕνεκα, ὅπου ἂν φαίνηται τέλος τι πρὸς ὃ ἡ κίνησις περαίνει μηδενὸς ἐμποδίζοντος. ὥστε εἶναι φανερὸν ὅτι ἔστι τι τοιοῦτον, ὃ δὴ καὶ καλοῦμεν φύσιν· οὐ γὰρ δὴ ὅ τι ἔτυχεν ἐξ ἑκάστου γίνεται σπέρματος, ἀλλὰ τόδε ἐκ τοῦδε, οὐδὲ σπέρμα τὸ τυχὸν ἐκ τοῦ τυχόντος σώματος.

beings, as Kahn puts it, "it is our rational nature to exercise moral and intellectual virtue, but the urge to realize this (our desire to do well) is the specifically human form of the universal tendency to move from potency to act."[56] According to Kahn's reading, the divine functions throughout nature as the final of final causes, providing a kind of atmospheric voltage that sparks each thing to aim to fulfill its particular "good," such as nature has constructed it, always or for the most part. Lets us call this the impulse hypothesis. This is my term, not Kahn's, and my reasons for it will become obvious below.

As Kahn says, Aristotle nowhere precisely says just this, but Kahn adduces nine texts from the corpus that are made very difficult to explain if the more restrictive reading of the Prime Mover is adopted, and his evidence is conclusive.[57] I set out one example here that gives a sense of them:

> We affirm that in all things nature always reaches for (ὀρέγεσθαί) what is better, and that being is better than not being. . . . But since it is impossible for being to be present always in all things, because they are far removed from the source, the divine has filled up the universe in the way that was left, by making coming-to-be perpetual. For this would be the best way for being to be connected together, because eternal generation and coming-to-be is the closest thing to being forever. And the cause of this, as we have repeatedly said, is the circular movement of the heavens. For circular movement alone is continuous. Hence all the other things which change into one another by their powers and passivities, such as the simple bodies, imitate the circular movement of the heavens. For when air is generated from water and fire from air, and in turn water from fire, we say they have completed the cycle of generation by returning back again. The result is that straight motion [of simple bodies in space] is continuous by imitating circular motion. (GC 336b27–37a7)

This text stipulates an internal "urge" on the part of the world of nature (that results in imitation of the divine, in order to be like it) to move

---

from potency to actuality and thereby enact the eternal process of becoming. The text refers to the divine "filling up" the universe, and thereby initiating a certain pattern of action among the entities that populate it: their perpetual "coming-to-be." This is not ascribable to nature or another causal structure; and it is not explicable via the passive reception of kinetic motion from the divine. It requires something else. Many variant readings of any of Kahn's nine texts are possible, when taken individually. When examined as a group, the range of potential difficulties in each one narrows upon consideration with the others, making the impulse hypothesis the most attractive way forward. Such phenomena require that the divine have a specific kind of causal presence in the natural world.

Kahn sets out the architectonic case for understanding the impulse hypothesis. These texts mostly pertain to the larger parts of Aristotle's cosmology and metaphysics where such a principle is needed to make sense of the argument. In his investigations into specific terrestrial phenomena across his corpus, Aristotle almost never directly invokes this "deep background" level of causation (Kahn does not point to any examples in his study). This is not surprising. In the familiar Aristotelian project of tracking out chains of causation in the natural world and in human behavior, he measures how the observable qualities and attributes, the natures, of substances interact with other natures. Nearly all things that move are moved by other moved movers. In such cases, one has no need to reference a broadly diffuse inclination toward actualizing potential, for which the Prime Mover is responsible. Of course, it is also true that a focus on the more observable levels of causation, examining the interactions of certain sets of qualities and attributes, would not supplant the lower level proposed here. The situation is to some extent comparable to a contemporary discussion by a physicist of features in the observable world via tools of Newtonian mechanics, which does not precisely take the place of the quantum level rules that govern subatomic minutiae, but often makes them not pertinent. Sometimes, though, a physicist will run into a phenomenon that is strange and inexplicable via the Newtonian rules.

According to the findings regarding the category of the demonic above, Aristotle turns to the demonic to talk about phenomena whose motion is not explicable *except* by invoking the divine as the immediate source of propulsion. This is the case with the heavenly bodies. When seen now via the preceding, this is a first example of the impulse hypothesis, at the highest levels of nature. While the rudimentary urge to actualize potential toward the good that we see across nature at the subsequent lower levels is universally at work, it is typically not necessary to appeal to it to explain specific phenomena. For example, we humans, as rational animals, typically actualize our potential for our good (that is, moral and intellectual virtue) through our self-conscious intellectual pursuit of it. Throughout his corpus, Aristotle shows himself to be mostly focused on gaining insight into the hundreds of complex, studiable, and answerable problems regarding our doing this. But what of the case of predictive dreams, resulting in a good outcome while we are sleeping, that is, when rationality is inactive (as it particularly is with empty-headed people)?

As we will turn to explore next, in this state, we enter a more rudimentary existence, in which our human nature is less fully realized. With the higher-order layers of the soul, that govern intellect, motion, rational desire, and so on, temporarily disabled, the lower orders are all that are left operating, and we temporarily engage in a life analogous to that of some much less sophisticated creature. According to the impulse hypothesis, even such lowly creatures, though, are steered from above. It is, of course, nature that has built into these meager souls the potentials that they actualize toward what is good for them, but the force superintending their consistent tendencies to actualize these potentials is the subterranean impulse for which the Prime Mover is ultimately responsible. After some further work, and a look at the scale of functions in the soul below, I will claim that his explanation of dreams invokes the subterranean urge that one particular piece of the natural world enacts: that is, the lowest order dimensions of the human creature, governed by the nutritive soul. The human organism itself, as an organism, and irrespective of our higher-order self-conscious goal-directed behaviors, exhibits also a lower-order set of impulses toward what is good for it. This will be the source of the surplus knowledge that divinatory dreams convey.

To sum up, we set out at the outset to uncover why in the world Aristotle, after he denies that dreams are god-sent, would assert the demonic character of them, and of nature as a whole to boot. We started by linking it to the direction he takes in his subsequent sentence, offering up a "proof" by stipulating that certain empty-headed people are sensitive instruments picking up signs in the nighttime atmosphere. Most modern interpretations adopt the randomness argument (reading that these souls experience only coincidentally correct dreams); hand-in-hand with this, they overlook the reference to the demonic (which is difficult to do given its appearance in both a pivotal sentence in the text and in Aristotle's short summary of it at the outset of the three treatises on sleep); and so they construe the proof offered as only having to do with the denial of the dream as god-sent. We saw serious problems with these interpretations above. A closer look at the demonic has shown that Aristotle uses it to mark parts of nature (the heavenly bodies) whose behavior is explicable *only* by the divine. This led to a further exploration of how the divine produces motion in nature, and next to the impulse hypothesis, which allows for a very narrow mode in which the divine directly causes motion across nature as a whole. This reading of the demonic gives a context that makes sense of the surprising claim that nature as a whole is demonic. Although it explains this broader proposition, and so warrants a claim that, in a way, any natural event could be called "demonic," it does not mark out any distinctive explanatory power for why Aristotle would use it with respect to divinatory dreams. After some further work, we will be in a position to claim that he invokes the demonic in the case of predictive dreams, as he did in the case of heavenly bodies, because no other causal structures, at the macro-level, will explain the event. It is one of the few cases where the impulse hypothesis is required to explain a specific observable phenomenon in nature.

On my reading, there are only very few occasions, precisely three as far as I am able to determine, on which Aristotle appeals to this deeper causal machinery to explain specific phenomena—making a turn to the quantum level, so to speak. In addition to the movements of the heavenly bodies, on further investigation, I will claim that there are actually two terrestrial examples. The case of divinatory dreams is one of these. The impulse hypothesis will give us a new and productive lens through which to understand the claim that dreams are demonic from *On Divination during Sleep*, which has guided the study this far. To see how, we must steer through the other terrestrial example, a deeply mutually illuminating phenomenon: the case of lucky people. It is a narrow topic in Aristotle's ethics, and embedded in his rich ideas on chance. To some surprise and continuing puzzlement for the many scholars who have wrestled with it, his consideration of luckiness opens into some of Aristotle's most fundamental questioning about why we do the things we do. Studies on the topic have converged on Aristotle's proposition of some kind of divine involvement, but without much progress on what that might be. I will work to show the advantages of the impulse hypothesis as a solution; and from there the question of divine involvement, via the demonic, in dreams will be ready for a proposed answer.

PART 3: ADVANCED DEMONIC STUDIES: LUCKY PEOPLE AND HUMAN BEHAVIOR BEYOND HUMAN CONTROL

In his effort to evaluate the praiseworthiness of actions, in his ethics, Aristotle works assiduously to calibrate the precise extent to which we are responsible for what we do. There are some things we do involuntarily, because of outside force. In these cases, it is clear that the person in question is not the initiator of the action, and so is not responsible for it. But there are also some actions that are due to forces inside us that are not subject to our self-conscious control. He is interested in these liminal areas of nonconscious behavior, carefully examining addiction, habit, and incontinence under the rubric of ἀκρασία (see NE 7.1–10). Such cases provide nuance for the idea that our self-conscious decision making functions as an autonomous executive center. There emerges from those discussions a class of events, performed by humans but precipitated by psychic movements that are outside of deliberate human control. In the *Eudemian Ethics*, Aristotle places luckiness, along with divination, among them. From observation, Aristotle is certain that there exists a class of people who are (oddly enough) consistently lucky. In trying to solve this riddle, he explicitly links the qualities that make them so to those that make some people capable of divinatory insight in their dreams, and both will rely on a certain quality and functionality of the divine.

He begins his ethical thinking from the premise that there is some end for which we do things, the good that we desire for its own sake. Mostly, we pursue the good via our highest and most godlike feature, our intellects, which we use to deliberate between courses of self-directed action.[58] But he is interested in exploring all ways that people do well and find good outcomes. At the opening of the *Eudemian Ethics* he makes a synopsis of potential sources of human happiness. He includes nature, learning, and good habits as bases of our thriving, and then adds two further possibilities:

> Or do men become happy in none of these ways, but in one of two others: either like those possessed by nymphs and deities, through an inspiration of some *daimôn*, just like inspired people, or through chance? For many declare happiness to be identical with good fortune.

> ἢ τούτων μὲν κατ' οὐδένα τῶν τρόπων, δυοῖν δὲ θάτερον, ἤτοι καθάπερ οἱ νυμφόληπτοι καὶ θεόληπτοι τῶν ἀνθρώπων, ἐπιπνοίᾳ δαιμονίου τινὸς ὥσπερ ἐνθουσιάζοντες, ἢ διὰ τὴν τύχην. (πολλοὶ γὰρ ταὐτόν φασιν εἶναι τὴν εὐδαιμονίαν καὶ τὴν εὐτυχίαν.) (*EE* 1214a21–25)[59]

After long considerations of nature, learning, and good habits, he treats the possibilities of chance and luck embraced by the Greek term τύχη in a few pages that close the work. This topic has been the subject of more than a dozen serious studies in the past few decades, but to my mind some advances in our understanding await.[60] The text is highly

---

[58] The divine character of our intellectual center is regularly made explicit; as when he calls it "the divine in us"; see *NE* 1177a13–17, 1177b27–31, 1179a27–28.

[59] Text: R. Walzer and J. Mingay, eds., *Aristotelis Ethica Eudemia*, Oxford Classical Text (Oxford: Oxford University Press, 1991), with emendations as noted. Translations my own, with help from many previous scholars noted in following fnn.

[60] Henry Jackson, "*Eudemian Ethics* θ i, ii (H xiii, xiv) 1246a26–1248b7," *Journal of Philology* 32 (1913): 170–221; M. J. Mills, "*Eudemian Ethics* θ, 2, 1247a7–13," *Hermes* 109 (1981): 253–56; M. J. Mills, "Aristotle's Dichotomy of *EUTUXIA*," *Hermes* 111 (1983): 282–95; G. Verbeke, "Happiness and Chance in Aristotle," in Gotthelf (1985), 247–58; van der Eijk (2005), 238–58; Richard Bodéüs, *Aristote et la théologie des vivant immortels* (Paris: Bellarmin, 1992), trans. by J. Garrett as *Aristotle and the Theology of the Living Immortals* (Albany: SUNY Press, 2000); D. Frede, "Necessity, Chance, and 'What Happens for the Most Part' in Aristotle's *Poetics*," in A. O. Rorty, ed., *Essays on Aristotle's* Poetics (Princeton: Princeton University Press, 1992), 197–219; Anthony Kenny, *Aristotle on the Perfect Life* (Oxford: Oxford University Press, 1992), 56–85; Kent Johnson, "Luck and Good Fortune in the *Eudemian Ethics*," *Ancient Philosophy* 17 (1997): 85–102; Monte Ransome Johnson, "Spontaneity, Democritean Causality and Freedom," *Elenchos: Rivista di studi sul pensiero antico* 30 (2009): 5–52; Friedemann Buddensiek, "Does Good Fortune Matter? *Eudemian Ethics* VIII.2 on *eutuchia*," in Fiona Leigh, ed., *The* Eudemian Ethics *on the Voluntary, Friendship, and Luck* (Leiden: Brill, 2012), 155–84; John Dudley, *Aristotle's Concept of Chance: Accidents, Cause, Necessity, and Determinism* (Albany: SUNY Press, 2012), 236–57; Monte Ransome Johnson, "Luck in Aristotle's Physics and Ethics," in D. Henry and

compressed, presents challenges of sense, and is likely corrupt at some points. This all presents serious difficulties, given the stretch in core concepts that emerge in it.

As the treatise advances, both divine guidance and fortune gain more serious consideration than the perhaps dismissive tone in the opening synopsis might indicate. One common way of imagining a divine role in luck holds no interest for Aristotle (and explains the dismissive tone). In a manner similar to his rejection of the idea that dreams are "god-sent," he is dismissive of appeals to the divine for explaining seeming breaks in the normal chains of causes. In both cases, and other similar ones,[61] his scruples have to do with popular conceptions of ad hoc divine intervention, and they reflect a wider Aristotelian distaste for the idea that inconsistency is a mark of the divine.[62] Quite the contrary; as in the case of the motions of the fixed stars, consistency is. Aristotle unfailingly rules out capricious and haphazard divine behavior; god does not intervene willy-nilly. The role of the divine for the fortunate, as he sets out to investigate whether it exists, will be of a different character.

Chance

The *Eudemian Ethics* discussion is part of a wider set of texts that consider fortune or chance in the corpus.[63] These ideas are most clearly articulated in the *Physics* 2.4–6, with some further guidance from

---

K. M. Nielsen, eds., *Bridging the Gap between Aristotle's Science and Ethics* (Cambridge: Cambridge University Press, 2015). Recent translations and commentary: Woods (1992); Anthony Kenny, *Aristotle: The Eudemian Ethics* (Oxford: Clarendon, 2011); Brad Inwood and Raphael Woolf, *Aristotle Eudemian Ethics*, Cambridge Texts in the History of Philosophy (Cambridge: Cambridge University Press, 2013).

[61] In the *Physics*, a broad discussion of chance, discussed below, starts off: "There are some for whom chance seems to be a cause, but a cause unclear to human reasoning on the grounds that it is something divine and rather demonic" (εἰσὶ δέ τινες οἷς δοκεῖ εἶναι μὲν αἰτία ἡ τύχη, ἄδηλος δὲ ἀνθρωπίνη διανοίᾳ ὡς θεῖόν τι οὖσα καὶ δαιμονιώτερον [*Phys.* 196b5–6]). He is similarly dismissive in the *Hist. an.* (636a24) of those who invoke the demonic as a cause of the phenomenon popularly known as "wind pregnancies"—in which women show false signs of pregnancy and attribute that to "the daemonic" (cf. *Frag.* 76.5).

[62] In evaluating the ideas of the Presocratics, for example, he rejects a link between the divine and the accidental (See *Phys.* 196a25–b4).

[63] On chance generally, see, recently, Dudley (2012).

Metaphysics 7.7 and 12.3, and *On Generation and Corruption* 333b55–59. I will be following the scholars who see these texts as, for the most part, not containing substantive contradictions. Chance has to do with the relationship of an event to the prior events that caused it. Aristotle analyzes end states reached as a result of being aimed for and end states reached while something else was aimed for. In the latter case, the prior events that cause them do indeed happen for the sake of something, but something else, a surplus, emerges from them as well. It is a surprise offspring, if you will, which is not the result of design. His famous example is a man who is owed money. He visits some place for an entirely different reason (say, goes to the marketplace to buy pomegranates), by accident runs into the man who owes him money, and is able to collect it. Getting back his money is the fulfillment of an end goal for the man (a final cause, or a "for the sake of which," in Aristotle's terminology), but it resulted from an event undertaken for a different "for the sake of which"—that is, getting the pomegranates—that had an entirely accidental relationship with what happened.

Strictly, Aristotle treats chance (τύχη) as a subset of a larger category of the "spontaneous" (τὸ αὐτόματον). This category will be familiar from early on in this study of Aristotle. It appears, linked to the demonic, in his short summary of the treatise on dreams, when he wonders, on my reading, whether seeing the future in dreams is a behavior within human control, or whether it is "among the things which have the demonic as the cause, and arise by nature or from the spontaneous."[64] Whereas chance refers only to cases in which purposeful human action is involved, initiated by the higher-order intellect, the spontaneous refers to any accidental event in nature (*Phys.* 2.6). Take, for example, the case of a tree that escapes a forest fire because a wind gust made the fire jump past it. Aristotle would call this a case of the spontaneous but not of chance. Again, the wind saved it, but it did not gust for the sake of the tree's being saved. Though a spontaneous event happens with nature as its cause, in a certain sense it happens not "according to nature" since it emerges from natural processes that were not aiming directly at it.[65] His

---

[64] See above, pp. 95–96.

[65] Aristotle also used the notion of the "spontaneous" in the case of spontaneous generation. He thought certain animals—mostly varieties of bugs and fishes—emerged spontaneously from matter. These qualify as spontaneous because there is no seed that reproduced them, and so they

reserving the term *chance* to describe events involving intelligent choosing agents is a bit clearer in the Greek, where τύχη contains what we mean by chance, but also means something closer to fortune or luck. Just as English speakers would mostly reserve the words *fortunate* or *unfortunate*, or *lucky* or *unlucky*, for results related to human action, so too Aristotle reserves τύχη for that class of actions as well.

The line separating out actions that are initiated by deliberative, goal-directed human agency from general events in nature is one Aristotle commonly draws. The distinction figures in his psychology, poetics, and in the rest of his ethics.[66] Aristotle typically reserves the verb πράττω and the cognate noun πρᾶξις for such actions.[67] Full-grown humans are capable of it. Other sorts of entities, including objects in the inanimate world, animals, and children, are not (*NE* 1112b31–32, 1129a20, 1139a17–b5; *EE* 1223a5; *Meta.*, 1025b18–24; *Phys.* 2.6). Objects incapable of πρᾶξις are more or less fully embedded in the kinetic causal chains that explain motion in nature. From the standpoint of Aristotle's ethical thinking, lower-order creatures are closer to inanimate things, flotsam and jetsam borne along by the currents of natural forces interacting with their own natures.

When prior events result in the events toward which they were explicitly aimed, Aristotle also has a preferred vocabulary. In the realm of

are the result of the materials coming together accidentally in the proportions and under the conditions necessary for a living thing to emerge. That the most common illustrative example is from biology is in keeping with his focus on living things as archetypal substances. The more general definition includes all events which result from a purposiveness that did not specifically aim for them.

[66] See H. Joachim, *The Nicomachean Ethics* (Oxford: Oxford University Press, 1955), 78. On poetics, a *mimêsis praxeôs* is the definition of tragedy, *Poetics* 1449b24; see G. F. Else, *Aristotle's Poetics: The Argument* (Cambridge, Mass.: Harvard University Press, 1963), 69–73, 241; Paul Ricoeur, *Time and Narrative*, vol. 1 (Chicago: University of Chicago Press, 1984), 31–50. For a view nuancing the common understanding of the implication of the poetics and ethics, see Elizabeth Belfiore, "Aristotle's Concept of Praxis in the Poetics," *The Classical Journal* 79.2 (1983–1984), 110–24. Belfiore is working from a stricter sense of the term, centering on culpability, whereas I am examining it from the dimension of agency, which is not in question. In a very broad statement elsewhere in the *Eudemian Ethics*, he mentions two sources of motion in the universe that qualify as first principles, humans and god (*EE* 1222b15–23).

[67] Only rational beings, and not children or animals, are capable of *praxis* (*EE* 1224a28–30; cf. *NE* 1139a20). While even the actions we initiate might ultimately find causes in the cosmological superstructure, they are of a sufficiently different quality as to sometimes be separated out as their own category. Here is the ground over which questions of determinism are debated, and again, it is not necessary to settle this question. For more, see Carlo Natali, *L'Action Efficace: Études sur la philosophie de l'action d'Aristote* (Louvain: Peeters, 2004).

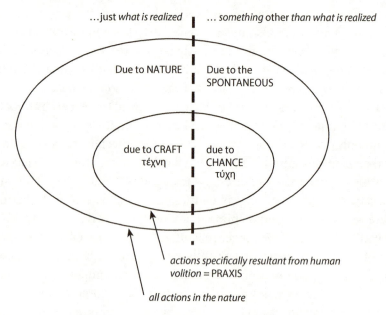

Figure 2. Aristotle on the causal backgrounds possible
for events—including accidents

human volition, he says they are due to *technê*, or craft. In nature as a
whole, such events are said to happen "according to nature." These considerations can be summarized in figure 2. This raises the question of
how one should consider nature as precisely "aiming" at things.

Nature's Purposes

Just after his discussion of the spontaneous in the *Physics*, in which the
idea of nature's purposes is central, Aristotle anticipates that some
might be wondering why nature belongs to the class of causes that act
"for the sake of" something.[68] This is a question to which we have already given some consideration in exploring the impulse hypothesis

---

[68] Particularly illuminating on this question is Victor Caston, "Aristotle's Two Intellects: A
Modest Proposal," *Phronesis* 44.3 (1999): 116–221.

above. Purposefulness in nature is a precondition for his template of the spontaneous and luckiness in the *Physics*, and so the question comes up. In a passage that has been much discussed by scholars, Aristotle takes the example that falling rain makes crops grow. Some people might think that rain simply falls with no purposiveness to it, he says, and the rain rains *not* in order to make crops grow. Consider, they might say, how the rain ruins crops if it falls after they have been reaped and are laying on the ground waiting to be gathered. These same people may also suggest that teeth come in not in order to facilitate mastication, and the ability to chew with them is just a coincidental benefit. Aristotle roundly disagrees with this argument.

He claims that it is simply absurd to say that such events are not purposive. His main argument is that these things happen always or for the most part. Our teeth come in in a way attuned to our digestive needs, he says, and falling rain helps crops grow and doesn't destroy them, for the most part. But when we speak of the results of chance and spontaneity, none of those things come about always or for the most part. Therefore, action for an end must be present in things that come to be and are by nature. The acorn example we cited above is pertinent here. The acorn always or for the most part turns itself into oak, and it never turns itself into a sunflower. This consistency is for Aristotle proof of purposiveness. Nature, like human artifice, is up to something. In an elegant statement from the *Physics* discussion, he develops these themes, comparing human action to the actions of nature as a whole (and, along the way, striking notes not so distant from the Hippocratic author of *On Regimen* that we saw above):

There is an "on account of something" in the things that come to be and exist by nature. Indeed, whatever things have a particular *telos*, what comes before in the succession is conducted on account of this. Now surely as in human action (πράττεται), so in nature; and as in nature, so it is in each action, if nothing interferes. Action is for the sake of an end; and nature in turn is for the sake of something. If a house, for example, were among the things that emerge by nature, it would be in the same state as it is now when made by art; and if things made by nature should be made not only by nature but also by art, they would emerge in that case, in just the same way in which they come to be by nature. And so one thing is for the sake of the other; and generally speaking art in some cases completes what nature cannot bring to a finish, and in others imitates nature. If therefore artificial products are for the sake of something, so clearly also are natural products.

ἔστιν ἄρα τὸ ἕνεκά του ἐν τοῖς φύσει γιγνομένοις καὶ οὖσιν. ἔτι ἐν ὅσοις τέλος ἔστι τι, τούτου ἕνεκα πράττεται τὸ πρότερον καὶ τὸ ἐφεξῆς. οὐκοῦν ὡς πράττεται, οὕτω πέφυκε, καὶ ὡς πέφυκεν, οὕτω πράττεται ἕκαστον, ἂν μή τι ἐμποδίζῃ. πράττεται δ' ἕνεκά του· καὶ πέφυκεν ἄρα ἕνεκά του. οἷον εἰ οἰκία τῶν φύσει γιγνομένων ἦν, οὕτως ἂν ἐγίγνετο ὡς νῦν ὑπὸ τῆς τέχνης· εἰ δὲ τὰ φύσει μὴ μόνον φύσει ἀλλὰ καὶ τέχνῃ γίγνοιτο, ὡσαύτως ἂν γίγνοιτο ᾗ πέφυκεν. ἕνεκα ἄρα θατέρου θάτερον. ὅλως δὲ ἡ τέχνη τὰ μὲν ἐπιτελεῖ ἃ ἡ φύσις ἀδυνατεῖ ἀπεργάσασθαι, τὰ δὲ μιμεῖται. εἰ οὖν τὰ κατὰ τέχνην ἕνεκά του, δῆλον ὅτι καὶ τὰ κατὰ φύσιν· (*Phys.* 199a7–18)

As many scholars have noted, one must be careful to distinguish Aristotle's position from some pan-psychic notion of a self-conscious raindrop guiding itself to fall on a farmer's plot of ground; or some demiurgic divinity, going about constructing everything in discreet acts of efficient causation. Instead, Aristotle is moved by the overall consistency in nature, which tends toward outcomes that "manifest goodness and beauty" (*Meta.* 984b12); or, as he puts it in *On Generation and Corruption*, "in all things, nature always reaches for the better (ἐν ἅπασιν ἀεὶ τοῦ βελτίονος ὀρέγεσθαί φαμεν τὴν φύσιν [336b27–28]). It is a fascinating and rich position, holding steadfastly to a sense of wonder at the simple fact that so much of what goes on in nature seems to work. Why not chaos all the time? This is a different, and more subtle position from the various arguments from design that emerge from William Paley and subsequent thinkers in the modern era, since Aristotle's idea does not rely on a notion of the divine as an efficient cause.[69]

In contrast to what happens according to nature, spontaneous outcomes occur by accident. These are attributable to the many layers of causation at work in the complex aggregation of nature's causes. Different

[69] See R. J. Hankinson, *Cause and Explanation in Ancient Greek Thought* (Oxford: Oxford University Press, 1997), 125. For a recent full consideration of the question, see Monte Ransome Johnson (2005).

vectors of causation will be percolating along at one level aiming toward their end points, and along the way they will produce ancillary accidental outcomes for others. These considerations provide a schematic outline of his common treatment of how accidents, both the spontaneous and luck, work in the natural world and in purposeful human action.

In the *Eudemian Ethics*, Aristotle presses the conversation further. He extends his discussion of chance to examine a rare class of it, the case of the behaviors of people who are consistently lucky. This leads him to appeal, beyond the level of causation at the macro level, to another, deeper layer of causation, which, I will claim, is an appeal to the impulse hypothesis we worked through above. Finally, during this discussion, Aristotle explicitly relates this rare phenomenon to another one, linking the strange case of the consistently lucky person to that of the person capable of divinatory foresight. Philip van der Eijk has studied this connection, and I have profited from his work.[70] I will mark points of disagreement.

A Second Chance

Anyone can experience luck. In the case of chance we just saw, for example, the person was lucky who went to the market to buy food, bumped into someone who owed him money, and got the money back. In going about the business he set himself on, he got his money back as an accidental bonus. This form of luck happens inconsistently. But Aristotle explores the possibility of a second kind of lucky person in the *Eudemian Ethics*. This one is consistently lucky, succeeds without recourse to rational deliberation, especially thrives in risky pursuits, and in matters where, although skill is decisive, a lot of luck is involved—for example in military affairs or piloting a ship. Aristotle has no doubt they exist, but the lucky are an odd group of people. They do something that seems impossible. They succeed by chance "always or for the most part," while chance will have as part of its definition precisely that it does *not* happen always or for the most part. Fascinatingly, he frames it as a question of internal desire. Consistently lucky people somehow

[70] Van der Eijk (2005), 238–58.

have an urge toward what is good for them, just what they should, when they should, and how they should.

Recent translators and commentators have taken distinctly different tacks on important parts of this gnarled and difficult section. For the text, I will rely on Walzer and Mingay's Oxford Classical Text, supplemented by van der Eijk for the section from 1248a16–41.[71] Deviations from this scheme are noted. I will bring out only those points of contest that are the most relevant to my main line of thinking. On my reading, Aristotle marks his attempt to account for the second class of luckiness as a kind of stretch in a manner similar to the one he uses to mark his account of predictive dreams, when he says it would seem to be "beyond human wit" to discover the cause of true predictive dreams (ὑπὲρ τὴν ἡμετέραν εἶναι δόξειεν ἂν σύνεσιν εὑρεῖν τὴν ἀρχήν [*Div. somn.* 462b25–26]):

> Since we observe that some people are lucky irrespective of all knowledge and correct reasoning, it is clear that something else should be the cause of their luckiness. Whether that luckiness exists or not, which desires what it ought and when it ought, there might not be a human reckoning of this.

> ἐπεὶ δ' ὁρῶμεν παρὰ πάσας τὰς ἐπιστήμας καὶ τοὺς λογισμοὺς τοὺς ὀρθοὺς εὐτυχοῦντας τινάς, δῆλον ὅτι ἕτερον ἄν τι εἴη τὸ αἴτιον τῆς εὐτυχίας. ἐκείνη δὲ πότερον [ἡ] εὐτυχία ἢ οὐκ ἔστιν, ἢ ἐπεθύμησεν ὧν ἔδει καὶ ὅτε ἔδει, ὁ λογισμὸς[72] ἀνθρώπινος οὐκ ἂν τούτου εἴη· (*EE* 1248a2–7)

He considers three possible causes: wisdom, a personal demon, and nature. He quickly rules out the personal demon. Some people claim that a certain guardian angel or *daimôn* guides the decisions of lucky

[71] Van der Eijk (2005), 248–56.

[72] The manuscripts here read, ὧν ἔδει καὶ ὅτε ἔδει τὸ λογισμὸς ἀνθρώπινος οὐκ ἂν τούτου εἴη. This is nonsensical. Walzer and Mingay (1991) place daggers around ὅτε ἔδει; Susemihl (1967) posits a lacuna between ὅτε ἔδει and the mss. τὸ λογισμὸς. Neither is satisfying. Rackham (1926) suggests a ᾧ for the τὸ and translates that a man "formed a desire for the right thing and at the right time when in his case human reasoning could not make this calculation." I suggest reading ὁ λογισμὸς for τὸ λογισμὸς which makes sense of the passage, echoes an earlier similar formulation, in a different context (1247b8–9), and corrolates with a similar sentiment, in slighly different terms, with respect to predictive dreams from *Div. somn.* (462b25–26).

people directly: "the lucky man has a good *daimôn* as his pilot" (see 1247a24–30). He dismisses this model along lines that are by now famil-iar. As in the divination text, it is simply absurd (ἄτοπον) for Aristotle that the divine would show particular favor to a foolish person, rather than to the best one. In both cases, the scenario he dismisses is that a divin-ity makes a discrete intervention, steering a person one way or the other.

He also rules out wisdom as the cause of consistent luckiness, be-cause, in another parallel with the treatment of dreams, it is precisely empty-headed people who are lucky, and they cannot give an account of their success, which they would be able to do if it had arrived from wisdom (1247a13–16). Aristotle then makes a further claim. It is not just that luckiness can't be explained by wisdom, but (again) just as with the case of predictive dreaming, lack of wisdom is a prerequisite for it. That people succeed in being fortunate consistently is for Aristo-tle correlative with their having an absence in higher-order intellectual activity in just the area in which they are lucky:

> Furthermore they are clearly senseless—not that they are concerning the rest of things . . .—but they are senseless precisely in things in which they are lucky. For in seafaring it is not the most skillful who are lucky, but just as in the fall of dice, one man throws nothing, and a different man throws a roll that corresponds with a naturally lucky man.

> ἔτι δὲ φανεροὶ ὄντες ἄφρονες, οὐχ ὅτι περὶ ἄλλα . . . ἀλλ᾽ {ὅτι} καὶ ἐν οἷς εὐτυχοῦσιν ἄφρονες. περὶ γὰρ ναυκληρίαν οὐχ οἱ δεινότατοι εὐτυχεῖς, ἀλλ᾽ ὥσπερ ἐν κύβων πτώσει ὁ μὲν οὐδέν, ἄλλος δὲ βάλλει καθ᾽ ἣν φύσει ἐστὶν εὐτυχής· (*EE* 1247a15–23)

The throwing of dice appears here, parallel to the reference to throwing in the discussion of divination by dreams. As we mentioned above, the con-text here sets it out as a, paradoxically, nonrandom sort of chance. Fur-ther, the characteristic of being consistently lucky is restricted to cases over which the subjects in question are intellectually weak. As in the case of dreaming, he counts the negative correlation with wisdom as evidence in trying to figure out what is going on. In each case, the cognitive functioning that is responsible for these behaviors needs to be located elsewhere.

Aristotle turns to his final proposal. He asks whether the consistently lucky are so by nature, and this possibility detains his attention longer. He starts by considering whether consistent luck comes from a naturally inclined disposition (a *hexis*), and compares it to the case of people who have sharp eyesight. This capacity is due to an individual's physical nature, and perhaps the case of consistently lucky people is like this. Their ability would be some quality of their natures, the knack to desire just what they should, when they should, and how they should. He says that many people think this is the case. But this runs into a problem because we would then need to say that men who are lucky are not so on account of luck, but just because their natures are a certain way, and this would mean there is no such thing as luck. But this is not acceptable to Aristotle because he is sure that luck exists, independent of nature—on the model of our example of serendipity in the marketplace—and if luck were a knack due to a natural disposition, one could then make a *technê* out of it. But there is no *technê* of luckiness (*EE* 1247a15). The kind of phenomenon he is looking at, he clarifies again by invoking dice, is when something happens "many times in succession to someone, not because it ought to happen this way, but it would be like always throwing dice in a lucky throw" (τινι ἐφεξῆς τὰ τοιαῦτα πολλάκις, οὐχ ὅτι οὕτως δεῖ,[73] ἀλλ' οἷον ἂν εἴη τὸ κύβους ἀεὶ μακαρίαν βάλλειν [1247b16–18]). Again, dice come in handy for him to illustrate nonrandom chance. He next moves off in a new and productive direction.

Impulses, Cognition, and the Divine

Aristotle introduces another way of talking about nature as the cause, beyond the particular natural disposition of this or that person. This sets him on a hunt for the source of lucky people's opportune desires, and into some of his broadest consideration of human desire in the corpus. He takes a perspective so broad, in fact, that he opens up an even

---

[73] Here following Sylburg's notation on Susemihl (1967)'s text (οὕτως δεῖ) in place of Walzer and Mingay (1991)'s (τοιοσδί); see Susemihl ad loc.

further dimension to the question—the background of *all* motion in the universe in general. On my reading, the impulse hypothesis is a critical part of this discussion. Lucky behaviors might work out the way they do, he proposes, because of the way actions in the whole cosmos in general tend to work out.

Aristotle begins his consideration of fortuitous desires by considering them against all the urges toward action that produce motion in humans. This builds on core Aristotelian positions we see in *On the Soul* and across the treatises of the *Parva Naturalia*. He wonders:

> Aren't there impulses in the soul, some from reasoning, others from irrational inclination? And aren't the ones from irrational inclination prior?

> ἆρ' οὐκ ἔνεισιν ὁρμαὶ ἐν τῇ ψυχῇ αἱ μὲν ἀπὸ λογισμοῦ, αἱ δὲ ἀπὸ ὀρέξεως ἀλόγου; καὶ πρότεραι αὗται; (*EE* 1247b18–20)

The proposed priority of irrational to rational movements inclines the investigation toward the more rudimentary levels of his well-attested hierarchy of functions in the soul.

In Aristotle's psychology, all living things have a soul. But souls have different capacities in different forms of life. At the highest level, he puts soul's intellectual function (διανοητικόν), which manifests uniquely in humans. It is responsible for self-conscious discursive reasoning and is associated with the νοῦς. Next comes the motive aspect (κινητικόν), which all creatures that possess the capacity for physical movements have. This function of the soul acts on desires that emerge from the soul's next layer, the appetitive (ὀρεκτικόν) faculty, the center of all desires, whether from rational thoughts, inclinations, or irrational passions. These desires are regularly formed in interaction with a still lower faculty, the perceptive capacity (αἰσθητικόν), which is present in creatures that can perceive things. At the lowest order sits the nutritive soul (θρεπτικόν), which is responsible for the simplest urges, visible in all living things, for nutrition and reproduction. Plants have only this lowest order. When present, the higher-order souls layer on top of, and do not displace, the lower ones. Calling the irrational movements of the soul prior to the rational ones, invokes this gradient and starts us on a downward path along it.

Next, Aristotle tells us what the prior irrational inclinations aim for by nature—it is a simple urge for pleasure—and he links this to his general principle that nature itself always reaches for the better:

> For if there is by nature an inclination on account of a desire of pleasure, everything would by nature proceed toward the good.

> εἰ γάρ ἐστι φύσει ἡ δι᾽ ἐπιθυμίαν ἡδέος {καὶ ἡ} ὄρεξις, φύσει γε ἐπὶ τὸ ἀγαθὸν βαδίζοι ἂν πᾶν.[74] (*EE* 1247b20–21)

Aristotle makes reaching for pleasure to be a co-expression of nature's tendency to manifest goodness and beauty, a principle that appears at multiple crux arguments elsewhere in the corpus, as we have already seen in discussion of the impulse hypothesis (e.g., *Phys.* 199a8–20, 199b26; *GC* 336b27–37a7; *Meta.* 984b12). All this begins to suggest to him another way in which nature could be behind consistent luckiness. Such people are operating more in the way that features of the natural world (which mostly do not have the capacity for rationality) generally operate. That is, via a system of subrational natural impulses that orients them toward the good:

> If some are well-suited by nature, just as singers sing, although they don't have knowledge, in this way they are naturally well-suited and they follow their impulse without reason, in the direction in which they are naturally oriented, and they desire what they ought, when they ought, and how they ought—these people succeed, although they are senseless and irrational, just as also people sing well although they are not able to teach it. These are the sort of people who are lucky—whoever without reason succeeds for the most part. It turns out that the lucky would be so by nature.

> εἰ δή τινές εἰσιν εὐφυεῖς ὥσπερ οἱ ᾠδικοὶ οὐκ ἐπιστάμενοι ᾄδειν, οὕτως εὖ πεφύκασι καὶ ἄνευ λόγου ὁρμῶσιν, <ᾗ> ἡ φύσις πέφυκε, καὶ ἐπιθυμοῦσι καὶ τούτου καὶ τότε καὶ οὕτως ὡς δεῖ καὶ οὗ δεῖ καὶ ὅτε, οὗτοι κατορθώσουσι, κἂν τύχωσιν ἄφρονες ὄντες καὶ ἄλογοι, ὥσπερ καὶ εὖ ᾄσονται οὐ διδασκαλικοὶ ὄντες. οἱ δέ γε τοιοῦτοι εὐτυχεῖς, ὅσοι ἄνευ

---

[74]Taking the πᾶν of the ms. and not following πᾶσα of Allan, whom Walzer and Mingay (1991) follow, see Walzer and Mingay, 117.

λόγου κατορθοῦσιν ὡς ἐπὶ τὸ πολύ. φύσει ἄρα οἱ εὐτυχεῖς εἶεν ἄν. (*EE* 1247b21–27)

He clarifies what he means here in what follows, by deepening the contrast with normal self-consciously guided human actions. He links the two different guiding systems of human behavior, rational and nonrational, to the two different kinds of luckiness he has already observed:

> Or do we talk about luckiness in multiple ways? For some acts are performed from impulse and others, if people choose to do them, are not, but are the opposite. We claim that they have been quite lucky when they succeed, both in the case of acts from impulse, in which they seem to have reasoned poorly, and again in those done by choice, if they wished for a good thing different from or less than they got.

> ἢ πλεοναχῶς λέγεται ἡ εὐτυχία; τὰ μὲν γὰρ πράττεται ἀπὸ τῆς ὁρμῆς καὶ προελομένων πρᾶξαι, τὰ δ' οὔ, ἀλλὰ τοὐναντίον. καὶ ἐν ἐκείνοις, <ἐν οἷς> κακῶς λογίσασθαι δοκοῦσι, κατορθοῦντας καὶ εὐτυχῆσαι[75] φαμέν· καὶ πάλιν ἐν τούτοις, εἰ ἐβούλοντο ἄλλο ἢ ἔλαττον <ἢ> ἔλαβον τἀγαθόν. (*EE* 1247b28–33)

The consistent kind of luckiness is not an epiphenomenon of rational self-aware choice: in such cases people are not following some deliberative action and getting an ancillary bonus. Instead they behave precisely *without* engaging their rational minds at all, and without self-consciously pursuing any particular goal. He has in mind a case like a ship's pilot entering an unknown port and twitching on the tiller at just the right times to avoid submerged rocks. A person in this situation will succeed without thought and instead because his actions are aimed the right way, at the right time.

The trajectory into rudimentary nature is anchored by the salience of the term *impulse* (ὁρμή) in this section of text. It is a rare category for Aristotle with distinctive uses. Over the corpus as a whole, the soul's movements that he discusses most are the result of self-conscious

---

[75] Following the ms. and not the κατευτυχῆσαι of Bussemaker, whom Walzer and Mingay (1991) follow.

factors, whether thoughts or passions.[76] They are divided into classes situated in the volition center, including wish (βούλησις), desire (ἐπιθυμία), and passion (θυμός). These are the central features of the systematic doctrine of his ethics and his theories regarding human action.[77] He typically reserves the term "impulse," by contrast, for a different class: automatic or involuntary urges. Particularly prominent in this group are the movements of the nutritive soul that regulate the organic processes of digestion and reproduction, in the more general discussions of living things (*Hist. an.* 572b8, 572b24, 573a27, 574a13, 575a15, 582a34, 581b12, 587b32; *GA* 750b20; cf. *NE* 1102b21). Urges like these emerge in all creatures, from plants all the way up to us.[78] They are a particularly embodied process. They are so rudimentary as to only be at the cusp of cognition.[79]

Other kinds of subvolitional semi-cognitive activity also fall into the impulse category. In the introduction to the *Politics*, the tendency of humans to live in groups is said to be an expression of an impulse (ὁρμή; 1253a29). It is not surprising that a whole range of involuntary actions are designated impulses in the Aristotelian *Problems*, like the movement of sweat out of the pores (867b7, 868b31), bedwetting (876a21), yawning (886a35), sneezing (961b25), hiccupping (962a5), and the stuttering of melancholics (903b21). These urges are directed toward goals that are for the most part in the creature's basic interest. Living in groups, digesting, and reproducing surely are, and even sweating, sneezing, and probably yawning (one has a harder time with bedwetting and stuttering).

---

[76] See the very helpful note from Woods (1992) on 1223a26–27 with many parallel citations. The soul's different levels are associated with certain kinds movements: choice and discursive thought are associated with the διανοητικόν aspect of the soul; inclinations (ὀρέξεις) emerge from the appetitive (ὀρεκτικόν) faculty, from a wish desire and passion. These all take place in the light of day, one might say.

[77] See *De anima* 3.10 for a summary account of the origins of motion from inclinations due to desire and thought. Cf. *EE* 1223a21–28.

[78] The *Politics* tells us that the human urge to reproduce is not the result of thought or desire: "This is not out of deliberate purpose, but with man as with the other animals and with plants there is a natural instinct to desire to leave behind one another being of the same sort as oneself" (καὶ τοῦτο οὐκ ἐκ προαιρέσεως, ἀλλ' ὥσπερ καὶ ἐν τοῖς ἄλλοις ζῴοις καὶ φυτοῖς φυσικὸν τὸ ἐφίεσθαι, οἷον αὐτό, τοιοῦτον καταλιπεῖν ἕτερον [1252a27–30]). Cf. *MM* 1213b18.

[79] Van der Eijk has done the most to help specify the ways in which Aristotle thinks of cognitive processes in physiological dimensions. See van der Eijk (2005), chaps. 5–8.

Further, he also uses the term regularly at an even lower rung in his ontological ladder, to label the most general kinds of leanings toward action that are built into even inanimate substances. The concept marks the tendency of fire to move up and a stone to move down.[80] These are his archetypal examples of the movements of simple substances in nature. That ὁρμή describes cases of even inanimate objects' propulsion makes its rudimentary quality even more striking. In the case of humans, these gravitational principles toward certain motions are humming away not because we desire them by rational choice, a passion, or a wish. They are just built into our sheer existence as substances in the world. And so, when Aristotle tells us that the starting points, at the most rudimentary levels, of any of our psychic chains emerge from impulse without reason, he is placing them within this class—just at the threshold of cognition itself.

Typically, Aristotle does not have a need to work out any particular relationship between such subvolitional impulses and the more complex behaviors that result from our self-conscious wishes, desires, and passions.[81] For the most part, the two systems operate on different levels. The self-aware system toward motion has its own modes and functions, which form the basis of most of Aristotle's consideration of human nature: we set out to make a deliberate decision, and engage the διανοητικόν aspect of the soul, by gathering information, applying rules of reason, and reaching a conclusion; we act on a passion or

---

[80] *An. pr.* 95a1, *Phys.* 192b18, *Meta.* 1023a9–23, cf. *Prob.* 937b36. The passage from the *Physics*, which opens book 2, illustrates the theme:

> Things that exist by nature have within them a principle of motion and of stationariness (in respect of place, or of growth and decrease, or by way of alteration). But a couch or a robe, insofar as they are objects of a craft, don't have any innate impulse of change. But insofar as they happen to be composed of stone or of earth or a mixture of the two, they do have it, which seems to indicate that nature is an origin and cause of being moved and of being at rest in that to which it belongs primarily.

> πάντα δὲ ταῦτα [τὰ ἐστι φύσει] φαίνεται διαφέροντα πρὸς τὰ μὴ φύσει συνεστῶτα. τούτων μὲν γὰρ ἕκαστον ἐν ἑαυτῷ ἀρχὴν ἔχει κινήσεως καὶ στάσεως, τὰ μὲν κατὰ τόπον, τὰ δὲ κατ' αὔξησιν καὶ φθίσιν, τὰ δὲ κατ' ἀλλοίωσιν· κλίνη δὲ καὶ ἱμάτιον . . . καθ' ὅσον ἐστὶν ἀπὸ τέχνης, οὐδεμίαν ὁρμὴν ἔχει μεταβολῆς ἔμφυτον, ᾗ δὲ συμβέβηκεν αὐτοῖς εἶναι λιθίνοις ἢ γηΐνοις ἢ μικτοῖς ἐκ τούτων, ἔχει, καὶ κατὰ τοσοῦτον, ὡς οὔσης τῆς φύσεως ἀρχῆς τινὸς καὶ αἰτίας τοῦ κινεῖσθαι καὶ ἠρεμεῖν ἐν ᾧ ὑπάρχει πρώτως καθ' αὑτό. (*Phys.* 192b18)

[81] The richest discussions close to the topic emerge from cases of *akrasia* in the ethical writings (*NE* 7.1–10).

desire, of which we are fully aware; and the ὀρεκτικόν functioning of the soul spurs the κινητικόν to produce a movement to actualize it. While these processes perform their functions, the lowest order soul carries out its activities by impulse, keeping our digestive track operating, steering us away from living alone, or seeing to it that we reproduce another like ourselves.

In his accounting, the two regions nearly always go about their business in distinct arenas. However, in the case of consistent luckiness, they come into contact. Now, actions and good outcomes that are typically only achievable via our self-conscious rationality wind up resulting from the lower order, impulse-driven system. We seem to have jumped categories here, which provokes the question of how these lower-order impulses could result in the more elaborate good outcomes they seem to.

Any result from the rudimentary tendencies toward motion in us should be tightly circumscribed. For example, the bulk of a standing human body, insofar as it is made up of earth, would tend toward its like, and so it will fall if the tension in the legs gives way. Then again, moving just up the chain of being, to the lowest ensouled entities, we do observe more complex examples of natural tendencies toward motion at the level of impulse. Without any higher-order thinking, a plant is somehow quite consistent in sending its roots toward water (*Phys.* 199a23–30). Turning to humans, the urge to live in groups and reproduce are not as simple as falling down; according Aristotle's notion of impulse, however, they are just as automatic.

To get to the core of how things tend to work out well for the consistently lucky, Aristotle makes a striking pivot in the argument. Just after he marks the difficulty of the question ("there might not be a human reckoning of this," *EE* 1248a7), he starts in a new direction by telling us there is in fact a way to explain it:

It is certainly not entirely without an account. Their self-conscious desire is not operating according to its natural function, but it is disabled by something.

οὐ γὰρ δὴ πάμπαν ἀλόγιστον τοῦτο, οὐδὲ φύσική <γ'> ἐστιν ἡ ἐπιθυμία, ἀλλὰ διαφθείρεται ὑπό τινος. (*EE* 1248a7–9)

He begins to envision the consistently lucky person as a stripped-down version of the human creature, with our distinctive higher-order cognition disabled. The underlying processes (present in all naturally existing things) are more visible in such humans because they are not overshadowed by the complex movements of self-conscious thinking and volition.

This next leads him to ask something that is typically unnecessary for him to ask. With the system of normal desire hampered, it must be some more rudimentary system that lies underneath it that is now initiating events. This raises the interesting question of where such preconscious, nonrational impulses come from, which then opens up a profound question of motion in humans at the most general level. He first considers whether luck could be the source:

> Is luck the cause of this very thing, of desiring what one ought when one ought? Or will it then be the cause of everything? For then luck will also be the cause of thinking and of deliberating, for a person certainly did not deliberate because of having deliberated earlier, and having deliberated about that—no, there is a certain starting point; nor did he think after having thought before thinking, and so on to infinity. So it turns out that thought is not the beginning of thinking, nor is deliberation the beginning of deliberating. Then what else is except fortune? With the result that everything will be from chance.

> ἆρ' αὐτοῦ τούτου τύχη αἰτία, τοῦ ἐπιθυμῆσαι οὗ δεῖ καὶ ὅτε δεῖ; ἢ οὕτως γε πάντων ἔσται; καὶ γὰρ τοῦ νοῆσαι καὶ βουλεύσασθαι· οὐ γὰρ δὴ ἐβουλεύσατο βουλευσάμενος καὶ τοῦτ' ἐβουλεύσατο, ἀλλ' ἔστιν ἀρχή τις, οὐδ' ἐνόησε νοήσας πρότερον <ἢ> νοῆσαι, καὶ τοῦτο εἰς ἄπειρον. οὐκ ἄρα τοῦ νοῆσαι ὁ νοῦς ἀρχή, οὐδὲ τοῦ βουλεύσασθαι βουλή. τί οὖν ἄλλο πλὴν τύχη; ὥστ' ἀπὸ τύχης ἅπαντα ἔσται.[82] (*EE* 1248a16–23)

This is an unsavory result that he will move away from quickly. In the mean time, given the turn in the argument, it is clear that what he is after will be the actuator of *all* our chains of reasoning and desire. The infinite regress argument has provoked the deeply interesting question of what causes us to think the things we do in the first place. Our strings

---

[82] Text follows van der Eijk (2005), 248–49.

of thought can't spring up *ex nihilo*, and so there must be a starting point. The search for the starting point of lucky people's actions has opened up a search for the starting point of any thought or desire that we might have. When he considers luck as a candidate for this starting point, the outcome is not persuasive, since then "everything" will be from chance, and luck obviously does not rule the cosmos. Then all would be chaos.

So he abandons fortune as a candidate, and the argument takes its next fascinating turn:

> Or is there some beginning beyond which there is no other, and is this beginning, on account of its being the way it is, able to produce this sort of effect [i.e., consistent luckiness]? This is the thing we are seeking, What is the starting point of motion in the soul? It is quite clear. Just as in the whole universe it is a god, also it is in the soul.[83]
>
> ἢ ἔστι τις ἀρχὴ ἧς οὐκ ἔστιν ἄλλη ἔξω, αὕτη δὲ διὰ τὸ τοιαύτη εἶναι τοιοῦτο δύναται ποιεῖν; τὸ δὲ ζητούμενον τοῦτ᾽ ἐστί, τίς ἡ τῆς κινήσεως ἀρχὴ ἐν τῇ ψυχῇ; δῆλον δὴ ὥσπερ ἐν τῷ ὅλῳ θεός κἂν ἐκείνῳ. (*EE* 1248a23–26)

What he means by this is the crux point at hand, and it is difficult to discern.[84] Scanning Aristotle's corpus, one proximate candidate for the starting point is our self-conscious διάνοια, which is engaged by the νοῦς. After all, Aristotle consistently correlates intellectual activity with the divine, as in *Metaphysics* 12.9, *De anima* 3, and *NE* 10 it is humans' distinctive activity by which we imitate the divine and partake of our highest, most godlike functions. And deliberative thought *is* almost always a completely adequate explanation of where our motions come from, discussed as human behavior under *praxis*. So, it may seem sensible that in claiming that the divine is the ultimate starting point, he is claiming that thought is the starting point. However, he has already ruled this out via both the observation that reason is disabled

---

[83] Following van der Eijk in translating the neuter demonstrative to refer back to the feminine noun, which, as he cites, is not uncommon in this chapter of the *Eudemian Ethics* (van der Eijk [2005], 249).

[84] The scholarly treatments mentioned above (n. 54) do not converge on a single reading of this text.

in lucky people, and via the infinite regress argument; and to make the case perfectly clear, he does so again in his very next statement. While thought begins our movements "in a certain way," it is not the ultimate beginning:

> Well, in a certain way the divine in us [i.e., νοῦς][85] moves everything. But the beginning of reasoning is not reasoning but something stronger. What then could be stronger than even knowledge except god? [It can't be virtue,] for virtue is a tool of intelligence. And on account of this, as I was saying earlier, they are called lucky who, if they follow their impulse, succeed although they are irrational, and to deliberate is not helpful to them. For they have the sort of a starting point which is something stronger than intelligence and deliberation (others have reasoning; but the lucky people do not possess this); they have divine inspiration.[86] But they are incapable of this [thinking and deliberation]: for it is by being without reason that they strike the mark.

> κινεῖ γάρ πως πάντα τὸ ἐν ἡμῖν θεῖον· λόγου δ' ἀρχὴ οὐ λόγος, ἀλλά τι κρεῖττον· τί οὖν ἂν κρεῖττον καὶ ἐπιστήμης εἴη πλὴν θεός; ἡ γὰρ ἀρετὴ τοῦ νοῦ ὄργανον· καὶ διὰ τοῦτο, ὃ [οἱ][87] πάλαι ἔλεγον, εὐτυχεῖς καλοῦνται οἳ ἂν ὁρμήσωσι, κατορθοῦσιν ἄλογοι ὄντες, καὶ βουλεύεσθαι οὐ συμφέρει αὐτοῖς. ἔχουσι γὰρ ἀρχὴν τοιαύτην ἢ κρεῖττον τοῦ νοῦ καὶ τῆς βουλεύσεως (οἳ δὲ τὸν λόγον· τοῦτο δ' οὐκ ἔχουσι) καὶ ἐνθουσιασμόν. τοῦτο δ' οὐ δύνανται· ἄλογοι γὰρ ὄντες ἐπιτυγχάνουσι.
> (*EE* 1248a26–34)

As was the case in the opening of his treatment of predictive dreams in chapter 2 of the *On Divination during Sleep*, the verb ἐπιτυγχάνω here means hitting the mark, by succeeding in a stochastic situation. The sense of the passage remains difficult, but the unmistakable central claim is that god ultimately serves as the starting point of all of our

---

[85] Following van der Eijk (2005), 250.

[86] For parallels to the language of inspiration see *Rhetoric* 1408b12–19, where Aristotle describes those in an elevated oratorical state as being divinely inspired; *Politics* 1340a11, 1342a7, 1341b34, 1342a4, 1340a11, 1340b4, where the effect of a certain inspirational kind of music on the soul is described this way.

[87] Following Walzer and Mingay (1991) here.

motions, and it is because god is in this role that the fortuitous outcomes result for the rare human that is consistently lucky.

This leads to the next problem, one on which the current scholarship is least satisfying. What is the mode by which god is supposed to be operating here? Scholarly debate in recent decades has tried to discern whether Aristotle means that the divine starts our motions via our intellects (the "god in us" or νοῦς position) or whether it does so independently. Due to the difficulties with the νοῦς idea that we have already shown, the consensus has settled on the hypothesis of independent divine involvement—but without much more specification as to precisely its mode. A free-floating divine operation would be a very strange idea for Aristotle. He has already ruled out that the divine would act in an ad hoc fashion. How else might it be involved? Most of the current scholarly discussion of divine involvement in nature, which we discussed above, yields no help. He cannot mean that the divine is involved because the fixed stars desire the Prime Mover. This is too narrow; it accounts only for their circular motion. Equally unhelpful would be a proposal that he means that, in some general way, since the divine is the indirect cause of all kinetic motion in the universe, via the movements of the heavens, it is also the ultimate indirect source of the motions that result in lucky psychic movement. Such a claim is much too broad to be of value. But as was explored above, there is another possibility.

The impulse hypothesis presents a promising path forward (and the reason I chose the name is by now clear). According to the account of luckiness, 1) as a co-condition of consistent luckiness, people need to be empty-headed; 2) when in this state, the higher-order centers that initiate motion are not operative, just bare impulses; and 3) to explain how these might incline toward good outcomes requires the divine. And, just so, the impulse hypothesis made room for a very narrow mode for the divine to be involved in the workings of the deep structure of all events in nature. According to it, movements from potentiality to act are precipitated via the Prime Mover. While nature sets out the circuits for these movements, the divine provides the voltage that actuates them. Further, like a vector that has both force and direction, this impetus to actualize has a consistent direction. It does not precipitate just any kind of actualizing of any kind of potential. It veers toward the good, always or for the most part. As we stipulated above, outside of describing the motions of the heavenly bodies, Aristotle mostly has no need to appeal to this hypothesis in his explanations of specific events. In my view the phenomenon of consistent luckiness requires it. It is an example of the general principle articulated by the impulse hypothesis at work in that specific part of the terrestrial natural world that is the human organism. Without the impulse hypothesis, we do not have an explanation for why bare impulses of substances in even rudimentary natures (in this case, ourselves as organisms) vector toward the good. With it, we do. In such a state we are akin to plants sending roots toward water.

We gain some further benefit by examining this phenomenon of consistent luckiness with respect to his carefully drawn categories of accidental and nonaccidental events. As we saw above, his main axes for those topics are craft/luck and natural/spontaneous. We can take these categories one by one. There is no possibility of these actions falling under a *technê*, of course, and the discussion rules this out explicitly (*EE* 1247a15). Next, the consistent kind of luckiness should, strictly speaking, no longer count as "luck" (τύχη) according to the taxonomy set out above. The category pertains only to goal-directed human action (*praxis*) which is accompanied by an accidental benefit. In the case of consistent luckiness, Aristotle has specifically ruled out the idea of any particular *praxis*, and instead speaks of benefits accruing to a human considered as a hunk of the natural world, without engaging any particular volition (*EE* 1247b28–33). As we saw above, the proper term for fortuitous outcomes in nature, divorced from purposeful human *praxis*, is the spontaneous (τὸ αὐτόματον). So the fact that these people operate entirely outside of self-conscious goal-directed action argues that these events would fall under the fourth category of the spontaneous.[88] But as a final consideration, there is at least some reason to think

---

[88] The reasons Aristotle keeps "luck" as the operative category in this context are not difficult to fathom. When he is examining luckiness, human-initiated action (*praxis*) is the central concern. After he removes *praxis* from his proposed second type, he sticks with the nomenclature of luck out of deference to the way such people are typically described (εὐτυχῆσαι φαμέν [1247b32]; εὐτυχεῖς καλοῦνται [1248a30]). Such a concession to common usage is characteristic

that such phenomena would qualify as being "according to nature," and so fall under the third category. We recall that when he explores three possible causes of consistent luckiness (wisdom, a personal demon, and nature) the first two are ruled out quickly. The latter is ruled out, in the sense of a natural disposition, but then returned to, and the treatment lacks conclusiveness with respect to whether his explanation is, strictly speaking, to be classified as within nature. Interpreting through the impulse hypothesis provides a clarifying vantage as to why.

Aristotle attributes consistent luckiness to an organizing principle *behind* nature as a whole (so in that sense natural) that is not exactly part of nature but prior to it (and in that sense *not* natural). Remember, Aristotle first rules out imagining that a certain kind of natural disposition causes lucky behaviors, meaning some people would have natures that result in luckiness. He reasons that then there would be no such thing as luck, because it would be subsumed into a natural process (but luck does exist), and one could make a *technê* out of it (but one can't). Rather it derives from the underlying principle, god, that keeps nature actualizing its potential, toward the good. Consistently lucky people are under the guidance of a nonvoluntary system, operating at the level of a physical organism and achieving outcomes that veer toward the good. Therefore, consistent luckiness, strictly speaking, breaks the rubric by which Aristotle typically measures accidents. It is strange behavior, indeed, and can only be explained by recourse to a layer of causation that lies behind all movement in the universe, both the "natural" and the "spontaneous."

Now, luckiness already shows some affiliation with the phenomenon of divination. We have people acting via cognitive states, albeit very rudimentary ones, over which the divine is ultimately responsible, causing a twitch of kinetic motion in just the right way to produce the

---

of Aristotle. His explicit spelling out of these cases leaves no doubt that while he uses "luck" for the second phenomenon, he is describing precisely a situation he defines as the spontaneous in the *Physics*. Shifting to the case of correct dreams, they are clearly distinct from Aristotle's first class of lucky behaviors. They aren't at all describable under the terms of self-conscious *praxis*, so the category of luck, strictly defined as belonging to the subcategory of *praxis*, is never pertinent to this, and there is no confusion of terminology. However, they are more thoroughly analogous to Aristotle's *second* form of luckiness, the consistent kind. Just as he said that the second class of luckiness was not the result of something being aimed for, so also in the case of dreams. This accounts for the difference in terms.

good outcome. These gives them a kind of ability to see around corners and move at the right time in the right way. So it should not be surprising, when, in the very next sentence in the discussion of luckiness, divination is precisely the direction Aristotle takes. He moves to the topic of divination by a comparison between the dual natures of each phenomenon. Just as there are two kinds of fortune—the consistent one that relies on impulse, and the fleeting one randomly emergent from a separate reason-directed *praxis*—so also there are two kinds of divination:

> Also it is necessary that the divination of those who are intelligent and wise is fleeting,[89] even that one ought almost to separate divination from reason, but in any case some make use of divination through empirical study others also through habitual acquaintance in observation, and these capabilities have to do with the divine. In addition, a person sees well both the future and the present, who is among those in whom this reasoning faculty is disengaged: which is why melancholics also see correct dreams. For it seems likely that the beginning is more powerful when reason is disengaged; exactly as the blind remember better when released from the element directed toward visible things, because the remembering element is more vigorous.

> καὶ τούτων φρονίμων καὶ σοφῶν ταχεῖαν εἶναι τὴν μαντικήν, καὶ μόνον οὐ τὴν ἀπὸ τοῦ λόγου δεῖ ἀπολαβεῖν, ἀλλ' οἱ μὲν δι' ἐμπειρίαν, οἱ δὲ διὰ συνήθειάν τε ἐν τῷ σκοπεῖν χρῆσθαι· τῷ θεῷ δὲ αὗται. τοῦτο καὶ εὖ ὁρᾷ καὶ τὸ μέλλον καὶ τὸ ὄν, καὶ ὧν ἀπολύεται ὁ λόγος οὗτος· διὸ οἱ μελαγχολικοὶ καὶ εὐθυόνειροι. ἔοικε γὰρ ἡ ἀρχὴ ἀπολυομένου τοῦ λόγου ἰσχύειν μᾶλλον· καὶ ὥσπερ οἱ τυφλοὶ μνημονεύουσι μᾶλλον ἀπολυθέντες τοῦ πρὸς τοῖς ὁρωμένοις, τῷ ἐρρωμενέστερον εἶναι τὸ μνημονεῦον. (1248a34–b3)

He maps the division he detects between normal, inconsistent luckiness and impulse-driven, consistent luckiness onto the two kinds of divination as they are commonly practiced: artificial divination based

---

[89] I am unaware of another translator that takes ταχεῖαν here to be fleeting. But it cannot mean swift in the sense of quick. Aristotle's point is to question the value of this form of divination, in favor of the other. Translators and commentators handle the whole of this difficult section in various ways. The variances here are as substantive as in any other section of the *Eudemian Ethics*.

on reasoning out patterns by observation of natural events vs. natural divination in those whose reasoning faculty is disengaged. Interestingly, his mapping directly echoes the division and relative evaluation of the modes of divination that we saw Plato set out in the *Phaedrus*, where he contrasts the irrational mode of divination favorably with the one based on sequential reason.[90] On the one hand, there is the inconsistent (fleeting) divination of those who use rational processes to analyze which sign events precede which future states. This is lined up with those who are in their right minds and gain occasional good fortune. But those whose reason is disengaged, like melancholics (also already familiar from the treatise on divination by dreams), are operating by a different system, by which they engage in a different kind of process. These people have an impulsive twitch in the right direction, consistently. And as we have already seen in the discussion of dreams, he again invokes the principle that beginnings are more powerful when the reasoning system is withdrawn. This brings us back to the main question at stake in Aristotle's discussion of dreams.

PART 4: FROM EXTERNAL MOVEMENTS TO ANTICIPATORY IMAGES: A RETURN TO THE SENSITIVE-INSTRUMENT ARGUMENT

By this reading, Aristotle's explanation of the strange case of consistent luckiness is a rare case of his appealing the notion of divine causation proposed by the impulse hypothesis to explain a specific phenomenon. Now, turning back to the treatise on predictive dreams, we have a new way to understand what Aristotle means in his claim that dreams are not "god-sent," however, "they are demonic; for nature is demonic, but not divine." The puzzle set out at the outset of this chapter centered on why he invokes the demonic. If Aristotle were mainly trying just to debunk divine causation, this category is left entirely without context. The work done up this point provides a solution to this crux of the *On Divination during Sleep*, as well as to the other problems

---

[90] See Bodéüs (2000), 166.

of interpretation in the sections that follow it. With the claim that dreams and nature as a whole are demonic, Aristotle is claiming that natural objects tend to reach for what is good for them, even in cases where these substances lack higher-order discernment of what that good is, because it is ultimately the divine that continuously precipitates the move from potential to actual along a vector toward the good, always or for the most part. There will be manifold qualifications and delimitations to this general principle as we re-work our way through the second section of the treatise.

Moving to the sentence immediately following the formula, as we saw above, Aristotle educes a "proof" of his broad claim that dreams are not godsent but, rather, demonic. He tells us that very simple people are clairvoyant (προορατικοί) and have correct dreams (εὐθυόνειροι).[91] We were struck earlier by the question of how such a proof was envisioned to work. Imagining it as just a debunking of the idea that dreams are godsent, and without reference to the demonic is ruled out by the logic of the subsequent sentences: he goes on to treat the correct dreamers as supersensitive instruments. He considers their profusion of dreams as genuine signs of future events and not as random fantasies. By reading through the gains made above, the logic by which the proof works now unfolds this way: the observable fact of clairvoyance among the empty-headed attests to an underlying process that must be steering it. Since such people are incapable of the distinctive higher-order human capacity of reason, they cannot achieve good outcomes that way (the way the rest of us do). They are closer to lower-order nature. And since they are, we need an explanation for why

---

[91] Translation agrees with Effe (1970), 85, n. 49, and not van der Eijk (2005), 145–46. Van der Eijk claims that the other appearances of the term in Greek literature prove it means vividness of dreaming. But these only include the texts of Aristotle on prescient dreams—*Div. somn.* 463b16, at stake here, and 463a25, 464a27, 464b7, 464b16 as well as the *EE* passage discussed above (1248a39–40)—plus the Plutarch passage also discussed above (*De def. or.* 437 d–f), which, as van der Eijk says, is not dispositive because it relies on Aristotle. On my translation, the idea of an accurate dream perfectly fits (see above n. 33). Etymologically, the prefix leans toward accuracy, but does not settle the question, since it just tells us that the action represented by the stem is done well. Among the passages in the *Div. somn.* 464a27, 464b7, and 464b16 all argue for the sense of the accuracy of a dream, not its vividness, and 463a25 is ambiguous. The text at stake here (463b16) makes sense by my reading only as indicating correctness of the dream.

they nevertheless veer toward what is good for them. The demonic is invoked to refer to this underlying process.

We have seen in the impulse hypothesis a very general accounting for why substances tend to actualize the reach toward the better that is part of their natures. The divine is not a direct efficient cause, but it provides a precipitating impulse to actualize potential, to fulfill the good of each entity that nature sets out for it. Because of their vacant intellects, correct dreamers, like lucky people, are more subject to this current, which directs all natural objects from potentiality to actuality along a vector toward the good. The result is a lower-order cognitive event, a flitting dream image, that is beneficial. Though it can then later enter into self-conscious thought and provoke discursive intellectual work, it comes from a source that is not within this system, but the more rudimentary one.

Dreams already carry a particular link to the lower orders of the soul since they happen in states of sleep. Aristotle explicitly links sleeping with the nutritive soul. After the higher-order systems shut down, it alone is active during sleep. *On Sleep and Waking* links sleep with the metabolism of food and growth, the critical processes overseen by the nutritive part of the soul:

> The nutritive part performs its own work during sleep, rather than during wakefulness.

> τὸ ἔργον τὸ αὑτοῦ ποιεῖ τὸ θρεπτικὸν μόριον ἐν τῷ καθεύδειν μᾶλλον ἢ ἐν τῷ ἐγρηγορέναι· (454b32–a1)

Discussion of nutrition is the main theme of the third part of that treatise (456a30–58a32). He even says that sleep and nutrition are coterminous; sleep ends when digestion is complete (458a10).[92]

Of further interest, the *Eudemian Ethics* offers further fascinating testimony (from much earlier in the text than the discussion of

---

[92] For more on the nutritive function of the soul, see *De anima* 415a22–b3, where he calls it the most primitive part, and the one most widely diffuse through all of nature. He speaks poetically of a divine inflection to this part, in the sense of its manifesting a creature's desire to be like the divine, by reproducing another like itself and so getting as close as it can to immortality.

consistent luckiness focused on above), in which he speaks generally of inspired prophecy, mapping it onto the soul's functions:

> On this account also, in the case of persons who are inspired and utter prophecies, although they perform an act of thought, nevertheless we deny that saying what they said and doing what they did was up to them. Nor is it a result of desire. Hence certain thoughts and certain affections are not under our control.

> διὸ καὶ τοὺς ἐνθουσιῶντας καὶ προλέγοντας, καίπερ διανοίας ἔργον ποιοῦντας, ὅμως οὐ φαμεν ἐφ᾽ αὑτοῖς εἶναι, οὔτ᾽ εἰπεῖν ἃ εἶπον, οὔτε πρᾶξαι ἃ ἔπραξαν. ἀλλὰ μὴν οὐδὲ δι᾽ ἐπιθυμίαν· ὥστε καὶ διάνοιαί τινες καὶ πάθη οὐκ ἐφ᾽ ἡμῖν εἰσίν. (1225a27–31)

Such inspired prophecy would include divinatory dreams (*Div. somn.* 464a25). He maps them onto a soul function that is out of our self-conscious control and not the result of desire; this sets them into the lower levels, the terrain from which surplus knowledge will emerge.

By understanding the reference to the demonic in *On Divination during Sleep* as a reference to the impulse hypothesis, we are able to make better sense of the remainder of the treatise. After educing that simple-minded dreamers are clairvoyant as proof that nature is demonic, we recall, Aristotle next explains why some of the dreams of empty-headed souls *don't* line up with what actually happens. He does this by invoking the complexity of causal chains all simultaneously operative—along the lines of his discussions of chance—and argues that the sometimes wrong dreams of the clairvoyant were indeed genuine prior signs, but not everything that was on its way to happening turns out to happen ("simply put, not everything that was going to happen happens" [463b22–31]). As we saw above, this discussion rules out the randomness argument. There would be no need to explain why some are incorrect if Aristotle were arguing that the correct ones resulted from coincidence. But the discussion makes perfect sense via the sensitive-instrument argument. These souls do not miss out on any vibration moving through the nightly air, including those that are, by chance, overrun by other causal chains, and so do not in the end happen.

So, chance is indeed a component of Aristotle's thinking here, but not in the way the randomness argument would have it. Rather, it is pertinent to the reality that is being correctly detected during the dream: different possible futures are buried in it. For the dreamer to succeed, he or she will be required to hit the mark, to pick out from among many causal chains manifest in the present, which one will be realized after they all collide. This reading demonstrates a further link with Aristotle's ideas on lucky people and provides a richer context for why consideration of the latter for him involved reference to the former. Further, it clarifies the dice example in the case of clairvoyant dreamers. They are able, somehow, to consistently "throw" so that they strike on the right causal chain, and then produce predictive images from it. The reading also underscores an important quality of the kind of prediction that one would expect from a dream, if it were properly to count as divination. It should operate not over cases of simple prediction that, for example, could be achieved by discursive reasoning. Dreaming that the sun came up in the morning (resultant from a very strong causal chain indeed), or that children playing with a precious piece of pottery broke it, or that the Spartans defeated the small village of Leuctra, would have hardly registered as a divinatory event. Whereas dreaming of something that could not be as easily foreseen by discursive reason would. Aristotle is thickening the context for seeing such souls as sensitive instruments.

He continues, we recall, on a mechanical note. Dream visions of events outside the body come from "movements" (κινήσεις) of air that are stirred up by faraway states of affairs that travel through the still night air and make contact with the sleeper's body. These produce images in the dreamer's souls:

And in the body they produce a perception through the dream (because people also perceive small internal movements when they are asleep rather than when they are awake); and these movements produce mental pictures, from which people foresee things that are going to happen also concerning those sorts of things [i.e., externally moved].

καὶ ἐν τῷ σώματι ποιεῖν αἴσθησιν διὰ τὸν ὕπνον, διὰ τὸ καὶ τῶν μικρῶν κινήσεων τῶν ἐντὸς αἰσθάνεσθαι καθεύδοντας μᾶλλον ἢ ἐγρηγορότας.

αὗται δ᾽ αἱ κινήσεις φαντάσματα ποιοῦσιν, ἐξ ὧν προορῶσι τὰ μέλλοντα καὶ περὶ τῶν τοιούτων. (464a15-19)

The sensitive instrument is able to detect the movements; and these produce mental images (φαντάσματα) on analogy with the mental images that internal states of the body sometimes produce in medical symptomology. The images of a distant present then lead to a predictive image:

> In this way it is reasonable that common people have foresight: for the discursive reasoning of these sorts of people is not thoughtful; but just on the grounds that it is bereft and empty of everything, it is also moved and led along according to the moving agent. It is also a cause why some of those who are out of their minds foresee things, since their internal movements do not trouble them but are driven away.

> οὕτω δ᾽ εἰκὸς τοὺς τυχόντας προορᾶν· ἡ γὰρ διάνοια τῶν τοιούτων οὐ φροντιστική, ἀλλ᾽ ὥσπερ ἔρημος καὶ κενὴ πάντων, καὶ κινηθεῖσα κατὰ τὸ κινοῦν ἄγεται. καὶ τοῦ ἐνίους τῶν ἐκστατικῶν προορᾶν αἴτιον ὅτι αἱ οἰκεῖαι κινήσεις οὐκ ἐνοχλοῦσιν ἀλλ᾽ ἀπορραπίζονται· (464a22-26)

Empty-headed people are more easily "carried along" by currents of nature. They are not disturbed by "internal movements," which here refers to mental events that would be initiated by a stronger self-directed intellect, if they had one.

Now, as we mentioned above, this physicalist explanation leaves two open questions for Aristotle's account, both of which explain why he needs the demonic to finish it off. There is first a need to sort out *how* successful dreamers strike on the causal chains that actually will happen; and second a need for a clearer understanding of how these images pertaining to the present result in forward-looking visions. Aristotle turns to these questions next, and further deepens the parallels with the discussion of consistently lucky people in the *Eudemian Ethics*:

> And the melancholic[93] on account of their impetuousness, just like people who hit the mark from far away, are good shots, and on account of their changeableness the thing that follows appears quickly to them; for just as also raving men do with the poems of Philaegides, they say

---

[93] On melancholy see van der Eijk (2005), 139-68; and W. V. Harris (2009), 256

and have in mind the things that follow from the thing that resembles them, for example, "Aphrodite *aphrosunên*," [erotic love is foolishness], and in this way they string together their thoughts into the future. Furthermore, on account of their impetuousness the subsequent movement derived from them is not knocked away by a different movement.

οἱ δὲ μελαγχολικοὶ διὰ τὸ σφοδρόν, ὥσπερ βάλλοντες πόρρωθεν, εὔστοχοί εἰσιν, καὶ διὰ τὸ μεταβλητικὸν ταχὺ τὸ ἐχόμενον φαντάζεται αὐτοῖς· ὥσπερ γὰρ τὰ Φιλαιγίδος ποιήματα καὶ οἱ ἐμμανεῖς,[94] ἐχόμενατοῦ ὁμοίου λέγουσι καὶ διανοοῦνται, οἷον Ἀφροδίτην ἀφροσύνην,[95] καὶ οὕτω συνείρουσιν εἰς τὸ πρόσω. ἔτι δὲ διὰ τὴν σφοδρότητα οὐκ ἐκκρούεται αὐτῶν ἡ κίνησις ὑφ᾽ ἑτέρας κινήσεως. (*Div. somn.* 464a32–b5)

We have already met the melancholic in the discussion of lucky people; and earlier in the treatise on divination as well, Aristotle invokes them, along with the talkative, as kinds of simple people that have correct dreams. The statement here makes two points about them, via two διά clauses. First, the melancholic are good shots on account of their impetuousness and the strength of their reactions; second, they get visions of what follows from the vibrations they receive on account of their changeableness.

The second claim is spelled out by an analogy with what some men do with poems of Philaegides (otherwise unknown): they are able to see what follows by stringing together resemblances into the future. The first is harder to discern, but we gain help from earlier in the treatise. He says their vehemence/impetuousness makes them good shots. This language is reminiscent of what he said earlier in the treatise about the melancholic. The key point there is that they are able to "hit the mark" (ἐπιτυγχάνουσιν) and be successful (ἐπιτυχεῖς ὄντες) despite a stochastic context in which they face a profusion of signs of possible future events, some of which will derail others (cf. *EE* 1248a34). Once more, there is no doubt that Aristotle considers the dream images they see are indeed signs, and not coincidences (*Div. somn.* 463b26, 30; cf. 463b23).

Just as in the case of consistent good fortune, Aristotle contemplates a situation in which unthinking people gain useful insight, via a

---

[94] Adding a comma here.
[95] Following van der Eijk's suggestion; van der Eijk (1994), 100, with commentary at 327–29.

twitchy system, that steers them through a chance-inflected environment to the advantageous route. The reason is, in both cases, because the human organism is "demonic," that is, on the reading presented here, it is steered by a divine impulse toward actualizing potential toward the good, beneath our self-conscious awareness. This governs our lowest subvolitional activities like nutrition and reproduction, where our behaviors are indistinguishable from those of plants. For those whose upper-order system is lacking, the lower orders take a stronger role. Just as lucky people gain from them a certain urge toward fortuitous kinetic movement, so also the accurate dreamers pluck out which image of the many possible futures contained in the current state of affairs will be the one that happens. Surplus knowledge arises from this.

The divine is required in both cases in order to explain why (in the world) these impetuous twitches would be toward the good. It supplies an explanation for the two questions left open by the physicalist explanation: after prescient dreamers pluck out the right present state of affairs, they project correctly toward the future state. After they have picked out of the profusion of signs the one that will result in the future toward which it points, they see unfold in their dreams what follows from it into the future event. These functions allow us to account for the missing piece in Aristotle's account of dreams. Divinatory dreams are demonic because even that part of us that is just a bare natural object tends to reach for the better. Our natures as bare organisms are looking out for what is good for them, projecting into the future just as the plant's roots project toward water.

Aristotle never proposes that this system would produce any particularly profound insights. And he surely gives no license for impulsive behavior. In fact, it seems clear that the results from such a cognitive system would be of a limited nature, enabling incremental course corrections resulting in self-preservation. Some people benefit from these twitches, and while the kinds of benefits they can receive could be consequential—in pursuits where a lot is riding on the right twitch at the right time—the comparative goods that accrue from our reasoning intellects, and self-conscious deliberations—which will include our ability to understand the shape of the cosmos and our place in it, just for example—will far outweigh the value of an opportune shudder.

However, none of these considerations obscure the wondrous character of the incremental good things achievable by those whose rational impairment enables them to listen to this root-level cognitive center. We have already seen his famous expression that "in all things always, nature reaches for the better" (GC 336b27). In the Nicomachean Ethics, such a meliorist principle applies up and down the scala naturae: "But perhaps even in inferior creatures there is some natural good stronger than themselves which aims at their proper good" (NE 1173a4–5). Humans are in a state analogous to these inferior creatures in the peculiar circumstance in which their upper-order cognitive activity is impaired by a kind of double-impediment. Very stupid people have little of it to begin with, and when they are asleep, what little they have is also dormant. They are living an existence in such moments that is like the most inferior of inferior creatures.

Conclusion: Returning to the Summary of *On Divination during Sleep*

We began this chapter noting that, at the opening of the first of his three treatises on sleep Aristotle frames what is coming, and he summarizes the subject of *On Divination during Sleep* this way:

καὶ πότερον ἐνδέχεται τὰ μέλλοντα προορᾶν ἢ οὐκ ἐνδέχεται, καὶ τίνα τρόπον εἰ ἐνδέχεται· καὶ πότερον τὰ μέλλοντα ὑπ' ἀνθρώπου πράσσεσθαι μόνον, ἢ καὶ ὧν τὸ δαιμόνιον ἔχει τὴν αἰτίαν, καὶ φύσει γίγνεται ἢ ἀπὸ ταὐτομάτου. (*Somn.* 453b)

Translators typically take the last clause as referring to a taxonomy of the kinds of events a dream might foresee, rendering an English translation like this: "And whether it is possible to foresee only future events that are performed by a human, or also those of which the demonic contains the cause, and come to be by nature or from the spontaneous." The Greek surely permits this translation, but as we noted it faces fatal difficulties of sense. The treatise *On Divination during Sleep*, is just never interested in this kind of taxonomy, let alone interested enough that it might serve as a summary statement. The work above provides new perspectives on how to interpret it.

The statement centers on a stem of two binaries: the main one is between what is due to our own intentional action versus the demonic; and then demonic events are divided into what happens according to nature's purposes vs. the spontaneous. Both these binaries are of central interest to Aristotle in the second chapter of the treatise. He uses them not to discern the kinds of events dreams might foresee, but rather in analyzing the causes of the dreams themselves. The question of whether predictive dreams are a human-initiated or demonic event is emphatically answered in favor of the demonic, according to the impulse hypothesis. This sets predictive dreams within a subterranean layer of causal mechanics, which undergirds nature itself, and is decidedly not within purposeful human *praxis*. Next, the question of nature's purposes vs. the spontaneous has a context now as well. We have seen these categories to be central to Aristotle's working through of the question of the kind of people that has predictive dreams. They are identical to the kind that has consistent good luck.

We saw that, properly speaking, in the discussion of consistent luckiness, the spontaneous is what we really have at stake, since Aristotle considered the human as a bare object in nature, and not as a participant in goal-oriented *praxis*. That the question is framed in the discussion on dreams by the category of the spontaneous is in accord with this. The question of "luck" does not enter at all here, since dormant humans are obviously not engaged in *praxis*, so they are not experiencing "good luck" when they dream correctly. The spontaneous, though, is entirely pertinent.

The stochastic dimension of the future, from the interacting vectors of causation that the sensitive instruments detect, is somehow negotiated by successful dreamers. They produce consistent good outcomes over domains marked by uncertainty, while they are closer to a state of nonsentient nature than to a state of human sentience. Both the advantageous visions of dreamers and twitches of consistently lucky people are not, strictly speaking, natural; that is, they are not under the purview of one or the other principle toward motion or rest built into any particular part of the natural world. They are surplus good things resultant from the underlying structure of the whole of nature. At the same time, it is also difficult to say that they properly belong to the realm of the spontaneous (since they are not exactly an accidental good thing accruing to a natural process aiming for something else). Aristotle needs to reckon with the pair (the spontaneous vs. what is according to nature), in order to discern something prior to them both, since it is prior to the natural processes themselves. It is only because of an even more general principle, underlying nature itself, that movement in the universe, in the most general sense, verges toward the good. Something this general is, of course, present to all of us; but, because it is so diffuse, it results in detectible, discrete good outcomes only for those whose more consequential (and on balance much more wondrous) power of reason is not strong enough to occlude it.

All these considerations suggest the other possible reading of the summary of the *On Divination during Sleep*, suggested at the opening, which is also allowed by the Greek:

> And whether it is possible to foresee the future or not possible, and if it is possible in what way. And whether, with respect to foreseeing future events, it is an act performed by humans on their own, or is also among the things which have the demonic as the cause, and arise by nature or from the spontaneous.

This rendering yields a summary of precisely the main points of the analysis, as interpreted above. The logic behind it falls into place from it, and reinforces insights from it. The diagram we produced above to map out luckiness now has a final piece of information to be added (in bold; see figure 3). In the summary of *On Divination during Sleep*, as well as in the treatise itself, Aristotle recapitulates the general taxonomy that he drew to describe all events in the cosmos, including accidents. But he adds the category of the demonic in a prominent place. We interpreted the statement in the treatise that "nature is demonic" as meaning that all events in nature have the divine as their ultimate precipitating cause, in the narrow sense that the divine actuates the movement from potentiality to actuality. The summary contains provocative evidence that leans toward this interpretation as well. (And this is true whether the suggested translation is accepted or not.) The place of the demonic in the formulation "things which have the demonic as the cause, and arise by nature or from the spontaneous" leaves no room for doubt that the

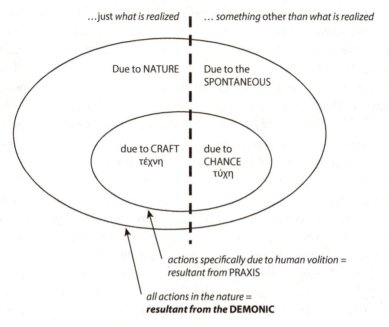

Figure 3. The place of the "demonic" in the causal backgrounds of possible events, according to Aristotle

demonic describes the causation of *all* events that happen in the natural cosmos—whether resulting from the internal teleology of a substance, its nature, or from an accidental meeting with another substance following its own end. The commentators have not made much headway on the sense of this passage.[96] To leave it unanswered leaves us in the difficult position of allowing Aristotle to make an uncharacteristically diffuse claim of divine activity. Unless we remove the divine from the demonic, something that in my view is indefensible, this provides a further suggestive testimony of the impulse hypothesis.

Moving forward from this observation, we gain a bit of further clarification on the demonic more generally. In the treatise *On Divination*

---

[96] Ross (1955) only includes a cross reference to the mention of the demonic in the *Div. somn.* 463b12; Gallop (1996) does the same, with a bit more discussion.

during Sleep, Aristotle makes the category distinct from the divine ("nature is demonic but not divine"); and elsewhere in the corpus, as we have seen, Aristotle finds the designation particularly useful to describe the heavenly bodies. Although they remain part of nature, the heavenly bodies gain the descriptor *demonic*, particularly when they are said to be in motion under the influence of their divine unmoved movers. This rounds out a consistency, noticed above, in Aristotle's usage. The demonic is his way of discussing those cases in which a particular kinetic motion in nature—the motions of the planets, lucky twitches, movements of the soul that result in predictive dreams, are the three examples for which I would argue—can only be understood by pointing to the underlying causal function of the divine within the natural world. As we stated above, this is rarely necessary for Aristotle to do since other, less remote causal structures, those in the internal teleologies due to nature, can mostly achieve good explanations.

Finally, the view of the involvement of the divine in nature—developed by Aristotle here to solve the riddle of predictive dreams—is also pertinent to a further, deeply unsettled area of scholarship on Aristotle. A short section of the third book of *On the Soul* (3.5) discusses the highest-order soul, *nous*, in terms whose ambiguity has defied consensus over the long history of commentary on Aristotle, since at least the time of Alexander of Aphrodisias. In 3.5 Aristotle speaks of a second *nous*, an "active intellect," which many scholars have taken to be a distinct region of the human *nous*, to which they then assign certain of the higher intellectual activities. This view generates a dyadic understanding of human *nous*, one piece of which is immortal, which presents difficulties for its supporters. In a striking study in 1999, Victor Caston proposed a solution in claiming that the two intellects from 3.5 belong to separate beings.[97] One is the human *nous*, the other the divine *nous* (that is, god itself) that precipitates the activities of human *nous*; and, equally, it precipitates all parts of nature to actualize their potentialities. On my reading, Caston's argument invokes the main tenets of what I have called the impulse hypothesis to make his point of

---

[97]Victor Caston, "Aristotle's Two Intellects: A Modest Proposal," *Phronesis* 44.3 (1999): 199–227.

divine involvement in human thought, and in the rest of the natural world as well.[98] His statement of the basic point is eloquent:

> In striving towards their own actualization, natural objects are in effect yearning after the godhead, that which is perfect actuality, being as such, "the one thing with respect to which all things are ordered" (πρὸς μὲν γὰρ ἓν ἅπαντα συντέτακται [*Meta.* 12.10, 1075a18–19]); and to this extent we can speak of God as what moves objects. Or so Aristotle is willing to put it in his more lyrical moments.[99]

Both Caston and Kahn cautiously qualify the "yearning" that can be claimed for natural objects, along the lines spelled out above.

It is perhaps fitting to close with a well-known citation from Sextus Empiricus, which is thought to refer mainly to the lost Aristotelian dialogues, written for a more popular audience, but the work above tells us that it could just as easily be referencing the subtle advances Aristotle makes in the *On Divination during Sleep*. He tells us that there are two things that make humans think of the gods, the stars and our dreams. Although the motions of the heavens, as a provocation toward real wonder, have received the share of attention they deserve from modern scholars, it is difficult to say the same for dreams. According to Sextus they are, however, striking enough to Aristotle to be half the equation that yields to humans their basic conception of the divine:

> Aristotle said that the idea of the gods has arisen from two origins in humans, from what happens concerning the soul and from the stars. Well, from what happens concerning the soul it is on account of those who become inspired in sleep with this and on account of their divination. For when, he says, the soul is on its own in sleep, at that time by recovering its particular nature it divines and foretells the future.
>
> Ἀριστοτέλης δὲ ἀπὸ δυοῖν ἀρχῶν ἔννοιαν θεῶν ἔλεγε γεγονέναι ἐν τοῖς ἀνθρώποις, ἀπό τε τῶν περὶ ψυχὴν συμβαινόντων καὶ ἀπὸ τῶν

---

[98] Caston quotes other work of Kahn, but not the article in question (1985). I assume Caston arrived independently at what I read as a congruent conclusion. Nor does he make reference to dreams, but he does carefully show the relevance of the *Eudemian Ethics* passages worked through above.

[99] Caston (1999), 217.

μετεώρων. ἀλλ᾽ ἀπὸ μὲν τῶν περὶ τὴν ψυχὴν συμβαινόντων διὰ τοὺς
ἐν τοῖς ὕπνοις γινομένους ταύτης ἐνθουσιασμοὺς καὶ τὰς μαντείας. ὅταν
γάρ, φησιν, ἐν τῷ ὑπνοῦν καθ᾽ ἑαυτὴν γένηται ἡ ψυχή, τότε τὴν ἴδιον
ἀπολαβοῦσα φύσιν προμαντεύεταί τε καὶ προαγορεύει τὰ μέλλοντα.
(*Frag.* 10)

This long route has brought us to a better appreciation of why Aristotle
and his students considered this phenomenon interesting enough to
consider in the first place. It pushes him into as speculative a region of
thinking on the central question of the origins of movement as we are
able to find; it opens up new vantages on the linkage between our intellects and the divine; and it shows how on some rare occasions a supplemental system, beneath our discursive intellects, can produce a surplus
of knowing.

CHAPTER 3

Posidonius and Other Stoics on Extra-Sensory Knowledge

It is a noble and beneficial thing, if in fact it exists, and one by which human nature is able to come closest to the power of the gods.

Magnifica quaedam res et salutaris, si modo est ulla, quaque proxime ad deorum vim natura mortalis possit accedere.

—Cicero, *De divinatione* 1.1 (trans. Wardle)

INTRODUCTION AND SOURCES

As we have seen, Plato and Aristotle treat divinatory insight as a curiosity, an epiphenomenon of human anatomy and cognition. For them, building a theory of it means proposing an alternative system of information-processing, paratactic to the everyday rational system. They revert to the lower orders of the soul by a process of elimination. Since divination seems not to have a place in the normal modes of thinking, they propose that some other form of insight dwells in the soul's other parts, situated closely to our creaturely selves. In Plato's case, we have the appetitive soul on occasion finding its alignment and so achieving a nondiscursive state of knowing that is beneath the ken of our rational soul. Aristotle's explanation relies on his idea of a gradient of the different levels of soul, and the sense that all these orders, even those operating below the level of self-conscious and goal-directed rationality, vector toward the good, always or for the most part, because nature itself tends toward the good. For both of them, explaining divination means tracing back to a predisposition built into the nature of the organism. Moving to the thought of the Stoics, there are many differences with these earlier ideas, though, oddly enough, given the dissimilarities of basic premises, a parallel underlying premise—that is, the logic and teleology of a living organism—plays the central role in understanding where divinatory insight might come from. Once again surplus knowledge is seen to emerge from the rudimentary impulses in a living thing.

In sharp contrast to their predecessors, the core thinkers of the early Stoic school understand the soul to be an undifferentiated whole. It is not a composite of different centers of impulse, desire, and reason, and it does not have a separate irrational side. The picture changes a bit with Posidonius,[1] the most important figure for Stoic thinking on divination, but the legacy of psychological monism will mean that the Platonic and Aristotelian territory of a discrete lower-order soul—which provided them a crucial space for theorizing about divinatory cognition—doesn't quite fit into the Stoics' thinking. However, they have a rather more robust structure of ideas to which they appeal. Briefly, they claim that we are able to know things beyond what we might expect because each of us has a center of cognition that is less discrete than simple observation might lead one to think.[2] As we will see below, in Stoic conceptions of divinatory knowing, they prominently promote the idea that the cosmos itself is a single unified animal. This notion is somewhat familiar, given the parallel conception in the *Timaeus*, a text that the Stoics use to build some of their own core views,[3] but it will require a substantial amount of unpacking to see all the ways it is pertinent to the Stoics' thinking on divination. When approaching the topic, their main unit of analysis is no longer the discrete individual human being, with this or that hidden process humming

[1] See Kidd (1999), F142–F146, with commentary.

[2] Particularly eloquent on this general view is Thomas Habinek, "Tentacular Mind: Stoicism, Neuroscience, and the Configurations of Physical Reality," in Barbara Stafford, ed., *A Field Guide to a New Meta-Field: Bridging the Humanities and Neuroscience Divide* (Chicago: University of Chicago Press, 2011), 64–83.

[3] Gretchen Reydams-Schils, "Posidonius and the *Timaeus*: Off to Rhodes and Back to Plato?" *Classical Quarterly*, N. S., 47.2 (1997): 455–76; Gretchen Reydams-Schils, *Demiurge and Providence, Stoic and Platonist Readings of Plato's* Timaeus, Monothéismes et Philosophie 2 (Turnhout: Brepols, 1999); Christopher Gill, *The Structured Self in Hellenistic and Roman Thought* (Oxford: Oxford University Press, 2006), 291–304; Ricardo Salles, "Introduction," in Salles, ed., *God and Cosmos in Stoicism* (Oxford: Oxford University Press, 2009), 3.

away, but rather the cosmos as a whole, which has its own internal activities that result in surplus knowledge for the human individuals embedded in it. In the Stoic view, the human creature amounts to a tiny corpuscle moving about inside a vast intelligent creature. Human sentience is embedded in the sentience of the larger whole, and in some circumstances the lines between the two are not meaningfully distinct.

The picture we are able to build of just about any aspect of Stoicism is more tentative than one would like. The primary sources for the most important Stoic thinkers are entirely lost. To reconstruct the views of Zeno, Cleanthes, and Chrysippus, the founding figures whose careers spanned the late fourth and most of the third centuries BCE, or of Posidonius (135–51 BCE), we are forced to rely on secondhand witnesses, who preserve their ideas under varying agendas. Even knowing the nuances between individual thinkers is difficult, since the fragments as often say "the Stoics" think x as they do "this or that individual Stoic" thinks x. Add to this that Von Arnim's definitive scholarly collection of Stoic fragments, on which the last century of scholarship is based, attributes to Chrysippus any fragment that is generally attributed to the school, and many details will be wanting. Cicero's interest in the school, Sextus Empiricus' vehement disagreements with it, some direct testimony from later Roman Stoics, along with the work of a few doxographers, save the ideas of the formative figures from oblivion.

Even despite their tattered nature, the sources leave no doubt that divination was a subject of abiding interest among the Stoics, and that it was no small concern, as it was for Plato and Aristotle, but a central one. We know as much about their views on divination as we do about almost anything else from the school. This is thanks in no small part to the survival of Cicero's *De divinatione*, to be sure, but given what we know of the Stoic corpus of writings, it's not a fluke. In fact, it is fair to say that no other ancient philosophical school took the topic as seriously as they did.[4] Cicero sets divination in "the very citadel of the

---

[4] Studies of Stoic views on divination are plentiful (something which may not be well known to the nonspecialist). Since Arthur Stanley Pease's monumental edition of Cicero's *De divinatione* over ninety years ago, the topic has become almost a subfield in itself, more often in connection with Cicero's text than not (A. S. Pease, *M. Tulli Ciceronis: De Divinatione* [Urbana, Ill.: 1920–1923]). It is therefore not surprising that the most current comprehensive bibliography on the topic is in D. Wardle's excellent translation and commentary, likely to ease Pease toward supplemental status, *Cicero: On Divination Book I* (Oxford: Oxford University Press, 2006).

Stoics" (1.10). They link the existence of divination to the existence of the gods themselves: "If there is divination there are gods, and if there are gods there is divination" (1.10). And the topic is well attested throughout the history of the school.[5] According to Cicero, Zeno (334– 262 BCE) "scatters seeds" of ideas on divination in his commentaries and Cleanthes (331–232 BCE) developed them a little more. Their successor Chrysippus (280–206 BCE), the prolific systematizer, published two works on divination, an additional work specifically devoted to oracles, and another to dreams. After these three founding figures, Zeno of Tarsus, Chrysippus' short-lived successor (head of school c. 206–c. 200 BCE), wrote nothing on it, but Chrysippus' pupil, Diogenes of Babylon (head c. 200–152 BCE), published one book on divination, though he also questioned the ability of astrologers to predict individual destinies (*De div.* 2.90). The next head of the school, Antipater of Tarsus (head 152–129 BCE), wrote two books on divination. His successor Panaetius (head 129–109 BCE) developed unorthodox views on a range of issues,[6] including divination, about which Cicero tells us that he "did not deny the power of divination but had his doubts." In the *Academica* (2.107), Cicero clarifies that this skepticism was exceptional— "every Stoic except him thought [the power of divination] was most certain"—and that it was also rather thoroughgoing, directed toward the haruspices, auspices, oracles, dreams, and prophecies. This brings us to Panaetius' pupil, Posidonius (c. 135–c. 50 BCE), a deeply learned man who traveled widely to pursue his scientific investigations, became well-known in his day as a polymath, founded his own Stoic school in Rhodes, and wrote five books on divination. He, with Chrysippus next, is the most important figure on the topic in the Stoic tradition.

From these works, some traces survive in various sources. We also have several pertinent passages from Epictetus, and in Seneca's *Natural Questions*, in the book he devotes to lightning and thunder. (The traditional ordering placed it as book two, but the most recent work has shown it to be the culminating book of the treatise.)[7] Overshadowing them all in size, coherence, and importance are Cicero's works on

---

[5] The following account is drawn from Cicero's *De div.* (1.6) and Diog. Laert. (1.147–49).

[6] Philodemus, *P. Herc.* 1018 col. LXI.

[7] See discussion, Harry Hine, "Translator's Introduction," in Hine, trans., *Seneca, Natural Questions* (Chicago: University of Chicago Press, 2010), 1 (and notes).

theological matters. His *De natura deorum* provides an invaluable overview of Stoic theology, put into the mouth of one Balbus, who presents an extended statement and a debate with representatives of Academic and Epicurean ideas. His *De divinatione* presents a wealth of material. The troubles one runs into by relying on Cicero are almost inviting compared to the problems of the patchiness and equal degrees of tendentiousness that arise in the other sources. And even though he conveys the case against divination in his own persona in book 2 of the *De divinatione*, it is fair enough to note that Cicero betrays a certain sympathy with Stoic ideas on matters of the divine, weighing in on the final line of the *De natura deorum* with the statement that the Stoic account "seemed to be more near to a semblance of the truth."[8]

Cicero structures the *De divinatione* as an extended debate. His brother Quintus is a surrogate for the Stoics, occupying most of book 1, and he himself represents the views of the skeptical academy in book 2. Cicero's main Stoic source is Posidonius, with whom he studied. We know from Plutarch that as part of an educational trip to study with various teachers of rhetoric, he visited Rhodes and attended Posidonius' lectures (*Life of Cicero* 4.5). There are also prominent currents in book 1 of the Peripatetic thinker Cratippus, whom Cicero calls "my intimate friend," and some lesser ones from Platonic sources. At some points, one or the other of these sources is mentioned explicitly, but mostly Cicero just puts them under the umbrella of a Stoic outlook, requiring some careful disambiguation of what is genuinely Stoic vs. Cratippean or Platonic. Cicero had Academic training in Athens from Antiochus, of whose famous turn away from skepticism Cicero expresses disapproval. Plutarch tells us that Cicero felt an enthusiasm for the skeptical academic views of Philo of Larissa, whose lectures, which he attended, likely inform the arguments of book 2.

From book 1 of the *De divinatione*, there are a handful of sections that are truly apposite to our present concerns, since for whole stretches, Quintus avoids theorizing and just relates famous past examples in which an observed sign correlated with some consequential future event. The

---

[8]The question of Cicero's own views on divination was subject to illuminating debate in a pair of articles in the *Journal of Roman Studies*. See Mary Beard, "Cicero and Divination: The Formation of a Latin Discourse," *Journal of Roman Studies* 76 (1986): 33–46; and Malcolm Schofield, "Cicero for and against Divination," *Journal of Roman Studies* 76 (1986): 47–65.

collecting of examples reflects a certain theoretical stance, of course, arguing on an empirical basis, that follows Stoic precedents. Cicero indicates that Chrysippus, Antipater, and Posidonius based their arguments on past examples, and that Chrysippus and Antipater did so from a great number of them ("by collecting many trivial examples").[9] Quintus anticipates the objection that correlation does not mean causation, and he concedes at several points that he may have to leave open the question of how it all works.[10] These aspects of the tradition make it likely that a certain amount of Stoic argumentation depended simply on lining up observations of successful examples, and leaning on an empiricist argument, without articulating theories to explain the background.

However, at a few places Quintus speaks directly of theoretical underpinnings (1.3–5, 64, 112–29). Since Cicero characterizes all of book 1 as Stoic, any of this material carries interest. But it is more prudent to prune these passages to a narrower set. A long tradition of scholarly *quellenforschung* has recognized the mix of non-Stoic thinking in these passages as well. I will here be taking a conservative approach and draw only on evidence that is widely agreed to be Stoic. In my view, such material is most likely to have come from, or at least by way of, Cicero's main Stoic source, Posidonius (following Reinhardt and now Wardle).[11] This puts me within a range of scholarly views on the Posidonian character of the material. On the one hand, there is the—for present purposes—quite narrow selection from the collection of Posidonian fragments assembled by Edelstein and Kidd.[12] On the other, there

[9] For Chrysippus and Antipater, see *De div.* 1.39; for Posidonius, see 1.64. See also examples given at 1.56, which are common Stoic ones, see Wardle (2006), 31. Compare Galen's characterization of Chrysippus on psychology, as relying on example after example from the poets (*De plac.* 3.2.1). The Stoics had a reason to rely on this structure of argument since they had a general sense that empiricism could work—in keeping with Aristotle and in contrast with Plato. While we human beings often fail in drawing the right conclusions from the information we gather from our senses, whatever knowledge we have must come through them (Sextus Empiricus, *Adv. math.* 8.56–58; Aetius, *De placitis reliquiae* 4.11.1–4). And sensation, by a logical soul, always involves a cognitive component of assent (Julia Annas, *Hellenistic Philosophy of Mind* [Berkeley: University of California Press, 1992]), 78.

[10] *De div.* 1.12, "I consider that the outcomes of these practices should be investigated rather than their causes," 1.12, 35, 84–86, 109.

[11] Karl Reinhardt, *Poseidonios* (Munich: Beck, 1921), 422–64; Wardle (2006), 28–36.

[12] For them, only *De div.* 1.6, 64, 125, 129–30; 2.33–35, 47, are included in the fragments (F26, F106–10).

are the more expansive views of Heeringa and Pease.[13] In any case, such difficulties are common given the state of the sources, and it is best to characterize the attribution of this material to Posidonius, as opposed to another Stoic, as probable.

There are some respects in which Posidonius differs from Chrysippus, and other Stoics; and where such differences are relevant and known, they will be pointed out. The extensive closing theoretical section is the most useful evidence for the current study. It begins toward the end of book 1, with an explicit turn in the argument, when Quintus says that it is time to address directly how divination works (1.118). He structures his treatment referencing a threefold theory of divination for which he credits Posidonius: arguments from god, fate, and nature (1.125). This division is by far the most specific and lengthy précis of any Stoic thinking that survives in the evidence, and will serve as the armature of the discussion that follows.[14]

Basic Physics

First, it's necessary to set out a few of the broader positions that inform the Stoics' understanding of the world. The Stoics are thoroughgoing materialists. Everything that can be said properly to exist is material.[15] Especially relevant for our purposes, even the divine is material. They define god as an extraordinarily fine mist, called *pneuma*, literally "breath," that permeates and suffuses inert matter, or *hylê*, bringing into being everything that exists in the cosmos. The *pneuma*, which is also co-extensive with *logos* or reason, steers the universe on its course.

[13] D. Heeringa, "Quaestiones ad Ciceronis de Divinatione Libros Duos pertinentes" (Dissertation, Gröningen University, 1906); Pease (1920–1923), 22. See further discussion at Wardle (2006), 31.

[14] Of the prior studies, particularly helpful for me have been R. J. Hankinson, "Stoicisim, Science, and Divination," *Apeiron* 21.2 (1988): 123–60; Carlos Lévy, "De Chrysippe à Posidonius: Variations Stoïciennes sûr le Thème de la Divination," in Jean-Georges Heintz, ed., *Oracles et Prophéties dans L'Antiquité* (Paris: De Boccard, 1997), 321–43; and Charles Brittain, "Posidonius' Theory of Predictive Dreams," *Oxford Studies in Ancient Philosophy* 40 (2011): 213–36.

[15] They allow four categories of nonmaterial things, which do not strictly exist, but subsist (*hyphistêmi*), mostly in the mode of coordinates attached to truly existing things—time, space, predicates ("*lekta*"), and the void.

It is, in fact, the sole active agent in the world. In speaking of this *pneuma* as "cause" Seneca tells us:

> Our Stoic philosophers, as you know, say that there are two things in nature from which everything is produced—cause and matter. Matter lies inert, an entity ready for anything, but destined to lie idle if no one moves it. Cause, on the other hand, being the same as reason, shapes matter and directs it wherever it wants, and from matter produces its manifold creations.[16]

Everything that moves, in other words, is moved by *pneuma*.

Entities in the world are understood to have a dual structure. Each existing thing, whether a rock, a tree, a mouse, or a human being, is structured by a portion of *pneuma* within. It operates like a vaporous body that coexists within the denser one, binding each thing as a whole and making it what it is. The *pneuma* blends thoroughly with the *hylê*, "through and through" [δι' ὅλων] is their typical formulation (*HP* 47H, 48C). They explain the different levels of complexity and capability that the pieces of the world display by asserting different levels of energy, measured in the degrees of tension, in the *pneuma* that structures them. The Stoics imagine a hierarchy according to these levels of tension. Starting at the low end, they assign the name of "tenor" (*hexis*) to the configuration of *pneuma* that holds together inanimate objects like stones and logs. They call *physis*[17] the *pneuma* in a slightly higher state of tension, which holds together plants and the human fetus between conception and birth. These are capable of the most basic functions of living things, nutrition and growth. Soul (*psychê*), a higher form of *pneuma*, has the powers of sensation and movement, and brings perception and locomotion to the *hylê* of which an animal is made up. The logical soul (*logikê psychê*), which is the most energetic form, holds together the inert matter that underlies the human body and uniquely manifests the characteristic of *logos*, or speech and reason.[18]

This basic structure, invisible *pneuma* structuring an entity from within and making it cohere into a single unity, holds true at the scale

---

[16]Seneca, *Letters* 65.2 = fragment 55E in A. A. Long and D. N. Sedley, eds., *The Hellenistic Philosophers* (Cambridge: Cambridge University Press, 1987). Hereafter referred to as *HP*.

[17]A specialized use of the general term.

[18]On this hierarchy of pneumatic configurations see *HP* 47O–Q, 53A–B and notes.

both of the microcosm and the macrocosm. The total collectivity of the internal structuring elements of all the entities in the cosmos is an entirely cohesive whole. The *pneuma* inside each thing is uncontained by the perimeter of whatever entity it shapes, and since even the atmosphere of the surrounding air itself is permeated by *pneuma*, it fills in all the gaps between discreet objects, making a single continuous flow of breathy, evanescent material throughout. This continuum of *pneuma* extends throughout the universe, and it is the divine, mentioned above.

The Stoics also speak of it as the soul of the world, and just as in the case of individual entities, the world soul makes the cosmos as a whole a massive unified living body. Since the macrocosm contains entities that show coherence, growth, locomotion, sensation, and even reason, its own soul must itself have all these capacities. So the degree of tension present in the soul of the world must be at least as high as the highest of entities within it. Because of this, it makes sense to them to speak of the cosmos as a living creature capable of motion and sensation, and permeated by a sensing, aware, intelligent, reasoning soul. The whole picture comes into focus in an attestation from Diogenes Laertius:

> Chrysippus says that the cosmos is a rational, ensouled, intelligent creature in the first book of his *On Providence*, and Apollodorus says it in his *Physics*, and Posidonius too. It is an animal in this way: it is a substance endowed with soul and perception. For the living creature is greater than what is not living; and nothing is greater than the cosmos. So the cosmos is a living creature. It is ensouled, as is clear from our soul's being a fragment from it.

> ὅτι δὲ καὶ ζῷον ὁ κόσμος καὶ λογικὸν καὶ ἔμψυχον καὶ νοερὸν καὶ Χρύσιππός φησιν ἐν πρώτῳ περὶ Προνοίας καὶ Ἀπολλόδωρός φησιν ἐν τῇ φυσικῇ καὶ Ποσειδώνιος· ζῷον μὲν οὕτως ὄντα, οὐσίαν ἔμψυχον αἰσθητικήν. τὸ γὰρ ζῷον τοῦ μὴ ζῴου κρεῖττον· οὐδὲν δὲ τοῦ κόσμου κρεῖττον. ζῷον ἄρα ὁ κόσμος. ἔμψυχον δέ, ὡς δῆλον ἐκ τῆς ἡμετέρας ψυχῆς ἐκεῖθεν οὔσης ἀποσπάσματος. (Diog. Laert. 7.142–43)

Studying the inclinations of the world, then, also means getting to know the wills, desires, and impulses of an exceptionally large creature whose soul is god. For theorists of divination, this is a rich terrain. A similar conception had already been present in Plato's *Timeaus* (see esp. 33c–d, 34b), but he did not develop his theories of divination in this direction. The Stoics do. Unlike Plato, they propose that the contiguous character of the whole creates otherwise inexplicable connections between things, analogous to the connections between sometimes distant parts of a single organism. Via the *pneuma*, all things are, in fact, connected to all things. This view, consistently articulated as a central piece of Stoic physics, provides a powerful premise for explaining divination. A Stoic thinker contemplating how a certain flight of a bird or cleft in a liver might link to some future event can rely on the capacious power of the divine, which flows from one point to the next, and furnishes the links in whole networks of causal chains that interconnect the cosmos. These interconnections are the central innovation of the Stoic school that is relevant to the topic of divination, and they consistently travel under the same technical term. The Stoics label this property of the cosmos "sympathy."

Sympathy

Sympatheia, literally co-feeling, is a prominent concept in antiquity, due primarily to the Stoics' interest in it.[19] For scholars working in the history of philosophy, it has, at least since Reinhardt's seminal works on Posidonius, had a twinge of the occult to it, but a half century of further evaluation has pulled back from this view, at least in regard to the Stoics. The concept has been anchored to ancient magic,

---

[19] Reinhardt (1921) attributed the notion to Posidonius, but see the reconsiderations by Josiah Gould, *The Philosophy of Chrysippus* (Leiden: Brill, 1970), 101 n. 1; Katerina Ierodiakou, "The Greek Concept of *Sympatheia* and Its Byzantine Appropriation in Michael Psellos," in Paul Magdalino and Maria Mavroudi, eds., *The Occult Sciences in Byzantium* (Geneva: La Pomme d'or, 2006), 97–106; and René Brouwer, "Stoic Sympathy," in Eric Schliesser, ed., *Sympathy*, Oxford Philosophical Concepts (Oxford: Oxford University Press, 2015), 15–35. The comparative adjective συμπαθέστερον (J. Von Arnim, ed., *Stoicorum Veterum Fragmenta*, 4 vols. [Stuttgart: Teubner, 1964], vol. 1, p. 596; hereafter referred to as *SVF*) and verb συμπάσχει (*SVF* 1.518) appear in Cleanthes. Many fragments of Chrysippus convey the idea (*SVF* 2.389, 416, 439, 441, 447, 449, 473, 546, 550, 716, 911, cited in Ierodiakou). The idea has re-emerged in contemporary philosophy among those interested in cognitive science and experimental psychology (Schliesser 2015).

but this has as much to do with Frazer's use of the term in the *Golden Bough* as it does with the ancient sources.[20] Of course, authorities on sympathies and antipathies developed the idea for magico-medical pharmaceuticals—including the likes of Bolus of Mendes (3/2 BCE?) and Nepualius (2nd c. CE?)[21]—but the notion appears more prominently in philosophical and medical contexts that provide more apposite, and also sober-minded, *comparanda*. The abstract nominalization in -ια is not commonly used until the Hellenistic period, which indicates a flowering of the concept then. We see a few precursors in the classical period, where cognate terms appear at points worthy of attention.

Plato's *Charmides* speaks of a contagious yawn via the verb συμπάσχω, and compares it to a state of confusion in Socrates provoking one in Critias (169c). In the comparison, co-feeling means a psycho-physiological action in one person triggering an identical response in a second—the point of the comparison makes clear that the provoked response is understood to be involuntary, it is a "compelled" behavior, since Plato's confusion is forced (ἀναγκασθῆναι), he says, on his interlocutor. The example marks sympathetic responses as taking hold irrespective of the volition of those involved. Each of these themes will be present in the Stoics' system. In the *Republic*, Plato uses the verb similarly to speak of an emotive state in fictional characters producing an identical state in the audience that hears the tale (*Rep.* 605c–d).

The notion appears in adjectival form in Aristotle's *Politics*, where he uses it to mark the effects of music on people. This rich and complex passage is well-studied because it provides useful evidence relating to

---

[20] See Fritz Graf's review of ancient theories of magic, where the term does not play a large role, Graf (2002).

[21] Bolus of Mendes' tract, *On Sympathies and Antipathies*, later attributed to Democritus, survives as not much more than a long list of which exotic ingredients remedy which bodily conditions, but it shows the notion of sympathy being used to describe a process in the physical world, in this case a change of state in the patient, brought about by the metabolizing of a physical cause, the drug or remedy. Later, Nepualius' work, also handed down under the title *Antipathies and Sympathies*, answers to the same description. It is entirely a list of what different animals eat or drink when they get sick, for example, a dog eats grass. After a short prologue, eighty-six sections list the behaviors of dozens of animals. This text uses the term *sympathy* as a label for the instinctual force that drives an animal toward something good for it.

the pivotal notion of catharsis in the *Poetics*.[22] He considers whether music should be understood as a form of education or entertainment. After speaking of the ways in which it delights us, he wonders whether it might do something more too, and affect the character of our souls:

But it is clear that we are affected in a certain manner, both by many other kinds of music and not least by the melodies of [the Phrygian composer] Olympus; for these admittedly make our souls enthusiastic, and enthusiasm is an affection of the character of the soul. And moreover everybody when listening to imitations becomes sympathetic, even apart from the rhythms and tunes themselves.

ἀλλὰ μὴν ὅτι γιγνόμεθα ποιοί τινες, φανερὸν διὰ πολλῶν μὲν καὶ ἑτέρων, οὐχ ἥκιστα δὲ καὶ διὰ τῶν Ὀλύμπου μελῶν· ταῦτα γὰρ ὁμολογουμένως ποιεῖ τὰς ψυχὰς ἐνθουσιαστικάς, ὁ δ' ἐνθουσιασμὸς τοῦ περὶ τὴν ψυχὴν ἤθους πάθος ἐστίν. ἔτι δὲ ἀκροώμενοι τῶν μιμήσεων γίγνονται πάντες συμπαθεῖς, καὶ χωρὶς τῶν ῥυθμῶν καὶ τῶν μελῶν αὐτῶν. (1340a8–14)

Music causes common effects on the ears of the listeners, and conveys shared emotional states. As Aristotle continues in this passage, he articulates a moral dimension with connections to the discussion of pity and fear in the *Poetics*. That this cluster of ideas enters his discussion here via sympathy is surely noteworthy. In addition, he uses the adjective to describe a connection between parts of a body (*Part. an.* 653b6, 690b5), and in the *On Sleep and Waking*, he uses the verb συμπάσχω to speak of different parts of the soul co-feeling things (*Somn.* 455a34).

Turning to the wider Peripatetic tradition, the term has a prominent spot in a section of the Aristotelian *Problems*. The author begins a chapter headed "Problems Arising from Sympathy" (ἐκ συμπαθείας; 886a25–87b7) with the same example Plato points out, of people co-yawning. This has led some to suggest that this section of the *Problems* was composed by Aristotle himself, and perhaps in proximity with

[22]For recent discussions of the passage, see Stephen Halliwell, *The Aesthetics of Mimesis: Ancient Texts and Modern Problems* (Princeton: Princeton University Press, 2002), 234–59; and Andrew Ford, "Catharsis: The Power of Music in Aristotle's *Politics*," in *Music and the Muses: The Culture of 'Mousikê' in the Classical Athenian City* (Oxford: Oxford University Press, 2004), 309–38. Translation below from Aristotle, *Politics*, trans. H. Packham (Cambridge, Mass.: Harvard University Press, 1944).

his learning from Plato.[23] This part of the text also speaks of how proximity to water provokes us to urinate, harsh sounds cause shuddering in the hearer, and the sight of someone in pain causes the observer to feel the pain. He also groups with these examples of sympathy the passing of diseases from one to another. And various medicines are said to produce the effects they do on patients by a similarity between their properties and the diseases they are meant to treat. In these texts, taken collectively, the two most prominent themes are the involuntariness and the physiological character of the activities—including urges to yawn, urinate, shudder, feel sympathetic pain, contract a disease, or become healed by the properties of a substance. It will be no surprise, given what we saw of Aristotle's views on *hormai*, or urges, that this notion comes up here as well (886a36). And, again, a physiological dimension to psychic experience is at stake in the Aristotelian *Physiognomonica*. The author claims that the body and soul are sympathetically connected with one another. Feelings of joy cause smiling and of grief grimacing (*Phgn.* 4). In the Hellenistic evidence, the notion will become particularly useful to articulate the connection between the physical body and (the by then physical) soul.[24]

The medical sciences made use of the notion of sympathy, particularly to express the interaction of bodily parts. Ancient physicians had long recognized the predictive power of signs within symptomology, and rashes, fevers, and countless other symptoms in one part of the body were well known to be related to conditions in others.[25] The Hippocratic author of *On Nutriment* uses the noun to discuss such interconnections,[26] as does Soranus, who recognizes a natural sympathy between uterus and breasts.[27] At points also, the medical treatises speak of "sympathy" between the body and soul, as when diseases

---

[23] Pierre Louis, ed., *Aristote: Problèmes*, Tome 1 (Paris: Budé, 1991), xxviii–xxxix. I owe the references to Brouwer. Van der Eijk has emphasized the continuity between the *Problems* and *Physiognomica* and the genuine treatises; *Medicine and Philosophy in Classical Antiquity: Doctors and Philosophers on Nature, Soul, Health, and Disease* (Cambridge: Cambridge University Press, 2005), 139–68, 236.

[24] See Brooke Holmes, "Disturbing Connections: Sympathetic Affections, Mental Disorder, and Galen's Elusive Soul," in W. V. Harris, ed., *Mental Disorders in Classical Antiquity* (Leiden: Brill, 2013), 147–76.

[25] See Holmes (2013), 149–55.

[26] Hippocrates, *On Nutriment* 23.

[27] Soranus, *Gynecology* 1.15.

interfere with the mind (*Hippocratic Letters* 23.10). Galen (c. 130–c. 200) in his principal work on pathology, *On Affected Parts*,[28] and in his commentaries on Hippocrates, uses sympathy widely as a way to explain connections between parts of the body.[29]

In the surviving Stoic evidence, the idea first appears in an argument assigned to Cleanthes. He speaks of the relation between body and soul, and claims that since it is impossible for an incorporeal to sympathize with [συμπάσχει] a corporeal, the soul must be a body. The soul clearly does show sympathy with the body, he says, as in the case when it is distressed when the body is diseased or cut; and the body with the soul, as in blushing from embarrassment or turning pale from fear[30] (*HP* 45C; *SVF* 1.518, cf. *SVF* 1.596). A congruent view is also identifiable in Epicurus (*DL* 10.63). In the case of both great Hellenistic philosophical schools, the soul is emphatically material, and so it makes sense that a term linking body parts in the medical texts also became more prominently used to describe the connection between body and soul.

With the testimony of Chrysippus, the scope of the idea expands mightily. He uses it to describe the whole of the interconnectedness in the cosmos via the pneuma that courses through it:[31]

> He posits that substance as a whole is unified, because a certain pneuma pervades throughout the whole of it, by which the whole is held together, is stable, and is sympathetic with itself. . . .

[28] Galen, *De locis affectis* 8.30.

[29] In addition, Galen's pharmacology, despite his own protests to the contrary, still works according to principles of sympathy and antipathy; see Paul T. Keyser, "Science and Magic in Galen's Recipes (Sympathy and Efficacy)," in Armelle Debru, ed., *Galen on Pharmacology* (Leiden: Brill, 1997), 175–198.

[30] On the argument, see Holmes (2013); and H. Dörrie, *Porphyrios' "Symmikta zetemata"* (Munich: Beck, 1959), 134–36.

[31] See extensive citations in Holmes (2013), 162, fn. 46. See Cicero, *De. div.* 2.33–34 (*SVF* 2.1211); *Nat. D.* 2.19; Cleomedes, *Caelestia* 1.1.13 (*SVF* 2.534), 1.1.69–73 (*SVF* 2.546); Diog. Laert. 7.140 (*SVF* 2.543); [Plutarch], *Fat.* 574E (*SVF* 2.912); Sextus Empiricus, *Math.* 9.78–80 (*SVF* 2.1013). On cosmic sympathy and the continuum, see S. Sambursky, *Physics of the Stoics* (London: Routledge & Paul: 1959), 41–44; and M. J. White, "Stoic Natural Philosophy," in Brad Inwood, ed., *Cambridge Companion to the Stoics* (Cambridge: Cambridge University Press, 2003), 124–52, esp. 128–33.

ἠνῶσθαι μὲν ὑποτίθεται τὴν σύμπασαν οὐσίαν, πνεύματός τινος διὰ πάσης αὐτῆς διήκοντος, ὑφ' οὗ συνέχεταί τε καὶ συμμένει καὶ σύμπαθές ἐστιν αὐτῷ τὸ πᾶν. . . . (*SVF* 2.473)

The connection between medical views of sympathy and those of the Stoics are particularly worthy of note. As noted above, the Stoics envision the cosmos as the corporeal body of a single creature, parallel to the medical context. One of the best known pieces of evidence for Stoic sympathy, from Sextus Empiricus, preserves a testimony that nicely co-implicates the two ideas:

> For in bodies formed of conjoined or separate things, the parts do not "sympathize" with each other. For example, if among all the soldiers in an army, it should happen that they all die, the one who survives does not appear to suffer anything passed on to him from the others. But in the case of unified things there is a kind of sympathy; for example, when the finger is cut, the whole body shares its condition. So the universe is a unified body. (Sextus Empiricus, *Math.* 9.80–81 = *SVF* 2.1013; trans. based on Bury [Loeb])

In my view this connection between Stoic somatism and Stoic sympathy, is pertinent for understanding what follows. It explains why a cluster of ideas that had been used to speak of emotional connection between individuals, and then connections within living bodies, can be transported to describing connections between parts of the cosmos. This provides a context for the notion of sympathy—an otherwise somewhat mysterious claim of cosmic connection—and situates it as just the kind of creative intellectual leap, grounded on scrupulously held prior positions, that characterizes Stoic thinking. It will be no surprise that when Cicero is looking for a translation of the Greek term, he chooses *contagio*, a term that already has a rich medical background within Latin when he uses it as a serviceable rendering.[32] Stoic sympathy is grounded in the idea of the cosmos as a single living organism.

---

[32] Cicero, *De div.* 2.33, 92; *De fato* 5. Cf. *De div.* 1.110 (following Falconer), though the text at 1.110 is argued over. See note 58 below for more discussion.

Posidonius' Threefold Argument for Divination

The closing theoretical section of *De divinatione*, book 1, covers 118–32. Cicero directly attributes it to Posidonius. Except for some inserted examples, like Caesar's fatal results in sacrificial divination, there is no good reason to doubt its authenticity. Its beginning is marked with a pivot in the argument in which Quintus interrupts himself, saying, "But it seems necessary to determine *how* it works" (*Sed distinguendum videtur quonam modo* [1.118]). At 125, he makes explicit reference to Posidonius' threefold treatment:

> It seems to me that, as Posidonius has done, the whole power and rationale of divination should be traced first from god, about whom enough has been said, secondly from Fate, and then from Nature. (1.125; cf. Posidonius *Aet. plac.* 1.28.5[33])[34]

Directly after this, Quintus moves into the arguments from fate (125–28) and then from nature (129–32). As to the argument from god, Quintus' statement that already "enough has been said" about it, invites a search for it earlier in the dialogue. Some have taken this to be a reference to a syllogistic argument, testified in the *De divinatione* (1.10, 82–83, 117; 2.41; cf. Cicero, *De legibus* 2.32–33), that co-implicates the existence of the gods and the existence of divination.[35] The argument is attributed to Chrysippus, Diogenes, Antipater, and Posidonius (1.84),[36] and it takes the following form:[37] If there are gods, and they do not give signs to humans of future events, then either they do not love humans, or they themselves do not know the future, or they think it of no advantage to us to know the future, or they think it beneath them to communicate with us, or they are incapable of communicating with us

---

[33] The fragment also appears at Stobaeus, *Anth.* 1.5.15.

[34] Translations taken from Wardle (2006), with minor adjustments.

[35] Wardle (2006) takes it this way, 408. Cf. Myrto Dragona-Monachou, "Posidonius' 'Hierarchy' between God, Fate, and Nature and Cicero's *De divinatione*," in *Philosophia* 4 (1974): 286–301, who conjectures that Quintus refers back to many earlier places in the dialogue (295, n. 40). See also Brittain (2011).

[36] A form of the argument may go back to Zeno as well, who links divine providence with divination (Diog. Laert. 7.149). For detailed discussion of Stoic views on providence, see Dragona-Monarchou, *The Stoic Arguments for the Existence and Providence of the Gods* (Athens: National and Capodistrian University of Athens, Faculty of Arts, 1976).

[37] The argument is answered at 2.101–2, 104–6.

by signs. The argument rules out all these possibilities, so the existence of divination is tied to the existence of the gods, and since the idea that the divine exists is a near given in philosophical accounts in antiquity, the argument holds.

Although it is clearly important, and well-attested, this is unlikely to be what Posidonius refers to in the threefold classification. First, its intent is to prove that divination exists, not to tell us how it works. It is not an argument tracing the "whole power and rationale of divination" (*vis omnis divinandi ratioque*) that his synopsis leads us to expect. Second, its positioning is not congenial. After referencing the syllogistic argument several times in book 1, Quintus makes a final summary of it to close off section 117, just *before* he introduces the new line of inquiry, saying it's now necessary to tell how divination works at 1.118. Third, there is other, more proximate material, set between 1.118 and the other two arguments that begin at 1.125, which is the better candidate for the argument "from god." Sections 118–24 address questions of divine action repeatedly, and they avoid the problems faced by the syllogistic argument. In my view, the three parts of the theoretical section run this way: 118–24 (god), 125–28 (fate), and 129–32 (nature), with the overarching statement about Posidonius as the source coming between parts 1 and 2. Some have tried to map the individual parts of the argument as applying to one or the other kind of divination, or onto just one part of the cosmos or the soul, but these are not supportable;[38] and further, in each part Posidonius makes a point of raising how his discussion applies across all divinatory types, making mention of examples from both technical and natural divination.

Argument from God

The argument from god begins with the following sentence at the opening of 118, which directly follows the pivot sentence:

> For it is not Stoic doctrine that the gods are concerned with every single fissure of livers, with every birdsong (for that is neither appropriate, nor

[38] See discussion in Reydams-Schils (1999), 471–73.

worthy, nor in any way possible), but that the world was created from the beginning in such a way that predetermined signs would precede predetermined events, some in entrails, others in birds, others in lightning, others in portents, others in the stars, others in the visions of dreamers, and others in the utterances of those inspired.

nam non placet Stoicis singulis iecorum fissis aut avium cantibus interesse deum; neque enim decorum est nec dis dignum nec fieri ullo pacto potest; sed ita a principio inchoatum esse mundum, ut certis rebus certa signa praecurrerent, alia in extis, alia in avibus, alia in fulgoribus, alia in ostentis, alia in stellis, alia in somniantium visis, alia in furentium vocibus. (De div. 1.118)[39]

Earlier Stoics, likely Chrysippus and Antipater, faced criticism from Carneades, the Epicureans and others—including one of their own, Panaetius—for having their divine principle too deeply implicated in the details of individual divinatory signs (1.12; 2.35). Their detractors characterize them as claiming that god was involved, ad hoc, in sending person-to-person messages, analogous to traditional accounts like Homer's. This invited the charge of cheapening the divine, making god into a kind of busybody concerned with quotidian minutiae. Posidonius is distancing himself from such a characterization. In his estimation, the machineries of the world are just set up such that events unfold with predictable precursors. The opening of the argument from god, then, is a limiting one. But two further points of note emerge from the opening statement.

First, the argument from god co-implicates at the outset both a notion of "predetermined events" (fate), and a statement about the way the world works (which is close to a statement about nature). It is clear from this beginning that the threefold argument will best be understood as a set of three perspectives on a single structure, rather than as a succession of treatments of discrete parts. This will be consistent throughout. Although the focus of attention will move, all three aspects will be apparent in each part of the argument. Second, in contrast to Plato and Aristotle for whom only dreams were of interest, Posidonius has an

[39] (= HP 42E); and SVF 2.1210.

overarching theory of all modes of divination in mind. While his statement about how the world was constructed, with an interlocking causal architecture, is noticeably relevant to artificial divination, he tells us explicitly it is also pertinent to natural divination: dreams and oracles are part of the predetermined setup of correlative events. This synthetic stance is interesting, especially since it will, in fact, be repeated in all parts of the threefold argument. We will see him making the claim that the logic he pursues will apply equally to natural and technical forms.

Posidonius' synthetic way of looking at these two modes is mostly unattested before him, and it is best seen as an expression of the Stoics' strongly materialist views of the soul. For both Plato and Aristotle, in their different ways, the soul is quite distinct from the material succession of causes according to which external events unfold.[40] So discussions of premonitions that arrive via a prescient soul (something in which they are both interested) will be something quite different from divination by signs embedded in the external world and interpreted by art (in which neither of them is much interested). By contrast, the Stoics' materialist view of the soul allows, and in fact requires, that the soul is now fully embedded within the interlocking set of physical causes that produce coming events. On these grounds, a Stoic argument that appeals to a consistent association between an outcome and a precursor in the natural world is not different in kind from an appeal to a precursor in an individual soul. A claim that certain birds are provoked to song by currents that also lead to certain future events, for example, is entirely analogous to a claim that certain souls are provoked to oracular utterances or dreams by such currents. It is also true that Stoic physics in general and sympathy in particular open up the opposite vantage on the synthesis. For them, just as the soul is now embedded in matter, so also the material world has a psychic dimension. Nothing in the external world is separate from the continuous flow of the world soul. This

---

[40] There is of course some parallel to be found in Aristotle, since he also sees a link between the distant causes that result in distant future events and the dream image, but it is so attenuated as to require an appeal to a deeply buried, underlying layer of divine activation in the world, and it relied on the teleology of the individual organism.

will become particularly pertinent when we arrive at Posidonius' third step, the argument from nature.[41]

So, the first point of Posidonius' argument from god tells us that the gods are not busybodies. On first look, it seems as though Posidonius is claiming that divine signs unfold without divine involvement at each step. But this would be odd, perhaps even a bit perverse, given the core Stoic idea of god as the sole active agent in the universe. Surely it couldn't be the case that every change that happens happens via the divine *except* divine signs. And, in fact, at each of his next steps in the argument from god, he speaks about how fully the divine *is* involved in each divine sign. Following his opening remarks, Quintus invokes the main argument of the section on god:

> Once this has been set down and agreed, that there is a certain divine power (*quandam vim divinam*)[42] which encloses the lives of men, it is not hard to imagine by what means those things happen which we clearly see do happen.[43]

> *Hoc autem posito atque concesso, esse quandam vim divinam hominum vitam continentem, non difficile est, quae fieri certe videmus, ea qua ratione fiant, suspicari.* (*De div.* 1.118)

---

[41] A further step along this line of synthesis emerges at a later point in the argument from god. A standard view since Plato held that true dreams were had by those with healthy souls (*Rep*, 571c–72b). Posidonius stretches this effect to the interpretive arts of technical divination:

> So just as the man who goes to sleep peacefully with his mind prepared both by fine thoughts and conditions appropriate to secure him serenity will have clear and reliable visions in his dreams, so the pure and undefiled soul of one who is awake is better prepared to interpret the truth of the stars, birds, all other signs and also of entrails. (*De div.* 1.121).

He understands a quiescence of the soul as a prerequisite for correct interpretation of external signs, and this puts the successful mantic interpreter on the same footing as the inspired dreamer or oracle.

[42] The phrase *quondam vim divinam* helps anchor this material to Posidonius specifically. At 2.33–35 (=F 106 E-K) Cicero invokes Posidonius by name using the similar phrase, *vim quantam sentientem atque divinam*, and also appeals to *sumpatheia*.

[43] C. Schäublin, "Cicero *De Divinatione* und Poseidonios," *Museum Helveticum* 42 (1985): 164–66, followed by Wardle (2006), suspects this passage as an intrusion into the manuscript on the basis of a redundancy (since the point of general divine involvement is already made), and that it represents an unsupportable variation on the formula, *vis sentiens*, that also appears in 1.118. In my view, it is hardly redundant, but it lays down the general premise, which the addition of *sentiens* later clarifies (more on this below), and a variation is not out of keeping with the variations in the formula apparent in other parts of the text (1.12, 1.120, and 1.125).

He goes on to make a series of direct appeals to the pervasive divine force that steers the universe, even in its smallest details. He considers divination by entrails, and tells us that:

> A sentient power (*vis sentiens*) which pervades the whole world can guide in the choice of a sacrificial victim and at the very moment when you intend to sacrifice, a change of entrails can take place so that something is either added or taken away.

> *nam et ad hostiam deligendam potest dux esse vis quaedam sentiens, quae est toto confusa mundo, et tum ipsam, cum immolare velis, extorum fieri mutatio potest, ut aut absit aliquid aut supersit.* (*De div.* 1.118)

The divine shapes the process at two levels. First, in guiding the choice of victim, and second in manipulations of the victim's organs. The point is made finer as Cicero continues, inserting discussion of the famous episode in which Caesar foresaw his death when a sacrificed bull was found with no heart, and the next day one was found with a liver missing a part. Since without the heart the bull could not have been alive before the sacrifice, which it clearly was, Posidonius reasons that it must have been somehow taken away, and the divine is the only possible cause of such a thing. He continues with a claim that the "divine spirit" does the same things in the case of birds (*eademque efficit in avibus divina mens* [1.120]) when it acts as the cause behind both their twitchy movements, and their impulsive screeches. It also is the agent sending signs (*idemque mittit et signa nobis* [1.121]) like eclipses, prodigious births, portentous dreams, and other strange occurrences.

These claims seem to run counter to Posidonius' opening claim, rejecting that god is concerned with every birdsong or fissure in a liver (*non placet Stoicis singulis iecorum fissis aut avium cantibus interesse deum*). A sharper focus on the formulation *interesse deum*, helps clarify. What he argues against is that each thing that happens in a divinatory moment is of interest, or concern, or importance to the divine. In other words, he is ruling out the idea of an individually oriented, ad hoc communication, which would be the result of some situation-specific desire by the god to send a message.[44] Rather, we

---

[44] This overall reading agrees with Schäublin (1985), 165.

have a pervasive divine presence that renders certain nodal points of seemingly unsystematic and aleatory events—like twitching birdsongs or movements, flitting dream images, odd births, choices of this or that sacrificial victim—into a large interconnected machine that is, in fact, not at all unsystematic. At each step, the divine is, as always, the ultimate active agent bringing about each outcome, and it functionally rules out happenstance. The divine steers the world as it always does, irrespective of the incremental good or bad outcomes that might accrue to the individual entities at the granular level.[45] As the sole agent of this large system, the divine provides the foundation for its staying organized at all levels. It undergirds the disparate events, renders what might seem a throng into an order, and so renders it predictable. The notion of sympathy is not far afield here. We see the internal workings of an organism, all of which interconnect.

Cicero's particular language yields some further insight. In the rest of the treatise, as he does in the citation above, he typically represents this function of the divine (that is, as the ordering power behind all things) via the term *vis*, which nearly all translators render into English as "force." It is easy enough on this translation to understand it as a generalized energy moving through the cosmos, but in my view there is likely something more specific behind the *vis*. Given the regularity with which Cicero uses the term in reference to the divine role in divination (esp. 1.12, 1.118, 1.125), it is likely that he is reflecting an underlying consistency in his Greek source material (again, mostly Posidonius).[46] The best

---

[45] See *Nat. D.* 2.167.

[46] Further uses of *vis* appear in book 1, each of which (see discussion to follow) is speaking of a power of *pneuma*, either an individual soul or the world soul, which will be the critical sense in the interpretation to follow: 1.6: Panaetius, the rare Stoic to take a skeptical view of divination: "did not dare to deny the existence of a divinatory power (*vim*), but said that he had his doubts"; 1.12: of both artificial and natural classes of divination: "There is a kind of natural power (*vis et natura quaedam*) which both through signs observed over a long time and through some impulse and divine inspiration announces the future"; 1.15: there is a "natural power in frogs for giving signs (*sed inest in ranunculis vis et natura quaedam significans*)"; 1.16: he speaks of some signifying power in winds and rain as a *vis*, saying he doesn't know how it works, just that it does work (*vim et eventum agnosco*), and lightning (*vis fulgurum*); 1.38: he mentions a terrestrial power that roused the mind of the Pythia (*vis illa terrae*); 1.66: contains a useful description, though without *vis*: "There is, therefore, in the soul a foreknowing-power (*praesagitio*) which is imposed from outside and which is kept in by divine influence"; 1.79, the gods do not appear to us directly, but they do "spread their power far and wide, enclosing it in caverns in the earth or fixing it in human nature" (*vim autem suam longe lateque diffundunt, quam tum terrae cavernis includunt, tum hominum naturis implicant*); 1.125: "the whole power and rationale of divination

candidate for the Greek equivalent for the Latin *vis* is δύναμις. Within Greek more broadly, this term speaks of a power, a capability, or a force, but within Stoicism it has an illuminating specific sense.

Stoic Psychology

The term takes on an important role in Stoic psychology.[47] They use it as a technical term in detailing how they understood the soul to function. While our souls are monistic configurations of the *pneuma*, extending uniformly throughout the body, they obviously have discrete modes of functioning. When the Stoics talk about these, they allow themselves to speak of certain distinctions in it. They make reference to two different kinds of taxonomies in this context. First, the sources attest to the idea of the soul having parts in the sense of its extending to various physical locations in the body. There is an eightfold discussion attested in two sources, speaking of a central part that remains in the chest, and seven parts extending out from there, one to each of the sensory organs, another to the throat, and another to the genitals (Aetius, *De placitis reliquiae HP* 53H; Galen, *PHP* 3.1.10–15). These tentacles of *pneuma* regulate different kinds of activities: those to the sense organs manage each kind of sensation, the one to the throat regulates speech, to the genitals reproduction, and that which stays in the center takes on the role of the commanding part in which executive functions take place.

From these different functions, the second form of taxonomy arises, by which they express different powers in the soul, and to label these the Stoics use the term δυνάμεις, which speaks of a power, capacity, faculty, or function. In this context, the Stoics speak of a δύναμις as a disposition of a soul that allows it to produce and regulate a certain discrete set of mental events.[48] The sources attest to four distinct classes

---

should be traced to god, fate, and nature"; 1.128: seeds are said to have a "vital power" (*vis*) of what they will produce in the future.

[47] See Brad Inwood, *Ethics and Action in Early Stoicism* (Oxford: Oxford University Press, 1985), 31.

[48] In his *Commentary* on Aristotle's *Categories*, Simplicius says the Stoics called a *dunamis* of a soul "that which brings on many events and controls the activities subordinate to it," Inwood (1985), 31, and Annas (1992), 65.

of psychic δυνάμεις: presentation (the capacity to display information via the senses); assent (the power to verify a particular appearance); impulse (a propulsion to action); and reason.[49] Following Brad Inwood's painstaking reconstruction of the details, the Stoics have a fully worked out idea of how these powers work in producing actions in ensouled creatures. Briefly, presentations arrive from the parts of soul extended toward senses, the commanding part at that point assents to the presentation or not, making a certification of its authenticity. The reasoning function then concludes what kind of action to take and sends out a triggering impulse to make it happen. This last δύναμις—impulse— will become more prominent later in the discussion. The term is the same as Aristotle's, ὁρμή, but it works quite differently for the Stoics. They use it as the general power that precipitates all forms of action in the world, a directive from reason to produce movement, and they do not favor it to describe subrational inclinations toward movement, as Aristotle did. There is a particularly pertinent subclass of it as well, we will see, that is oriented toward movements in the future.

Now, given that god is, by Stoic definition, precisely a soul, and further a rational soul, when Posidonius speaks of the way in which divination works as unfolding according to a divine δύναμις, one is tempted to seek clarification of this claim from broader ideas on how souls operate. And further, we are quite authorized to do just this by other well-attested views from Stoic physics and theology. According to the Stoics, the world is not just like a creature, from the vantage of its larger architectural organization. It also functions like a creature in the mechanics of its behaviors. In his *De natura deorum*, Cicero quotes Zeno as calling nature "a craftsmanlike fire," and he continues:

> The nature of the world itself, which encloses and contains all things in its embrace, is styled by Zeno not merely "craftsmanlike" but actually "a craftsman," whose foresight plans out the work to serve its use and purpose in every detail. And as the other natural substances are generated, reared, and sustained, each by its own seeds, so the world-nature experiences all those motions of the will, those impulses of conation and desire, that the Greeks call ὁρμαί, and it follows these up with the

---

[49] Iamblichus, *De anima* (cited in Stobeaus, *Ecl.* 1.369) = *SVF* 2.831; plus the discussion of Inwood (1985), 29–32.

appropriate actions in the same way as do we ourselves, who experience emotions and sensations. Such being the nature of the world-mind, it can therefore correctly be designated as prudence or providence (for in Greek it is termed πρόνοια).

ipsius vero mundi, qui omnia conplexu suo coercet et continet, natura non artificiosa solum sed plane artifex ab eodem Zenone dicitur, consultrix et provida utilitatum oportunitatumque omnium. atque ut ceterae naturae suis seminibus quaeque gignuntur augescunt continentur, sic natura mundi omnis motus habet voluntarios, conatusque et adpetitiones, quas ὁρμὰς Graeci vocant, et is consentaneas actiones sic adhibet ut nosmet ipsi qui animis movemur et sensibus. Talis igitur mens mundi cum sit ob eamque causam vel prudentia vel providentia appellari recte possit (Graece enim πρόνοια dicitur). (De natura deorum 2.58; trans. follows Rackham [Loeb])

So the universe works like a sentient creature in its details too. It is not just that the world as a whole has abstract wills and desires, it also has an apparatus for executing actions based on these wills and desires that parallels what we see in individuals. The world behaves with rational thinking, but also with perception and even the impulse that we learn about in Stoic psychology. I will here proceed by considering that when Cicero refers to divination as operating according to a *vis*, he is reflecting a Greek δύναμις in his source, which is a reference to a psychic mechanism of the cosmic creature. Up to this point, the most that could be claimed is that Posidonius' argument allows such a reading, but as his argument continues, in my view, it requires it. Taking into account the psychology will provide resources to sort out two further claims, one each in the arguments from fate and nature, which are otherwise impenetrable.

Argument from Fate

With the argument from fate, Posidonius links his explanation of divination to a widely-attested Stoic idea of the deterministic, and so predictable, character of the cosmos. What happens in the universe does not just come out of nowhere, it arises from prior causes.

Things which are to be do not suddenly spring into existence, but the evolution of time is like the unwinding of a cable: it creates nothing new and only unfolds each event in its order.

non enim illa, quae futura sunt, subito exsistunt, sed est quasi rudentis explicatio sic traductio temporis nihil novi efficientis et primum quidque replicantis. (*De div.* 1.127)

Stoic ideas of determinism flow from the positions we have already seen them stake out. Since nothing happens outside of the divine architecture of interlocking causes, nothing happens that is causally underdetermined from what came before. This means that knowledge of the state of affairs at one time allows for projections about what the state of affairs will be at a future time. Full knowledge would mean an ability to make perfect projections:

If there were a man whose soul could discern the links that join each cause with every other cause, then surely he would never be mistaken in any prediction he might make. For he who knows the causes of future events necessarily knows what every future event will be. But since such knowledge is possible only to a god, it is left to humans to presage the future by means of certain signs that indicate what will follow them.

si quis mortalis possit esse, qui colligationem causarum omnium perspiciat animo, nihil eum profecto fallat. qui enim teneat causas rerum futurarum, idem necesse est omnia teneat, quae futura sint. quod cum nemo facere nisi deus possit, relinquendum est homini, ut signis quibusdam consequentia declarantibus futura praesentiat. (1.127)

The argument envisions a gradient and not a rupture, between everyday kinds of prediction and a god's knowledge, positioning divinatory knowledge somewhere in between. This is another sharp difference from Plato and Aristotle. To illustrate this, Posidonius makes reference to a hypothetical figure, with total knowledge. Such a person comes up in multiple areas of Stoic thought, in other texts they call him a "wise man," who is a person who has learned to live in perfect accordance with nature.[50] The wise man is a *telos* of enlightenment, and one

---

[50] Being a wise man yields perfect contentment and a life permanently in line with virtuous action, and closer to the matter at hand, it yields a person capable of foreseeing future states. On

may never have been actually spotted in real life, but such a figure is possible as a further extension of the powers of knowing that are innate to us all. In other texts, we learn that a wise man is able to "do everything well" (*HP* 61G = *SVF* 3.560). He is the only true statesman, priest, king, orator, military strategist, poet, and grammarian. He is also the only true diviner (*SVF* 2.654). Divination, as practiced by those who are not wise men (that is, just about everyone) is offered here as a kind of concession. Lacking fully realized wisdom like god's, we find a usefulness in certain signs as indicators of the future. They are not erratic interventions into an otherwise normal course of events. The machineries of fate, and the predictable patterns it determines, make the system of signs work in the first place.

This raises a problem. Starting from the argument from fate, one might begin to wonder not what counts as divination for the Stoics, but what would *not* count. If divination is the attempt to develop a predictive system by recording what signs precede what outcomes, how will it be different from any of the observational sciences? Such a broad explanation of it risks explaining it away. The question is especially near the surface with respect to natural divination. In fact at several points in the *De divinatione*, typically when he expresses limitations on his ability to explain how it works, Cicero has his Stoic spokesman, Quintus, feel little urgency to disambiguate divination from prediction via natural sciences. Just as certain other, obviously useful and reputable sciences are unable to be fully explained, so also should it be allowed that divination is reasonable, even if one is unsure of its explanation:

> I see the efficacy of the scammony root for purging and birthwort for countering snake bites . . . and this is sufficient; I do not know why they work. In the same way I do not understand adequately the explanation for the signs of wind and rain which I have mentioned; I recognize, I

---

this figure, see recently Katja Vogt, *Law, Reason, and the Cosmic City* (Oxford: Oxford University Press, 2008), 111–60. Vogt takes it that even a wise man cannot know the causes of things (p. 128 n. 28), with reference to Michael Frede on the Stoic emphasis on the obscure and hidden character of causes: Frede, "The Original Notion of Causes," in *Essays in Ancient Philosophy* (Minneapolis: University of Minnesota, 1987), 125–50. This is perfectly in keeping with the relative stretch involved in the idea that during divination it sometimes *is* indeed possible for humans to discern causes (see below). Divination is distinctive in this way for Posidonius.

know, and I vouch for the force and the result of them. Likewise I accept what "the fissure" in entrails means or what "a thread" means; I do not know their cause. Life is indeed full of these things. (*De div.* 1.16)[51]

Although he says he does not know *why* such connections exist, Quintus knows from centuries of recorded observation *that* these connections exist.

Of course, he must make some distinction regarding divine signs, or else any kind of definition is muddled. He does so, but more with statements than arguments, as at 1.112: "Doctors, pilots, and also farmers all sense many things in advance, but I call none of them divination" (*Multa medici, multa gubernatores, agricolae etiam multa praesentiunt, sed nullam eorum divinationem voco* [cf. 1.13, 24, 111]). One might be inclined to wonder, *on what grounds* is the entrail reader engaged in something distinct from the farmer who senses rain? No help will come from suggesting divine involvement in the first but not the second. Given that the divine is indiscriminately involved in the movements of all things in the world, as the sole active agent, such a distinction has no relevance. Nor can a Stoic rely on the traditional idea of a disruption via a divine intention to communicate a message, for the reasons already set out.

Quintus' argument suggests, but does not develop, that the Stoics, in fact, did have at least an imperfect means to limit the domain of possible divine signs in order to delimit the range of divination. It shows up at the very opening of his remarks. In a sentence that has the rhetorical force of a formula, Quintus defines divination as: "the prediction of those things which are thought (*putantur*) to occur by chance" (1.9). After he references this, he does not mention it again, and when the topic of chance comes up again in the first book, it is only in a different context, in claims that correlations between signs and future events are not capable of being explained away by chance (1.23, cf. 1.71, 125). But a suspicion that the appeal to chance is in fact significant for the Stoics is confirmed by the way Cicero makes hay of it in book 2. A series of problems deriving from it gets a lavish airing there (2.14–19; cf. 2.47, 48,

---

[51] Cf. *De div.* 1.13, 15; *De fato* 11.

66, 67, 75, 83, 121, 141). The main ones are as follows: If an event happens truly by chance, what else could that mean than that it is precisely not predictable, because it is causally underdetermined, no matter what the method of trying to predict it? Second, why would the divine in particular be involved in things that happen willy-nilly? And third, since the Stoics see the world as unfolding in a deterministic order, where possibly could be the room for chance? But all these questions from Cicero-the-character in book 2 ignore two important pieces of context, of which Cicero-the-author was surely aware.

First, they ignore the *putantur* in Quintus' formulation. The definition that speaks of things "*thought to be* by chance" is a different kind of proposition from the one Cicero rebuts. It makes no claim about the ontological status of the events in question but instead about the human knowledge of the causal background that led to them. The Cicero that is the main speaker of book 2 consistently ignores the difference, and even misquotes what Quintus said, leaving out the *putantur* at 2.14 and again at 2.19. To account for the variance in the definitions used by Quintus (with the *putantur*) and Cicero (without) some have proposed that earlier Stoics, like Chrysippus, had introduced chance into the definition of divination, and having seen this position criticized by the likes of Carneades, along the lines of Cicero's criticisms, the later Stoic Posidonius introduced the *putantur*.[52] This hypothesis has limited appeal. It assumes a level of sloppiness in Chrysippus' earlier formulation, which is difficult (though not impossible) to embrace. More important, it undervalues the second piece of context on the topic of chance.

The Stoics offer a definition of chance handed down in the fragments that clarifies the matter. Several texts tell us the Stoics defined chance [*tychê, fortuna*] as a cause which is unclear [*aition adêlon*] to human reason:[53]

The Stoics say that chance is a cause obscure to human reasoning.

οἱ Στωικοὶ [τύχην] ἄδηλον αἰτίαν ἀνθρωπίνῳ λογισμῷ·

---

[52] Pease (1920–1923) thinks the misquotation is inadvertent and "due to garbled sources," but this is not credible given the rhetorical importance of the slip.

[53] Aetius, *De placitis reliquiae* 1.29.7; cf. Alex. Aphrod., *De fato* 7.

If this definition does indeed date back to Chrysippus, to whom it is attributed by Von Arnim, it is possible that something slightly more is afoot when Stoics invoke chance to define divination. Claiming chance as a cause in a Stoic context means nothing more than saying that the real cause lies beyond human reason. The addition of the qualifier from Quintus, about things "thought" to happen according to chance, adds rhetorical emphasis to a subtle point already built into the technical Stoic definition. A claim of chance indicates an observer ignorant of a true cause. Chance, in the sense of causal indeterminacy, does not exist at all.

These considerations clear up the questions raised in Cicero's arguments from book 2. The question of how a state of affairs resulting from chance could be predicted is removed, since causal indeterminacy is not at stake. Whether the divine is involved is not really at stake either; rather, the salient factor is our ignorance of the causal underpinnings. Third, when chance is a statement about the observer's state of knowledge rather than the underlying event, there is no incompatibility between chance and determinism. Returning more closely to present purposes, if divination is by definition the predicting of outcomes due to chance, in the Stoic technical sense, then divination is the art of predicting those outcomes whose causes are beyond our knowledge (that is, leaving aside the legendary wise man). It lines up without remainder with the definition of divination pressed in this study. The Stoics see it as precisely an extension of our cognition into a realm that is otherwise beyond us, or by the terms used here, as the production of surplus knowledge. There is of course a certain weakness to this argument, which is likely why Cicero-the-author, who is interested in presenting a dialogue, not an invective, does not have his brother rely on it heavily in book 1.[54] We can already see from Quintus' list above—the one that includes the scammony root and the effect of birthwort—that he has some difficulties. He claims not to know many causal connections, but he would presumably not want to make all of these into moments of divination.

[54] On this character of the *De div.*, Mary Beard is particularly illuminating, "Cicero and Divination," *Journal of Roman Studies* 76 (1986): 33–46.

Discerning the Cause

As Posidonius' argument from fate continues, a development of greater interest appears on the side of natural divination. Both artificial and natural diviners are aware of the consistently correlated sequences that warrant the taking of prior states of affairs as signs. Artificial diviners see only the correlations, not underlying causes: "Although the latter [artificial diviners] do not see the causes themselves, none-theless they do see the signs and marks of the causes" (1.127). How-ever, Posidonius claims, those performing natural divination, likely *do* see the causes:

> So it comes about that on the one hand it can be known by observation what effect generally follows each cause, even if it doesn't always follow (for it is difficult to affirm that); on the other hand, it is probable that the very causes of future effects are perceived by those who see them in frenzy or in sleep.

> *ita fit, ut et observatione notari possit, quae res quamque causam plerumque consequatur, etiamsi non semper (nam id quidem affirmare difficile est), easdemque causas veri simile est rerum futurarum cerni ab eis, qui aut per furorem eas aut in quiete videant.* (1.126)

This requires a bit of clarification. As others have shown, discerning a cause of things is something quite distinct in Stoicism.[55] What is it that Posidonius is claiming those dreaming or in a frenzy see (*videant*) or discern (*cerni*)? To understand this requires a deeper sense of Stoic ideas of a cause.

A cause for the Stoics is emphatically a material body that acts on another material body. They speak of causation always by making ref-erence to two bodies:

> The Stoics say that every cause is a body which becomes the cause to a body of something incorporeal. For instance, the scalpel, a body, be-comes the cause to the flesh, a body, of the incorporeal predicate "being

---

[55] Cf. n. 50 above.

cut." And again, the fire, a body, becomes the cause to the wood, a body, of the incorporeal predicate, "being burnt."

<οἱ> Στωικοὶ μὲν πᾶν αἴτιον σῶμά φασι σώματι ἀσωμάτου τινὸς αἴτιον γίνεσθαι, οἷον σῶμα μὲν τὸ σμιλίον, σώματι δὲ τῇ σαρκί, ἀσωμάτου δὲ τοῦ τέμνεσθαι κατηγορήματος, καὶ πάλιν σῶμα μὲν τὸ πῦρ, σώματι δὲ τῷ ξύλῳ, ἀσωμάτου δὲ τοῦ καίεσθαι κατηγορήματος. (Sextus Empiricus, *Math.* 9.211 = *HP* 55B)

It is unlikely that Posidonius means that those who are sleeping see the material bodies in a simple sense, as images in their dreams. This leaves no solution for how a visual mental picture of an object would lead to a knowledge of its causal dimension in producing a future state.

This brings up further considerations on cause. Both the body that acts as a cause and the body that receives the action, according to the Stoics, will each be held together by their own configuration of *pneuma* at a certain degree of tension. These internal natures determine the future state in a case of causation. As Suzanne Bobzien has explored, Chrysippus develops a language for talking about two classes of cause.[56] We have external causes that produce effects from the outside, and internal ones that do so from within the structure of the affected body (Cicero, *De fato* 41–43).[57] Beginning at a rudimentary level, applicable to the simplest kind of internal pneumatic configuration, Chrysippus uses the example of a cylinder atop an incline. On one level a finger, if it pushes, is the cause of its rolling, but the cylinder's own disposition, that it is round with respect to its horizontal axis, is also a cause. Just as the cylinder's rolling contains a cause built into it, so also, all bodies have built into them the dispositions that will unfold in the causal chains to come. This will be just as true in the case of bodies more complex than the cylinder. In fact, the point of the cylinder example is to argue on analogy to internal causes in humans. Chrysippus uses it to advance the case that our acts of assent are not determined only by external causes, but that our internal disposition is equally part of the story; and he references this as a ground of our being

---

[56] Suzanne Bobzien, "Chrysipppus' Theory of Causes," in Katerina Ierodiakonou, ed., *Topics in Stoic Philosophy* (Oxford: Clarendon, 1999), 196–242.

[57] For more discussion see Bobzien (1999); and Dorothea Frede, "Stoic Determinism," in Inwood (2003), 198–200.

ethically responsible, even despite the deterministic nature of the cosmos. This is of course perfectly consonant with the Stoic view of the *pneuma* as the sole active agent in the cosmos, since in each case, both internal and external, a cause is attributable to characteristics of each body, all of which are determined by *pneuma*. (The point was already made sharply in the citation from Seneca above in which the Stoics can call this suffusing divine *pneuma*, simply, "cause" [*HP* 55E].)

Looking from the standpoint of fate, the Stoics imagine the rollability of the cylinder as a kind of pent-up future toward which it is inclined. In the case of more complex bodies, with pneumatic configurations at higher states of tension, one finds analogous inclinations. To speak of these, the Stoics typically use the category of the seed, on which Posidonius relies in the next step of the argument from fate. He continues:

> It is not amazing that those things which exist nowhere are known in advance by diviners; all things "exist," but they are absent from the standpoint of time. As in seeds there is present the power (*vis*) of those things which are produced from the seeds, so in causes are stored the future events which the soul discerns, either when in frenzy or set free in sleep, or which reason or conjecture sense in advance.

> *Non est igitur ut mirandum sit ea praesentiri a divinantibus, quae nusquam sint; sunt enim omnia, sed tempore absunt. atque ut in seminibus vis inest earum rerum, quae ex eis progignuntur, sic in causis conditae sunt res futurae, quas esse futuras aut concitata mens aut soluta somno cernit aut ratio aut coniectura praesentit.* (*De div.* 1.128; cf. 1.117)

This statement comes in answer to an unstated question that arises from the Stoics' own views of time. Since (providing a precursor to Augustine's *Confessions* 11) the Stoics see an infinitesimal present and a past and future that do not properly exist, but only subsist, in the strange mode of the few incorporeals they allow (*HP* 51), an interesting problem is raised when it comes to divinatory knowledge. These sentences show Posidonius providing an answer to this question: If something has only a quasi existence (the future), what is there to be comprehended by the observer? The answer comes in the form of the seed.

At several consequential points in their thinking, the Stoics use the seed analogy to talk about future-oriented causation. In fact, Sextus Empiricus tells us that the idea of the seed is so implicated in their idea of causation that it is able to stand as a proxy for cause itself: "If seed exists, they say, cause also exists, since seed is the cause of the things which grow and are generated from it" (Sext. Emp., *Math.* 9.196).[58] The Stoics' mode of speaking about the male seed as an extension of *psychê* to the genitals is relevant here, as is their custom of talking about the underlying reason that guides the universe as a collection of *spermatikoi logoi*.[59] These are the principles that govern normal, unexceptional growth and development, as well as all the other seemingly aleatory events we considered above. The divine has planted seeds in the cosmos that operate in and through the medium of *pneuma*, and all these seeds unfold together in an interconnected whole. A poetic statement of this survives in a citation of Cleanthes preserved in Stobaeus:

> Just as all the parts of a single thing grow from seeds at the proper times, so too the parts of the world, which include animals and plants, grow at their proper times. Further, just as the particular *logoi* of the parts, coming together in a seed, mingle and in turn separate as the parts are generated, so all things arise from one thing, and from all things one thing is composed, as the cycle proceeds systematically and harmoniously.

> ὥσπερ γὰρ ἑνός τινος τὰ μέρη πάντα φύεται ἐκ σπερμάτων ἐν τοῖς καθήκουσι χρόνοις, οὕτω καὶ τοῦ ὅλου τὰ μέρη, ὧν καὶ τὰ ζῷα καὶ τὰ φυτὰ ὄντα τυγχάνει, ἐν τοῖς καθήκουσι χρόνοις φύεται. καὶ ὥσπερ τινὲς λόγοι τῶν μερῶν εἰς σπέρμα συνιόντες μίγνυνται καὶ αὖθις διακρίνονται γινομένων τῶν μερῶν, οὕτως ἐξ ἑνός τε πάντα γίνεσθαι καὶ ἐκ πάντων [εἰς] ἓν συγκρίνεσθαι, ὁδῷ καὶ συμφώνως διεξιούσης τῆς περιόδου. (*SVF* 1.497; trans. from Long [1996])

Future states, then, exist insofar as they are buried as seeds inside material bodies. By this logic, the quasi-existence of the future that would be capable of being detected in the present is the anticipatory set of

---

[58] See also Eus., *Praep. evang.* 15.20.1; Diog. Laert. 7.158–59.

[59] On this, see the concise synthesis of Marcia Colish, *The Stoic Tradition from Antiquity to the Early Middle Ages* (Leiden: Brill, 1990), 31–34; with copious references.

causal vectors built into the *pneuma* within each body. I propose that this is what Posidonius means when he speaks of a natural diviner as perceiving the "very causes," which are not perceptible to others. But a few final steps in the argument are required to get to this point.

Internal causes will vary. On one level, this means one thing will be round, another square. But they will also vary, more consequentially, according to degree of the tension they carry. Physical shape is an example at the low end of the scale of nature, exhibited even by a *pneuma* whose tension is at the level of a *hexis*. Its seedlike dimension is not much more complex than the cylinder's quite observable rollability. According to the example above, it indicates a predisposition, a future waiting to happen. Now, moving up the scale—from *hexis*, to a *physis*, to a *psychê*, to a *logikê psychê*—each of these contain more complex futures in the seeds they carry. Within the highest order, the *logikai psychai*, we find dispositions toward action that are built into them, just as the cylinder's propensity to roll is built into it. The Stoics have a well-developed set of thoughts regarding these.

Recalling the Stoic discussion of a soul's four *dunameis*, or powers, among them is impulse—Greek *hormê*—which they thought of as a movement of the soul toward something. A detailed testimony on impulse from Arius Didymus' doxography of Stoic ethics is preserved by Stobaeus (9–9a [Wachsmuth (1882), 86–87]). A careful reading of this difficult text by Brad Inwood has teased out a dozen classes of impulse in a tiered hierarchy. Different classes emerge according to the different degrees of tension in an internal *pneuma*. Instinctual movement in an animal, for example, is one thing, and movement resulting from logical consideration by a human another. Looking more closely at the rational *hormê*, there are further subclasses of it as well. For example, one class produces motion now, called the *orexis*; another, most interesting for the present purposes, is an inclination toward action in the future, known as an *orousis*. An example Inwood offers is helpful. One has a presentation of a neighbor burying treasure in his yard; one reasons (mistakenly) that it is right to steal it when possible, assents to this, and by that assent forms an impulse to dig it out as soon as the neighbor leaves town. This impulse will be a material configuration of the internal *pneuma*. This opens a rich source of predictive data buried inside *logikai psychai*, not as apparent as the external shapes of inanimate objects, but equally material and equally due to a specific configuration of *pneuma*. The Stoics imagine all of these impulses specifically as causes.[60]

Returning to the *De div.* text above, the power of the seed is expressed with the term *vis*: "As in seeds there is present the power (*vis*) of those things which are produced from the seeds, so in causes are stored the future events which the soul discerns" (*De div.* 1.128). If for *vis* we read the Greek *dunamis*, we have evidence of a formidable set of ideas in psychology being invoked here. Speaking of the seed as an expression of a *dunamis* would be the normal Stoic way of referencing a disposition of a *pneuma* by which it produces and regulates a certain discrete set of events. The seed analogy clearly makes the most pertinent kind of *dunamis* under discussion to be that toward motion, impulse (*hormê*), and not a power of sensation, assent, or reason; and within the class of impulse, more particularly, the subclass toward future motion (*orousis*). The argument from fate, then, is a discussion of the soul of the world, and its individual parts exhibiting inclinations toward future states. We recall above the Stoic invitation to consider the whole world as operating like a unified organism, even down to the mechanics. The testimony bears repeating in total:

> The nature of the world itself, which encloses and contains all things in its embrace, is styled by Zeno not merely "craftsmanlike" but actually "a craftsman," whose foresight plans out the work to serve its use and purpose in every detail. And as the other natural substances are generated, reared and sustained each by its own seeds, so the world-nature experiences all those motions of the will, those impulses of conation and desire, that the Greeks call ὁρμαί, and it follows these up with the appropriate actions in the same way as do we ourselves, who experience emotions and sensations. Such being the nature of the world-mind, it can therefore correctly be designated as prudence or providence (for in Greek it is termed πρόνοια). (*Nat. D.* 2.58)

The key pieces of the picture are already in place in this evidence, down to and including the idea of the seed itself. The universe as a whole creature experiences motions of will and ὁρμαί, impulses; and it follows these up with the appropriate actions. Since it is a *logikê psychê*,

---

[60]Inwood (1985), 53.

the world itself will contain, among its impulses, a variety of types, including those aimed at present action, or *orexeis*, and since it moves according to purpose, foresight, and planning, it must also contain specifically that class of impulses called *orouseis*, or inclinations toward future action. Even out in the capillaries of the universe, involving the most remote and intricate states of inanimate and animate objects, the world soul's impulses are present, shaping the inclinations of the whole. Analogous to the bones and sinews, material objects with their own internal *hexeis*, so too the hunks of the larger cosmos—some of which are animate, some of which are not—are all parts of the same unified creature with a much more complex *logikê psychê* suffusing it as a whole. This yields the best accounting of the evidence to explain the "very causes" that the divining soul sees. They are the impulses toward future action that are embedded in the world soul.

A final part of the story, not yet addressed, is how Posidonius proposes that the sensing (under the verb *cerno*) of the impulse is supposed to happen. That we have a transfer of information encoded in *pneuma* is not a problem. This is standard Stoic thinking. But typically, these bits of data are sent and received via the sense organs; and the soul divining by dreams or frenzy does not have functional sensory mechanics. The verb describing the picking up of these piece of information by the diviner, in each instance, is *cerno*. Its generality suggests that it will not be perception of the normal sort, and its etymology is surely pertinent. The verb *cerno* means to sift, precisely to isolate seeds from the chaff.[61] The argument from nature makes it clearer what kind of apperception he has in mind, and we turn to it next, in examining the argument from nature.

Before we do it is worthwhile addressing one question that may have come up with regard to fate. The account assembled here, has centered on an idea of fate as having as much to do with the synchronic interlocking of causes, in a large web, at any given time, as it does with a diachronic unwinding. While it may seem at variance with common notions of fate, this, in fact, perfectly coincides with a recent reassessment of Stoic fate by Susan Sauvé Meyer.[62] More often than an unwinding

---

[61] I thank Dennis Feeney for the insight.
[62] Susan Sauvé Meyer, "Chain of Causes: What is Stoic Fate?" in Salles (2009), 71–90.

rope, the sources have the Stoics speaking of a chain (*series*; εἱρμός), the term Quintus uses in introducing the argument from fate (*De div.* 1.125). Now, the idea of a chain is of course congenial with a temporal sequence, but it does require a metaphorical move (one that we so commonly make as to hardly notice it). Since a chain is an interlocking totality of elements all present to each other at a particular time, it is even more hospitable to the idea of a simultaneous interlocking system. Sauvé-Meyer has convincingly shown the many points in the sources at which the Stoic "chain" of fate is conceived of this way.[63] This is a system in which the horizontal interlinking of objects, each containing its forward-leaning seeds, will be the crucial way of envisioning sequences, and fate, which result from each immediately prior state. Each cause (that is, material body) fully embedded with all the other causes in the universe, will have its own internal seeds expressed through the active tenor of its *pneuma*.

Argument from Nature

When Quintus proceeds to Posidonius' argument from nature, we get the final piece of the picture. The argument from nature is much more compressed than the other two. The core of it is stated in one short section of text:

> From Nature comes another particular argument, which teaches us how great the power (*vis*) of the soul is when it is separated from the physical senses, which happens most of all either when people are sleeping or mentally inspired. Because, as the minds of the gods understand what each other is thinking without eyes, ears, and tongues (on the basis of this men, when they make a silent wish or vow, do not doubt that the gods hear them), so men's souls, which when released by sleep

[63] Further to this point, as Sauvé Meyer argues, the typical way of understanding a chain of cause and effect, in which an event is a cause of what comes after it, and an effect of what came before it, already presents difficulties for understanding the Stoics. Because, by Stoic reasoning, an effect is an incorporeal state of affairs expressed by a predicate (a *lekton*), it cannot ever itself become a cause. For anything to be a cause it must be a body, so it cannot be the case that they conceive of the chain in the cause-and-effect way we most commonly do, with effects becoming causes to successive effects. See Sauvé-Meyer (2009).

are free of the body or stirred by inspiration and roused move freely of their own accord, discern (*cernunt*) those things which they [souls] cannot see when they are mixed up with the body.

A natura autem alia quaedam ratio est, quae docet quanta sit animi vis seiuncta a corporis sensibus, quod maxime contingit aut dormientibus aut mente permotis. ut enim deorum animi sine oculis, sine auribus, sine lingua sentiunt inter se, quid quisque sentiat (ex quo fit, ut homines, etiam cum taciti optent quid aut voveant, non dubitent, quin di illud exaudiant), sic animi hominum, cum aut somno soluti vacant corpore aut mente permoti per se ipsi liberi incitati moventur, cernunt ea quae permixti cum corpore animi videre non possunt. (De div. 1.129)

It is highly unlikely that the claim of the soul moving freely of its own accord is meant as an out-of-body experience. There are a handful of mentions in the Stoic sources of free-floating demons—possibly the souls of the dead[64]—and nothing that speaks of people's souls temporarily leaving the bodies they structure. It's easy to understand why. Although Plato's dualism, for example, could allow such a situation to be entertained, in the image of a chariot, for instance, the Stoics have no way of doing that, even poetically or speculatively. If the *pneuma* inside of any entity somehow left it, all that would remain is the grey ash its unformed *hylê*, and this never happens. Instead, Posidonius is telling us we have a pneumatic principle untethered from the day-to-day functions it is normally required to superintend, and so in that sense, it is free to be affected (that is, to move) in interaction with the atmospheric eddies of the other configurations of *pneuma* in its proximity. Note again the verb is *cerno*, inviting us to picture the isolating of seeds, and contributing to the idea that the dreamer is gaining information about forward-leaning causes pent up within the *pneumata* of entities outside the dreamer. The reference is not as clear as one would like, but a few things are clear. We have an apprehension of information

---

[64]On Stoic demons, see Keimpe Algra, "Stoics on Souls and Demons," in Dorothea Frede and Burkhard Reis, eds., *Body and Soul in Ancient Philosophy* (Berlin: De Gruyter, 2009), 359–87; and Frederick E. Brenk, "In the Light of the Moon: Demonology in the Early Imperial Period," in *ANRW* II.16.3 (Berlin: De Gruyter, 1986), 2068–145. Posidonius had some interest in the topic. We know he wrote a work that does not survive under the title *On Heroes and Demons*.

without the senses—this is not in doubt—and so we have a reference to direct *pneuma-pneuma* transfer of information.[65]

That a power of the soul (*vis*) is again referenced here likely invokes another of the soul's four *dunameis*. We recall above that in addition to impulse, the logical soul is capable of presentation (with the powers of assent and reason rounding out the list). Here the power referred to most likely exists in the presentation class of the soul's functions. In addition to the soul's ability to gain information from the senses about its environment, we now have a soul capable of discerning pneumatic information somehow without the senses. How this works remains opaque, but within strict Stoic understanding, it would not require fairy dust to happen, just contact; and since, via sympathy, all things are in contact with all things, that problem is already solved. Another testimony from earlier in the *De divinatione*, very likely from Posidonius,[66] makes a point along these lines, and on my reading brings in reference to sympathy:

> As I have said before, the second type of divination is natural and with the subtle reasoning applied to physics should be ascribed to the nature of the gods, from which, as the most learned philosophers agree, our own souls are drawn and gathered. Since the universe is filled and packed with eternal intelligence and the divine mind, human souls are necessarily affected by their sympathy[67] with divine souls. But when

---

[65] Likely to be pertinent here as well is another discussion earlier in the *De div.* of dream theory, which Cicero attributes to Posidonius. Quintus references a threefold analysis of divinatory dreams:

> He [Posidonius] maintains that there are three ways in which men dream under divine impulse. In the first the soul foresees all by itself because of the relationship with the gods it possesses; in the second, the air is full of immortal souls on which the marks of truth are clear, as though hallmarked; in the third, the gods themselves speak with people as they sleep.

> *Sed tribus modis censet deorum appulsu homines somniare: uno, quod praevideat animus ipse per sese, quippe qui deorum cognatione teneatur; altero, quod plenus aër sit inmortalium animorum, in quibus tamquam insignitae notae veritatis appareant; tertio, quod ipsi di cum dormientibus colloquantur.* (1.64)

[66] See Wardle (2006)'s gathering of the scholarly evidence, ad loc.

[67] The manuscripts at this point read *cognitione*, which is clearly a corruption. Falconer, followed here, follows Davies, Christ, Baiter, and Thoresen, with *contagione*. Wardle (2006) and Pease (1920-1923) prefer *cognatione*, "relationship," and argue for it on the strength of the Posidonian parallel at 1.64. More strongly in favor of the *contagione*, is Cicero's testimony in

they are awake our souls are subject to the necessities of life and, hampered by the restraints of the body, are hindered from association with the divine.

Altera divinatio est naturalis, ut ante dixi; quae physica disputandi subtilitate referenda est ad naturam deorum, a qua, ut doctissimis sapientissimisque placuit, haustos animos et libatos habemus; cumque omnia completa et referta sint aeterno sensu et mente divina, necesse est contagione divinorum animorum animos humanos commoveri. sed vigilantes animi vitae necessitatibus serviunt diiunguntque se a societate divina vinclis corporis impediti. (De div. 1.110)

The idea that our souls, when freed up from their business of tending to waking necessities, are capable of being moved along with the motions of the divine, here according to the dimensions of a sympathy with the divine, brings us around to the same proposition made in the argument from nature.[68] During divination, souls acquire presentations without the senses via sympathetic connection.

This reading also provides a hint to another a part of the Posidonian argument that has been puzzling to commentators. Just after he sets out the argument from nature above, and specifies its relevance particularly to natural divination, he makes a statement that it is also pertinent to artificial divination:

And, although it is perhaps difficult to transfer this natural explanation to the kind of divination which we say derives from a technique, nonetheless Posidonius has explored this question as far as is possible. He holds that there are in nature particular signs of future events.

atque hanc quidem rationem naturae difficile est fortasse traducere ad id genus divinationis, quod ex arte profectum dicimus, sed tamen id quoque rimatur, quantum potest, Posidonius. esse censet in natura signa quaedam rerum futurarum. (De div. 1.130)

---

book 2, at sections 33 and 92, along with *De fato* 5, which are not in dispute, in which he uses *contagio* as a way to translate Stoic *sympatheia*.

[68] Several smaller considerations also argue for this statement as a parallel testimony to the argument from nature above: the ascription of the argument to physics (the investigation of *natura*), the discussion of the *natura* of the gods, along with a discussion of the physical dimension and character (nature) of the soul.

The account goes on to discuss an unhelpful example, of the tradition at Ceos of examining the dog star each year and making a conjecture from it whether the year ahead will be healthy or pestilential. Quintus reports, as an application of the argument from nature, that the light of the star functions as an instrument to read the quality of the atmosphere. If it is dim, the atmosphere is thick and so unhealthy; bright indicates a clear atmosphere and so a healthy year to come. Similarly, he cites Democritus making a connection between the observable health of entrails and the general health of the ecosystem of which they are a part. This line of thinking is obviously out of context with the prior one. With the readable atmosphere we have signs observed by the senses, whereas the sole point of the prior argument is the transfer of information without the senses. And even prior to this problem, the examples adduced for atmospheric conditions seem not to need any particular divinatory explanation. They do not depart from scientifically observable phenomena. The most likely solution here is that Cicero's presentation has missed the mark. The prior presentation of Posidonius' argument from nature makes only one point—that sometimes souls gain information from other souls (or other configurations of *pneuma*) without the use of senses—and this is not present in the examples Cicero adduces.

A short closing of the argument helps a bit.

> Why, then, since there is one abode for all things and it is common to all, and since the souls of men have always been and will be, why can they not understand what follows from each event and what signifies each event? (1.131)

This framing of the issue and the "common abode" statement bring us back to the argument from nature, with souls discerning causes via sympathetic contact with entities in their proximity. It brings us back to the common, animated creature that is the cosmos. The cosmos is moved by a unified soul that itself has *dunameis*, which include future-oriented impulses. These are causal structures buried inside the *pneumata* of surrounding entities. Some of these will be as obvious as the round shape of the cylinder. Others, like those within humans for example, will be much more complex and hidden. Under certain circumstances, for certain souls, these seeds become discernable (*cerno*), even though they are not sensible. The argument from nature, when Posidonius extends it to technical divination, displaces the idea that repeated patterns allow for inferential thinking with the much more powerful and intriguing idea of discerning the underlying causal structures that lie underneath the patterns in the first place.

This reading also solves another difficulty in Quintus' presentation of the Stoic argument. It gives a way to understand how Posidonius imagined technical divination to be distinct from empirical sciences. The information we gather in divination is different from that which we draw out from the other signs we might observe, and from which we might draw conclusions, precisely and by definition, because its workings lie beyond our regular inferential reason. This lines up perfectly with Quintus' definition of divination as "the prediction of those things which are thought to occur by chance" (1.9). As we saw, to say that an event is thought to occur by chance is to say that it has a cause that we cannot grasp. It lies outside the reach of our calculating, reasoning powers. The argument from nature has shown us how knowledge of such things typically outside our grasp might happen. It comes in a surplus, beyond the reach of our customary systems.

Before closing off this discussion of the Stoics, it is also worth the risk of stating the obvious. Taking a step back and looking at the macrocosm once more, the entire system of the cosmos is built to be a single body, connections within which are grounded in the communicative channels of the organism. When the cosmos speaks to us, it does so through a mechanism that is analogous to (or precisely is) one body part communicating with another. We are the corpuscles receiving the message of the somatic cosmos. The receptors, if you like, taking in the body's signals. Our position inside it, animated by our logical souls, makes us capable of picking up its information by our senses, and sometimes by surplus means as well.

CONCLUSION

The substantial differences on basic ontology and metaphysics among the Stoics, Aristotle, and Plato have the effect of making even more remarkable an underlying similarity. Given how distinct are the premises on which these systems of explanation are built, it is noteworthy that each school of thought, in its own way, embeds the semantic connections that link divine signs to their meanings within the teleology of the organism. For Plato, the gods grant that even the baser, corporeal side of our beings, in which the irrational soul is embedded, have a share in the good, and so grant the power of divination, as a simulacrum of reason, to our creaturely natures. For Aristotle, even the lowliest of living things, whose organic functions also hum away unconsciously inside us, tend toward the good. And we, complex and elegantly organized beings that we are, on occasion gain benefits from the innate orientation of our instinctual natures toward the good. In the Stoic universe, the links between signs and their meanings are again understood in terms of a semiotic system that is internal to an organism, and in this case, the organism is the cosmos itself. As I have tried to show, several features of the Stoic system entail a questioning of the proper boundaries of individual organisms. There are dimensions of our natures that are not any longer properly understood to end with our own physical selves. At some rudimentary level, a sliver of our functioning is now, more or less, to be understood as a behavior embedded in the behavior of the cosmos.

CHAPTER 4

Iamblichus on Divine Divination
and Human Intuition

ONE MAY ENTER THE WORLD OF THE NEOPLATONISTS expecting that
traditional divinatory thinking will find fertile ground. This ancient
school, after all, advanced ideas on union with the divine, spiritual ascent through contemplative *askêsis*, and the practice of theurgy. But the
expectation is not exactly met. It is something of a enigma, which the
prior work allows us to understand better. The most serious Neoplatonic thinker on the question, Iamblichus, will advance restrained
views toward traditional divination, and will even be ready to toss aside
the whole practice. He expresses these nuances while vigorously embracing a newly configured notion of divination, whose departures
from Classical and Hellenistic ideas come into sharper focus through
the perspective granted by the prior chapters.

As we have seen, up through the Stoics, Greek philosophers considered that divination might offer insights that were quite narrow. The
knowledge gains they theorize about are situational, having to do with
increments related to upcoming events. Further, each school, in its different way, consistently understood such insights to arrive via psychophysi-
ological systems embedded in an organism; they emerge from a physiological cusp into the cognitive world. The cases of Aristotle and the Stoics
are quite clearly this way; they embed it in the human animal and the
living animal that is the cosmos, respectively, and consider discrete information about coming events. The case of Plato is a bit more complicated since he makes divination a metaphor for sometimes grand kinds
of knowledge, beyond the incremental and situational. But as we saw in
chapter 1, in the end, it accords with this description. First, as far as the
scope of knowledge, despite his entertaining sometimes fulsome ideas,

we showed Plato to be interested in divination not because he thought it revelatory of philosophical insight, but because it was nondiscursive; and knowledge of the forms, to which philosophers aspire, must be like that too. He uses divination, in the *Republic, Phaedrus, Phaedo*, and *Symposium*, as a *comparandum* to explore the distinctive mode of nondiscursive knowing that would be required to know the transcendent forms. He does not position divination proper as a way to philosophy. This is confirmed in the *Timaeus* discussion, his most direct consideration of the topic, where we have no indication that the lower soul spends its time at night meditating on the nature of the universe. Second, the fact that Plato centers his discussion of divination on the liver, embedded in his most extended consideration of physiology in the corpus, makes a strong statement about the physiological character of divination proper in Plato's thinking.

With the Neoplatonists, we move into a different territory altogether, opened up through a particular reading of Plato. They take the discussions of the master as an invitation to understand a newly reconfigured idea of divination as much more than a *comparandum*, but as itself a vehicle to reveal philosophical knowledge on large questions—in works like Porphyry's *Philosophy from Oracles*, the Neoplatonists' commentaries on the *Chaldean Oracles*, and Iamblichus' *De mysteriis*. Iamblichus speaks about a new, "true" kind of divination, through assimilation to the divine, which yields sweeping knowledge of the philosophical underpinnings of the universe as a whole, and which is possible only through the most thorough eschewing of any bodily connection. We will see that, in the school's most robust discussion, Iamblichus defines this new kind, consistently, *in contrast to* the tentative knowledge available by traditional divinatory practices. The earlier work in this study sharpens the contrast between the Neoplatonists and the schools preceding them, and allows us to see the distinctiveness of Iamblichus' insistence both on the antimaterialist and antiphysiological nature of the true form; and the expansive, functionally limitless, reach of the knowledge thought possible to be generated. At the same time, in keeping with his predecessors, he continues to see the *traditional* forms of divination through the lens of physiology. But for him, the proximity of such knowledge to the physical world now leads him to propose replacing it with something better. The Neoplatonists' true form of divination is only possible by entire escape from the material world, and it is revelatory of the deepest secrets of the structure of the cosmos and the human place in it. This is not the kind of information that earlier Greeks would appeal to diviners to uncover.

As was argued in the introduction to this study, the domain available to divinatory insights persistently has to do with proximate concerns about specific courses of action, not underlying ontology. This is the case in the evidence that survives up through the Hellenistic period, both among philosophers and in more general, nonphilosophical Greek understandings. We simply do not find claims for this kind of knowledge in this period collecting around the figures stationed in Delphi, Delos, Dodona, or Cumae. Were they thought to have access to such wisdom, it is not credible that it would go unattested in the relatively abundant remains of evidence.

Even if one widened the consideration, to include more marginal and more expansive thinkers, like those of Magna Graecia, and the popular traditions surrounding them—Empedocles or Pythagoras, for example—the picture of divination proper would not be substantially different. The testimony around such figures styles them as savants infused with the divine, not unlike Plato's Diotima, and positions them to transcend the knowledge *anyone* else—whether diviner, healer, politician, or magician—might achieve.[1] This is consistent with the Classical and Hellenistic habit of mind that esoteric wisdom about the workings of the universe, when it could be reached, belonged to the philosopher, not the oracle.

The change apparent in Neoplatonic texts stems not just from Plato. It is also a culmination of currents of thought developing in the later classical world, since the close of the Roman Republic, when more expansive views on the philosophical reach of divinatory knowledge begin to appear. A third-century CE inscription found high on a wall of the city of Oenoanda, down the coast of Asia Minor from Claros, which Merkelbach and Stauber included as #25 in their collection of Clarian oracles, will introduce the tone:[2]

[1] On their claims to transcending the merely human abilities of priests and diviners, see Empedocles, F 112; on Pythagoras see Iamblichus, *VP* 31, 140; Aristotle, *Frag.* 191.

[2] R. Merkelbach and J. Stauber, "Die Orakel des Apollon von Klaros," *Epigraphica Anatolica* 26 (1996): 1–53; see Sarah Iles Johnston, *Ancient Greek Divination* (Oxford: Wiley-Blackwell,

"Self-born, untaught, born without a mother, undisturbable,
Unable to be named, many-named, dwelling in fire,
That is god: we are a small part of god, his angels."
This, then to those who asked about god's nature
The god replied, calling him all-seeing Aether: look to him
And pray at dawn, looking to the east.

The inscription has been a source of continuous scholarly attention, since at least 1971 (with its publication by an intrepid epigrapher who had accessed it, suspended by a rope),[3] not least because it coincided with a text cited by Lactantius,[4] attributed to Apollo, and invoked to show the way in which famous oracles were now agreeing more with Christian ideas than classical pagan ones. The first three lines also coincide with a citation in a collection by a late fifth-century Christian handed down under the title, *Prophecies of the Greek Gods*,[5] assembled also to prove that pagan oracles started to see the light and agree with the Christians. The anonymous collector tells us he extracted it from yet another text, a collection by the third-century Neoplatonist, Porphyry, called *On Philosophy from Oracles*. Several points of interest for the present purposes emerge from this cluster of observations.

Most important, in this period, the oracle is turned to for something different from advice about what to do next. It is thought to provide insight into the nature of the divine itself. This is characteristic of a change in the scope of knowledge oracles were thought to have. Also, the shared interest in this oracle among resolutely antipagan Christian commentators and the equally resolutely anti-Christian Neoplatonist Porphyry hints at the interconnection of different traditions in the evolution in thinking on divination during the period. This embrace of

---

2008), 78–82, translation from Johnston. For further consideration, see Robin Lane Fox, *Pagans and Christians in the Mediterranean World from the Second Century AD to the Conversion of Constantine* (New York: Penguin, 2006), 168–84.

[3] G. E. Bean, *Journeys in Northern Lycia: 1965–67*, Österreichische Akademie der Wissenschaften philosophisch-historische Klasse 104 (Vienna: Böhlau, 1971): 20–22.

[4] *Divine Institutes*, 1.7.

[5] This text has also been known as the *Theosophy of Tübingen*, unfortunately so named after its first modern publication, as an appendix to the dissertation of Karl Buresch, *Klaros: Untersuchungen zum Orakelwesen des späteren Altertums* (Leipzig: Teubner, 1889). For the text, see Harmut Erbse, *Theosophorum Graecorum Fragmenta* (Leipzig: Teubner, 1995), 13. For a thorough modern study, see Pier Franco Beatrice, *Anonymi Monophysitae Theosophia: An Attempt at Reconstruction* (Leiden: Brill, 2001).

the revelatory, a change for the Greeks, is visible across the post-Hellenistic Mediterranean world. To understand it presents a scholarly project of intellectual history that has not achieved clarity, and will require much more work to unravel. It will surely include consideration of mutual influence between schools of thinking otherwise opposed to each other, including developments in Pythagoraenism and Neoplatonism, Christianizing adaptation of Hebrew prophetic traditions, and Jewish apocalypticism.[6] The notion that oracles begin to contain insights of broad scope becomes widely shared.

I will begin this part of the discussion by pointing to just a few of the most prominent pieces of evidence in this change in the post-Hellenistic classical tradition: in literary works of Cicero and Vergil, in the changing Sibylline tradition, and in a few points in the history of philosophy in this period. These texts testify to a shift in ideas about the kind of knowledge divination might offer, from the incremental to the revelatory. They will provide some context for a second step, a closer look at the Neoplatonists' embrace of oracles as a vehicle for philosophy, evident in their reception of the *Chaldean Oracles* and Porphyry's *Philosophy from Oracles*. And these considerations will prepare the way for a closer look at the most important evidence, book 3 of Iamblichus' *De mysteriis*, in which traditional notions of divination are set in the role of an antithesis to this new, more expansive vision.

From Incremental Insight to Revelatory Vision

Two foundational literary texts are a good place to begin. Both Cicero's "Dream of Scipio," from *Republic*, book 6, and Vergil's *Aeneid*, book 6, articulate an otherworldly journey specifically as enabled by divination,

[6]See the fascinating discussion between Jan Bremmer and Nicholas Horsfall, in which Bremmer has been making a persuasive case for understanding lines of influence on Vergil. Jan Bremmer, "Orphic, Roman, Jewish and Christian Tours of Hell: Observations on the *Apocalypse of Peter*," in Tobias Nicklas et al., eds., *Other Worlds and Their Relation to This World* (Leiden: Brill, 2010), 305–21; Bremmer, "Tours of Hell: Greek, Roman, Jewish and Early Christian," in Walter Ameling, ed., *Topographie des Jenseits: Studien zur Geschichte des Todes in Kaiserzeit und Spätantike* (Stuttgart: Steiner, 2011), 13–34; Bremmer, "Descents to Hell and Ascents to Heaven," in John J. Collins, ed., *Oxford Handbook of Apocalyptic Literature* (Oxford: Oxford University Press, 2014); Bremmer, "Post Scriptum: Virgil and Jewish Literature," *Vergilius* 59 (2013): 157–64; and Horsfall, "Virgil and the Jews," *Vergilius* 58 (2012): 67–80.

that allows the main figures to gather knowledge on a massive scope, about the deep structure of the cosmos, eschatology, the general fate of souls, and universal human history. Scipio's enlightenment comes through the standard divinatory form of the dream and the passage to Vergil's underworld relies on the oracle herself, the Sibyl, as the critical intermediary. The two most salient prior texts, Plato's Myth of Er from book 10 of his *Republic* and book 11 of Homer's *Odyssey*, furnish well-studied source material for the later texts, and they also help illuminate differences, which come into sharper view through the lens provided by the current study.

Of course, the scope of knowledge conveyed in Plato's story of Er, the most prominent intertext for Cicero's dream of Scipio, is wide indeed. It tells of an otherworldly journey, including an eschatological dimension on the fate of souls and extended comment on the fundamental structure of the cosmos. However, Plato does not shape this episode as having anything to do with divination. While the links with Plato have anchored scholarly understanding of Cicero's text, the novelty of the divinatory component has been underappreciated.[7] Plato's Myth of Er is a story, a *mythos* (621b), from which we are invited to learn through analogy, on par with such powerful accounts as those in the *Statesman* about the deep history of the planet, in the *Phaedo* about the structure of the earth, and of the cave in the *Republic*.[8] Diviners are not cast as the sources of the insights conveyed through any of these other Platonic stories, and, in keeping with this, neither does Er gain his knowledge from a diviner. The closing myth of the *Republic* fits into a different tradition, rather long even by Plato's time, of esoteric philosophical discussion on the hidden structure of the world, by the likes of Empedocles and Parmenides, but does not make links with oracular diviners. Cicero takes

[7] See, for example, the subtle discussion, with thematic focus, of James E. G. Zetzel, "Introduction," in Zetzel, ed., *Cicero: De Re Publica* (Cambridge: Cambridge University Press, 1995), 15; and John Penwill, "Myths, Dreams, and Mysteries," in Penwill, *Two Essays on Virgil: Intertextual Issues in* Aeneid 6 *and* Georgics 4, Studies in Western Traditions Occasional Papers 2 (Bendigo: La Trobe University Press, 1995).

[8] For a standard overview, see K. Morgan, *Myth and Philosophy from the Pre-socratics to Plato* (Cambridge: Cambridge University Press, 2000); C. Partenie, ed., *Plato's Myths* (Cambridge: Cambridge University Press, 2009); and C. Collobert, P. Destrée, and F. J. Gonzales, eds., *Plato and Myth: Studies on the Use and Status of Platonic Myths,* Mnemosyne Supplements 337 (Leiden: Brill, 2012).

up this literary *topos* of the otherworldly journey, which is revelatory of the cosmos, and re-situates it into a divinatory form. The considerations of the preceding chapters reveal the distinctiveness and importance of such a move. Cicero's work testifies to a shift in imagining the scope of insight that could credibly be situated within a divinatory dream.

Odyssey 11, the most salient of the many intertexts for Vergil's book 6, provides analogous points of contrast.[9] There is no question that Vergil's text is centered on divination. The Sibyl enables and continuously guides Aeneas on his journey. In contrast, while Odysseus' journey to make contact with the underworld of course has to do with a prophet, the full explanation of this linkage is the awkward fact that Teiresias happens to be dead. To learn the answer to his question—How do I get home?—Odysseus must consult this greatest of diviners, and he is only available via a trip to the realm of Hades. In other words, access to divination necessitates the otherworldly trip; it does not enable it. In contrast to Aeneas, Odysseus' way there is not through a seer's temple with a prophet as guide, but alone and by knowledge of the secret location of the entrance and the rites required to draw out the shades. This is provided by Circe, who is not a *mantis*. When he arrives, the question he asks, and the information he gains from the prophet, is narrow and tactical. After expressing surprise to see him, Tiresias

---

[9] A fuller consideration would also treat Vergil's connection with the extended prophecy of Cassandra in Lycophron's *Alexandra*. In this work, whose dating and true authorship remain under scholarly disagreement, there is no question of the status of divination. The poem is couched as the report of an extended prophetic statement, in 1400 lines, by Cassandra. It has to do with the aftermath of Troy and looks forward into history from there. Toward the close of the poem are obscure references that Willamovitz understood to point to Alexander the Great, as well as some reference to a rising power in the West, which may be an interpolation by a later figure to insert Rome into the poem's future—though the scholarship is not settled. The poem shows a characteristic Alexandrian learning, with a particular interest in strange words and the display of oblique references to sometimes recherché places, people, and events. The extended time horizon for the prophetic statements aligns with Vergil's. But it is missing the larger insights into the structure of the universe that make Vergil's underworld distinctive. For dating and connections with Vergil, see Nicholas Horsfall, "Virgil, History and the Roman Tradition," *Prudentia* 8 (1976): 73–89; and Horsfall, "Lycophron and the *Aeneid*, Again," *Illinois Classical Studies* 30 (2005): 35–40. See the recent literary analysis of Evina Sistakou, *The Aesthetics of Darkness: A Study of Hellenistic Romanticism in Apollonius, Lycophron, and Nicander*, Hellenistica Groningana 17 (Louvain: Peeters, 2012). On potential connections with the Sibyl, see Christophe Cusset, "Cassandre et/ou la Sibylle: Les voix dans l'«Alexandra» de Lycophron," in Monique Bouquet and Françoise Morzadec, eds., *La Sibylle: Parole et représentation* (Rennes: Presses Universitaires de Rennes, 2004), 53–60.

warns him in a compact informational section, running 40 lines, that Poseidon is angry for the blinding of the cyclops, and that Odysseus should avoid the Cattle of the Sun, watch out for the suitors when he gets home, and then appease Poseidon by building a temple to him far away from the sea. While the episode as a whole surely has to do with ideas of large scope—there is an entrance to the underworld far to the West, being dead is unpleasant and all dead shades would rather be living, a handful of famously egregious offenders are tortured in the afterlife, and details of the recent past abound from individual reporters among the shades—in each case, we learn about these matters not through prophetic insight, but through the direct witness of Odysseus, standing on ground near the Cimmerians at the edges of the world, being attentive to what is in front of him. There is no question we have a variation on the form of *katabasis*—one in which the hero sees characters from under the world come up rather than descend himself—but there is no good reason to propose that Homer, outside of the consultation with Teiresias, understands the rest of this as a divinatory or prophetic event. Not all strange journeys have to do with divination.[10] Bracketing Tiresias' 40 lines, Odysseus' story fits well within the tradition of tales of famous descents, by Heracles and Theseus for example, which are not configured as journeys enabled by, or imbedded in, the cultural form of divination.

The shift from incremental to revelatory insight is equally apparent in the development of the Sibylline tradition. As John Collins has argued, and J. L. Lightfoot has expanded on persuasively, the movement from Republican-era Sibylline oracles to the later tradition is marked by a distinctive shift in the oracles' scope.[11] The crucial rupture between these two phases is the loss of all the Sibylline books in the fire that destroyed the Temple of Jupiter Optimus Maximus on July 6, 83 BCE. The evidence base for the early oracles is meager (especially when compared with the importance of the tradition), but the surviving

[10] Sarah Johnston takes a similar interpretation of this, and of necromancy in general, in Johnston (2008), 97–98. See also her review of Daniel Ogden, *Greek and Roman Necromancy* (Princeton: Princeton University Press, 2001), *Bryn Mawr Classical Review* (June 19, 2002).

[11] John J. Collins, *Seers, Sibyls, and Sages in Hellenistic Roman Judaism*, Supplements to the Journal for the Study of Judaism (Leiden: Brill, 1997), 181–97; J. L. Lightfoot, ed. and trans., *The Sibylline Oracles: With Introduction, Translation, and Commentary on the First and Second Books* (Oxford: Oxford University Press, 2007), 6–7, and 51–93.

examples from the Sibylline books from Republican times are quite different from those attributed to the Sibyl in the later pseudepigraphical writers.[12] The former exclusively have to do with particular responses to specific situations, predictions of warfare, or natural disasters. They yield advice regarding plagues, famines, or the appearance of prodigies, and may prescribe a ritual to deal with the problem. They are interested, in other words, in discrete matters of particular concern. In the later tradition, the Sibyl will speak with a new, expansive voice about all of world history, the fate of souls, and the structure of the universe.[13] Further, in a precursor to Iamblichus' approach (as we will see), the later Sibylline texts shift away markedly from the traditional way of talking about divination, that is, with terminology cognate with *mantikê*. As Lightfoot has pointed out, instead of calling her a μάντις, the later texts much more regularly refer to her as a προφῆτις. With respect to the verbs used, the prophetess describes what she does as προφητεύομαι rather than μαντεύομαι. And when μάντις vocabulary is used (just twice), just as in the case of Iamblichus, it is joined with the further adjective "true" (4.3; 11.316–17), as if to signal that the term alone could be misconstrued for something false.[14] This evolution in terminology is no doubt influenced by currents of thinking from the Eastern Mediterranean that come into view in the texts of the Septuagint and the New Testament, and reflect the ties of the later Sibylline texts to Jewish and early Christian traditions. The biblical texts generally avoid μάντις and μαντεύομαι, except in cases of false prophets,[15] whereas προφῆτις and προφητεύομαι are the preferred language for true prophecy. These developments within the Sibylline tradition fit perfectly under the arc being described here, and suggest the historical importance of Jewish and Christian notions of prophecy in changing ideas about divination visible in pagan thinkers.[16]

---

[12] Collins (1997), 182–84.

[13] The thorough discussion in Collins and Lightfoot makes the case persuasively.

[14] Lightfoot (2007), 20–21.

[15] See, for example, the case of the Witch of Endor at 1 Sam 28:8 and the Gentile slave girl possessed by a demon at Acts 16:16. Citations taken from, and further discussion and references in, Lightfoot (2007), 21.

[16] The irony that Christian prophecy, against which a Neoplatonist like Porphyry was a savage critic, could be an important influence on Neoplatonic ideas fades a bit as we continue to see the ways in which the traditions mutually interact. A congruent line of scholarship has long

Before turning to the Neoplatonists, there are other developments within the philosophical writings of the first centuries of the Roman Imperial period, in which one can discern innovations testifying to a movement from incremental knowledge to a preoccupation with revelation of philosophical insight. Plutarch, for example, writes extensively on divinatory topics, from his position as a priest at Delphi itself. As scholars have discussed, it is surely significant that he decides to set philosophical discussion of many wide-ranging issues in the context of the oracle, using the temple site as a background for a diffuse conversation, on topics ranging from the age of the earth to the fate of souls, in several dialogues (*On the Obsolescence of Oracles, On the Oracle at Delphi, On the E*, and *Isis and Osiris*).[17] Importantly, though, in this case, the linkage between the philosophical insights of the discussants and the oracle is limited to setting. The oracle is not positioned as a font of such wisdom. Added to this, the references to divination in the *Lives*, discuss poignant instances of foreshadowing by portents and oracles, which are describable as instances of incremental insight about the proximate future, rather than any larger view.[18]

More movement toward expansiveness of divinatory insight comes in a text of Apuleius, *On the God of Socrates*. He tells us that Socrates' *daimôn* is among a set of intermediate divinities, with characteristics he maps onto Middle Platonist metaphysics, in the realm between humans and gods. They are capable of conveying profound wisdom to those humans that can lead lives conducive to such potential insight ("omnia visitet, omnia intellegat" [*De deo Soc.* 16.25]). A revelatory character to divination is even more apparent in the hagiographic biography of a first-century Pythagorean in Philostratus' *Life of Apollonius of*

---

understood the importance of Neoplatonic influence on Christian thinkers like Augustine and Pseudo-Dionysius, but we have only begun to reckon with influences in the reverse direction. The case of divination is a likely example. See, for example, Peter Brown, *Augustine of Hippo* (Berkeley: University of California Press, 1967), 79–92; and Peter Struck, "Pagan and Christian Theurgies: Iamblichus, Pseudo–Dionysius, Religion and Magic in Late Antiquity," *Ancient World* 32.2 (2001): 25–38.

[17] See Crystal Addey, *Divination and Theurgy in Neoplatonism: Oracles of the Gods* (Surrey: Ashgate, 2014), 15; Lane Fox (2006), 185.

[18] Frederick Brenk's thorough treatment makes this clear. See Brenk, *In Mist Apparelled: Religious Themes in Plutarch's Moralia and Lives* (Leiden: Brill, 1977), 184–213. Plutarch also conveys several views about how the oracle works, in line with questions motivating the present study, though less trenchant than those focused on here (ibid.).

Tyana. This understudied text attests to a new way of understanding divination.[19] It follows Apollonius' life in the mode of a holy man, traveling across the Mediterranean world, and surpassing the wisdom and spiritual power of the wisest representatives of cultures renowned among the Romans for their acumen in such matters. He outdoes the Brahmans, Egyptians, and Babylonians. He has foresight over matters large and small, but denies that what he is doing should count as divination (*VA* 4.44). The insights he receives, he prefers to categorize under the category of *prognôsis* (a category we will meet again in Iamblichus), a cognitive capacity emerging from wisdom, capable of revealing philosophical wisdom as well as incremental insight. Apollonius' mode supersedes traditional mantic practices, and the wisdom he gains derives from his closeness to the gods.[20] By the time we reach Iamblichus, the knowledge available by his own distinctive form of divination will seem to him so different from that derivable by traditional techniques as to cause him to propose a rupture. The old techniques will be seen to produce strictly limited results, and a new "true" or "authentic" form of revelatory insight will offer expansive wisdom, which, further, has a soteriological power.

PHILOSOPHY FROM ORACLES AMONG THE NEOPLATONISTS

The *Chaldean Oracles*, a collection of uncertain provenance, joins the core Platonic dialogues as a central text of interest for Neoplatonists from Porphyry onward.[21] In the late second century CE, the gods had handed the oracles down to Julian the Chaldean and his son, Julian the Theurgist. It is unknown whether the designation Chaldean is meant to refer to geographical origin or the region's reputation for mystical

---

[19] This is the compelling view of Roshan Abraham, in "Magic and Religious Authority in Philostratus' *Life of Apollonius of Tyana*" (Ph.D. dissertation, University of Pennsylvania, 2009). On the topic of divination in this text, see also V. Fromentin, "La divination dans la *Vie d'Apollonios de Tyane* de Philostrate," *Etrusca Disciplina* 8 (1997): 71–79.

[20] See Abraham (2009), 82–131.

[21] See E. R. Dodds, "Theurgy and Its Relationship to Neoplatonism," *Journal of Roman Studies* 37 (1947): 57–60.

wisdom and magic.[22] We have access to them in fragments in quotations by later figures.[23] The oracles are written in hexameters, and are mainly short and enigmatic expressions on ontology, cosmology, and metaphysics. They are informed by Platonism, on a par with other collections of texts on esoteric wisdom of the period, including the Hermetic corpus and the writings of the Gnostics. Fragment 5 is a characteristic example:

> For the first transcendent fire does not enclose its own power in matter by means of works, but by Intellect. For intellect derived from intellect is the craftsman of the fiery cosmos.[24]

> οὐ γὰρ ἐς ὕλην
> πῦρ ἐπέκεινα τὸ πρῶτον ἐὴν δύναμιν κατακλείει
> ἔργοις, ἀλλὰ νόῳ· νοῦ γὰρ νόος ἐστὶν ὁ κόσμου
> τεχνίτης πυρίου (= Proclus, *In Tim.* 2, 57.30–58.3)

This oracle survives because the fifth-century Neoplatonist Proclus finds that it helps him discern the true meaning in a part of the *Timaeus* (32c–d). There Plato speaks of the four elements pervading the universe as a whole, without any part of them external to the created universe. For Proclus this raises a question. The *Timaeus* text seems not to consider that material elements have higher-order dimensions, their forms, that would be external to the created world. Proclus discovers interpretive help in the wisdom the Chaldean oracle provides. When the *Timaeus* speaks of nothing external, it must be speaking of it in the way the oracle does. That is, it must mean nothing is external specifically with respect to the intellectual dimension of the universe, not with respect to its material dimension. This is characteristic of the kinds of insights the Neoplatonists find in the *Oracles*. Their use of the collection attests to a phenomenon, parallel to the development of the Sibylline tradition, in which oracles are understood to deliver wide-ranging wisdom, of a philosophical inclination. The mysterious compression

---

[22] For the arguments, see J. Bidez, *La Vie de L'empereur Julien* (Paris: Les Belles Lettres, 1930), 75, who suggests a geographic origin for the father; and H.-D. Saffrey, "Les Néoplatoniciens et les Oracles Chaldaïques," *Revue des etudes anciennes* 26 (1981): 225, who attributes the name to its connection with magic, and proposes a Syrian provenance.

[23] The most thorough modern treatment remains Ruth Majercik, *The Chaldean Oracles: Text, Translation, and Commentary* (Leiden: Brill, 1989).

[24] Translation by Majercik (1989).

in their style provoked the likes of Porphyry, Iamblichus, and Proclus to interpret them expansively, reading them through the lenses of a Plotinian-inspired Neoplatonism.

In a similar vein, we also find Porphyry's text *On Philosophy from Oracles*.[25] Porphyry wrote some sixty works; and left perhaps his most profound mark on the history of philosophy as the editor of Plotinus' *Enneads*. Few of Porphyry's own works survive except in fragments, and this is the case with *Philosophy from Oracles*. Mainly in Christian opponents, these fragments show it as an assemblage of oracles said to be delivered by Hecate, Hermes, and Serapis, as well as by Apollo.[26] The following example, in dactylic hexameter, is characteristic:[27]

> And again, when asked for what reason they say there are many heavens, [Apollo] uttered these things:

> In the entire world there is one circle, but it is carried
> With seven belts on the starry roads,
> Which Chaldeans and the enviable Hebrews
> Named heavenly, to go on a sevenfold circuit.

> καὶ πάλιν ἐρωτηθεὶς τίνι λόγῳ πολλοὺς λέγουσιν οὐρανούς, ἔχρησε τάδε·

> εἷς ἐν παντὶ πέλει κόσμου κύκλος, ἀλλὰ σὺν ἑπτὰ
> ζώναισιν πεφόρηται ἐς ἀστερόεντα κέλευθα,
> ἃς δὴ Χαλδαῖοι καὶ ἀριζήλωτοι Ἑβραῖοι
> οὐρανίας ὀνόμηναν, ἐς ἑβδόματον δρόμον ἕρπειν. (Smith 324F)

Porphyry cites such oracles, and then explicates them, finding links between them and Neoplatonic principles. From this work, it is evident that Porphyry, whose hard-nosed rationalism is evident in his *Letter to Anebo* and his work *Against the Christians*, thought oracles competent in philosophical questions. This has presented a challenge to modern scholars. A standard narrative of the last century made a chronological

---

[25] A. Smith, *Porphyrius: Fragmenta* (Leipzig: Teubner, 1993), 351–407.

[26] For further consideration, see Aaron Johnson, "Arbiter of the Oracular: Reading Religion in Porphyry of Tyre," in Andrew Cain and Noel Lenski, eds., *The Power of Religion in Late Antiquity* (Surrey: Ashgate, 2009), 103–15. And for Porphyry in general, see Aaron Johnson, *Religion and Identity in Porphyry of Tyre: The Limits of Hellenism in Late Antiquity*, Greek Culture in the Roman World (Cambridge: Cambridge University Press, 2013).

[27] Translation from Johnson (2013), 339.

reckoning. Porphyry was thought to have dabbled in this religious material early in his life, but then after coming under the influence of Plotinus is said to have left such things behind and become a more serious philosopher.[28] There are problems with this. It is too quick to elide an interest in religion with superstition, and, more important, we have no firm evidence for the chronological sequence of his writing, so such arguments are unable to avoid some degree of circularity. More recent appraisals have explored the view that Porphyry's rationalism may well have been compatible with his interest in things like oracles and the question of the proper orientation toward the divine.[29] It is undoubtedly true that Porphyry's *Letter to Anebo* takes strong views against most any kind of ritual activity directed toward the divine.[30] Manipulation of anything material is thought to lead practitioners inevitably away from, not toward, the divine. The current study makes more comprehensible how such views could be consistent with the project of the *Philosophy from Oracles*. Given the general currents within the later classical world, and among the Neoplatonists in particular, a new kind of nonmaterial, nonphysiological divination, which is based on direct contact with the divine, not on ritual manipulation of materials, now comes to supplant traditional views of divination. Porphyry's *Philosophy from Oracles* is in accord with this new form, and is also compatible with the vigorous antiritualist, contemplationist program of his *Letter to Anebo*.

IAMBLICHUS' *DE MYSTERIIS*

Iamblichus, of the late third and early fourth century, hands down the most thorough treatment of divination we have from his school, in book 3 of the *De mysteriis*. This work is many things. For Ficino, who gave it the title by which it is still known, it was a kind of key to unraveling the secrets of the cosmos. For E. R. Dodds in his Sather lectures of

---

[28] The *locus classicus* is J. Bidez, *La vie de Porphyre: Le philosophe néo-Platonicien* (Leibner: Teubner, 1913).

[29] Addey (2014); and see further Johnson (2009), and especially Johnson (2013), 102–45.

[30] The polemical character of the work has recently been recast as a willing contribution to making a dialectic about the topic. See Addey (2014).

1950, it was, pungently, "a manifesto of irrationalism."[31] Whatever else it is, it is also a dense meditation on the question of links between the mundane and divine worlds. To understand what is at stake for the topic of divination in this work, we require some further reference to the larger philosophical conversation under scrutiny here. With all their differences, the prior theories we have examined converge on the proposal that bodies have certain receptivities, which allow them to function as circuitry for a subterranean mode of signaling, inflected by a (more or less) divine element. This question, the mix of the corporeal and divine dimensions of how we know through divination, is precisely what is at stake in *De mysteriis*, book 3. Like Plato, Aristotle, and the Stoics, Iamblichus will carry forward the general sense that traditional divination yields insights that emerge from the organism in its interconnections with the *physis*. But in the distinctive world of Neoplatonic thinking, the polarity surrounding thoughts on the somatic dimensions of the world is dramatically heightened, forcing the Neoplatonists to devalue insights traceable to it more strenuously than their predecessors did.

The *De mysteriis* is Iamblichus' defense of a range of rites that he and his followers knew as the program of theurgy. He writes it in response to objections that Porphyry, his fellow intellectual heir to Plotinus, raises in the polemical *Letter to Anebo*. The nature of these rites is still not fully understood.[32] Porphyry called them magic, a characterization

---

[31] E. R. Dodds, *The Greeks and the Irrational* (Berkeley: University of California Press, 1951), 287.

[32] Hans Lewy advanced modern work on the subject in his *Chaldaean Oracles and Theurgy* (Cairo: Inst. Français d'Archéologie Orientale, 1956), revised and expanded by Michel Tardieu (Paris: Études Augustiniennes, 1978). Since them, work has carried on apace. See Anne Sheppard, "Proclus' Attitude to Theurgy," *Classical Quarterly* 32 (1982): 212–24; Sarah Iles Johnston, *Hekate Soteira: A Study of Hekate's Roles in the Chaldean Oracles and Related Literature* (Atlanta, Geor.: Scholars' Press, 1990); Gregory Shaw, *Theurgy and the Soul: The Neoplatonism of Iamblichus* (State College: Penn State Press, 1995); and John Dillon, "Iamblichus' Defence of Theurgy: Some Reflections," *International Journal of the Platonic Tradition* 1 (2007): 30–41. Of particular importance in recent years has been the much needed new translation into English of Emma C. Clarke, John M. Dillon, and Jackson P. Hershbell, *Iamblichus: De mysteriis* (Atlanta: Society of Biblical Literature, 2003). Indispensible for understanding the text is Martin Sicherl, *Die Handschriften, Ausgaben und Übersetzungen von Iamblichos De Mysteriis: Eine kritisch-historische Studie* (Berlin: Akademie-Verlag, 1957). Work on other Neoplatonists has continued as well. See, for example, Radek Chlup, *Proclus: An Introduction* (Cambridge: Cambridge University Press, 2012); and the edition of Porphyry's *Letter to Anebo* from Henri Dominique Saffrey and Alain-Philippe Segonds, eds., *Porphyre: Lettre à Anébon l'Égyptien* (Paris: Les Belles Lettres, 2012).

Dodds endorsed, but Iamblichus emphatically denied that, and spoke of them as a ritual supplement to the general Neoplatonic program of soteriological contemplative philosophy.[33] For Platonists of any stripe, of course, any embrace of ritual, and the material world in which it is embedded, risks a problem. Plato had set out the terms, with his view that material things in the world around us are fallen imitations of higher realities. This means that an appeal to the material as an aid to spiritual ascent will face an impediment, a fact made blisteringly clear in Porphyry's polemic. He makes strenuous arguments against the theurgic rituals just on the grounds that they employ matter. He directly targets Iamblichus' specific program, but the argument is so wide-ranging that it amounts to a broadside against any kind of ritual action at all: any of it will rest on a turn to the physical world and so should be avoided. Prominently coming in for criticism from Porphyry is the domain of traditional divinatory rites.

In his critique, Porphyry preserves what I have characterized as the general outlook that preceded him. Traditional *manikê* operates along physiological and physical circuitry. But he brings to the conversation ideas of the division between the divine and the material more stringent than previous iterations, even than Plato's own. The transcendence of the divine of course has good Platonic roots, but Plato on rare occasions entertains the idea of a divine trace in the material world, as we have seen in the *Timaeus*, for example. He also allows that, through participation in the forms, some glimpses of the divine might be visible down here. There are provocative suggestions in the visions of true Beauty in the *Symposium*, or of the Good in the *Republic*, book 6, or the theory of recollection, or the longing that initiates the ascent of the soul in the *Phaedrus*. But in the *Letter to Anebo*, Porphyry carries forward the stricter view, also a legitimate part of Plato's legacy, and does not allow for *any* kind of divine hue to processes of the *physis*. He repeatedly characterizes the kind of knowing in which diviners are engaged, since it is derived from humans' physical natures, as deficient. It always represents a turn away from, not toward, the divine and the truth.[34] Iamblichus' answer is as fascinating as it is consequential.

[33] Iamblichus, *De myst.* 3.25, line 52 (Des Places).

[34] This view is evident throughout the relatively short *Letter to Anebo*. For a text, translation, and commentary, see Henri Dominique Saffrey and Alain-Philippe Segonds, eds., *Porphyre: Lettre à Anébon l'Égyptien* (Paris: Les Belles Lettres, 2012).

First, Iamblichus follows Porphyry, and the tradition, and characterizes knowledge from divinatory practices as emerging through our more creaturely selves—at least for divination that is practiced in an unenlightened (and traditional) way. Second, and somewhat counterintuitively, he also mostly, like Porphyry, departs from the tradition by claiming that because of the prominence of the material, divine power cannot be any part of such phenomena. As we will see below, he characterizes the traditional practices as an extension of the mundane human ability to make predictions about affairs in the material world. They might yield murky and tentative knowledge, but are mostly not worthwhile. However, along lines that are common in his overall argument in favor of theurgy, he proposes a distinct and more powerful kind of divinatory phenomenon. This claim lines up with a central theme of the *De mysteriis*, in which he proposes the existence of special nodes of divine presence, situated like traces in the material world. Those who have expertise with these nodes are able to tap into true and unmediated divine presence in the rites they perform.[35] This is the novelty that makes theurgy in general distinct from prior Greek modes of understanding ritual, and it is emblematic of a critical turn in the tradition of thinking on divination. He claims there is a higher form of divination that makes use of real divine presence and is, in fact, *not* mediated through material. It is attributable solely to divine power, yields extraordinary insight, and transcends well beyond any physiological or psychological mechanism.

To understand the divine traces and how they work requires a wider view of Neoplatonism. All those working in the wake of Plotinus focus on a better understanding of the particular modes by which the divine could be connected to the material world. One can understand the interest. Plotinus' system thoroughly remakes such connections without specifying them in detail.[36] In the third century, he proposes that the cosmos itself results from the emanation of an utterly transcendent first principle. He draws from the idea of the Good beyond being in the *Republic*, which enables other objects to be known and even provides

---

[35] See Peter T. Struck, *Birth of the Symbol* (Princeton: Princeton University Press, 2004), 204–26.

[36] The puzzle is analogous to a very old one in the school. Plato himself did not make much progress on the notion of how the material world might "participate" (μετέχει) in the forms. The tentative nature of the idea is a central unsolved puzzle in the *Parmenides*.

them with being itself (509b), and from consideration of the form of the One in the *Parmenides*.[37] Strictly speaking, Plotinus' first principle is so transcendent as to be entirely beyond any predicates we could derive from human language and understanding, but calling it "the One" is the least inadequate description. The entire universe is traceable back to this source. In an act of overflowing plenitude, the One pours out the rest of the cosmos in a set of tiered manifestations. It manifests pure intellect first, then a realm of pure soul. Underneath soul, the material world comes into being, but it is so far removed from the source of reality and truth that it hardly has any of the real or the true left in it. All motion and desire are traceable back to the One. As the layers of reality radiate out from it, at the same time, all parts of the universe, including humans, contain an urge or inclination to revert back to it. These centrifugal and centripetal vectors, procession from the One and reversion back to it, form the main principles of movement in the cosmos.

As a philosopher, Plotinus was committed to more than describing this system; his works also convey a distinct urgency in trying to discern how best for humans to act in it. Plotinus saw spiritual ascent toward the One as the point of living. There will be degrees of success in achieving the urge for union built into us. The route to the One that Plotinus points to moves upward exclusively via a discipline of contemplation. Matter was mostly figured as an impediment, and fixing one's sights on the immaterial as a necessary move to save oneself from the pollution of the world down here. We know from Porphyry's biography that Plotinus ascended spiritually with success. He even achieved the very highest form of it, and attained union with the One itself, four times during his life.[38]

The corpus of Plotinus (again, edited by Porphyry) shows no interest in ritual as a means to ascent. However, he does not settle on a single valuation of matter (and so he leaves the door open a crack for the enterprising Iamblichus to build up a program of ritual action that focuses on the material world, a point to be reconsidered in a moment). While, at some points, Plotinus refers to matter as identical with evil

---

[37] On the links to Plato, the most lucid general treatment remains E. R. Dodds, "The *Parmenides* of Plato and the Origin of the Neoplatonic One," *Classical Quarterly* 22 (1928): 129–42.

[38] *Life of Plotinus* 23.15–18.

and the complete privation of form and intelligibility (*On Matter* 2.4.16), he was also cautious to eschew the views of the Gnostics, who attributed matter to an evil demiurge. In *Against the Gnostics*, a well-studied treatise devoted entirely to his disagreements with the school, he insists that matter does indeed come from the One itself, and not from some other evil principle, and so it *must* carry at least some trace of the One's magnificence (see esp. 2.9.16–18). The debate between Porphyry and Iamblichus brings to a culmination this tension in Plotinus' work. Porphyry's strongly and explicitly antiritualist statements reflect more the spirit of *On Matter*, while Iamblichus' readiness to make use of the material world in theurgy finds at least some connection to the attitude toward matter arrived at in *Against the Gnostics*.

Theurgy made use of certain pieces of the material world to aid spiritual ascent. Iamblichus can speak of "divine matter" (a Neoplatonic oxymoron) because "matter also issues from the father and creator of all, and thus gains its perfection, which is suitable to the reception of gods" (*De myst.* 5.23.17–20). But, in Iamblichus's reckoning, divine presence in the world is not uniform. It shows through a bit more brightly in some spots. Some pieces of matter, "such of it as is perfect and pure and of good type," serve as nodes for the divine presence (*De myst.* 5.23.23–24). This stance carries forward a view from the *Chaldean Oracles*. In one of the oracles, we hear that during the creation, "the Paternal Intellect has sown symbols throughout the cosmos" (*Chald. or.* 108). In the vocabulary of the Neoplatonists, "*symbola*" or "*synthemata*" are tangible, physical traces of the divine itself.[39] They are secret, hidden divine shards or sparks, and they serve as the basis for the theurgic rites:

> Observing this [that the divine has a presence in matter], and discovering in general, in accordance with the properties of each of the gods, the receptacles adapted to them, the theurgic art in many cases links together stones, plants, animals, aromatic substances, and other such things that are sacred, perfect and godlike, and then from all these composes an integrated and pure receptacle.[40]

---

[39] See Struck (2004), 204–26.

[40] Iamblichus continues the focus on origins. Translations based on Clarke, Dillon, and Hershbell. I have relied on their text, which is based on Des Places' edition in the Belles Lettres series, *Jamblique: Les mystères d'Égypte* (Paris: Les Belles Lettres, 1966).

Ταῦτα τοίνυν κατιδοῦσα ἡ θεουργικὴ τέχνη, κοινῶς τε οὑτωσὶ κατ᾽ οἰκειότητα ἑκάστῳ τῶν θεῶν τὰς προσφόρους ὑποδοχὰς ἀνευρίσκουσα, συμπλέκει πολλάκις λίθους βοτάνας ζῷα ἀρώματα ἄλλα τοιαῦτα ἱερὰ καὶ τέλεια καὶ θεοειδῆ, κἄπειτα ἀπὸ πάντων τούτων ὑποδοχὴν ὁλοτελῆ καὶ καθαρὰν ἀπεργάζεται. (De myst. 5.23.29-34)

These give Iamblichus a basis for promoting the rituals, which centrally feature an invoking of real divine presence into material objects:

> One must not, after all, reject all matter, but only that which is alien to the gods, while selecting for use that which is akin to them, as being capable of harmonizing with the construction of dwellings for the gods, the consecration of statues, and indeed for the performance of sacrificial rites in general. For there is no other way in which the terrestrial realm or the men who dwell here could enjoy participation in the existence that is the lot of the higher beings, if some such foundation be not laid down in advance. We must, after all, give credit to the secret discourses when they tell us how a sort of matter is imparted by the gods in the course of blessed visions; this is presumably of like nature with those who bestow it.

> Οὐ γὰρ δὴ δεῖ δυσχεραίνειν πᾶσαν ὕλην, ἀλλὰ μόνην τὴν ἀλλοτρίαν τῶν θεῶν, τὴν δὲ οἰκείαν πρὸς αὐτοὺς ἐκλέγεσθαι, ὡς συμφωνεῖν δυναμένην εἴς τε θεῶν οἰκοδομήσεις καὶ καθιδρύσεις ἀγαλμάτων καὶ δὴ καὶ εἰς τὰς τῶν θυσιῶν ἱερουργίας. Οὐδὲ γὰρ ἂν ἄλλως τοῖς ἐπὶ γῆς τόποις ἢ τοῖς δεῦρο κατοικοῦσιν ἀνθρώποις μετουσία ἂν γένοιτο τῆς τῶν κρειττόνων λήψεως, εἰ μή τις τοιαύτη καταβολὴ πρώτη προενιδρυθείη· πείθεσθαι δὲ χρὴ τοῖς ἀπορρήτοις λόγοις ὡς καὶ διὰ τῶν μακαρίων θεαμάτων ὕλη τις ἐκ θεῶν παραδίδοται· αὕτη δέ που συμφυής ἐστιν αὐτοῖς ἐκείνοις τοῖς διδοῦσιν· (De myst. 5.23.35-45)

All of this is strong language, considering the legacy of Plotinus, and one can understand the strength of Porphyry's reaction in the *Letter to Anebo*. Under its pressure, Iamblichus is at pains to try to separate his program from manipulative sorcery and mere wonder working. Along with Porphyry (and Augustine, to whom we will pay some attention below), Iamblichus had no doubt that certain kinds of manipulations of the world were possible by communicating with and harnessing lower-order spiritual or material powers. But Iamblichus, and surely the other two as well, was disparaging of such things.[41] The concern to separate himself thoroughly from magicians makes him particularly careful to attribute any such power that derives from theurgic practice to the divine and the divine alone, activated by the *symbola*, and not to manipulations of lower, demonic or material powers.

As we will see next, in the turn to divination, the ongoing discussion of the place of the divine in the material world will affect Iamblichus' proposals on how true communication with the divine world should be understood to work. Further, as we will see in closing, this also results in a noteworthy development at the other pole. He will tuck away true divination in a realm that belongs solely to the gods, and leave behind a whole tradition of thinking on a certain kind of human cognition, embedded in physiology, that we see in the earlier philosophers. This now gets reconfigured. With the *divine* power removed, what is left is a much more flimsy human power to know things in oblique ways. The polemic with Porphyry has sharpened the categories. Iamblichus in fact is ready to remove the divine completely from traditional *mantikê*, even out of the deep background. Where earlier philosophers mostly found at least some kind of place for it, he pushes it out of the picture altogether. What remains now gets a name. He creates a de-divinized realm of oblique human cognitive function, precisely under a notion akin to what modern observers would call intuition.

Divine and Nondivine Divination in the De Mysteriis

Iamblichus begins his treatment of divination, which occupies book 3 of the *De mysteriis*, by ruling out just about every previous idea for where divine signs come from. He tells us that "the origin and governing principle of divination" (τὴν ἀρχὴν τῆς μαντικῆς):

> neither originates from bodies, nor from bodily affections, nor from any nature, nor from powers that have to do with nature, nor from human disposition, nor from the conditions that have to do with a human

---

[41] See for example, his reluctant acquiescence to his followers' bids for him to summon water spirits, Eros and Anteros, at the hot springs of Gadara (Eunapius, *Vita soph.* 458–59).

disposition, but neither is it from any acquired external technical practice, performed for some part of the human way of life.

οὔτε ἀπὸ σωμάτων ἐστὶν ὁρμωμένη οὔτε ἀπὸ τῶν περὶ τοῖς σώμασι παθημάτων, οὔτε ἀπὸ φύσεώς τινος καὶ τῶν περὶ τὴν φύσιν δυνάμεων, οὔτε ἀπὸ τῆς ἀνθρωπίνης παρασκευῆς ἢ τῶν περὶ αὐτὴν ἕξεων, ἀλλ' οὐδ' ἀπὸ τέχνης τινὸς ἔξωθεν ἐπικτήτου περί τι μέρος τῶν ἐν τῷ βίῳ διαπραγματευομένης. (De myst. 3.1.14–20)

The negativity in the rhetoric, apparent from this beginning, is the most salient aspect of Iamblichus' ideas on *mantikê*. His discussion is prominently one of limits. Those who have looked to explain divine signs by our bodily natures, by invisible currents in the physical cosmos, by local terrain or atmosphere, by the characters and dispositions of different organisms, or by the natural qualities of the cosmos itself have been misguided. In place of this series of ideas, Iamblichus proposes that (real) divination works solely because it is a divine gift:

Rather, all of its supreme power belongs to the gods, and is bestowed by the gods. . . . All the rest is subordinate, instrumental to the gift of foreknowledge sent down by the gods: everything that concerns our soul, our body, everything that is inherent in the nature of the universe, and in the particular constitution of each thing.

τὸ δὲ πᾶν κῦρος αὐτῆς ἀνήκει εἰς τοὺς θεοὺς καὶ ἀπὸ τῶν θεῶν ἐνδίδοται. . . . τὰ δ' ἄλλα πάντα ὡς ὄργανα ὑπόκειται τῇ ἐκ θεῶν καταπεμπομένῃ τῆς προγνώσεως δόσει, ὅσα τε περὶ τὴν ψυχὴν ἡμῶν ἐστι καὶ τὸ σῶμα καὶ ὅσα ἐν τῇ φύσει τοῦ παντὸς ἢ ταῖς ἰδίαις ἑκάστων φύσεσιν ἐνυπάρχει· (De myst. 3.1.20–27)

From this starting point, Iamblichus moves on to do something his predecessors had never done. He makes two broad categories in divination, and draws a distinct line between "true" or "divine" or "authentic" *mantikê*, of the kind which he has been describing, as opposed to the lesser forms of sign reading that derive from the material world. One split seems obvious: this could be mapped onto the traditional distinction between inspired vs. technical divination. But this is not what Iamblichus claims, in the end. He moves serially through genres of divinatory practice of all kinds, including the inspired and technical varieties, and claims that each one has a truly divine form and a merely human form. While the material forms might be explicable using the various theories prior schools and thinkers had proposed, the most intelligible thing one can say about "true" divine signs is that they come from the gods alone, without any taint of the material world. This is closer to Homer's notion of how signs work than to the intervening thinkers we have examined. In levering out legitimate vs. illegitimate forms, Iamblichus adds new vocabulary to the discussion. He invokes with noteworthy frequency the idea of "true divination" (*De myst.* 3.3.25; 3.8.3; 3.26.23; 3.27.2) or "divine divination" (3.4.2; 3.10.2; 3.17.51; 3.27.6, 9, 12, 37, 45, 56; 3.31.41, 58; 9.3.33; 9.5.19; 10.4.1; 10.5.2; 10.8.2). These categories have an overall effect of making one suspicious of "divination" without any qualifier. They come up nearly always in contrast with the nondivine kind that is enmeshed in the material world.

He begins by looking at natural divination, which has to do with direct and internal inspiration—dreams, divine possession, and oracles—and later looks at divination that reads signs in the external world—like birds, entrails, and all the rest. He starts with dreams. He distinguishes true and divine dreams from a class he calls human dreams (ἀνθρώπινοι ὄνειροι). The latter are sometimes able to tell true things about the future, but are sometimes inaccurate (ἃ τότε μέν ἐστιν ἀληθῆ τότε δὲ ψευδῆ, καὶ ἐπί τινων μὲν τυγχάνει τοῦ ὄντος, ἐπὶ δὲ τῶν πολλῶν ἀποτυγχάνει [3.2.9–11]). By contrast, divine dreams are quite different. For starters, they do not even come during sleep, but at the stage between sleep and waking when the intellect is just becoming active. This claim steps over the longstanding tradition of explanation, as we have seen, coming from Plato and Aristotle, which begins from the premise that, since dreaming comes when the higher-order cognitive systems are not active, it is evidence of a lower part of the mind at work. But Iamblichus eschews the idea that true divination could come from any lower-order, or more somatically engaged, part of the mind, but rather it must come from the higher, more divinely inflected part. For him, divine dreams are the result of a direct union of the dreamer's highest mind with the first divine principles. So he is, in fact, required to claim that the upper soul is not dormant while these divine dreams happen. He explicitly says that divine dreams have nothing to do with

sleep: "Remove, then, from divine dreams in which divination especially occurs, 'sleep' in any way whatsoever" (Ἄνελε οὖν ἐκ τῶν θείων
ὀνείρων, ἐν οἷς δὴ καὶ μάλιστά ἐστι τὸ μαντικόν, τὸ καθεύδειν ὁπωσοῦν
[3.2]). So comes his proposal that they occur on the precipice between
sleep and waking.

The mode of divine presence during these dreams is a bit hard to
fathom (just as it is, indeed, in the case of the other theurgic rituals). He
calls it a "certain rushing voice" (3.2). The immaterial divine presence
sometimes makes a rushing sound (ῥοιζόμενος). It results in a "possession of the eyes" (κατοχὴ τῶν ὀμμάτων). It resembles a blackout trance
and a seizure (ἡ κάρῳ προσεμφερὴς κατάληψις). It is sent from the gods
themselves and is a share of divine epiphany (ἀπ' αὐτῶν τε ἐπιπέμπεται
τῶν θεῶν, μέρος τε τῆς θείας ἐπιφανείας). Analogously to his defense of
theurgic claims based on true divine presence in certain materials, so
also in these kinds of dreams the divine is present. It is a "uniting" with
the divine. Such dreams have no trace of any somatic mechanism. They
come from the gods alone, and their efficacy rests in the gods alone. He
equates their power with the healing dreams of traditional Asclepius
cult (3.3.43–55).

Iamblichus makes a similar kind of bifurcated mapping of both divination by frenzy and by oracles. He starts off this way: "In this area
also, I want to make clear the characteristic signs of those who are truly
possessed by the gods" (Βούλομαι δὴ καὶ ἐν τούτοις τὰ τεκμήρια τῶν
ὀρθῶς κατεχομένων ὑπὸ τῶν θεῶν παραδεῖξαι [3.4.7–9]). Once again,
his main point is to articulate the signs of true possession, so that it
may be distinguished from the lower-order forms of frenzy that emerge
from natural states, such as melancholy (3.8) or passion (3.8), or are produced by agitating music or dancing (3.9). Truly inspired people are
wholly in the possession of the god and are impervious to bodily pleasure and pains. They feel no effect from fire, from being stuck through
with a spit, or even being struck on the back with an axe (3.4.21–36)—they
feel nothing bodily because they are wholly beyond their bodies. In
true divination by inspired trance, those who are moved by the divine
become its instruments and are wholly subordinate to it. Some bodily
agitations may be visible, but these are only incidental to the state of
true possession. In contrast, those under the influence of a merely
bodily frenzy mainly show just these kinds of bodily disturbances, and

consort with lower spirits, not gods. Further, they manipulate the divinities to whom they appeal, and what they learn is compromised:

But those who perform conjuring of spirits in an unclear way, without these blessed visions, grope, as it were, in darkness, and know nothing of what they do, except for some very small signs which appear in the body of the frenzied one, and some other signs that show themselves clearly; but they are ignorant of the whole of divine inspiration, which is hidden in obscurity.

Οἱ δ' ἄνευ τῶν μακαρίων τούτων θεαμάτων ἀφανῶς ποιούμενοι τὰς ἀγωγὰς τῶν πνευμάτων ὥσπερ ἐν σκότῳ ἀφάσσουσι καὶ οὐδὲν ἴσασιν ὧν ποιοῦσι, πλὴν πάνυ σμικρῶν τῶν διὰ τοῦ σώματος φαινομένων σημείων τοῦ ἐνθουσιῶντος καὶ τῶν ἄλλων τῶν ἐναργῶς ὁρωμένων, τὰ ὅλα τῆς θείας ἐπιπνοίας ἐν ἀφανεῖ κεκρυμμένα ἀγνοοῦντες. (3.6.10–16)

These inferior forms of possession yield only a few obscure signs, and a few clear ones. Iamblichus then goes on to discuss and dismiss many prior theories of divine possession, including any idea that possession is connected with places, or particular atmospheres, or that it is an effect of agitation of the soul (3.10). These denials rule out traditional explanations, as well as philosophical ones we have looked at, for how the large temple-based oracles operated. He closes the consideration of oracles this way:

For such a power [divination by oracles], if inseparable from the nature of places and of bodies subject to it, or if it advances according to a motion limited by quantity, cannot know beforehand things everywhere and always in the same manner. But if separate and free from places and times measured by quantity (since it is superior to things that come to be in time and occupy a place), it is equally present with beings wherever they are, and is always simultaneously present to those that are born in time, and embraces in one the truth of the universals because of its own separate and superior existence.

Ἀχώριστος μὲν γὰρ οὖσα τῆς φύσεως τῶν τόπων καὶ τῶν ὑποκειμένων αὐτῇ σωμάτων ἡ τοιαύτη δύναμις, ἢ προϊοῦσα κατὰ κίνησιν τὴν ἀφοριζομένην ἀριθμῷ, οὐ δύναται τὰ πανταχοῦ καὶ ἀεὶ προγιγνώσκειν ὡσαύτως· ἀφειμένη δ' ἀπόλυτος τῶν τόπων καὶ τῶν διαμεμετρημένων τοῖς ἀριθμοῖς χρόνων (ἅτε δὴ κρείττων οὖσα τῶν γιγνομένων κατὰ χρόνον καὶ τῶν ὑπὸ τόπου κατεχομένων) τοῖς πανταχοῦ οὖσιν ἐξ ἴσου πάρεστι, καὶ τοῖς κατὰ χρόνον φυομένοις πάντοτε ἅμα σύνεστιν, ἐν ἑνί τε συνείληφε τῶν ὅλων τὴν ἀλήθειαν διὰ τὴν χωριστὴν ἑαυτῆς καὶ ὑπερέχουσαν οὐσίαν. (3.12.3–14)

So, just as in the case of dreams, there is a split in the classes of foresight around frenzy and oracles. There are some powers into which one can tap that dwell here in the material world. But true divination exists as a purely divine power, on a higher plane and is removed from the material world.

And so one would not rightly suppose divine possession to belong to the soul nor any of its powers, nor to intellect nor any of its powers or activities, nor to bodily weakness or its absence. Nor would one reasonably suppose that it would occur in this way, for being transported by a god it is neither a human accomplishment, nor does it base its power in human parts (of the body) or activities. But, on the one hand, these are otherwise subordinate, and the god uses them as instruments; on the other hand, the entire activity of divination comes to its fulfillment through the god acting by himself, purely detached from other things, without the soul or body moving in any way. Hence, divination done rightly, as I say, really and truly happens. But when the soul takes the initiative, or is disturbed during divination, or the body interrupts and perverts the divine harmony, the divination becomes turbulent and false, and the possession is no longer true nor genuinely divine.

ψυχῆς μὲν οὖν καί τινος τῶν ἐν αὐτῇ δυνάμεων, ἢ νοῦ καί τινος τῶν ἐν αὐτῷ δυνάμεων ἢ ἐνεργειῶν, ἢ σωματικῆς ἀσθενείας ἢ ἄνευ ταύτης οὐκ ἄν τις ὑπολάβοι δικαίως τὸν ἐνθουσιασμὸν εἶναι, οὐδ' ἄν οὕτω γίγνεσθαι εἰκότως ἄν ὑπόθοιτο· οὔτε γὰρ ἀνθρώπινόν ἐστι τὸ τῆς θεοφορίας ἔργον, οὔτε ἀνθρωπίνοις μορίοις ἢ ἐνεργήμασι τὸ πᾶν ἔχει κῦρος· ἀλλὰ ταῦτα μὲν ἄλλως ὑπόκειται, καὶ χρῆται αὐτοῖς ὁ θεὸς ὡς ὀργάνοις· τὸ δὲ πᾶν ἔργον τῆς μαντείας δι' αὐτοῦ πληροῖ, καὶ ἀμιγῶς ἀπὸ τῶν ἄλλων ἀφειμένος οὔτε ψυχῆς κινουμένης οὐδ' ὁτιοῦν οὔτε σώματος ἐνεργεῖ καθ' αὑτόν. Ὅθεν δὴ καὶ ἀψευδῶς γίγνονται τὰ μαντεῖα τὰ οὕτως ὡς λέγω κατορθούμενα. Ἐπειδὰν δ' ἡ ψυχὴ προκατάρχῃ ἢ μεταξὺ κινῆται, ἢ τὸ σῶμά τι παρεμπίπτῃ καὶ τὴν θείαν ἁρμονίαν ἐπιταράττῃ, θορυβώδη γίγνονται καὶ ψευδῆ τὰ μαντεῖα, καὶ ὁ ἐνθουσιασμὸς οὐκέτι ἀληθὴς ὑπάρχει οὐδὲ γνησίως θεῖος. (3.7.15–31)

Given this general push against materialist-based theories of divine signs, there is an entire class of divinatory activity that one would anticipate would not fare too well—and indeed it does not. He carries forward the distinction between those forms that are the result of an internal divine possession of the soul, such as we have already addressed, versus those that are the result of a technical skill, an expertise at reading signs that appear in the material world. Iamblichus takes a rather dismissive view of the whole of these forms of divination.

He makes a summary statement at the opening of chapter 15 of book 3, in which he says: "Come, then, let us turn to the mode of divination, accomplished by human technical skill, which partakes largely of guessing and supposition" (Φέρε δὴ οὖν ἐπὶ τὸν διὰ τέχνης ἀνθρωπίνης ἐπιτελούμενον τρόπον μετέλθωμεν, ὅστις στοχασμοῦ καὶ οἰήσεως πλείονος εἴληφε [3.15.1–3]). He continues, emphasizing its tentative nature: the technical kind "somehow draws conclusions and guesses at divination, inferring it from certain probabilities" (συμβάλλει πως ἡ τέχνη καὶ στοχάζεται τὴν μαντείαν, ἐξ εἰκότων τινῶν αὐτὴν συλλογιζομένη [3.15.9–10]). He discusses signs in entrails, birds, and astrology as a part of the natural world, which the gods produced either via nature or via the demons that oversee it. Certain occurrences will consistently precede others and so will function as signs from which we can make inferences. But as was the case with "human dreams" or frenzies produced by agents other than the divine, these forms of information are embedded in the natural world and are unreliable. The natural world and demons stand in intermediary position. They make possible a less reliable form of divination, for those who deign to investigate the material world.

During the extended discussion on these techniques, as he considers the principles by which the forms of predictive thinking embedded in the natural world operate, Iamblichus forwards a negative evaluation of sympathy, which had, since the Stoics, as we saw, been a first line of explanation for divinatory signs of all kinds. After considering the idea that different kinds of physical affections produce divinatory insight, he rules these out as causes of true or divine mantic knowledge.

But even if they are to the greatest degree subject to the influence of sympathy, I do not see in what way they will know anything true about the future. For foreknowledge and predicting what is going to happen is not the province of a power exerting sympathetic influence or of something enmeshed in matter and held fast in a specific place and body, but, on the contrary it is characteristic of a power that is freed from all these.

Εἰ δὲ δὴ ὅτι μάλιστα καὶ οὕτως εἰσὶ συμπαθεῖς, οὐχ ὁρῶ τίνα τρόπον εἴσονταί τι περὶ τοῦ μέλλοντος ἀληθές. Οὐ γὰρ συμπαθοῦς δυνάμεως οὐδ' ἐνύλου καὶ κατεχομένης ἔν τινι τόπῳ καὶ σώματι τὸ προγιγνώσκειν τε καὶ προμηνύειν τὸ μέλλον, ἀλλὰ τοὐναντίον τῆς ἀπὸ πάντων τούτων ἀπολελυμένης. (3.22.40–46)

When Iamblichus evaluates sympathy as a power, active on the level of the material, he is actually in keeping with Stoic views, which held fast to a materialist view of the cosmos. It is just that now Iamblichus is committed to the idea that true divination must rely on a divine that is imagined to exist wholly immaterially and entirely removed from the natural world.

It is also worth noting here that when Iamblichus anchors true divination to divine power, and separates it from the powers of the material world, he makes less salient a problem that other theorists of it have faced. As we saw crop up in Cicero's *De divinatione*, ideas about divination eventually run into the problem of separating the kinds of predictions it makes from the kinds of predictions natural scientists make.[42] The more the theorist makes technical divination comprehensible, via explanations that appeal to terrain, or animal behaviors, or physical dispositions, the more difficult it becomes to mark out a distinct kind of inference that is specifically divinatory. If, in the natural world, certain events just tend to precede others, prediction based on such signs makes one look a lot like an empirical natural scientist of some sort, rather than a diviner.

For Iamblichus the problem becomes moot. He is all too happy to stipulate that forms of foresight based on observing external signs are in fact on equal footing with the observational natural sciences

---

[42]See Cicero, *De div.* 2.34; 1.112; cf. 1.13–14.

generally. And in his view both of these are inferior forms of prediction, based on connections in the physical world, and they both contrast with true divinely based foreknowledge. The collection of traditional divinatory techniques that are used to observe nature, he says,

> calculates the future from probabilities and estimates by certain signs, and these are not always trustworthy, nor, in like manner, do they have what is signified properly connected with that of which the signs are evidence. But divine foreknowledge of future events is directed by a firm knowledge, and an unshakeable assurance deriving from the causes, an indissoluble comprehension connecting all things to all. . . .

> ἐξ εἰκότων γὰρ ἀναλογίζεται τὸ μέλλον καὶ σημείοις τισὶ τεκμηριοῦται καὶ τούτοις οὐκ ἀεὶ πιστοῖς οὐδ' ὡσαύτως συνηρτημένον ἔχουσι τὸ δηλούμενον, οὗπέρ ἐστι τὰ σημεῖα δείγματα. Τῆς δὲ θείας προνοίας τῶν ἐσομένων βέβαιος ἡ εἴδησις προηγεῖται, καὶ ἀπὸ τῶν αἰτίων ἀμετάπτωτος ἡ πίστωσις, συνηρτημένη τε πάντων πρὸς ἄπαντα ἀδιαλύτως κατάληψις. . . . (3.26.37–43)

Divination based on the material world, then, is functionally coextensive with the physical sciences. Neither of these modes yields unshakable insight, only conjecture and guesswork. When Iamblichus argues against materially facilitated divination and toward contemplative, intellectually driven gnosis, he is working with presuppositions as to these two different kinds of knowledge that are consistent with the earlier philosophical traditions of thinking. He takes it for granted that traditional *mantikê* operates through the corporeal. The difference in his case is a stronger reluctance to consider such knowledge as useful.

True Divination and Prognôsis

What is left, after Iamblichus prunes away the material dimensions, is a notion of true divination as a meditative exercise, in which the divine and the highest human mind are understood to make a connection. It has some relation with Plotinus' contemplation, and with the outlining of the relation between oracles and philosophy in Porphyry's *On*

Philosophy from Oracles. A recent monograph has explored the particular contours of this newly formed vision of what divination can be.[43]

We add here just a few more points at which a congruent kind of intellectual move is recognizable in other developments of Late Antiquity. Oddly enough, Iamblichus' ideas are in general quite in line with those of a thinker like Origen and roughly anticipate ideas in Augustine.[44] He is surely consistent with Origen and Augustine in attempting to separate traditional *mantikê* from a truer form of revelatory divine communion. Both Iamblichus and the Christian thinkers look at a host of traditional pagan mantic practices and characterize them as unsure, tentative groping through material prognostication. Origen argues that pagan *mantikê* results in unreliable knowledge (*Contr. Cel.*, 4.92), deriving from the material world, anchored to specific times and places (7.4), is overseen by demons (now cast as agents of evil; 7.3, 4.92), and is nothing like the revelatory power of the Christian God, which transcends time, place, and all material realities (8.48). The Platonist bifurcation, which leads Iamblichus to a flight away from the traditional technologies, works congruently to a different impulse among the Church Fathers to denigrate traditional pagan forms of religious authority. In each case, physicalist explanations are eschewed in favor of a model of prophetic encounter that is wholly a divine power and activity, in which the human being is a mere conduit. In the case of the Christians and Iamblichus, while the *theos* is different, the theological structure is similar.

As part of his forwarding of this new idea of completely transcendent divination, Iamblichus introduces a new vocabulary to the discussion. He speaks frequently of *prognôsis*, carrying forward a vocabulary we saw above to be already visible in Philostratus' *Life of Apollonius of Tyana*.[45] It is ubiquitous in Iamblichus' discussion, and almost

---

[43] Addey (2014), who draws out persuasive and fascinating similarities with Porphyry's *On Philosophy from Oracles*, 127–69.

[44] For Augustine, the main evidence is *On Christian Doctrine* (2.23–24) and *City of God* (mainly 9.21–23) and a short work, *On Divination by Demons*. Pagan divinatory practices offer limited knowledge, only of the material world, and are governed by demons, whereas true divine foreknowledge is secure and oriented toward the immaterial, and god. For Origen, see *Contr. Cel.* 7.3, and esp. 4.88–92.

[45] See pp. 224–25 above. The salience of this term in the treatise was pointed out to me in a reading group at the University of Pennsylvania by Roshan Abraham. Also participating in the seminar were Todd Krulak and Professor Annette Yoshiko Reed.

entirely absent from earlier philosophical considerations of divination we have examined. It is the general term with which he launches
the whole investigation (*De myst.* 3.1.2, 5); it is explicitly that kind of
knowledge one is able to gain from true divination, inspired by the
gods, and as opposed to the unreliable forms that turn to the material
world (3.1.25, 49; 3.18.19; 3.19.26; 3.24.5, 17, 19, 20; 3.26.30, 37; 3.30.38;
3.31.70; 6.4.14; and esp. 10.4.3, 9, 12, 20); it is the pure power of the
higher-order divinities to see the future (3.1.40; 3.12.25). Where, one
might wonder, did this idea come from? This will be a question for another study, but for now, one could just note that the term comes up in
connection with Jewish prophecy in the Septuagint, though only in the
deuterocanonical Book of Judith (9:6; 11:19), and in the New Testament
(Acts 2:23 and 1 Peter 1:2); it designates the foreknowledge of God.
And, back to Origen, the notion comes in use for him in separating the
true prophetic insights of the Christians from pagan divination in the
Contra Celsum (4.88–92). This may give some philological underpin-
ning to the claim of a tie between early Christian and Neoplatonic
views of *mantikê*.

Iamblichus is often seen as a traditionalist, fighting to save pagan
theology and cultic practices by refurbishing them and making a more
coherent whole out of them. But his program is actually much more
radical than this. It is worth noting that the two groups of people sufficiently offensive to Porphyry to provoke him to write his famous
polemics were the Christians and the circle around Iamblichus. Along
the way to re-invigorating the ancient ways, which is his overt purpose,
Iamblichus needs to jettison some traditional views in order to preserve
what he sees as the core of the whole. Divinatory knowledge, as traditionally understood, is one such piece of ballast tossed overboard. The
end state of all of this is a decided turning of the page on a rather long
philosophical history of study on ancient mantic practices. True oracular insight is no longer thought to emerge from our physiological selves
embedded in nature. Several of the basic building blocks of Greek and
Roman public religion—the observation of birds and entrails, not to
mention the movements of the stars—are seen to be inferior techniques based on guesswork and supposition. This looks like a quite
pristine example of the move from locative to utopian religions, which
has been investigated so fruitfully within the history of religions by

Jonathan Z. Smith and Peter Brown.[46] Iamblichus leaves behind quite a different terrain from the one he inherited.

Mantikê *and Intuition*

In making his definitive separation of divine divination from insight that can be gained from the material world, Iamblichus produces a noteworthy result for the other end of the pole as well, and this development makes a fitting closing. When he separates out divine divination, he leaves behind the lower kind—or, that is, all the traditional forms by which Greeks had understood the strange abilities of some people to gain incremental knowledge of things via instinctual, nondiscursive insights, extracted from the natural world. Since these do not involve the divine, according to Iamblichus, it is reasonable enough to expect that it would no longer make sense to talk about them using the term *mantikê*. So at a few moments in his treatise, we see Iamblichus exercising a need to find a new vocabulary for this kind of thing. Here is an example:

> If then these things we are talking about are true, we should not, if we receive a certain intuition from nature (τινα ἐκ φύσεως ἐπιβολὴν) regarding the way things are or an apprehension of the future (τοῦ μέλλοντος ἐπαφήν), judge this as divinatory foreknowledge; rather while it has a similarity to divination, except that this latter lacks nothing of certainty and truth, intuition chances upon the truth for the most part, but not always, and gains understanding in the case of some things but not in the case of all.

---

[46] Jonathan Z. Smith, "The Influence of Symbols upon Social Change: A Place on Which to Stand," in Smith, *Map Is Not Territory: Studies in the History of Religions*, Studies in Judaism in Late Antiquity 23 (Leiden: Brill, 1978), 129–46; and Smith, *To Take Place: Toward Theory in Ritual* (Chicago: Chicago University Press, 1987). On the holy man as new oracle, see Peter Brown, "The Rise and Function of the Holy Man in Late Antiquity" in *Society and the Holy in Late Antiquity* (Berkeley: University of California Press, 1982), 132–34; David Frankfurter, *Religion in Roman Egypt* (Princeton: Princeton University Press, 1998), 184–93; and Frankfurter, "Syncretism and the Holy Man in Late Antique Egypt," *Journal of Early Christian Studies* 11 (2003): 339–85.

Εἰ δὴ ταῦτα ἀληθῆ λέγομεν, οὐ δεῖ, εἴ τινα ἐκ φύσεως ἐπιβολὴν εἰς τὰ ὄντα παρειλήφαμεν ἢ τοῦ μέλλοντος ἐπαφήν, ἐγκρίνειν ταύτην ὡς μαντικὴν πρόγνωσιν· ἀλλ' ὁμοία μέν ἐστι μαντικῇ, πλὴν οὐδὲν αὕτη βεβαιότητος ἢ ἀληθείας ἀπολείπεται, τὸ δ' ὡς ἐπὶ τὸ πολὺ τυγχάνον οὐκ ἀεὶ δὲ καὶ ἐπί τινων μὲν οὐχὶ δ' ἐπὶ πάντων αἱροῦσα· (*De myst.* 3.26.28–34)

When Iamblichus uses *epibolê* and *epaphê*, it is a bit of a stretch. These terms had meant things like touching or applying one's mind to something in the classical period. And in Iamblichus' own text, *epaphê* remains linked to its root sense of touching and contact (3.2.22) and interestingly serves to describe contact of demons with divinatory bodily organs that result in debased divination (6.3.12). And this is precisely what is interesting. As mentioned in the introductory chapter, the Greek language does not, in fact, have a well-established vocabulary for naming this kind of thing. There had been occasional appeal to something like a direct apprehension of certain fundamental intellectual realities in prior thinkers, as with Aristotle's *nous*, and the term *epibolê* was sometimes used in such contexts.[47] (This is what we called rational intuition in the introduction.) But Greek did not have a way of talking about just knowing something quotidian or mundane without really thinking about it (what we called cognitive intuition). Iamblichus is producing that here. The term *epibolê* as he uses it can mean any kind of noninferential knowing (on one occasion, Iamblichus uses it for the kind of knowledge that god can have [3.17.44]), but it develops a particular special sense in his discussion of divination. It shows in contexts in which someone has a hunch that does not come from the divine, nor is it the result of deliberative thought, and it is just as easily false as it might have some truth in it (3.26.9, 29; 3.6.22). A summary section of book 10, produces a particularly well-turned testimony, phrased as a rebuttal to Porphyry, which repays lengthy citation:

> I would like in the next instance to run through the other slanders which you direct against divine foreknowledge, when you compare it with certain other methods that concern the prediction of future events. For me, not even if there is some instinctive ability from nature for

---

[47] See Epicurus, *Epistula ad Herodotum* (in Diog. Laert. 10.38) and Plotinus 4.4.1. Aristotle uses νοῦς at *Posterior Analtyics* 100b and *NE* 6.6 (1141a) and 6.8 (1142a).

signaling what will be, just as a foreknowledge of earthquakes, wind, or storms occurs among animals, does this seem to be worthy of respect. For such an innate faculty of divining occurs according to a keenness of perception or sympathy, or some other movement of natural powers, containing nothing holy or supernatural—any more than, if somebody, through human reasoning or skilled observation, deduces from signs those things which the signs indicate (just as doctors predict an ensuing fever from a spasm or shivering), does he seem to me to possess anything venerable or good. For he conjectures after a human fashion and infers with the aid of our reasoning things that, we all acknowledge, occur naturally, and forms a diagnosis not far removed from the corporeal order. In this way, even if there is within us a certain natural intuition (φυσική τις ἐπιβολή) of the future, just as this power is clearly seen to be active in all other animals, this does not, in reality, possess anything that is worthy of celebration. For what could there be that is genuine, perfect, and eternally good among us that is implanted by nature within the realms of generation?

Βούλομαι δὴ τὸ μετὰ τοῦτο καὶ τὰ ἄλλα ἐπιδραμεῖν, ὅσα διαβάλλων τὴν θείαν πρόγνωσιν ἄλλας τινὰς μεθόδους αὐτῇ παραβάλλεις, περὶ τὴν τοῦ μέλλοντος προμήνυσιν διατριβούσας. Ἐμοὶ γάρ, οὔτε εἴ τις ἐκ φύσεως ἐπιτηδειότης εἰς σημασίαν τοῦ ἐσομένου παραγίγνεται, ὥσπερ ἡ τοῖς ζῴοις τῶν σεισμῶν ἢ τῶν ἀνέμων ἢ τῶν χειμώνων συμπίπτει πρόγνωσις, τίμιος εἶναι δοκεῖ· κατ' αἰσθήσεως γὰρ ὀξύτητα ἢ κατὰ συμπάθειαν ἢ κατ' ἄλλην τινὰ φυσικῶν δυνάμεων συγκίνησιν ἡ τοιαύτη ἔμφυτος συνέπεται μαντεία, οὐδὲν ἔχουσα σεμνὸν καὶ ὑπερφυές· οὔτε εἴ τις κατὰ λογισμὸν ἀνθρώπινον ἢ τεχνικὴν παρατήρησιν ἀπὸ σημείων τεκμηριοῦται ἐκεῖνα ὧν ἐστι τὰ σημεῖα δηλωτικά (ὡς ἀπὸ συστολῆς ἢ φρίκης τὸν μέλλοντα πυρετὸν προγιγνώσκουσιν οἱ ἰατροί), οὐδὲν οὐδὲ οὗτός μοι δοκεῖ τίμιον ἔχειν καὶ ἀγαθόν· ἀνθρωπίνως τε γὰρ ἐπιβάλλει καὶ συλλογίζεται τῇ ἡμετέρᾳ διανοίᾳ, περί τε τῶν ἐν τῇ φύσει τοῖς γιγνομένοις ὁμολογουμένως οὐ πόρρω τῆς σωματοειδοῦς τάξεως ποιεῖται τὴν διάγνωσιν. Ὥστε οὐδ' εἰ φυσική τις ἔνεστιν ἐν ἡμῖν ἐπιβολὴ τοῦ μέλλοντος, ὥσπερ καὶ ἐν τοῖς ἄλλοις ἅπασιν ἡ δύναμις ἥδε ἐναργῶς ἐνεργοῦσα διαφαίνεται, οὐδὲν οὐδὲ αὕτη μακαριστὸν τῷ ὄντι κέκτηται· τί γὰρ ἂν εἴη γνήσιον καὶ τέλειον καὶ ἀΐδιον ἀγαθὸν τῶν ὑπὸ τῆς φύσεως τῆς ἐν γενέσει εἰς ἡμᾶς ἐμφυομένων; (10.3)

Considering the earlier tradition of thinking to which Iamblichus re-acts, and the novelty of this *nondivine* form of such knowledge, we are again led to the suggestion that such things as we call intuition had been until Iamblichus subsumed under the large and robust Greek cul-tural form of divination, in which cracks were beginning to form.

CONCLUSION

When Iamblichus separates out human intuition from truly divine divination, we have reached a turning point in ancient thinking on di-vine signs. Up through the Hellenistic period, according to what pre-cedes, they were mostly not construed as separate in ancient Greek thinking. With Iamblichus they are. The two new categories do not re-sult in a sum equal to what preceded them. On the one side, a divination removed from questions of locality, physiology, and cognitive mecha-nisms of any kind becomes a resolutely and exclusively theological and antimaterial question. It was not this before. The question of closeness to the divine will now become the key for understanding the source of this surplus knowledge. On the other, a now de-divinized, merely human intuition appears as a new kind of foundling. Construed pre-cisely this way, it had not been thought about rigorously before this and would have appeared unformed and somewhat odd. Iamblichus' link with animals in the final quotation considered above is noteworthy. We will now be left in a realm of instinct and animal cognition. We have already seen a certain pertinence to questions of animal knowing in both Plato and Aristotle, though not in the Stoics. The question of a human version of this, deracinated from the long tradition of attempts to understand surplus knowledge in prior ancient schools of thought, has little hope of flourishing after Iamblichus; and in fact it doesn't. A whole tradition of study on physiologically based knowledge could have been brought to bear, but mostly won't be, since the category of a nondivine, human mode of surplus knowing remains of little interest until many centuries later, along the lines sketched out in our introduc-tion, at which point its deep ancient past is occluded by the rupture to which Iamblichus attests.

Finally, it is also of some interest to recall that we have already seen one other narrowing of scope of the category of *mantikê* in what precedes. In the work of Plato, we proposed, the categories of rational and cognitive intuition were not separated, and both these were subsumed under the category of divination at the time. He was required to use the language of divination to articulate something like rational intuition. This changes after Aristotle separates out rational intuition, that is, the direct apprehension of certain fundamental intellectual prerequisites for reasoning, via his appeal to a certain capacity of *nous*. In further study in the Greek corpus, we will likely continue to find what we might see as three separate classes of cognitive activity circulating through the category of *mantikê*: knowledge from the gods, knowledge of the necessary prerequisites for rationality, and uncanny and unexplained insight regarding proper courses of action in the proximate future. Of course, these are today emphatically separate questions, worked on from within widely variant intellectual histories and disciplinary habits of mind, and from this perspective, the ancient history traced out here could be understood as an ongoing disambiguation of these facets of surplus knowledge.

They were already recognized two and a half millennia ago as curious things. And since then, I think it is safe to say, the mechanisms of each of them remain unfathomed—leaving behind an ongoing testimony to the axiom with which this study started. It is likely to be the case that not only does our ability to know exceed our capacity to understand that ability, but it will continue to do so. But who could know the future?

Reconsidering Penelope

THOUGH THEY HAVE DIFFERENT IDEAS ON HOW EXACTLY IT WORKS and how to value it, the Greek philosophers considered here show a consistent understanding of traditional divinatory insight as the result of an ancillary form of cognition that takes place outside our self-conscious, purposive thinking. It enters into our awareness and offers incremental insight into what is around the corner. They construe it as a feature of human nature, as embedded in physiological processes that have to do with our status as embodied organisms situated in a surrounding atmosphere of stimuli. It relies on mechanisms buried deep in our natural structures, and the philosophers allow that some people will have a better mechanism for it than others. I have tried to show that its cognitive status is consistently congruent to what most contemporary English speakers would call intuition, and that it is best understood as a cultural formation responding to the provocative nature of surplus knowledge. The valuations that the schools give this kind of knowledge vary widely. Posidonius understands knowledge that results from μαντική to be well-grounded and reliable. Iamblichus takes it, because of its rootedness in the body, to be so unreliable as to be no better than a guess, and recommends avoiding it in favor of a new kind of divine knowledge based on revelation (θεία μαντική; πρόγνωσις). Both Plato and Aristotle, take knowledge that arrives through our dreams as the only possibly serious mode of traditional divinatory insight, and they each explain how it might in some cases be right, but they are somewhat tentative.

The account in this book has been of philosophical schools trying to make sense of a puzzling phenomenon. As is always the case in looking at an intellectual history from this perspective, one may rightly raise the question of whether it has pertinence outside these rarified circles.

Do the perspectives apparent in those texts allow us to gain new insights in other domains of culture? I think they could. Take the historical case of the famous wooden wall, in Herodotus' telling, for example. If we look at it through the lens developed here, we have the Athenians deliberating over what to do about the coming onslaught of the Persians. They interrupt their discursive thinking by sending for an oracle. That then comes back with the parameter of the wooden wall that, while on its own solves nothing, gives a space for new thoughts to catalyze around it. The rearrangement is not the result of deliberation, exactly. Rather, the introduction of a new orthogonal voice triggers the seeing of new resemblances, and invites nondiscursive insight to rejigger the pieces of the deliberation. What before had been a discussion that Herodotus does not describe as having any particular shape now crystallizes around two options: a navy or refuge in the Acropolis. This enables the Athenians to reenter a clarified field of deliberation. On the side of classical drama, the story of Oedipus would on this view include a layer of commentary on Oedipus' particular failings. His renown for his ability to win a confrontation of wits with the sphinx shows him as an acute thinker in a discursive mode. But his ongoing confrontation with the messages from Delphi, particularly brought to a head by Tiresias, would, by the perspective worked through here, show him to be deficient at another kind of cognition, the nonconscious insight that comes from what we would call intuition. He has discursive rational capacity aplenty but is lacking something else. This study could help us get a clearer fix on what Sophocles and his audience would have understood to be his deficiency. His inability to gain knowledge from oracles looks like the distinctive cultural expression that we might call a lack of intuitive insight. One could imagine a longer list of texts, setting up a series of potential studies to test the possibility of consonant manifestations of the ideas set out here, in nonphilosophical cultural production. I will close by offering a slightly closer look at one such case study, which provides an example for the kinds of insights that may be available. The vantage provided here gives us a new purchase on the divine signs in the culminating books of Homer's *Odyssey*, which by my reading are sending us a slightly richer message about Penelope than we have yet fully appreciated.

In books 15 through 21 of the *Odyssey*, Homer shows Odysseus disguised as a beggar in the thick of navigating his way back into his place

at home. The narrative thread of Agamemnon and his particular wel-
coming home, made emphatic in his face-to-face meeting with Odysseus
in book 11, has sharpened Odysseus' sense of danger; and Penelope
is deeply wary of imposters. The two together make up a pair that is
actively guarded against each other, while at the same time, fully aware
that each of their purposes will be fulfilled only by a mutual knowledge
of each other. As has been well-appreciated in the modern scholarship,
only a subterranean language marked by hints, signs, and enigmas will
suit their purposes.[1] Odysseus knows more in this game, since he is
certain of both players—himself and Penelope. The puzzle of recognition through hinting and surmising on hunches is particularly acute
for Penelope. She is faced with coming to some kind of conclusion about
his identity. Mostly, this is not presented as a discursive set of inferences
in Penelope's mind. There is a powerful exception in book 23, with the
test of the bed, which is a coup de grâce of self-conscious discursive
planning and execution. But prior to this, we have instead a whole series of glimmers and hints that would be best characterized not as acts
of inference, but more like an aggregate of intuitive moments. By the
thesis proposed here, it would make sense for Homer to encode such a
mode of thinking in terms of divine signs and divination. As has long
been recognized, divine signs are thick on the ground in the pertinent
part of the text, and the work in the prior chapters opens a new way to
understand it.

The dramatic tension of the second half of the *Odyssey* requires of
course that Penelope not recognize him yet. At the same time, Homer
also provides a series of uncanny hints that she does, in fact, have in-
klings, at some level, that this stranger is her husband. Homer has several nondivinatory signs from which we can discern Penelope's state of
knowledge. Those around Penelope make passing references to the resemblances between this beggar and Odysseus (19.379–81; 20.205); and
when she declares the axe contest, she has granted advanced warning
of it only to one person, the stranger, whom she tells in her audience
with him (19.570–81). Why she should tell him is not clear, and invites

[1]See John Finley, *Homer's Odyssey* (Cambridge, Mass.: Harvard University Press, 1978);
Sheila Murnaghan, *Disguise and Recognition in the Odyssey* (Princeton: Princeton University
Press, 1987); Richard Heitman, *Taking Her Seriously: Penelope and the Plot of Homer's Odyssey*
(Ann Arbor: University of Michigan Press, 2005).

us to surmise—though it does not tell us outright—that she is at some level seeing through the disguise. Slightly more interesting, but also more opaque is Penelope's public announcement in the middle of book 18. Inspired by Athena, she tells the crowd of suitors (and the beggar-Odysseus whom Penelope can see among them) that she will now relent and take one of them as a husband, but only after they have brought her many gifts. Odysseus' reaction to this is odd. He rejoices:

> Staunch Odysseus glowed with joy to hear all this—
> his wife's trickery luring gifts from her suitors now,
> enchanting their hearts with suave seductive words
> but all the while with something else in mind.[2]

> ὣς φάτο, γήθησεν δὲ πολύτλας δῖος Ὀδυσσεύς,
> οὕνεκα τῶν μὲν δῶρα παρέλκετο, θέλγε δὲ θυμὸν
> μειλιχίοις ἐπέεσσι, νόος δέ οἱ ἄλλα μενοίνα. (18.281–83)

His lack of suspicion of Penelope is out of character with his deeply wary caution, always on guard against danger. Why does he not suspect she is capitulating to the suitors? How could he be sure that this is Penelope tricking (θέλγε) the suitors, and so an occasion for him to rejoice? Homer provides at least one reasonable explanation. In her address to the suitors, he has her declare as a prelude that, before he left, Odysseus had given her permission to take a new husband if he was still gone when Telemachus' beard came in. She declares that now that that time has arrived, she will accept one of them. Through this statement, an explanation regarding Odysseus' confidence comes into view. It could be explained if she is lying to them, and Odysseus never said such a thing. If it is a lie, it would be one that only she and the real Odysseus could recognize. According to this possibility, she is attaching a kind of packet of metadata to her announcement about capitulating: "If you're really Odysseus, you'll know I'm tricking the suitors."[3] But whatever knowledge he or she does have is not explicitly stated, nor at this point is any particular inferential string set out in Penelope's

---

[2] Translation from Robert Fagles, *Homer: The Odyssey* (New York: Penguin, 2002).
[3] For a different reading of this passage, see Heitman (2005), 34–49. Heitman's reading is not fully satisfying, since it does not have an answer for Odysseus' lack of suspicion.

mind. The kind of cognitive event coalescing around Penelope's discernment of Odysseus would be more a gut feeling or an intuition.

According to the template outlined here, there would be no more apt Greek mode in which Homer could express her hunch than divination. And turning now to the kind of signs on which we are focused, there is a pronounced salience of divine signs around the Odysseus/Penelope axis, while divine signs are not abundant in the rest of the story. I have summarized the signs in the *Odyssey* in table 1.

If we rearrange the material so that it is grouped by the kinds of insights provided by each sign, it becomes clear that moments of divination in the *Odyssey* as a whole cluster around books 15–21, and particularly around an expression of Penelope's intuitive sense that this stranger is indeed Odysseus (see table 2).

Book 19 and the opening of book 20 provide perhaps the most concentrated and powerful examples, centered on Penelope's dreaming. She invites the beggar into her household chambers at the start of 19 for a private conversation. She has a discussion with him, in which the beggar claims to have seen Odysseus. When he seems to give her a hint of his identity, Homer embeds the hint in a divinatory context. He tells her that he has seen Odysseus and he is on his way home, but he has stopped off at the oracle at Dodona to inquire whether he should come home plainly or disguised. In other words, he's telling her that an oracle may be telling the real Odysseus that it's better to come home in secret, as he has indeed come. This is the passing along of a hint, not a sharing of straightforward information. That he would tell this particular lie by invoking a divine sign from Dodona is entirely in keeping with the larger thesis. It is an expression by Homer, in the expected cultural idiom, that the information being passed between the two of them will be nondiscursive and intuitive, and not at the level of sharing straightforward knowledge. The scar episode ensues.

She then, almost as a afterthought, asks him to interpret one of her dreams. Her dream is a redundant form of divination, a prophetic dream of a bird omen—which picks up one of the two earlier bird omens (15.160), since again an eagle attacks geese. The geese eat at her trough, and the eagle swoops down out of nowhere and kills them all. This makes her upset in the dream, which is not entirely expected, and her handmaids console her. The eagle then comes back to her and

TABLE 1

Sign	Book, Line	Who Sees/Hears	What Sign Means	Context
Eagles collide, thrash each other	2.146	Telemachus and suitors	Suitors doomed.	Telemachus has just made a prayer that they face vengeance.
Tiresias' oracle	11	Odysseus	What Tiresias says.	Odysseus needs help getting home.
Eagle on right clutching white goose	15.160	Telemachus, Menelaus, Helen	Odysseus is coming home.	Helen reads it as Telemachus starts home from Sparta.
Hawk on right clutching dove	15.526; 17.160	Telemachus and Theoclymenus; then Theoclymenus reports to Penelope at 17.160	The family will be safe; Odysseus is here.	Arriving at Ithaca, Telemachus prays Zeus will bring death to suitors; Theoclymenus reports to Penelope as proof that Odysseus is here.
Sneeze, like thunder	17.545	Penelope	Odysseus is here.	Penelope notices beggar for first time, tells Eumaeus she wants to speak to him, closes with wish that Odysseus were back and would kill suitors, at which point Telemachus sneezes.
Odysseus at Dodona asking about strategy: return openly or secretly (lie)	19.296	Penelope	Odysseus may come secretly.	Disguised Odysseus tells Penelope lie about real Odysseus.

Dream	19.535	Penelope	Odysseus is here.	Eagle kills geese, interprets story, "I am Odysseus"; then Penelope asks disguised Odysseus to interpret story, she's asking him to be the Odysseus in her dream.
Further dreams and daydream	20.88, 94	Penelope and Odysseus	Odysseus is here; Penelope knows it.	Extends Penelope's dream.
Thunder and kledonomancy	20.100	Odysseus	Odysseus will succeed.	Odysseus asks for it from Zeus, directly following on daydream.
Eagle on left clutching dove	20.243	Odysseus, cowherd, Eumaeus	Odysseus will succeed.	Beggar, Odysseus, swears Odysseus will return and kill suitors; cowherd, Eumaeus, seconds it; Zeus sends eagle.
Direct vision of death and blood	20.351	Theoclymenus, announces to suitors	Suitors will die.	Suitors ignore it and go on feasting.
Thunder	21.413	Odysseus	Zeus on his side.	Odysseus strings bow; thunder follows.

TABLE 2

Sign	Book, Line	Who Sees / Hears	What Sign Means	Context	Category of Insight
Tiresias' oracle	11	Odysseus	What Tiresias says.	Odysseus needs help getting home.	Directions home
Eagles collide, thrash each other	2.146	Telemachus and suitors	Suitors doomed.	Telemachus has just made a prayer that they face vengeance.	A sign the suitors can't read
Direct vision of death and blood	20.351	Theoclymenus, announces to suitors	Suitors will die.	Suitors ignore it and go on feasting.	
Eagle on right clutching white goose	15.160	Telemachus, Menelaus, Helen	Odysseus is coming home.	Helen reads it as Telemachus starts home from Sparta.	Encourage Telemachus
Thunder and kledonomancy	20.100	Odysseus	Odysseus will be succeed.	Odysseus asks for it from Zeus, directly following on daydream.	
Eagle on left clutching dove	20.243	Odysseus, cowherd, Eumaeus	Odysseus will succeed.	Beggar Odysseus swears that Odysseus will return and kill suitors; cowherd, Eumaeus, seconds it; Zeus sends eagle.	Encourage Odysseus
thunder	21.413	Odysseus	Zeus on his side.	Odysseus strings bow; thunder follows.	

					Penelope's insight about Odysseus
Hawk on right clutching dove	15.526, 17.160	Telemachus and Theoclymenus; Theoclymenus reports to Penelope at 17.160	The family will be safe; Odysseus is here.	Arriving at Ithaca, Telemachus prays Zeus will bring death to suitors; Theoclymenus reports to Penelope as proof that Odysseus is here.	
Sneeze, compared to thunder	17.545	Penelope	Odysseus is here.	Penelope notices beggar for first time, tells Eumaeus she wants to speak to him, closes with wish that Odysseus were back and would kill suitors, at which point Telemachus sneezes.	
Odysseus at Dodona asking about strategy: return openly or secretly (lie)	19.296	Penelope	Odysseus may come secretly.	Disguised Odysseus tells Penelope lie about real Odysseus.	
Dream	19.535	Penelope	Odysseus is here.	Eagle kills geese, interprets story, "I am Odysseus"; then Penelope asks disguised Odysseus to interpret story; she's asking him to be the Odysseus in her dream.	
Further dreams and daydream	20.88, 94	Penelope and Odysseus	Odysseus is here / Penelope knows it.	Extends Penelope's dream.	

speaks in a human voice that she says soothed her. The eagle tells her that this is not a dream, but a true waking vision, that will come true for her. The geese are the suitors, he says, and the eagle interprets himself to be her husband back at last and about to kill them all. Hearing this account of the dream from Penelope, the disguised Odysseus is left, almost for the first time in the epic, speechless, or without much to add. Then, we recall how the dream scene starts, with Penelope asking the beggar to interpret her dream. Well, the dream already has an interpreter, the eagle. So when Penelope asks the beggar to be the dream's interpreter, she is asking the beggar to be the eagle, and she is asking him to be Odysseus. No wonder he doesn't have much to add. The story interleaves the threads of divination into a veil of enigmatic knowingness on Penelope's part. Her own internal hunch is externalized through her reported witnessing of a redundantly divinatory event, provoked as well as affirmed by her husband, all three manifestations of her husband: the eagle, the beggar, and the hero in disguise. Book 20 then opens with an oscillating set of scenes parceled up to be a continuation of the prophetic dream.

We leave Penelope in the closing lines of 19 having gone to bed, but sleeplessly weeping for Odysseus. Book 20 opens with Odysseus also sleepless, lying only some dozens of feet from Penelope in her entrance hall, trying to figure out how to kill the suitors. Athena appears precisely as dreams do; she swoops down from the sky, presenting a vision to him by hovering at his head. She speaks to him as dreams do: wondering about the status of his sleep, and then soothes him by assuring him that he'll be able to kill the suitors. She then sends him to sleep. At that moment Penelope wakes up in her chamber, dozens of feet away, begins weeping, and calls out in a prayer to Artemis, saying that she has just awoken from a dream in which she saw the form of Odysseus as he was when he left for Troy. She reports in the prayer that within the dream she mistakes it for the truth and celebrates that Odysseus is really home. Then dawn comes; and still the dreaming continues. At the point of Penelope's waking up and weeping, Odysseus is also awake, and begins to have a daydream. She seems to be standing next to him and to know that it is really him.

All of this together has a beguiling uncanniness to it, of course, but by the lens developed here, it has also a statement about the status of their aggregating knowledge of one another. Here the divine message (which by this reading is to say, the intuition) that Penelope was conveying (that the beggar really is Odysseus) is matched by Odysseus' divine message (intuition) that Penelope is catching on and knows (at least intuitively) that this is really him. Right at this point in the narrative, 100 lines into book 20, Odysseus asks for a divine sign from Zeus. In fact, Odysseus asks for a double divine sign of a peculiar kind, in another example that is redundantly divinatory. He wants to hear a good omen from someone inside the house—this is kledonomancy, or divination by overheard words—and he wants a sign from outside as well. Zeus answers with thunder, at which point Odysseus overhears a woman grinding grain inside the house wishing out loud that this be the last day of the suitors. This then shows Odysseus self-consciously reckoning with an intuition that is taking shape in his own mind: Penelope is coming to the conclusion that he is Odysseus. There are a few more signs that move book 20 along. An eagle flies by clutching a dove, just as the good cowherd and Eumaeus, Odysseus's chief allies, wish that Odysseus would come back and kill the suitors, and Theoclymenus has a visceral vision that he narrates to the suitors as he is having it, of them all being ghosts and blood dripping from the walls, which they ignore. By the terms of this study, this would be an expression equivalent to calling out a lack of intuitive insight among them.[4]

Then there is a final dream sign, of a kind. Along with the prior dreams at the close of 19 and start of 20, it forms the other bookend around the scenes in between: the descriptions of preparation and slaughter in books 21 and 22, from which divine signs are absent. After the deed is done, the old nurse Eurycleia comes to Penelope's bed to wake her up and tell her that the beggar really is Odysseus and that he has killed all the suitors. Homer has her do this by taking the form of a dream. She swoops over to Penelope's bed and hovers at her head to give her the message. In other words, Homer has decided to shape the confirmation that the beggar really is her husband in the form of a dream come true, or an intuition confirmed. The idea that divination is an expression of a kind of knowing that we would call intuition helps us better

---

[4] An equivalent case could be made for Agamemnon's false dream at the opening of *Iliad* 2, an insight for which I thank Jay Boggis.

understand the richness of Homer's work in these closing books of the *Odyssey*.

By contrast, if one approaches this section of text from the other two main scholarly viewpoints on divination, which were considered in the introduction, the way would be paved for what in my view would be a rather narrow reading of what is going on. Were we, for example, to begin from the premise that divination mostly pertains to social history in antiquity, the examples in Homer's poetry look like the product of a literary craftsman who has shaped and tailored a cultural form, used most consequentially in political contexts, into the realm of issues of personal concern. Or if we work through these scenes from a perspective shaped by the magic and divination lens, we see a perhaps enchanting, but surely alien, set of beliefs to which Homer turns in order to invest an event of profound human emotion with a divine and uncanny hue. Neither of these views would be wrong, exactly, but both claim a certain distance between Homer's literary use of a phenomenon—in continuous connection with subtle internal cognitive states of Penelope and Odysseus—and that phenomenon's actual cultural reality. The preceding work gives us a better appreciation of how fully Homer's divine signs will be able to express the awareness Penelope in particular is assembling.

In my view, for Homer's ancient audience, the aptness of divinatory signs for expressing Penelope's intuitions will have nothing unexpected or uncanny about it. This evidence, and the consistent kernel of the philosophers' views in the previous chapters, align perfectly, and support instead the idea that there is *no* difference between the way Homer uses the phenomenon in advancing his plot and the way in which divination mainly and most consequentially was understood in the cultural reality of Greece up through the Hellenistic period. It was exactly the way a person would talk about moments of knowing that creep in and then crystallize, the kind of knowing still familiar to us, and not at all reducible either to superstition or social trickery and gamesmanship. Like the Greek philosophers of the classical and Hellenistic period studied here, Homer treats potential insights from divination analogously to an expression of intuitive insight about the proximate future. It is a way to talk about surplus knowledge.

BIBLIOGRAPHY

Original texts are listed below, under "Ancient Texts." Translations and commentaries are listed under "Modern Authors."

Ancient Texts

Aristotle. *Aristoteles Werke in deutscher Übersetzung: Parva Naturalia. De insomniis. De divinatione per somnun*, vol. 14, part 3. Philip J. van der Eijk, ed. Berlin: Akademie Verlag, 1994.

——. *Aristotelis qui ferebantur librorum fragmenta*. V. Rose, ed. Leipzig: Teubner, 1886. Repr. Stuttgart, 1967.

——. *Ethica Eudemia*. R. Walzer and J. Mingay, eds. Oxford Classical Texts. Oxford: Oxford University Press, 1991. [I also draw on Franz Susemihl, ed. Leipzig: Teubner, 1884. Repr. Amsterdam: Hakkert, 1967.]

——. *De la Génération et de la Corruption*. Charles Mugler, ed. Collection des universités de France. Paris: Les Belles Lettres, 1966.

——. *Météorologiques*. Pierre Louis, ed. Collection des universités de France. Paris: Les Belles Lettres, 1982.

——. *De Motu Animalium*. Martha Nussbaum, ed. Princeton: Princeton University Press, 1985.

——. *Les Parties des Animaux*. Pierre Louis, ed. Collection des universités de France. Paris: Les Belles Lettres, 1956.

——. *Parva Naturalia graece et latine*. Paul Siwek, ed. Rome: Desclée, 1963. [I also draw on W. D. Ross, ed. Oxford: Clarendon Press, 1955.]

——. *Physics*. W. D. Ross, ed. Oxford: Clarendon, 1998.

——. *Prior and Posterior Analytics*. W. D. Ross, ed. Oxford: Oxford University Press, 1949.

Cicero. *De Divinatione*. 2 vols. Arthur Stanley Pease, ed. Urbana: University of Illinois Press, 1920–23.

The Hellenistic Philosophers. 2 vols. A. A. Long and D. N. Sedley, eds. Cambridge: Cambridge University Press, 1987.

Hippocrate: Du régime. Corpus medicorum graecorum 1.2.4. Robert Joly, ed. Rev. ed. with Simon Byl. Berlin: Akademie-Verlag, 2003.

Homeri Opera. Thomas Allen, ed. Oxford Classical Texts. Oxford: Oxford University Press, 1966.

Jamblique: Les mystères d'Égypte. E. Des Places, ed. Paris: Les Belles Lettres, 1966.

Posidonius. 3 vols. L. Edelstein and I. G. Kidd, eds. 2nd. ed. Cambridge: Cambridge University Press, 1989–99.

Platonis Opera. J. Burnet, ed. Oxford Classical Texts. Oxford: Oxford University Press, 1967.

———. *Phaedrus*. Harvey Yunis, ed. Greek and Latin Classics. Cambridge: Cambridge University Press, 2011.

Porphyrius: Fragmenta. A. Smith, ed. Leipzig: Teubner, 1993.

Sophoclis Fabulae. H. Lloyd-Jones and N. G. Wilson, eds. Oxford Classical Texts. Oxford: Oxford University Press, 1990.

Stoicorum Veterum Fragmenta. 4 vols. J. Von Arnim, ed. Stuttgart: Teubner, 1964.

MODERN AUTHORS

Abraham, Roshan. "Magic and Religious Authority in Philostratus' *Life of Apollonius of Tyana*." Ph.D. dissertation, University of Pennsylvania, 2009.

Addey, Crystal. *Divination and Theurgy in Neoplatonism: Oracles of the Gods*. Surrey: Ashgate, 2014.

Alexandru, S. *Aristotle's Metaphysics Lambda: Annotated Critical Edition Based upon a Systematic Investigation of Greek, Latin, Arabic and Hebrew Sources*. Leiden: Brill, 2014.

Algra, Keimpe. "Stoics on Souls and Demons." In *Body and Soul in Ancient Philosophy*, ed. Dorothea Frede and Burkhard Reis, 359–87. Berlin: De Gruyter, 2009.

Ambady, Nalini, and John Skowronski, eds. *First Impressions*. New York: Guildford, 2008.

Annas, Julia. *Hellenistic Philosophy of Mind*. Berkeley: University of California Press, 1992.

Archer-Hind, R. D., ed. *The Timaeus of Plato*. London: MacMillan, 1888. Repr. New York: Arno, 1973.

Ashbaugh, Anne Freire. *Plato's Theory of Explanation: A Study of the Cosmological Account in the Timaeus*. Albany: SUNY Press, 1988.

Baltussen, Han. "Did Aristotle Have a Concept of 'Intuition'? Some Thoughts on Translating *nous*." In Close, Tsianikas, and Couvalis (2007), 53–62. Adelaide: Department of Languages–Modern Greek, Flinders University, 2007.

Barnes, Jonathan. "Metaphysics." In *Cambridge Companion to Aristotle*, ed. Jonathan Barnes, 66–108. Cambridge: Cambridge University Press, 1995.

Barnes, Jonathan, ed. *The Complete Works of Aristotle*. Bollingen. 2 vols. Princeton: Princeton University Press, 1984.

Bean, G. E. *Journeys in Northern Lycia: 1965–67*. Österreichische Akademie der Wissenschaften, philosophisch-historische Klasse 104. Vienna: Böhlau, 1971.

Beard, Mary. "Cicero and Divination: The Formation of a Latin Discourse." *Journal of Roman Studies* 76 (1986): 33–46.

Beare, J. I., trans. Aristotle, "On Sleep." In Barnes (1984), 1:721–35.

Beatrice, Pier Franco. *Anonymi Monophysitae Theosophia: An Attempt at Reconstruction*. Leiden: Brill, 2001.

Belfiore, Elizabeth. "Aristotle's Concept of Praxis in the Poetics." *The Classical Journal* 79.2 (1983–1984): 110–24.

Bidez, J. *La Vie de L'empereur Julien*. Paris: Les Belles Lettres, 1930.

———. *La vie de Porphyre: Le philosophe néo-platonicien*. Leipzig: Teubner, 1913.

Bobzien, Suzanne. "Chrysipppus' Theory of Causes." In *Topics in Stoic Philosophy*, ed. Katerina Ierodiakonou, 196–242. Oxford: Clarendon, 1999.

Bodéüs, Richard. *Aristote et la théologie des vivant immortels*. Paris: Bellarmin, 1992.

———. *Aristotle and the Theology of the Living Immortals*. Trans. J. Garrett. Albany: SUNY Press, 2000.

Bolton, Robert. "Intuition in Aristotle." In Osbeck and Held (2014), 39–54.

Bottéro, J. *Mesopotamia: Writing, Reasoning, and the Gods*. Chicago: University of Chicago Press, 1992.

Bremmer, Jan. "Descents to Hell and Ascents to Heaven." In *Oxford Handbook of Apocalyptic Literature*, ed. John J. Collins, 340–57. Oxford: Oxford University Press, 2014.

———. "Orphic, Roman, Jewish and Christian Tours of Hell: Observations on the *Apocalypse of Peter*." In *Other Worlds and Their Relation to This World*, ed. Tobias Nicklas, Joseph Verheyden, Erik Eynikel, and Florentino García Martínez, 305–21. Leiden: Brill, 2010.

———. "Post Scriptum: Virgil and Jewish Literature." *Vergilius* 59 (2013): 157–64.

———. "Tours of Hell: Greek, Roman, Jewish and Early Christian." In *Topographie des Jenseits: Studien zur Geschichte des Todes in Kaiserzeit und Spätantike*, ed. Walter Ameling, 13–34. Stuttgart: Steiner, 2011.

Brenk, Frederick E. *In Mist Apparelled: Religious Themes in Plutarch's Moralia and Lives*. Leiden: Brill, 1977.

———. "In the Light of the Moon: Demonology in the Early Imperial Period." In *ANRW* II.16.3, 2068–145. Berlin: De Gruyter, 1986.

Brickhouse, T. C., and N. D. Smith. "Socrates' *Daimonion* and Rationality." In *Socrates' Divine Sign: Religion, Practice, and Value in Socratic Philosophy*, ed. Pierre Destrée and Nicholas D. Smith. Special issue, *APEIRON: A Journal for Ancient Philosophy and Science* 38.2 (2005): 43–62.

———. *Socrates on Trial*. Princeton: Princeton University Press, 1989.

Brisson, Luc. *How Philosophers Saved Myths*. Chicago: University of Chicago Press, 2004.

———. "Socrates and the Divine Signal According to Plato's Testimony: Philosophical Practice as Rooted in Religious Tradition." In *Socrates' Divine Sign: Religion, Practice, and Value in Socratic Philosophy*, ed. Pierre Destrée and Nicholas D. Smith. Special issue, *APEIRON: A Journal for Ancient Philosophy and Science* 38.2 (2005): 1–12.

Brittain, Charles. "Posidonius' Theory of Predictive Dreams." *Oxford Studies in Ancient Philosophy* 40 (2011): 213–36.

Brouwer, René. "Stoic Sympathy." In Schliesser (2015), 15–35.

Brown, Jerome V. "Henry's Theory of Knowledge: Henry of Ghent on Avicenna and Augustine." In *Henry of Ghent: Proceedings of the International Colloquium on the Occasion of the 700th Anniversary of His Death, 1293*, ed. W. Vanhamel, 19–42. Louvain: Louvain University Press, 1996.

Brown, Peter. *Augustine of Hippo*. Berkeley: University of California Press, 1967.

———. "The Rise and Function of the Holy Man in Late Antiquity." In Peter Brown, *Society and the Holy in Late Antiquity*, 103–52. Berkeley: University of California Press, 1982. Repr. *Journal of Roman Studies* 61 (1971): 80–101.

Buddensiek, Friedemann. "Does Good Fortune Matter? Eudemian Ethics VIII.2 on *eutuchia*." In *The Eudemian Ethics on the Voluntary, Friendship, and Luck*, ed. Fiona Leigh, 155–84. Leiden: Brill, 2012.

Buresch, Karl. *Apollon Klarios: Untersuchungen zum Orakelwesen des späteren Altertums*. Leipzig: Teubner, 1889.

Burkert, Walter. *Homo Necans: The Anthropology of Ancient Greek Sacrificial Ritual and Myth*. Trans. Peter Bing. Berkeley: University of California Press, 1983. Repr. Berlin: De Gruyter, 1972.

——. *The Orientalizing Revolution*. Cambridge, Mass.: Harvard University Press, 1992.

Bury, R. G. *Plato IX: Timaeus, Critias, Cleitophon, Menexenus, Epistles*. Loeb Classical Library 234. Cambridge, Mass.: Harvard University Press, 1929.

Busse, Adolfus. *Commentaria in Aristotelem graeca*, vol. 18.2. Berlin: Reimer, 1904.

Cambiano, G. "Une interpretation 'materialiste' des rêves: Du Régime IV." In *Hippocratica: Actes du Colloque Hippocratique de Paris*, ed. Mirko Drazen Grmek, 87–96. Paris: Centre National de la Recherche Scientifique, 1980.

Carey, Benedict. "Brain Power: In Battle, Hunches Prove to Be Valuable." *New York Times*, July 27, 2009.

Carpenter, William Benjamin. *Principles of Human Physiology*. Philadelphia: Blanchard and Lea, 1842.

——. *Principles of Mental Physiology*. London: H. S. King & Co., 1874; repr. Cambridge: Cambridge University Press, 2009.

Cartledge, P. A., and F. D. Harvey, eds. *Crux: Essays in Greek History Presented to G.E.M. de Ste. Croix*. London: Duckworth, 1985.

Caston, Victor. "Aristotle's Two Intellects: A Modest Proposal." *Phronesis* 44.3 (1999): 199–227.

——. "The Spirit and the Letter: Aristotle on Perception." In *Metaphysics, Soul, and Ethics, in Ancient Thought*, ed. Ricardo Salles, 245–320. Oxford: Clarendon, 2005.

Chlup, Radek. *Proclus: An Introduction*. Cambridge: Cambridge University Press, 2012.

Clarke, Emma C., John M. Dillon, and Jackson P. Hershbell, eds. and trans. *Iamblichus: De mysteriis*. Atlanta: Society of Biblical Literature, 2003.

Clay, Albert T. *Epics, Hymns, Omens and Other Texts: Babylonian Records in the Library of J. Pierpont Morgan*, vol. 4. New Haven: Yale University Press, 1923.

Close, E., M. Tsianikas, and G. Couvalis, eds. *Greek Research in Australia: Proceedings of the Sixth Biennial International Conference of Greek Studies, Flinders University June 2005*. Adelaide: Department of Languages-Modern Greek, Flinders University, 2007.

Colish, Marcia. *Medieval Foundations of the Western Intellectual Tradition: 400–1400*. New Haven: Yale University Press, 1997.

——. *The Stoic Tradition from Antiquity to the Early Middle Ages*. Leiden: Brill, 1990.

Collins, Derek. "Mapping the Entrails: The Practice of Greek Hepatoscopy." *American Journal of Philology* 129.3 (2008): 319–45.

Collins, John. J. *Seers, Sibyls, and Sages in Hellenistic-Roman Judaism*. Supplements to the Journal for the Study of Judaism. Leiden: Brill, 1997.

Collobert, C., P. Destrée, and F. J. Gonzales, eds. *Plato and Myth: Studies on the Use and Status of Platonic Myths*. Mnemosyne Supplements 337. Leiden: Brill, 2012.

Cook, Patrick J. "Intuition, Discourse, and the Human Face Divine in *Paradise Lost.*" *Essays in Literature* 23 (1996): 147–64.

Cornford, Francis MacDonald. *Plato's Cosmology: The Timaeus of Plato Translated with a Running Commentary.* London: Kegan Paul, Trench, Trubner & Co., 1937.

Courcelle, Pierre. *Connais-toi toi-même de Socrate à Saint Bernard.* 3 vols. Paris: Études Augustiniennes, 1974.

Cusset, Christophe. "Cassandre et/ou la Sibylle: Les voix dans l'«Alexandra» de Lycophron." In *La Sibylle: Parole et representation,* ed. Monique Bouquet and Françoise Morzadec, 53–60. Rennes: Presses Universitaires de Rennes, 2004.

Damasio, Antonio. *Descartes' Error: Emotion, Reason, and the Human Brain.* New York: Putnam, 1994. Rev. ed. New York: Penguin, 2005.

———. *Looking for Spinoza: Joy, Sorrow, and the Feeling Brain.* New York: Harcourt, 2003.

Descartes, René. *Descartes: Selected Philosophical Writings,* vol. 2 Ed. and trans. John Cottingham, Robert Stoothoff, and Dugald Murdoch. Cambridge: Cambridge University Press, 1988.

Detienne, Marcel. *Les Maîtres de vérité dans la grèce archaïque.* Paris: Maspéro, 1967.

———. *Masters of Truth in Archaic Greece.* New York: Zone, 1996.

Diès, Auguste. "La transposition platonicienne." *Annales de l'Institut de philosophie de l'université de Bruxelles* 2 (1913): 267–308.

Dillery, John. "*Chresmologues* and *Manteis*: Independent Diviners and the Problem of Authority." In Johnston and Struck (2005), 167–231.

Dillon, John. "Iamblichus' Defence of Theurgy: Some Reflections." *International Journal of the Platonic Tradition* 1 (2007): 30–41.

Dodds, E. R. *The Greeks and the Irrational.* Berkeley: University of California Press, 1951.

———. "The *Parmenides* of Plato and the Origin of the Neoplatonic One." *Classical Quarterly* 22 (1928): 129–42.

———. "Theurgy and Its Relationship to Neoplatonism." *Journal of Roman Studies* 37 (1947): 57–60.

Donini, P. L. *Aristotle and Determinism.* Louvain: Peeters, 2010.

Dörrie, H. *Porphyrios' "Symmikta zetemata."* Munich: Beck, 1959.

Dragona-Monachou, Myrto. "Posidonius' 'Hierarchy' between God, Fate, and Nature and Cicero's *De divination.*" *Philosophia* 4 (1974): 286–301.

———. *The Stoic Arguments for the Existence and Providence of the Gods.* Athens: National and Capodistrian University of Athens, Faculty of Arts, 1976.

Dudley, John. *Aristotle's Concept of Chance: Accidents, Cause, Necessity, and Determinism.* Albany: SUNY Press, 2012.

Effe, Bernd. *Studien zur Kosmologie und Theologie der Aristotelischen Schrift "Über die Philosophie."* Munich: Beck, 1970.

Else, G. F. *Aristotle's Poetics: The Argument.* Cambridge, Mass.: Harvard University Press, 1963.

Epley, Nicolas. *Mindwise: Why We Misunderstand What Others Think, Believe, Feel, and Want.* New York: Knopf, 2014.

Erbse, Harmut. *Theosophorum Graecorum Fragmenta.* Leipzig: Teubner, 1995.

Evans-Pritchard, E. E. *Witchcraft, Magic, and Oracles among the Azande.* Oxford: Clarendon, 1937.

Falconer, W. A., trans. *Cicero, On Divination*. Loeb Classical Library 154. Cambridge: Harvard Univerity Press, 1923.

Fazzo, Silvia. *Il libro Lambda della Metafisica di Aristotele*. Elenchos 61. Naples: Bibliopolis, 2012.

Fine, Gail. "Aristotle on Determinism." *Philosophical Review* 90.4 (1981): 561–79.

Finley, John. *Homer's* Odyssey. Cambridge, Mass.: Harvard University Press, 1978.

Flower, Michael. *The Seer in Ancient Greece*. Berkeley: University of California Press, 2008.

Fonenrose, Joseph E. *The Delphic Oracle: Its Responses and Operations*. Berkeley: University of California Press, 1978.

Ford, Andrew. "Catharsis: The Power of Music in Aristotle's *Politics*." In *Music and the Muses: The Culture of Mousike in the Classical Athenian City*, ed. Penelope Murray and Peter Wilson, 309–36. Oxford: Oxford University Press, 2004.

Fowler, H. N., ed. and trans. *Plato I: Euthypro, Apology, Crito, Phaedo, Phaedrus*. Loeb Classical Library 36. Cambridge, Mass.: Harvard University Press, 1926.

Frankfurter, David. *Religion in Roman Egypt*. Princeton: Princeton University Press, 1998.

———. "Syncretism and the Holy Man in Late Antique Egypt." *Journal of Early Christian Studies* 11 (2003): 339–85.

Frede, Dorothea. "Necessity, Chance, and 'What Happens for the Most Part' in Aristotle's *Poetics*." In *Essays on Aristotle's Poetics*, ed. A. O. Rorty, 197–219. Princeton: Princeton University Press, 1992.

———. "Stoic Determinism." In Inwood (2003), 198–200.

Frede, Michael. "The Original Notion of Causes." In Michael Frede, *Essays in Ancient Philosophy*, 125–50. Minneapolis: University of Minnesota, 1987.

Frede, Michael, and David Charles, eds. *Aristotle's* Metaphysics Lambda: *Symposium Aristotelicum*. Oxford: Clarendon, 2000.

Fromentin, V. "La divination dans la *Vie d'Apollonios de Tyane* de Philostrate." *Etrusca Disciplina* 8 (1997): 71–79.

Gallop, David, trans. *Aristotle, On Sleep and Dreams: Text and Translation with Introduction, Notes, and Glossary*. Oxford: Aris & Phillips, 1996.

Gigerenzer, Gerd. *Gut Feelings: The Intelligence of the Unconscious*. New York: Penguin, 2008. Repr. 2007.

Gill, Christopher. *The Structured Self in Hellenistic and Roman Thought*. Oxford: Oxford University Press, 2006.

Gill, M. L. *Aristotle on Substance*. Princeton: Princeton University Press: 1989.

Goris, Harm. "The Angelic Doctor and Angelic Speech: The Development of Thomas Aquinas's Thought on How Angels Communicate." *Medieval Philosophy and Theology* 11 (2003): 87–105.

Gould, Josiah. *The Philosophy of Chrysippus*. Leiden: Brill, 1970.

Graf, Fritz. "Theories of Magic in Antiquity." In Mirecki and Meyer (2002), 93–104. Leiden: Brill, 2002.

Gram, Moltke S. "Intellectual Intuition: The Continuity Thesis." *Journal of the History of Ideas* 42.2 (1981): 287–304.

Griffiths, Devin S. "The Intuitions of Analogy in Erasmus Darwin's Poetics." *Studies in English Literature, 1500–1900* 51.3 (2011): 645–65.

Habinek, Thomas. "Probing the Entrails of the Universe: Astrology as Bodily Knowledge in Manilius' *Astronomica*." In *Ordering Knowledge in the Roman Empire*, ed. Jason König and Tim Whitmarsh, 229–40. Cambridge: Cambridge University Press, 2007.

Habinek, Thomas. "Tentacular Mind: Stoicism, Neuroscience, and the Configurations of Physical Reality." In *A Field Guide to a New Meta-Field: Bridging the Humanities and Neuroscience Divide*, ed. Barbara Stafford, 64–83. Chicago: University of Chicago Press, 2011.

Halliday, W. R. *Greek Divination: A Study of its Methods and Principles.* London: Macmillian, 1913.

Halliwell, Stephen. *The Aesthetics of Mimesis: Ancient Texts and Modern Problems.* Princeton: Princeton University Press, 2002.

Hankinson, R. J. *Cause and Explanation in Ancient Greek Thought.* Oxford: Oxford University Press, 1997.

———. "Stoicism, Science, and Divination." *Apeiron* 21.2 (1988): 123–60.

Harris, W. V. *Dreams and Experience in Classical Antiquity.* Cambridge, Mass.: Harvard University Press, 2009.

Harris-McCoy, Daniel E., trans. *Artemidorus, Oneirocritica.* Oxford: Oxford University Press, 2012.

Haussoullier, Bernard. "Inscriptions de Didymes." *Revue du Philologie* 44 (1920): 271–74.

Heeringa, D. "Quaestiones ad Ciceronis de Divinatione Libros Duos pertinentes." Ph.D. dissertation, Gröningen University, 1906.

Heitman, Richard. *Taking Her Seriously: Penelope and the Plot of Homer's Odyssey.* Ann Arbor: University of Michigan Press, 2005.

Hett, W. S., trans. *On the Soul, Parva Naturalia.* Loeb Classical Library 391. Cambridge, Mass.: Harvard University Press, 1936.

Hine, Harry. "Translator's Introduction." In Harry Hine, trans., *Seneca, Natural Questions*, 1–18. Chicago: University of Chicago Press, 2010.

Holmes, Brooke. "Disturbing Connections: Sympathetic Affections, Mental Disorder, and Galen's Elusive Soul." In *Mental Disorders in Classical Antiquity*, ed. W. V. Harris, 147–76. Leiden: Brill, 2013.

Holowchak, M. A. "Aristotle on Dreaming: What Goes On in Sleep When the 'Big Fire' Goes Out." *Ancient Philosophy* 16 (1996): 420–22.

Horky, Phillip. "Persian Cosmos and Greek Philosophy: Plato's Associates and the Zoroastrian *Magoi*." *Oxford Studies in Ancient Philosophy* 37 (2009): 47–103.

———. *Plato and Pythagoreanism.* Oxford: Oxford University Press, 2013.

Horsfall, Nicholas. "Lycophron and the *Aeneid*, Again." *Illinois Classical Studies* 30 (2005): 35–40.

———. "Virgil and the Jews." *Vergilius* 58 (2012): 67–80.

———. "Virgil, History, and the Roman Tradition." *Prudentia* 8 (1976): 73–89.

Howland, Jacob. "Plato's *Apology* as Tragedy." *Review of Politics* 70 (2008): 519–46.

Ierodiakou, Katerina. "The Greek Concept of Sympatheia and Its Byzantine Appropriation in Michael Psellos." In *The Occult Sciences in Byzantium*, ed. Paul Magdalino and Maria Mavroudi, 97–106. Geneva: La Pomme d'or, 2006.

Ingham, Mary Beth, and Mechthild Dreyer. *The Philosophical Vision of John Duns Scotus: An Introduction.* Washington, D.C.: Catholic University Press, 2004.

Inwood, Brad. *Ethics and Action in Early Stoicism.* Oxford: Oxford University Press, 1985.

Inwood, Brad, ed. *The Cambridge Companion to the Stoics.* Cambridge: Cambridge University Press, 2003.

Inwood, Brad, and Raphael Woolf. *Aristotle* Eudemian Ethics. Cambridge Texts in the History of Philosophy. Cambridge: Cambridge University Press, 2013.

Irwin, Terrance. "Aristotle's First 'Intuition'? Some Thoughts on Translating *nous.*" In Close, Tsianikas, and Couvalis (2007), 53–62.

———. *Aristotle's First Principles.* Oxford: Oxford University Press, 1989.

Jackson, Henry. "Eudemian Ethics θ i, ii (H xiii, xiv) 1246a26–1248b7." *Journal of Philology* 32 (1913): 170–221.

Jaeger, Werner. *Paideia: The Ideals of Greek Culture,* vol. 3, *The Conflict of Cultural Ideals in the Age of Plato.* Oxford: Oxford University Press, 1986.

James, Henry. *The American.* Oxford World's Classics. Oxford: Oxford University Press, 1999.

Joachim, H. H. *Aristotle on Coming-to-Be and Passing-Away.* Oxford: Clarendon, 1922.

———. *The Nicomachean Ethics.* Oxford: Oxford University Press, 1955.

Johnson, Aaron. "Arbiter of the Oracular: Reading Religion in Porphyry of Tyre." In *The Power of Religion in Late Antiquity,* ed. Andrew Cain and Noel Lenski, 103–15. Surrey: Ashgate, 2009.

———. *Religion and Identity in Porphyry of Tyre: The Limits of Hellenism in Late Antiquity.* Greek Culture in the Roman World. Cambridge: Cambridge University Press, 2013.

Johnson, Kent. "Luck and Good Fortune in the *Eudemian Ethics.*" *Ancient Philosophy* 17 (1997): 85–102.

Johnson, Monte Ransome. *Aristotle on Teleology.* Oxford Aristotle Series. Oxford: Clarendon, 2008.

———. "Luck in Aristotle's Physics and Ethics." In *Bridging the Gap between Aristotle's Science and Ethics,* ed. D. Henry and K. M. Nielsen, 254–75. Cambridge: Cambridge University Press, 2015.

———. "Spontaneity, Democritean Causality and Freedom." *Elenchos: Rivista di studi sul pensiero antico* 30 (2009): 5–52.

Johnston, Sarah Iles. *Ancient Greek Divination.* Oxford: Wiley-Blackwell, 2008.

———. *Hekate Soteira: A Study of Hekate's Roles in the Chaldean Oracles and Related Literature.* Atlanta: Scholars' Press, 1990.

———. "Introduction: Divining Divination." In Johnston and Struck (2005), 1–28.

———. "Lost in the Shuffle: Roman Sortition and Its Discontents." *Archiv für Religionsgeschichte* 5 (2003): 146–56.

———. Review of Daniel Ogden, *Greek and Roman Necromancy. Bryn Mawr Classical Review* (June 19, 2002).

Johnston, Sarah Iles, and Peter T. Struck, eds. *Mantikê: Studies in Greek and Roman Divination.* Leiden: Brill, 2005.

Jones, W.H.S. *Hippocrates I.* Loeb Classical Library 147. Cambridge, Mass.: Harvard University Press, 1923.

Jouanna, Jacques. "L'interprétation des rêves et la théorie micro-macrocosmique dans le traité hippocratique de *Régime:* Sémiotique et mimesis." In *Text and Tradition: Studies in Ancient Medicine and Its Transmission,* ed. K. D. Fischer, D. Nickel, and P. Potter, 161–74. *Studies in Ancient Medicine* 18. Leiden: Brill, 1998.

———. "The Theory of Sensation, Thought, and the Soul in the Hippocratic Treatise *Regimen*: Its Connections with Empedocles and Plato's *Timaeus*." In *Greek Medicine from Hippocrates to Galen: Selected Papers*, ed. Philip J. van der Eijk, 193–228. Trans. Neil Allies. Leiden: Brill, 2012.

Kahn, Charles H. "The Place of the Prime Mover in Aristotle's Teleology." In *Aristotle on Nature and Living Things: Philosophical and Historical Studies*, ed. Allan Gotthelf, 183–205. Bristol: Bristol Classical Press, 1985.

Kahneman, Daniel. *Thinking, Fast and Slow*. New York: Farrar, Straus, & Giroux: 2011.

Kal, Victor. *Aristotle on Intuition and Discursive Reason*. Leiden: Brill, 1988.

Kany-Turpin, Jose, and Pierre Pellegrin. "Cicero and the Aristotelian Theory of Divination by Dreams." In *Cicero's Knowledge of the* Peripatos, ed. W. W. Fortenbaugh and P. Steinmetz, 220–45. New Brunswick, NJ: Transaction, 1989.

Kenny, Anthony. *Aristotle on the Perfect Life*. Oxford: Oxford University Press, 1992.

———. *Aristotle: The Eudemian Ethics*. Oxford: Clarendon, 2011.

Keyser, Paul T. "Science and Magic in Galen's Recipes (Sympathy and Efficacy)." In *Galen on Pharmacology: Philosophy, History, and Medicine*, ed. Armelle Debru, 175–98. Leiden: Brill, 1997.

Knoper, Randall. "American Literary Realism and Nervous 'Reflexion.'" *American Literature* 74.4 (2002): 715–45.

Kock, T., ed. *Comicorum Atticorum Fragmenta*, vol 3. Leipzig: Teubner, 1888.

Lane Fox, Robin. *Pagans and Christians in the Mediterranean World from the Second Century AD to the Conversion of Constantine*. New York: Penguin, 2006.

Lee, Henry D. P. *Aristotle Meteorologica*. Cambridge, Mass.: Harvard University Press, 1952.

Lee, Yungwhan. "Aristotle and Determinism: An Interpretation of Aristotle's Theory of Causation, Necessity, and Accidents." Ph.D. dissertation, Princeton University, 2009.

Leszl, Walter. "I messaggi degli dei e i segni della natura." In Manetti (1996), 43–85.

Levin, S. "Know Thyself: Inner Compulsions Uncovered by Oracles." In *Fons perennis: Saggi critici di filologia classica raccolti in onore di Vittorio d'Agostino*, 231–57. Turin: A Cura della Amministrazione della RSC, 1971.

Lévy, Carlos. "De Chrysippe à Posidonius: Variations Stoïciennes sûr le Thème de la Divination." In *Oracles et Prophéties dans L'Antiquité*, ed. Jean-Georges Heintz, 321–43. Paris: De Boccard, 1997.

Lewy, Hans. *Chaldaean Oracles and Theurgy*. Cairo: Inst. Français d'Archéologie Orientale, 1956.

———. *Chaldaean Oracles and Theurgy*. Ed. Michel Tardieu. Rev. ed. Paris: Études Augustiniennes, 1978.

Lightfoot, J. L., ed. and trans. *The Sibylline Oracles: With Introduction, Translation, and Commentary on the First and Second Books*. Oxford: Oxford University Press, 2007.

Linderski, Jerzy. "The Augural Law." *ANRW* II.16.3, 2146–312. Berlin: De Gruyter, 1975.

Lloyd, Geoffrey E. R. *Aristotle: The Growth and Structure of His Thought*. Cambridge: Cambridge University Press, 1968.

Louis, Pierre, ed. *Aristote. Problèmes*, vol. 1. Paris: Budé, 1991.

Lovejoy, Arthur O. *The Great Chain of Being: A Study of the History of an Idea*. Cambridge, Mass.: Harvard University Press, 1936.

Mahootian, Farzad, and Tara-Marie Linné. "Jung and Whitehead: An Interplay of Psychological and Philosophical Perspectives on Rationality and Intuition." In Osbeck and Held (2014), 395–420.

Majercik, Ruth. *The Chaldean Oracles: Text, Translation, and Commentary.* Leiden: Brill, 1989.

Manetti, Giovanni. *Theories of the Sign in Classical Antiquity.* Bloomington: Indiana University Press, 1993.

Manetti, Giovanni, ed., *Knowledge through Signs: Ancient Semiotic Theories and Practice.* Turnhout: Brepols, 1996.

Marden, Orison Swett. *How They Succeeded: Life Stories of Successful Men Told by Themselves.* Boston: Lothrop, 1901.

Marmodoro, Anna. *Aristotle on Perceiving Objects.* Oxford: Oxford University Press, 2014.

Maurizio, Lisa. "A Reconsideration of the Pythia's Role at Delphi: Anthropology and Spirit Possession." *Journal of Hellenic Studies* 115 (1995): 69–86.

McPherran, Mark. *The Religion of Socrates.* University Park: Penn State Press, 1996.

Mensch, Jennifer. "Intuition and Nature and Kant and Goethe." *European Journal of Philosophy* 19 (2011): 431–53.

Merkelbach, R., and J. Stauber. "Die Orakel des Apollon von Klaros." *Epigraphica Anatolica* 26 (1996): 1–53.

Miller, Dana R. *The Third Kind in Plato's Timaeus.* Göttingen: Vandenhoeck & Ruprecht, 2003.

Mills, M. J. "Aristotle's Dichotomy of *EUTUXIA.*" *Hermes* 111 (1983): 282–95.

———. "*Eudemian Ethics* θ, 2, 1247a7–13." *Hermes* 109 (1981): 253–56.

Mirecki, Paul, and Marvin Meyer, eds. *Magic and Ritual in the Ancient World.* Leiden: Brill, 2002.

Mitchell, J. C. *The Yao Village.* Manchester: Manchester University Press, 1956.

Montiglio, Silvia. *Wandering in Ancient Greek Culture.* Chicago: University of Chicago Press, 2005.

More, Brookes, trans. *Ovid's Metamorphoses.* Boston: Cornhill, 1957.

Morgan, Kathryn. "The Voice of Authority: Divination and Plato's *Phaedo.*" *Classical Quarterly* 60.1 (2010): 63–81.

———. *Myth and Philosophy from the Presocratics to Plato.* Cambridge: Cambridge University Press, 2000.

Mugnier, René. *Aristote: Petits traités d'histoire naturelle.* Paris: Les Belles Lettres: 1953.

Murnaghan, Sheila. *Disguise and Recognition in the Odyssey.* Princeton: Princeton University Press, 1987.

Nadler, Steven M. *Spinoza's Ethics: An Introduction.* Cambridge: Cambridge University Press, 2006.

Natali, Carlo. *L'Action Efficace: Études sur la philosophie de l'action d'Aristote.* Louvain: Peeters, 2004.

———. "Le cause del Timeo et la teoria delle Quattro cause." In *Interpreting the Timaeus—Critias: Proceedings of the IV Symposium Platonicum,* ed. Tomás Calvo and Luc Brisson, 207–13. St. Augustin: Academia Verlag, 1997.

Oberhelman, S. M. "Dreams in Graeco-Roman Medicine." *ANRW* II.37.1, 121–56. Berlin: De Gruyter, 1993.

Ogden, Daniel. *Greek and Roman Necromancy*. Princeton: Princeton University Press, 2001.

Osbeck, Lisa M., and Barbara S. Held, eds. *Rational Intuition: Philosophical Roots, Scientific Investigations*. Cambridge: Cambridge University Press, 2014.

Park, George K. "Divination and its Social Contexts." *Journal of the Royal Anthropological Institute* 93.2 (1963): 195–209.

Parke, H. W., and D.E.W. Wormell. *The Delphic Oracle*. Oxford: Oxford University Press, 1956.

Parker, Robert. "Greek States and Greek Oracles." In *Crux: Essays in Greek History Presented to G. E. M. de Ste. Croix*, ed. P. A. Cartledge and F. D. Harvey, 298–326. London: Duckworth, 1985. Repr. In *Oxford Readings in Greek Religion*, ed. R. Buxton, 76–108. Oxford: Oxford University Press, 2000.

Partenie, C., ed. *Plato's Myths*. Cambridge: Cambridge University Press, 2009.

Pasnau, Robert. "Cognition." In *The Cambridge Companion to Duns Scotus*, ed. Thomas Williams, 285–311. Cambridge: Cambridge University Press, 2002.

Peek, Philip. "Introduction: The Study of Divination, Past and Present." In Philip Peek, *African Divination Systems: Ways of Knowing*, 1–22. Bloomington: Indiana University Press, 1991.

Penwill, John. "Myths, Dreams, and Mysteries: Intertextual Issues in *Aeneid* 6." In John Penwill, *Two Essays on Virgil: Intertextual Issues in Aeneid 6 and Georgics 4*, 6–27. Studies in Western Traditions Occasional Papers 2. Bendigo: La Trobe University Press, 1995.

Pritchett, Kendrick. *Greek State at War: Part 3*. Berkeley: University of California Press, 1979.

Rackham, H. *Aristotle XIX: Nicomachean Ethics*. Loeb Classical Library 73. Cambridge, Mass.: Harvard University Press, 1926.

Raven, J. E. *Plato's Thought in the Making: A Study of the Development of His Metaphysics*. Cambridge: Cambridge University Press, 1965.

Reiner, Erica, and David Pingree. *Babylonian Planetary Omens: Part Four*. Cuneiform Monographs 30. Leiden: Brill, 2005.

Reinhardt, Karl. *Poseidonios*. Munich: Beck, 1921.

Repici, L. *Aristotele: Il sonno e i sogni*. Venice: Marsilio, 2003.

Reydams-Schils, Gretchen. *Demiurge and Providence: Stoic and Platonist Readings of Plato's Timaeus*. Monothéismes et Philosophie 2. Turnhout: Brepols, 1999.

———. "Posidonius and the Timaeus: Off to Rhodes and Back to Plato?" *Classical Quarterly*, N. S., 47.2 (1997): 455–76.

Ricoeur, Paul. *Time and Narrative*, vol. 1. Chicago: University of Chicago Press, 1984.

Rives, James. "Aristotle, Antisthenes of Rhodes, and the *Magikos*." *Rheinisches Museum für Philologies*, n. F., 147.1 (2004): 35–54.

Rochberg, Francesca. "'If P, Then Q': Form and Reasoning in Babylonian Divination." In *Divination and Interpretation of Signs in the Ancient World*, ed. Amar Annus, 19–27. Oriental Institute Seminars 6. Chicago: The Oriental Institute, 2010.

———. *The Heavenly Writing: Divination, Horoscopy, and Astronomy in Mesopotamian Culture*. Cambridge: Cambridge University Press 2004.

Rosenstein, N. "Sorting Out the Lot in Republican Rome." *American Journal of Philology* 116 (1995): 43–75.

Ross, W. D. *Aristotle*. 5th ed. London: Methuen, 1949.

Rotondaro, Serafina. "Il ΠΑΘΟΣ della ragione e i sogni: Timeo 70d7–72b5." In *Interpreting the Timaeus—Critias: Proceedings of the IV Symposium Platonicum*, ed. Tomás Calvo and Luc Brisson, 275–80. St. Augustin: Academia Verlag, 1997.

Ryan, Vanessa. *Thinking without Thinking in the Victorian Novel.* Baltimore: Johns Hopkins University Press, 2012.

Saffrey, H.-D. "Les Néoplatoniciens et les Oracles Chaldaïques." *Revue des études anciennes* 27 (1981): 209–25.

Saffrey, Henri Dominique, and Alain-Philippe Segonds, eds. *Porphyre: Lettre à Anébon l'Égyptien.* Paris: Les Belles Lettres, 2012.

Salles, Ricardo, ed. *God and Cosmos in Stoicism.* Oxford: Oxford University Press, 2009.

Salles, Ricardo. "Introduction: God and Cosmos in Stoicism." In Salles (2009), 1–19.

Sambursky, S. *Physics of the Stoics.* London: Routledge & Paul, 1959.

Sauvé Meyer, Susan. "Chain of Causes: What is Stoic Fate?" In Salles (2009), 71–92.

Schäublin, C. "Cicero *De Divinatione* und Poseidonios." *Museum Helveticum* 42 (1985): 164–66.

Schliesser, Eric, ed. *Sympathy: A History.* Oxford Philosophical Concepts. Oxford: Oxford University Press, 2015.

Schofield, Malcolm. "Cicero for and against Divination." *Journal of Roman Studies* 76 (1986): 47–65.

Segal, Charles. "Pentheus and Hippolytus on the Couch and on the Grid: Psychoanalytic and Structuralist Readings of Greek Tragedy." *The Classical World* 73.3 (1978): 129–48.

Segev, Mor. "The Teleological Significance of Dreaming in Aristotle." *Oxford Studies in Ancient Philosophy* 43 (2012): 107–41.

Sharmdasani, Sonu. *Jung and the Making of Modern Psychology: The Dream of a Science.* Cambridge: Cambridge University Press, 2003.

Shaw, Gregory. *Theurgy and the Soul: The Neoplatonism of Iamblichus.* State College: Penn State Press, 1995.

Sheppard, Anne. "Proclus' Attitude to Theurgy." *Classical Quarterly* 32 (1982): 212–24.

Shorey, Paul. *Plato: The Republic, Books I–V.* Loeb Classical Library 237. Cambridge, Mass.: Harvard University Press, 1969.

Sicherl, Martin. *Die Handschriften, Ausgaben und Übersetzungen von Iamblichos De Mysteriis: Eine kritisch-historische Studie.* Berlin: Akademie-Verlag, 1957.

Sistakou, Evina. *The Aesthetics of Darkness: A Study of Hellenistic Romanticism in Apollonius, Lycophron, and Nicander.* Hellenistica Groningana 17. Louvain: Peeters, 2012.

Sluiter, Ineke. "The Greek Tradition." In *The Emergence of Semantics in Four Linguistic Traditions: Hebrew, Sanskrit, Greek, Arabic,* ed. Wout van Bekkum, Jan Houben, Ineke Sluiter, and Kees Versteegh, 147–224. Amsterdam: John Benjamins, 1997.

Smith, Jonathan Z. "The Influence of Symbols upon Social Change: A Place on Which to Stand." In Jonathan Z. Smith, *Map Is Not Territory: Studies in the History of Religions,* 129–46. Studies in Judaism in Late Antiquity 23. Leiden: Brill, 1978.

———. *To Take Place: Toward Theory in Ritual.* Chicago: Chicago University Press, 1987.

Snow, Dale E. *Schelling and the End of Idealism.* Albany: SUNY Press, 1996.

Solmsen, Friedrich. *Aristotle's System of the Physical World: A Comparison with His Predecessors.* Ithaca, N.Y.: Cornell University Press, 1960.

Sorabji, Richard. *Necessity, Cause, and Blame*. Chicago: University of Chicago Press, 1980.

Spencer, Herbert. *An Autobiography*. 2 vols. London: Williams and Norgate, 1904.

Stafford, Barbara, ed. *A Field Guide to a New Meta-Field: Bridging the Humanities and Neuroscience Divide*. Chicago University of Chicago Press, 2011.

Steel, Carlos. "The Moral Purpose of the Human Body: A Reading of Timaeus 69–72." *Phronesis* 46.2 (2001): 105–28.

Struck, Peter T. *Birth of the Symbol: Ancient Readers at the Limits of Their Texts*. Princeton: Princeton University Press, 2004.

———. "Pagan and Christian Theurgies: Iamblichus, Pseudo–Dionysius, Religion, and Magic in Late Antiquity." *Ancient World* 32.2 (2001): 25–38.

Taylor, A. E. *A Commentary on Plato's* Timaeus. Oxford: Clarendon, 1928.

Tortzen, Christian Gorm. "'Know Thyself': A Note on the Success of a Delphic Saying." In *"Noctes Atticae": Thirty-Four Articles on Graeco-Roman Antiquity and Its Nachleben: Studies Presented to Jørgen Mejer on his Sixtieth Birthday, March 18, 2002*. Copenhagen: Museum Tusculanum, 2002.

Tränkle, Hermann. "Gnothi seauton: Zu Ursprung und Deutungsgeschichte des delphischen Spruchs." *Würzburger Jahrbücher für die Altertumswissenschaft*, n. F., 11 (1985): 19–31.

van der Eijk, Philip J. *Medicine and Philosophy in Classical Antiquity: Doctors and Philosophers on Nature, Soul, Health, and Disease*. Cambridge: Cambridge University Press, 2005.

Vanhamel, W., ed. *Henry of Ghent: Proceedings of the International Colloquium on the Occasion of the 700th Anniversary of his Death, 1293*. Louvain: Louvain University Press, 1996.

Verbeke, G. "Happiness and Chance in Aristotle." In *Aristotle on Nature and Living Thing: Philosophical and Historical Studies*, ed. Allan Gotthelf, 247–58. Bristol: Bristol Classical Press, 1985.

Vernant, Jean-Pierre, and Marcel Détienne, eds. *La cuisine du sacrifice en pays grec*. Paris: Gallimard, 1979.

Vlastos, Gregory. "Cornford's *Principium Sapientiae*." *Gnomon* 27 (1955): 65–76.

———. "Cornford's *Principium Sapientiae*." *Studies in Greek philosophy*, vol. 1, *The Presocratics*, ed. Daniel W. Graham, 112–23. Princeton: Princeton University Press, 1995.

———. *Socrates, Ironist, and Moral Philosopher*. Ithaca, N.Y.: Cornell University Press, 1991.

Vogt, Katja. *Law, Reason, and the Cosmic City*. Oxford: Oxford University Press, 2008.

Wachsmuth, C. *Studien zu den griechischen Florilegien*. Berlin: Weidmann, 1882.

Wardle, D. *Cicero: On Divination Book I*. Oxford: Oxford University Press, 2006.

Wedin, Michael V. *Aristotle's Theory of Substance: The* Categories *and* Metaphysics Zeta. Oxford Aristotle Studies. Oxford: Oxford University Press, 2000.

Werner, Daniel S. "Plato on Madness and Philosophy." *Ancient Philosophy* 31.1 (2011): 47–71.

White, M. J. "Stoic Natural Philosophy." In Inwood (2003), 124–52.

Wilkins, Eliza. "'Know Thyself' in Greek and Latin Literature." Ph.D. dissertation, University of Chicago, 1917.

Wilson, Malcolm. *Structure and Method in Aristotle's Meteorologica*. Cambridge: Cambridge University Press, 2014.

Wilson, Timothy. *Strangers to Ourselves: Discovering the Adaptive Unconscious*. Cambridge, Mass.: Belknap, 2002.

Wolfsdorf, David. "Timaeus' Explanation of Sense-Perceptual Pleasure." *Journal of Hellenic Studies* 134 (2014): 120–35.

Woods, Michael, trans. and comm. *Aristotle: Eudemian Ethics, books I, II, and VIII*. Clarendon Aristotle Series. Oxford: Clarendon, 1992. Repr. 1982.

Yovel, Yirmiyahu. *Spinoza and Other Heretics*, vol. 1, *The Marrano of Reason*. Princeton: Princeton University Press, 1989.

Zeller, E. *Die Philosophie der Griechen in ihrer geschichtlichen Entwicklung*, vol. 2. 3rd ed. Leipzig: Fues, 1879.

Zetzel, James E. G. "Introduction." In *Cicero: De Re Publica*, ed. James E. G. Zetzel, 1–34. Cambridge: Cambridge University Press, 1995.

INDEX LOCORUM

Acts
  2:23   245

Aeschylus
Supplices (Supp.)
  17   83

Aetius
De placitis reliquiae (Diels, ed.)
  1.29.7   199n.53
  4.11.1–4 (= *HP* 39E)   176n.9
  4.21.1–4 (= *HP* 53H)   193

Arius Didymus
  9–9a   205

Alexander of Aphrodisias
De fato
  7   199n.53

Anselm
Proslogion
  14   26n.50
  18   26n.50

Apuleis
On the God of Socrates (De deo Soc.)
  16.25   224

Aristotle
De anima   93
  407a24   98n.10
  415a22–b3   158
  415a26–b2   127n.57
  433a10–434a21 (= 3.10)   146n.77

De caelo (Cael.)
  279a22–30   127n.57
  285a29   119
  286a9–11   119
  292a20–b2   119
  292a22–b25   127n.57
  292b32   119

Categories (Cat.)
  10a1   100n.13

On Divination during Sleep (Div. somn.)
  462b20   96n.7

  462b20–22   116n.38
  462b23   162
  462b24–26   95
  462b25–26   140, 140n.72
  462b26   162
  462b30   162
  463a7–11   105
  463a18–20   105
  463a20–21   105
  463a25   96n.7, 157n.91
  463a28   96n.7
  463a28–29   97
  463b12   167n.96
  463b1   95n.6
  463b12–15   95
  463b15–22   113
  463b16   157n.91
  463b22–31   114, 159
  464a12   96n.7
  464a15–19   160
  464a19   96n.7
  464a22–24   100
  464a32–b5   161–62
  464b2   96n.7
  464b7   157n.91
  464b16   157n.91
  464a22–26   161
  464a25   159
  464a27   157n.91
  464b8–9   105
  464b15–18a   101
  465a3–7   97

On Generation and Corruption (GC)
  333b7–9   126
  333b55–59   134
  336b27   164
  336b27–28   138
  336b27–37a7   127, 144
  337a21   127n.57

De generatione animalium (GA)
  731b20–32a9   127n.57

750b20   146
789b5   98n.10

De juventute et senectute (Juv.)
469a8   98n.10

Eudemian Ethics (EE)
1214a21–25   132
122b15–23   135n.66
1223a3   94
1223a5   135
1223a21–28   146n.77
1223a26–27   146n.77
1224a28–30   135n.67
1225a27–31   159
1225a29   94
1229a25   100n.13
1139a20   135n.67
1247a13–16   141
1247a15   142, 153
1247a15–23   141
1247a21–23   115–16
1247a24–30   140–41
1247b8–9   140
1247b16–18   142
1247b18–20   143
1247b20–21   144
1247b21–27   144–45
1247b28–33   145, 153–54
1247b32   153n.88
1248a2–7   140
1248a7   148
1248a7–9   148–49
1248a16–23   149
1248a23–26   150
1248a26–34   151
1248a30   153n.88
1248a34   162
1248a34–b3   155

Fragments (Rose)
6.3   117
10   169
76.5   133n.61
44.21   117
191   217n.1
192.3   117
193.13   117
487.4   117
490.2   117

History of Animals (Hist. an.)
572b8   146
572b24   146

573a27   146
574a13   146
575a15   146
581b12   146
582a34   146
587b32   146
636a24   133n.61

Metaphysics (Meta.)
981a14   115n.35
984b12   138, 144
1023a9–23   147n.80
1025b18–24   135
1026a18–20   121
1028b9–13   120n. 45
1028b34–36   118n.40
1032a19   118n.43
1035b6–12   118n.42
1042a7–11   120n. 45
1050a9   98n.10
1050b5–6   127n.57
1072b14   124
1074a30–31   119

Meteorologica (Meteor.)
339a19–32   123–24, 127n.57

On the Movement of Animals (Mot. an.)
700a5   124

Nicomachean Ethics (NE)
1017b10–14   118
1094a15   98n.10
1097a18   98n.10
1102b21   146
1106b33   115n.35
1112b31–32   135
1122b21   117
1129a20   135
1139a17–b5   135
1141a   247n.48
1141a34–b1   119
1142a   247n.48
1142a23–30   21n.39
1143b6   21n.39
1145b11   100n.13
1146a23   115n.35
1173a4–5   164
1176b30   98n.10
1177a13–17   132n.58
1177b27–31   132n.58
1179b21–22   94
1179a27–28   132n.58

On the Parts of Animals (Part. an.)
644b22–45a6   119–20
651a4   100n.13
653b6   182
690b5   182

Physics (Phys.)
192b18   147n.80
196a25–b4   133n.62
196a31–32   126
196a34   119
196b5–6   133n.61
199a7–18   137–38
199a8–20   144
199a23–30   148
199b26   144
222b16   100
226a35   94
259b11   94

Physiognomica (Phgn.)
4   183

Poetics
1340a8–14   182
1459a8   101n.15

Politics (Pol.)
1252a27–30   146n.78
1253a29   146
1280b40   98n.10
1322b31   117
1325a7   98n.10
1331b33   115n.35
1339b36   98n.10

Posterior Analytics
100b   247n.48

Prior Analytics
95a1   147n.80

Problemata (Prob.)
867b7   146
868b31   146
876a21   146
886a25–87b7   182
886a35   146
886a36   183
903b21   146
937b36   147n.80
961b25   146
962a5   146

Rhetoric (Rhet.)
1354a9   115n.35
1360a1   94

De sensu et sensibilibus (Sens.)
436b6–8   93

On Sleep and Waking (Somn.)
453b   164
453b21–25   93, 95–96
455a34   182
456a30–68a32   158
458a10   158

Augustine
On Christian Doctrine
2.23–24   244n.45

City of God
9.21–23   244n.45

Confessions
11   203

Chaldean Oracles
5   226
108   233

Chrysippus
SVF 1.518   180n.19
SVF 2.389   180n.19
SVF 2.416   180n.19
SVF 2.439   180n.19
SVF 2.441   180n.19
SVF 2.447   180n.19
SVF 2.449   180n.19
SVF 2.473   180n.19, 184–85
SVF 2.546   180n.19
SVF 2.550   180n.19
SVF 2.716   180n.19
SVF 2.911   180n.19

Cicero
Academica
2.107   174

De divinatione (De div.)
1   175, 200
1.1   171
1.2–4   17n.28
1.3   10n.14
1.3–5   176
1.6   16, 174n.5, 176n.11, 192n.46
1.9   198, 213
1.10   173, 186
1.12   176n.10, 188, 190n.43, 192
1.13   198
1.13–14   242n.43
1.15   192n.46, 198n.51
1.16   192n.46, 197–98
1.18   16

1.24   198
1.35   176n.10
1.38   192n.46
1.39   176n.9
1.56   176n.9
1.64   176, 210n.65, 210n.66
1.66   192n.46
1.71   198
1.79   192n.46
1.82–83   186
1.84   186
1.84–86   176n.10
1.109   176n.10
1.110   185n.32, 210–11
1.111   198
1.112   198
1.112–29   176,186
1.117   186, 187, 203
1.118   177, 187–88, 190, 191, 192
1.118–24   187
1.118–32   186
1.120   190n.43, 191
1.121   190n.41, 191
1.125   176n.11, 177, 186, 187, 190n.43, 192, 192–93n.46, 198
1.125–28   186, 187
1.126   201
1.127   195–96, 201
1.128   193n.46, 203, 206
1.129   208–9
1.129–30   176n.11
1.129–32   186, 187
1.130   211
1.131   212
2   175, 199, 200
2.11   16
2.14   199
2.14–19   198
2.19   199
2.33   185n.32, 210n.67
2.33–34   184n.31
2.33–35   176n.11
2.35   188
2.40   10n.14
2.41   186
2.47   176n.11, 198
2.48   198
2.66   198
2.67   199
2.83   199
2.90   174

2.92   185n.32, 211n.67
2.101–2   186n.37
2.104–6   186n.37
2.121   199
2.141   199

De fato
5   185n.32, 211n.67
11   198n.51
41–43   202

De legibus
2.32–33   186

De natura deorum (Nat. D.)
2.19   184n.31
2.58   194–95
2.167   192n.45

Cleanthes
HP 45C   184
SVF 1.497   204
SVF 1.518   184
SVF 1.596   184

Cleomedes
Caelestia
1.1.13 (SVF 2.912)   184n.31
1.1.69–73 (SVF 2.546)   184n.31

Democritus
Diels-Kranz 68 A 77–79   99n.12
Diels-Kranz 68 B 34   78n.35
Diels-Kranz 68 B 164   79n.36
Diels-Kranz 68 B 166   99n.12

Diogenes Laertius (Diog. Laert.)
1.147–49   174n.5
7.140   184n.31
7.142–43   179
7.149   186n.36
7.158–59   204n.58
9.46   99n.12

Empedocles
Diels-Kranz 31 B 112   217n.1

Epicurus
Epistula ad Herodotum
Diog. Laert. 10.38   247n.48
Diog. Laert. 10.63   184

Eunapius
Vitae sophistarum (Vita soph.)
458–59   235n.41

Euripides
Electra (El.)
826–29   81

Eusebius
Praeparatio evangelica (Praep. evang.)
   15.20.1   204n.58

Galen
De locis affectis
   8.30   184n.28

The Doctrines of Hippocrates and Plato (PHP)
   3.1.10–15   193

Herodotus
   1.157.3   11n.17
   7.140–41   39

Hephaistion of Thebes
Apotelesmatica
   3   36n.67

Hipparchus
   9.9   11n.17

Hippocrates
On Nutriment
   23   183

On Regimen (On Reg.)
   1   106
   1.4   107
   1.5   107–8, 109
   1.11   109
   1.12   1
   1.14   108
   1.23   108
   1.24   108
   2   109
   2.40   109n.29
   2.45   109n.29
   2.54   109n.29
   4   105, 106, 109
   4.86   110
   4.87   107, 111

Hippocratic Letters
   23.10   183–84

Homer
Odyssey
   2.146   256, 258
   15.160   256, 258
   15.526   256, 258
   17.160   256, 258
   17.545   256, 258
   18.281–83   254
   19.296   256, 258
   19.379–81   253
   19.535   257, 258
   19.570–81   253
   20.88   257, 258
   20.94   257, 258
   20.100   257, 258
   20.205   253
   20.243   257, 258
   20.351   257, 258
   21.413   257, 258

Iamblichus
De mysteriis (De myst.)
   3   219
   3.1.2   245
   3.1.5   245
   3.1.14–20   236
   3.1.20–27   236
   3.1.25   245
   3.1.40   245
   3.1.49   245
   3.2   238
   3.2.9–11   237
   3.2.22   247
   3.3.25   237
   3.3.43–55   238
   3.4.2   237
   3.4.7–9   238
   3.4.21–36   238
   3.6.10–16   238
   3.6.22   247
   3.7.15–31   240–41
   3.8   238
   3.8.3   237
   3.9   238
   3.10   239
   3.10.2   237
   3.12.3–14   239–40
   3.12.25   245
   3.15   241
   3.15.1–3   241
   3.15.9–10   241
   3.17.44   247
   3.17.51   237
   3.18.19   245
   3.19.26   245
   3.22.40–46   242
   3.24.5   245
   3.24.17   245
   3.24.19   245
   3.24.20   245
   3.25   230n.33
   3.26   21
   3.26.9   247

3.26.23   237
3.26.28–34   246–47
3.26.29   247
3.26.30   245
3.26.37   243, 247
3.27.2   237
3.27.6   237
3.27.9   237
3.27.12   237
3.27.37   237
3.27.45   237
3.27.56   237
3.30.38   245
3.31.41   237
3.31.58   237
3.31.70   245
5.23.17–20   233
5.23.23–24   233
5.23.29–34   234
5.23.35–45   234
6.3.14   247
6.4.14   245
9.3.33   237
9.5.19   237
10.3   248–49
10.4.1   237
10.4.3   245
10.4.9   245
10.4.12   245
10.4.20   245
10.5.2   237
10.8.2   237

Vita Pythagorae (VP)
31   217n.1
140   217n.1

Judith
9:6   245
11:19   245

Milton
Paradise Lost
5.488–90   27
8.352–54   27

Onasander
The General
10.10   32n.65

Origen
Contra Celsum (Contr. Cel.)
4.88–92   244n.45, 245
4.92   244
7.3   244

7.4   244
8.48   244

Ovid
Metamorphoses (Met.)
6.510   21n.39

1 Peter
1:2   245

Philodemus
P. Herc.1018   174n.6

Philostratus
Life of Apollonius of Tyana (VA)
4.44   225

Plato
Apology (Apol.)
17d   38
20d–e   39
21b   38, 39
21b–d   38
22a   37
22b–c   72
23a–b   39–40
23b–c   38
24a   38
27a   38
27d   38
28c   37
31d   68
39c–d   50
40a   69n.28
40a–b   68

Charmides
169c   181
173c   45

Cratylus (Crat.)
383b–84a   49
396d–e   48
399a   83n.41
405a–c   44
411b   21n.39
411c   49
428c   49

Crito
44b   50

Euthydemus (Euthyd.)
272e   68

Euthyphro
3e   48, 69n.28
9c   56n.15

Ion   73
   531b   44
   538e–39d   44

Laches
   195e–96d   45
   199a   44

Laws
   634e   52
   642d7   44
   686a4   44
   694c   52
   700b   52
   722d   52
   734e   52
   738c   83n.41
   747e   83n.41
   772d   46
   792d   46
   800a–c   52
   811c   83n.41
   828a–b   46
   871d   46
   885c–d   46
   908d   46
   913b2   45–46
   914a   46
   933a   46
   950b   21n.39
   952d   52

Lysis
   216   48

Meno
   85c   60n.21
   92c   48
   99b–c   60

Phaedo
   69c   52n.14
   72e–77a   65
   73c–75c   64n.25
   84d–85d   73
   84e–85b   50
   96a–c   74
   106e–7a   51
   111b   51–52
   118a   40n.4

Phaedrus
   229e   61
   238c–d   61
   241e–42d   61

   242b–d   68–69
   244   16
   244c–d   17n.28, 62
   247c   64
   248d   90
   249c–d   64
   249e–50a   65
   262d   61
   265b   83n.41
   275b   43
   279a   47

Philebus (Phil.)
   20b   56n.17
   44c   72
   64a   58, 60
   66b   58
   67b   73

Republic (Rep.)
   349a   47
   364b5   45
   370a   56n.15
   383b6   44
   389d3   45
   394d   48
   430e   54
   431e   21n.39, 54
   443c   54
   496c   68
   499c   83n.41
   505e–6a   57–58, 60
   508d   59
   509b   231–32
   510a   59
   516d   59
   521d   55–56
   523a   56, 60
   531d   57
   538a   57
   538b   57
   571c–72b   190
   586b   54–55
   599d3   42n.7
   605c–d   181n.41
   614a–621d   220
   614b   37
   621b   220

Statesman
   260e   44
   289c   47
   290d   44

299d   44
309c   60n.20

Symposium (Symp.)
180b   66
181c   83n.41
188c   66
192d   53
197a   44
198a   47
198a–b   66
202e–3a   70–71
206b   67
210d   67
210e   67
212a   67n.26

Theaetetus (Theaet.)
142c   47
150d   65
151a   68
179a   48

Timaeus (Tim.)
27a–b   75
27c–41d   75
29b   78
30b   76
32c–d   226
33c–d   179–80
34a–b   76
34b   179–80
35   77
36e   76
39a–b   77
39c   78
39e   78
40d   71
41d   77
43a–b   85
44a–d   78
44b   86
46c7   88
46d1   88
47c   78
51d   64
69   76
69b   75
69e   79
70b   79–80
70e   80
71a   80
71c   81, 86

71c–d   82
71d–e   89
71e   84
72b   82, 87
76d6   88
81a–b   78–79
89d–90d   86–87
90a   71n.31, 83, 87
90c   83, 87
90c–d   87

Plotinus
Enneads
2.9.16   233
2.9.16–18   233
4.4.1   247n.48

Plutarch
De defectu oraculorum (De def. or.)
437f   115n.36

[Plutarch]
De Fato (Fat.)
574E   184n.31

Porphyry
On Philosophy from Oracles
324F (Smith)   227

Life of Plotinus
23.15–18   232n.38

Proclus
Commentary on Plato's Timaeus (In Tim.)
57.30–58.3   226

1 Samuel
28:8   223n.15

Seneca
Letters
65.2 (HP 55E)   178

Sextus Empiricus
Against the Professors (Math.)
8.56–58   176n.9
9.78–80 (=SVF 2.1013)   184n.31
9.80–81 (=SVF 2.1013)   185
9.196   204
9.211 (=HP 55B)   201–2

Sibylline Oracles
4.3   223
11.316–17   223

Sophocles
Oedipus Tyrannus (OT)
964–72   38–39

Soranus
Gynecology
  1.15   183n.27

Thomas Aquinas
Summa Theologica
  1a56.1   26
  1a58   27
  55.2   26
  58.6–7   26

Vergil
Aeneid
  6   219

Xenophon
Apology (Apol.)
  14   40

Cyropaedia (Cyr.)
  1.6.46   11n.17

Memorabilia (Mem.)
  1.4.15   11n.17

Symposium (Symp.)
  4.47–47   49n.Index

SUBJECT INDEX

Cave, allegory of the, 55–59, 220
Christianity, 218–19, 223, 227, 244–45
coincidence, 34, 97–98, 113–14, 129–30, 137, 159, 162
cosmos, 87, 88, 123, 163, 187, 192, 215, 228, 233, 236, 242; as deterministic, 195, 203; creation of the, 75–78, 89; divination as semiotic machinery of the, 34, 35; as emanation of a first principle, 231–32; as ensouled, 77, 179, 189, 192n.46, 207; material, 44, 59, 63, 65, 67, 74, 75–76, 80, 85, 89, 189, 216–17, 230–33, 235–237, 240–246; microcosm and macrocosm, 78–79, 106, 107–10, 178–79; as organism bound by *pneuma*, 76, 172, 177–80, 184–85, 128, 204, 207, 212–13, 214; structure of the, 33, 104, 105, 217, 220–21, 225, 226
craft. See *technê*
craftsman, 89–90; diviner as, 43–47, 89–90; nature as, 194–95, 206, 226

daimon (demon), and the demonic, 27, 68–71, 83, 87, 94–95, 98–99, 103–4, 112–22, 128–31, 134, 140–41, 154, 156–57, 159–60, 161, 163, 164–68, 209, 224, 235, 241, 244, 247
discursive reasoning, 14, 18, 20, 22, 27, 54, 58–65, 69, 73, 80–84, 87, 100, 143, 158, 160–61, 170, 252–53
divination: as corporeal, 35–36; as direct revelation, 223, 236; divine, true, 237–43, 245; through dreams (see *dreams*); and the gods, 173–74, 186–87; as innate, 171–72; and intuition, 11, 22, 52–61, 69–70, 249; and luckiness, 154–56, 165; and magic, 6–9, 10, 45–46; natural, 16–17, 187–92, 197, 201, 237; and politics, 5–6, 8–9; and rationality, 8–9, 12–13, 62–63, 83–84; as *technê*/skill, 8, 16–17, 43–47, 72, 187–189, 201, 211, 213, 237, 241–46
dreams, 82, 83, 93–102, 169, 174, 188, 238, 240; as demonic, 113, 117–22, 128–31,

156–57, 163; as not god-sent, 102–3, 112–13, 122, 130, 156–57; and empty-headed people, 96–97, 99, 116, 129, 159–61, 164; in medicine, 103–6; predictive, 54, 93, 96, 99–101, 104, 113, 129, 130, 140, 141, 151, 156, 160, 161, 165, 168, 183; as revelatory, 221–29

eidôlon (phantom image), 42, 80–81, 89
elenchus (cross-examination), 40, 50–52, 53, 55, 57, 84, 90
Epicureans, 10, 25, 175, 184, 188,
Er, myth of, 37, 220

fate, 107–8, 177, 186, 187, 188, 195–200, 203, 206, 207–8
Forms, Platonic, 26, 40, 53, 55, 58, 59, 61, 64–66, 67, 74, 76, 216, 226, 230, 232, 237, 238–39

Good, the, 45, 53, 55, 57–58, 60, 67, 77, 129, 141–42, 144, 153–54, 157–58, 163–164, 171, 214, 230–31

hexis (disposition), 142, 178, 205
hylê (matter), 59, 177–78, 189, 209, 230, 232–34, 242

impulse, 53, 92, 172, 193–94, 195, 205–7, 210
impulse hypothesis, 125–31, 136–37, 139, 143–48, 152–59, 162–63, 165–68
intuition, 16, 20–33, 69–70, 235; cognitive, 23–28, 31–33, 54; rational, 22–28, 52–54, 246–49, 249–50, 251–52, 255, 261–62

knowledge: discursive (*see* discursive reasoning); non-discursive, 17, 18, 22, 23, 25–27, 28, 33, 42, 43, 47–50, 52–61, 63–67, 73, 83, 90, 91–92, 104, 110, 171, 215–216, 246, 252, 255; surplus, 15–16, 20, 22, 23, 28, 32, 35, 54, 91–92, 104, 129, 159, 163, 170, 172, 200, 213, 249–51, 262

liver-reading, 18, 42–43, 73, 80–82, 84, 87–88, 89–90, 180,187–88, 191, 216
luckiness, 92, 144–45, 160, 165, 166, 168; and impulse, 142–45, 152; consistent, 115–16, 130–32, 139–42, 148–155, 156, 158, 161–63

magic, 5–10, 16, 45–46, 51, 92, 180–81, 217, 225, 229–30, 235, 262
mantis (diviner), 44, 45, 48, 52
matter. See *hylê*
medicine, 7, 66, 76, 92, 96–97, 99, 102–6, 111–12, 161, 181, 183–85
movement: and the divine, 122–25, 126–30, 135, 152, 154, 166, 168, 170, 232; and impulse, 147–50, 194, 206; of the cosmos, 77–79, 121, 122–23, 125, 179, 232; of the soul, 85, 87, 110, 148, 152, 178, 205; and dreams, 99, 101, 114, 162–63, 165–66

nous, 20, 25–27, 53, 64, 143, 149–152, 168, 247, 250

Odysseus, 37, 221–22, 252–62
Oedipus, 5, 7, 37–40, 252
oracles, 16, 46, 49, 55, 61, 71–72, 174, 217–219, 224, 244, 252, 256, 258; Chaldean, 225–26, 233–34; Delphic, 1–2, 4, 7, 9, 37, 38–41, 47, 50, 61, 224; of Dodona, 7, 43, 255; Sibylline, 7, 220, 222–23

Penelope, 252–62
phantasma (mental image), 80, 82, 89, 99, 102, 160–161
physis (nature), 178, 205, 229, 230
pneuma (Stoic soul), 177–80, 184–85, 193, 202–10
praxis (deliberate action), 20, 95n.6, 135, 136, 150, 153–55, 165, 167
Prime Mover, 100, 121–29, 152
prognôsis (prophetic foreknowing), 225, 243–46

prophecy, 11–12, 56, 62, 66, 174, 219, 221–23, 244–45
psychê. See soul

randomness, 85, 113–17, 122, 129–30, 155, 159–60
rationality, 12–14, 43, 62, 86, 129, 144, 148, 181, 214, 250. See also intuition, rational; soul, rational
reason, 20, 25–27, 58–59, 61, 64, 76, 77, 80–88, 144, 147–51, 155–56, 157, 160, 166, 172, 177–79, 193–94, 199–200, 203–4, 206, 210, 213–14

skill. See *technê*
soul, 44, 64–65, 75, 77, 79, 85–86, 93, 97, 101–2, 107, 109–10, 143, 145–46, 148, 168, 178, 180, 182, 183–85, 93–95, 204, 208, 212, 241; fate of the, 51, 219–20, 223, 224; irrational, 86, 214; lower, 79–89, 91–92, 129, 148, 158, 171–72, 216; nutritive, 129, 143, 146, 158; powers of the, 205–6, 208–9, 210, 212; rational, 82, 85, 171,178, 194, 205–7; upper, 83–87, 129, 237–38
spontaneity, 93–96, 126n.55, 134, 136–39, 153, 154, 164–67
Stoics, 17, 122, 171–214, 215, 242
sympathy, 76, 175, 180–85, 189, 192, 210–11, 241–42, 248

technê (craft), 7–8, 43–45, 47, 60, 66, 72, 100–1, 108, 135–36, 139, 141–42, 147n80, 153–154, 167, 241, 248
teleology, 34–35, 43, 52, 98–99n11, 166, 168, 172, 199n40, 214
theurgy, 215, 229–235, 238
Tiresias, 7, 38, 221–22, 252, 256, 258
tychê (luck, fortune), 116, 125n.36, 126n.55, 130–36, 137, 139–42, 149–50, 155–56, 159, 163, 167, 172–73, 198–200, 213

wisdom, 11–12, 30, 39, 44–45, 47, 48, 140–41, 154, 197, 217, 224–26

CPSIA information can be obtained
at www.ICGtesting.com
Printed in the USA
JSHW041208270620
6366JS00003B/173